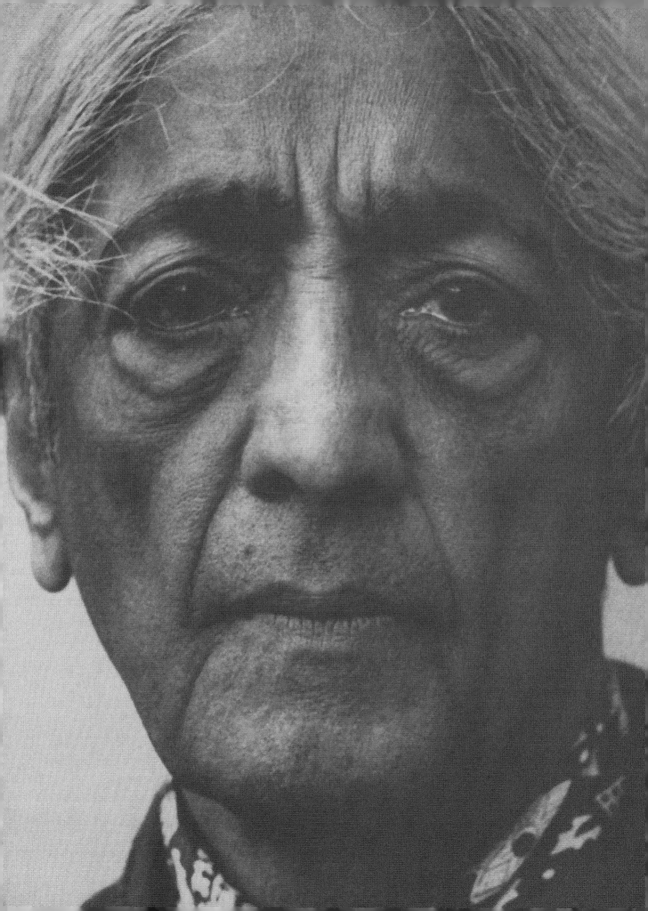

The Collected Works
of
J. Krishnamurti

Volume XVII

1966–1967

Perennial Questions

COLLECTED WORKS VOLUME 17

Photo: J. Krishnamurti, ca 1972 by Mark Edwards © Krishnamurti Foundation Trust, Ltd.

Copyright © 2012 by Krishnamurti Foundation America
P.O Box 1560, Ojai, CA 93024

Website: www.kfa.org

Printed in the United States of America

ISBN 13: 9781934989500
ISBN: 1934989509

Contents

Preface

Jiddu Krishnamurti was born in 1895 of Brahmin parents in south India. At the age of fourteen he was proclaimed the coming World Teacher by Annie Besant, then president of the Theosophical Society, an international organization that emphasized the unity of world religions. Mrs. Besant adopted the boy and took him to England, where he was educated and prepared for his coming role. In 1911 a new worldwide organization was formed with Krishnamurti as its head, solely to prepare its members for his advent as World Teacher. In 1929, after many years of questioning himself and the destiny imposed upon him, Krishnamurti disbanded this organization, saying:

Truth is a pathless land, and you cannot approach it by any path whatsoever, by any religion, by any sect. Truth, being limitless, unconditioned, unapproachable by any path whatsoever, cannot be organized; nor should any organization be formed to lead or to coerce people along any particular path. My only concern is to set men absolutely, unconditionally free.

Until the end of his life at the age of ninety, Krishnamurti traveled the world speaking as a private person. The rejection of all spiritual and psychological authority, including his own, is a fundamental theme. A major concern is the social structure and how it conditions the individual. The emphasis in his talks and writings is on the psychological barriers that prevent clarity of perception. In the mirror of relationship, each of us can come to understand the content of his own consciousness, which is common to all humanity. We can do this, not analytically, but directly in a manner Krishnamurti describes at length. In observing this content we discover within ourselves the division of the observer and what is observed. He points out that this division, which prevents direct perception, is the root of human conflict.

His central vision did not waver after 1929, but Krishnamurti strove for the rest of his life to make his language even more simple and clear. There is a development in his exposition. From year to year he used new terms and new approaches to his subject, with different nuances.

Because his subject is all-embracing, the *Collected Works* are of compelling interest. Within his talks in any one year, Krishnamurti was not able to cover the whole range of his vision, but broad applications of particular themes are found throughout these volumes. In them he lays the foundations of many of the concepts he used in later years.

The *Collected Works* contain Krishnamurti's previously published talks, discussions, answers to specific questions, and writings for the years 1933 through 1967. They are an authentic record of his teachings, taken from transcripts of verbatim shorthand reports and tape recordings.

The Krishnamurti Foundation of America, a California charitable trust, has among its purposes the publication and distribution of Krishnamurti books, videocassettes, films and tape recordings. The production of the *Collected Works* is one of these activities.

New York City, New York, 1966

✳

First Talk in New York

It is always rather difficult to communicate. Words must be used, and each word has a certain definite meaning, but we should bear in mind that the word is not the thing; the word does not convey the total significance. If we semantically stick to words, then I'm afraid that we shall not be able to proceed much further. To communicate really deeply needs not only attention but also a certain quality of affection—which doesn't mean that we must accept what is said or that we must not be critical. We must not only be alert intellectually but we must avoid the pitfall of words. To really communicate with another about anything, there should also be a certain quality of direct affection, a certain quality of exchange, with full capacity to investigate, to examine. Then only can communication take place. Perhaps there will be a communication with each other here, because we are going to deal with many subjects, many problems during these talks. We are going to go into them fairly deeply. To understand what the speaker is saying, there must be a certain quality of attention in listening.

Very few of us listen because we ourselves have so many ideas, so many opinions, so many conclusions and beliefs, which actually prevent the act of listening. To listen to another is one of the most difficult things to do. We are so ready with our own opinions, our own conclusions. We are likely to interpret, agreeing or disagreeing, taking sides, or saying, "I don't agree," and quickly brushing aside what is being said. All that, it seems to me, prevents the act of actually listening. Only when there is a listening which is not merely intellectual is it possible to commune with each other. Any clever person can listen to a certain argument, to a certain exposition of ideas; but to listen with the mind and the heart, with one's total being, requires a great deal of attention. To attend implies not only knowing one's own beliefs, concepts, conclusions, what one wants, and so on, but also putting those aside for the time being, and listening.

We have to talk over a great many things because life has so many problems; we are all so confused. Very few have any belief in anything, or faith. There is war; there is insecurity, great anxiety, fear, despair, the agony of daily existence, and the utter boredom and loneliness of it. Beyond all this are the problems of death and love. We are caught in this tremendous confusion. We must understand the totality of it, not the fragment which is very clear, which we want to achieve; not the special conclusion which we think is right, or an opinion, or a belief.

We must take the whole content of existence, the whole history of man: his suffering, his loneliness, his anxiety, the utter hopelessness, meaninglessness of life. If we can do that, not take any particular fragment which may for the time being appeal to us or give us pleasure, but rather, as it were, see the whole map, not partially, not fragmentarily, then perhaps we shall be able to bring about a radical revolution in the psyche. That's the main crisis of our life, though there are vast changes going on in the world of science, of mathematics, and all the rest. Technologically there is tremendous change going on, but in the psyche of the human being there is very little change. The crisis is not in the outward technological advancement but rather in the way we think, the way we live, and the way we feel. That is where a revolution must take place. This revolution cannot be according to any particular pattern because no revolution, psychologically, is possible if there is merely the imitation of a particular ideology. To me, all ideologies are idiotic; they have no meaning. What has meaning is *what is,* not, 'what should be'. And to understand *what is,* there must be freedom to look, not only outwardly, but also inwardly.

Really there is no division as the outer and the inner. It's a process, a unitary movement; and the moment we understand the outer, we are also understanding the inner. Unfortunately we have divided, broken up life into fragments: the outer, the inner, the good and the bad, and so on. As we have divided the world into nationalities, with all their miseries and wars, we have also divided our own existence into inward and outward. I think that is the worst thing we can do: break up our existence into various fragments. That's where contradiction lies, and most of us are caught in this contradiction, and hence in conflict.

With all the complications, the confusions, the misery, the enormous human effort that has gone to build a society which is getting more and more complex, is it possible, living in this world, to be totally free of all confusion, and therefore of all contradiction, and hence to be free of fear? A mind that is afraid obviously has no peace. Only when the mind is completely and totally free of fear can it observe, can it investigate.

One of our major problems is violence, not only outwardly, but also inwardly. Violence is not merely physical violence, but the whole structure of the psyche is based on violence. This constant effort, this constant adjustment to a pattern, the constant pursuit of pleasure and therefore the avoidance of anything which gives pain, discarding the capacity to look, to observe *what is*—all these are part of violence. Aggression, competition, the constant comparison between *what is* and 'what should be', imitation—all are surely forms of violence. Because man, since historical times, has chosen war as a way of life, our daily existence is a war, in ourselves as well as outwardly. We are always in conflict with ourselves and with others. Is it possible for the mind to be totally free of this violence? We need peace, outwardly as well as inwardly, and peace is not possible if there is not freedom, freedom from this total aggressive attitude toward life.

We all know that there is violence, that there is tremendous hate in the world, war, destruction, competition, each one pursuing his own particular form of pleasure. All that is a way of life which breeds contradiction and violence. We know this intellectually; we have thought about it; statistically we can examine it; intellectually we can rationalize the whole thing, and say, "Well, that's inevitable; that is the history of man for the last two million years and more, and we'll go on that way." Is it possible to bring about a total revolution in the psyche, in oneself—

not as an individual? The individual is the local entity: the American, the Indian, the Russian. He can do very little. But we are not local entities. We are human beings. There is no barrier as an Indian, an American, a Russian, a communist, and so on if we regard the whole process of existence as that of a human being, which you and I are, and if we can bring about a revolution there, not in the individual. After all, if you go beyond nationalities, the absurdities of organized religion, and superficial culture, as human beings we all suffer; we go through tortures of anxiety. There is sorrow; there is the everlasting search for the good, the noble, and what is generally called God. We are all afraid. If we can bring about a change in the human psyche, then the individual will act quite differently. This implies that there is no division between the conscious and the unconscious. I know it is the fashion to study a great deal about the unconscious. Really there is no such thing. We'll discuss all this later. I'm just outlining what we are going to talk over together during the next five talks.

Is it possible for the human being to totally empty the past so that he is made new and looks at life entirely differently? What we call the unconscious, whether it is fifty years past or two million years past, the racial residue, the tradition, the motives, the hidden pursuits, the pleasures—all this is not the unconscious. It is always in the consciousness. There is only consciousness, although you may not be aware of the total content of that consciousness. All consciousness is limitation, and we are caught in it. We move in this consciousness from one field to another field, calling them by different names; but it is still the conscious. The game we play, as the unconscious, the conscious, the past, the future, and all the rest, is within that field. If we are very aware of our own process of thinking, feeling, acting, we can observe for ourselves how we deceive ourselves, move from one field, from one corner to another. This consciousness is always limited because in this consciousness there is always the observer. Wherever there is the observer, the censor, the watcher, he creates limitation within that consciousness.

Any change or revolution brought about by will, by pleasure, by an avoidance or an escape, by pressure, by strain, by convenience is still within that limit, within that consciousness, and therefore it is always limited, always breeding conflict. If we observe this, not through books, not through psychologists and analysts, but actually, factually, as it takes place in ourselves as human beings, then the question will inevitably arise whether it is possible to be conscious where it is necessary to be conscious—going to the office and similar activities—and to be free of it where consciousness is a limitation. It is not that we go into a trance or amnesia, or some mystical nonsense; but unless there is freedom from this enclosing consciousness, this time-binding consciousness, we shall not have peace. Peace is not dependent on politicians, on the army; they have too much vested interest. It is not dependent on the priests, nor on any belief. All religions, except one or two perhaps, Buddhism and Hinduism, have always talked peace and entered into war. That's the way of our lives. I feel that if there is no freedom from this limitation of consciousness as time-binding, with its observer as the center, man will go on endlessly suffering.

Is it possible to empty the whole of consciousness, the whole of the mind, with all its tricks and vanities, its deceptions, pursuits and moralities, and all that, based essentially on pleasure? Is it possible to be totally free of it all, to empty the mind so that it can look and act and live totally differently? I say that it is possible, but not out of vanity or some superstitious, mystical nonsense. It is possible only when there is a realization that the observer, the center, is the observed.

It requires a great deal of understanding to come to this. It isn't a matter of your sentimentally agreeing or disagreeing. Do you know what understanding means? Surely, understanding is not intellectual, not saying, "I understand your words, the meaning of your words." That's not understanding, nor is it an emotional agreement, a sentimental affair. There is understanding of any problem, of any issue, when the mind is totally quiet, not induced quietness, not disciplined quietness, but when the mind is completely still. Then there is understanding. Actually this takes place when we have a problem of any kind. We have thought a great deal about it, investigated, examined back and forth, and there is no answer. We more or less push it aside, and the mind becomes quiet with regard to that problem. Suddenly we have an answer. This happens to many people; it is nothing unusual. Understanding can only come when there is direct perception, not a reasoned conclusion.

Our question then is: How is a man, a human being—not American, not English, nor Chinese—how is a human being to create a new society? He can only create that when there is a total revolution in himself as a human being, when he has no fear at all because he understands the nature of fear, what the structure of fear is, and the meaning of fear. He comes directly into contact with it, not as a thing to be avoided, but as a thing to be understood. Is that possible? Is it possible to understand the whole structure of thought, which is always functioning round a center? Is it possible to understand the whole machinery of thinking, which is the result of memory, since thought is the reaction of memory, and hence the limitation of consciousness? Is it possible to totally not think, to totally function without memory as it now functions?

This brings us to a point: What is the function of idea, idea being the prototype, the formula, the ideal, the concept? Has it any function at all? For us idea is very important, and we act, we function on idea, on concepts, on formulas. A belief is a formula. All our activity is from ideas, or based on ideas, and hence there is a contradiction between act and the idea. I have an idea, an ideal, a belief, and I act according to that, or approximate my action to that. Action can never be the idea. The idea is unreal; the action is real. The idea of a nation, the idea of a certain dogma, such as belief in God, and all other ideas are purely ideological. Is it possible to act without the idea?

Please, this requires a great deal of inquiry because as long as there is conflict in any form, there must be pain and sorrow, and there must be conflict just as long as there is contradiction. The nature of contradiction is essentially the idea and the fact, the *what is.* If there is no idea at all, no belief, no dogma, no tomorrow, which is always the ideal, then I can look at *what is* actually—not translate it in terms of tomorrow, but see actually *what is.* To understand *what is,* one need not have ideas. All that one has to do is to observe.

That brings us to the next point, which is: What is observing? What is seeing? I wonder if we ever see, observe, or do we see with the word, with a conclusion, with a name, and therefore they become barriers to seeing? If you say, "Well, he's an Indian from India with all his mystical ideas, or romantic ideas," and so on, you're not actually seeing. It is only possible to see when thought doesn't function. If you are listening, expecting something, I don't know what, the expectation is preventing you from listening; the idea, the concept, the knowledge prevents you from observing. If you look at a flower, a tree, a cloud, or a bird, whatever it is, immediately your reaction is to give it a name; you like it or dislike it; you have categorized it, put it away as a memory, and you have stopped looking.

Is it possible to look, to see, without all the mentation taking place? Mentation is always thought as an idea, as memory; and there is no direct perception. I do not know if you have observed your friend, your wife, or your husband, just looking. You look at another or listen to another with all the memories of misfortunes, insults, and all the rest. You actually are not listening or seeing. This process of nonobservance is called relationship. (Laughter) Please don't laugh it away, because all this is very serious. This isn't a philosophical lecture which you listen to, and then go home and carry on. Only to the very serious man is there living, is there life. One cannot, with all this appalling confusion, misery, just laugh it away, or go to a cinema and forget all about the beastly stuff. It requires extraordinary, earnest, attentive seriousness, and seriousness is not a reaction. All reactions are limitations, but when one observes, listens, looks, one begins to understand whether it is at all possible for man to be totally free of his conditioning. We are all conditioned: by the food, the clothes, the climate, the culture, the society in which we live. Is it possible to be free of that conditioning, not in some distant future, but instantly? That's why I asked whether it is possible to free the mind totally, empty it completely, so that it is something new. If this does not take place, we are committed to sorrow; we are committed to everlasting fear.

Is it possible to free the mind of the past, totally, and if it is, how can one empty it? In certain fields, past knowledge is essential. One must know where one is going. One can't forget and put aside all the technological knowledge which man has acquired through centuries, but I am talking about the psyche, which has accumulated so many concepts, ideas, experiences, and is caught

within this consciousness with the observer as its center.

Having put this question, what is the answer? It is the right question, not an irrelevant question. When one puts the right question, there is the right answer; but it requires a great deal of integrity to put the right question. We have put the right question: Is it possible for man, who has lived for so many centuries and millions of years, who has pursued a path of violence, who has accepted war as a way of life, in daily life as well as on the battlefield, who is everlastingly seeking peace and denying it—is it possible for man to transform himself completely so that he lives totally differently?

Having put the question, who will answer it? Will you look to someone to answer it, some guru, some priest, some psychologist, or are you waiting for the speaker to answer it? If you put the question rightly, the answer is in the question, but very few of us have put that question. We have accepted the norm of life, and to change that requires a great deal of energy. We are committed to certain dogmas, certain beliefs, certain activities as the way of life. We are committed, and we are frightened to change it, not knowing what it will breed.

Can we, realizing the implications of all this, can we honestly put that question? Surely, how we put it matters also. We can put it, ask ourselves intellectually, out of curiosity, out of a moment which we can spare from the daily routine, but that will not answer it. What will answer that question depends on the mind: how earnest it is, how lazy it is, or how indifferent it is to the whole structure and the misery of existence.

Having put that question, we are going to find out. We are going to talk over together, during these five more talks that are to come, how to discover the answer for ourselves, not depending on anyone. There is no authority; there is no guru, no priest who will answer this; and to come to the point where we are not dependent on anyone psychologically is the first, and probably the last step. Then, when the mind has freed itself from all its diseases, it can find out if there is a reality which is not put together by thought; it can find out if there is such a thing as God. Man has searched, sought after, and hunted that being, and we have to answer that question. Also we have to answer the question of what death is. A society, a human being that does not understand what death is will not know what life is, nor what love is. Merely to accept or deny something which is not of thought is rather immature, but if we would go into it, we must lay the foundation of virtue, which has nothing to do with social morality. We must understand the nature of pleasure, not deny pleasure or accept pleasure, but understand its nature, its structure. And obviously there must be freedom from fear, and hence a mind that is completely free from discontent and wanting more experience. Then only, it seems to me, is it possible to find out if there is something beyond the human fear which has created God.

Question: Would you please repeat that very important question the way you asked it?

KRISHNAMURTI: I'm afraid I couldn't do that, could I? That means going all over it again. I will perhaps another day.

Question: What is the state of the mind, body, and brain which is energy, the state in which self is not?

KRISHNAMURTI: It is very easy to ask questions, but who is going to answer them? Please do take seriously what I'm saying. Who is going to answer? To put the right question demands a great deal of intelligence. I'm not saying that you're not intelligent, but it requires a great deal of understanding. If you ask a question to confirm your own ideas, if you're asking for confirmation, you're not really asking a question. If you're asking the question to clarify your own confusion, will you ask a question if you know you're confused? Because out of your confusion you may ask a question, and you will listen to the reply only according to your confusion; therefore, it's not an answer. Or you ask a question because you can't look, you can't understand, and therefore you want someone's help. The moment you seek help from another psychologically, you're lost. Then you set up the whole structure of hierarchical thinking—the gurus, the priests, the analysts, and all that.

To ask a right question is one of the most difficult things, and the moment you have asked the right question, there is the answer—you don't have to ask it even. (Laughter) No, please, this is really serious.

Question: Are you setting as the goal of human experience the contemplation of infinity and perfection?

KRISHNAMURTI: I'm afraid I'm not, sir. (Laughter)

Question: What do you mean when you talk about the mind being quiet, but not an induced quiet?

KRISHNAMURTI: Sir, I can discipline the mind to be quiet, force it, control it, because I have an idea that the mind should be quiet, because out of that quietness I hope to achieve something, or gain something, or realize something, or experience something. All that is induced quietness; therefore, it's sterile. But quietness is something entirely

different, which we can't go into now because it requires a great deal of examination
and understanding. That silence comes
naturally when there is understanding, when
there is no effort.

*Question: What relation has the observer,
my observer, to other observers, to other
people?*

KRISHNAMURTI: What do we mean by that
word *relationship?* Are we ever related to
anyone, or is the relationship between two
images which we have created about each
other? I have an image about you, and you
have an image about me. I have an image
about you as my wife or husband, or
whatever it is, and you an image about me
also. The relationship is between these two
images and nothing else. To have relationship with another is only possible when there
is no image. When I can look at you and you
can look at me without the image of
memory, of insults, and all the rest, then
there is a relationship, but the very nature of
the observer is the image, isn't it? My image
observes your image, if it is possible to observe it, and this is called relationship, but it
is between two images, a relationship which
is nonexistent because both are images. To
be related means to be in contact. Contact
must be something direct, not between two
images. It requires a great deal of attention,
an awareness, to look at another without the
image which I have about that person, the
image being my memories of that person—
how he has insulted me, pleased me, given
me pleasure, this or that. Only when there
are no images between the two is there a
relationship.

*Question: Could you comment on the
present use of LSD. . .*

KRISHNAMURTI: Ah! (Laughter)

*Question: . . . for creating that state of
imageless relationship?*

KRISHNAMURTI: LSD is the newest drug to
produce certain effects. In ancient India there
existed another of these drugs called soma.
The name doesn't matter. Man has tried
everything to bring about right relationship
between man and man: drugs, escapes,
monasteries, dozens and dozens of ideals,
which one hopes will unify man—the communist ideal, this ideal, or that ideal. Now
there is this drug. Can an outside agency
bring about right relationship, which is imageless relationship? You know we have
tried, not chemicals, but a belief as a drug.
People in the West have had a belief in
Christ, the Buddhists in the Buddha, and so
on. They all hoped that their belief would
bring people together, but it has not. On the
contrary, by their exclusive belief they have
created more mischief. As far as I'm concerned, no outside agency, such as a drug,
can bring about right relationship. You cannot, through drugs, love another. If you
could, then everything would be solved. Why
do we give much more importance to a drug
than to a belief, to a dogma, to the one
savior who is going to bring right relationship? Why emphasize a drug or a belief?
Both are detrimental to right relationship.
What brings about right relationship is to be
totally aware of all one's activities, one's
thoughts, one's feelings, and to observe
choicelessly what's going on in all relationships. Then out of that comes a relationship
which is not based on an idea.

*Question: You spoke of the relationship of
an observer of one human being with that of
another, saying that they were both images.
Would that not also hold true in yourself in*

the alienation of the observer from the rest of the psyche?

KRISHNAMURTI: Of course, surely.

Comment: I believe that you said that a quiet mind is a natural state, that I don't have to induce it.

KRISHNAMURTI: Is a quiet mind a natural thing? Does it come easily? Obviously not. We want little pills to achieve everything. I said it is a natural outcome when there is the right foundation.

Question: You spoke of consciousness being limited. Do you mean that this quiet mind is not limited?

KRISHNAMURTI: I'm afraid one has to go into this question of whether it is possible for a mind to be quiet from different facets, different angles. Is it possible for the mind to be quiet? Must it be everlastingly chattering? To understand that, one has to go into the question of thought, and whether the mind, in which is contained the brain, can be quiet though it has its reactions. I'll go into all that later.

Comment: It's very hard to be honest, and I have the strangest feeling that the only reason we're gathered here in this room is because you are here. I think that's rather sad. Before we come again, if we come again, I think we ought to be a little bit clearer about your role, because we come with a motive; we didn't come here spontaneously.

KRISHNAMURTI: I wonder why you attend any gathering of this kind, any meeting at all. Is it out of curiosity, because you've heard of someone's reputation, and you say, "Well,

let's go," or are you serious in wanting to find out? That of course depends on you; no one can answer that.

Question: I would like to know about the people who go into samadhi *in India, or in America. Isn't that the true aspect of the expression of the inner soul of man, and therefore very important in his surroundings?*

KRISHNAMURTI: The gentleman wants to know what the Hindus mean by the word *samadhi*. I'm afraid you'll have to look it up in a book to find out, sir. I am not belittling the questioner, but what matters most? Is it more important to find out what *samadhi* is, a trance, or whatever it may mean, or to find out for oneself the misery in which one lives, the confusion, the endless conflict within oneself, and to find out whether it can be ended? If it can be ended, then you will find out for yourself, whatever that word may mean, and then it won't matter at all. We're always wandering off from the central issue. The central issue is so colossal, so enormous, so confusing that we'd rather not face it. But unfortunately we have to see it; we have to look at it; and by looking at it very closely, without any image, perhaps the mind can be free from this contagion of life, with its misery.

September 26, 1966

Second Talk in New York

As human beings we do not seem to be able to solve our problems totally. We move from one problem to another endlessly. Man has tried every way to escape from these problems, to avoid them or to find some excuse for not resolving them. We probably do not have the capacity, the energy, the drive to resolve them, and we have built a network of escapes so cunningly that we do not even know that we are escaping from the main issue. It seems to me that there must be a total change, a total revolution in the mind, not a modified continuity, but a total psychological mutation so that the mind is entirely free from all the bondage of time, so that it can go beyond the structure of thought, not into some metaphysical region, but rather into a timeless dimension where the mind is no longer caught in its own structure, in its own problems. We see the absolute necessity of complete change. We have tried so many ways, including LSD, beliefs, dogmas, joining various sects, going through various disciplines of meditation. The mind, at the end of all this, remains just the same: petty, narrow, limited, anxious, but it has had a period of enlightenment, a period of clarity. That's what most of us are doing: pursuing a vision, a clarity, something that is not entirely the product of thought, but we come back again and again to this confusion. There seems to be no freedom. As we were saying the other day, is it possible for man to be totally free, psychologically? We don't know what that freedom means. We can only build an image, or an idea, a conclusion as to what freedom should be or should not be. To actually experience it, to actually come upon it requires a great deal of examination, a great deal of penetration into our process of thinking.

This evening I would like to go into whether it is possible for man, for a human being to have entire freedom from all fear, from all effort, from every form of anxiety. It must be unconscious in the sense that it is not deliberately brought about. To understand this question we must examine what change is. Our minds are bound, conditioned by society, by our experience, by our heredity, by all the influences that man is heir to. Can a human being put all that aside and discover for himself a state of mind where there is a quality which has not been touched by time

at all? After all, that is what we are all seeking. Most of us are tired of the daily experiences of life, its boredom, its pettiness; and we are seeking something through experience, something much greater. We call it God, a vision, or whatever name we can give it—the name doesn't matter.

How can a mind that has been so conditioned by everyday experience, by knowledge, by social and economic influences, by the culture in which that mind lives—how can such a mind bring about a total revolution, a mutation in itself? Because if it is not possible, then we are condemned to sorrow, to anxiety, to guilt, to despair. It's a valid question, and we must find a right answer, not a verbal answer, not a conclusion, not an ideation, but actually find the answer to that question and live in that.

We have to go into the question of what change is, who the entity is that's going to change, and who is going to be conscious or aware that it has changed. The word *change* implies a movement from what has been to what will be. There is a time sequence: what was, what is, and what should be. And in this time interval, from what is to what should be, there is effort to achieve the 'what should be'. What should be is already preconceived, predetermined by what has been. So the movement from what has been to what should be is no movement at all; it is merely a continuity of what has been.

I think it would be worthwhile if we could treat this, not as a talk to which you are listening and with which you are agreeing or disagreeing, but rather as the means you can use to actually observe the whole process of your own thinking, the process of your own reactions. We are not trying to have group analysis but rather to investigate factually what is being said. If you are investigating what is being said, then you are actually listening, not coming to any conclusion of agreement or disagreement. It really is a matter of examining yourself as a total human being, not as an American, or an Indian, and all the rest of that silly nonsense. You are actually observing the total movement of your own mind. If you do that, it has enormous significance. The speaker is only a mirror in which, or through which you are observing the whole content, the movement of yourself. The speaker doesn't matter at all. What is important is to observe, to be completely aware, without any choice—just to observe what's going on. Then you are bound to find out for yourself the meaning and the structure of change.

We must change. There is a great deal of the animal in us: aggression, violence, greed, ambition, the search for success, the effort to dominate. Can those remains of the animal be totally eradicated so that the mind is no longer violent, no longer aggressive? Unless the mind is at complete peace, or completely still, it is not possible to discover anything new. Without that discovering, without the mind being transformed, we shall merely live in the time process of imitation, continuing with what has been, living always in the past. The past is not only the immediate, but the immediate is the past.

What does one mean by change? That is an imperative necessity because our life is pretty shoddy, empty, rather dull and stupid, without meaning. Going to the office every day for the next forty years, breeding a few children, seeking everlasting amusement, either through the church or the football field—to a mature man all that really has very little meaning. We know that, but we don't know what to do; we don't know how to change, how to put an end to the time process. Let's go into it together. First we must be very clear that there is no authority, that the speaker is not the authority. Therefore the relationship between you and the speaker changes entirely. We are both investigating, examining, and therefore both of us

are partaking of what is being said, like taking a journey together. Therefore your responsibility is much greater than that of the speaker. We can go into this, take this journey, only when we are very, very serious, because it entails a great deal of attention, energy, clarity.

For most of us change implies a movement toward what is known. It isn't an actual change but a continuity of what has been, in a modified pattern. All sociological revolutions are based on that. There is the idea of what should be, what a society should be, and the revolutionists try to bring about that idea in action; that, they call revolution. There is society, with its classes, and they want to bring about a totally different structure of society. They have the pattern of what should be, and that's no change at all. It's merely a reaction, and reaction is always imitative.

When we talk about change, it is not change or mutation from what has been to what should be. I hope you are observing your own process of your thinking and are aware not only of the necessity of change but also of your conditioning, the limitations, the fears, the anxieties, the utter loneliness and boredom of life. We are asking ourselves whether that structure can be totally demolished and a new state of mind come into being. That state of mind is not to be preconceived; if it is, it's merely a concept, an idea, and an idea is never real.

We have this field in which we live, an actual fact. How can a mutation take place in that fact? We only know effort to bring about any change, through pleasure or through pain, through reward or through punishment. To understand change in the sense which we are talking about, in the sense of mutation, with a totally different mind happening, we have to go into the question of pleasure. If we do not understand the structure of pleasure, change then will merely depend on pleasure and pain, on a reward or a punishment.

What we all want is pleasure, more and more pleasure, either physical pleasure through sex, through possessions, through luxury, and so on, which can easily be transcended, which can easily be understood and set aside, or the psychological pleasure on which all our values are based: moral, ethical, spiritual. All our relationship is based on that—the relationship between two images, not two human beings, but the two images that human beings have created about each other.

The animal wants only pleasure. And as I said, there is a great deal of the animal in us. Unless one understands the nature and the structure of pleasure, change or mutation is merely a form of the continuity of pleasure, in which there is always pain.

What is pleasure? Why does the mind constantly seek this thing called pleasure? By pleasure I mean feeling superior, psychologically, feeling anger, violence, and the opposite, nonviolence. Each opposite contains its own opposite; therefore, nonviolence is not nonviolence at all. Violence gives a great deal of pleasure. There is a great deal of pleasure in acquiring, in dominating, and psychologically in the feeling of having a capacity, the feeling of achievement, the feeling that one is entirely different from someone else. On this pleasure principle our relationships are based; on this principle our ethical and moral values are built. The ultimate pleasure is not only sex but the idea that one has discovered God, something totally new. We are making constant efforts to achieve that ultimate pleasure. We change the patterns of our relationships. I don't like my wife; I find various excuses and choose another wife; and this is the way we live, in constant battle, in endless strife. We never consider what pleasure is, whether there is an actual state such as pleasure, psychologically,

or we have conceived, formulated pleasure through thought, and we want to achieve that pleasure—so pleasure may be the product of thinking.

We must understand this very deeply, see the whole structure very, very clearly, not get rid of pleasure—that's too immature. That is what the monks throughout the world have done. We are using the word *understand* nonintellectually, nonemotionally, in the sense of seeing something very clearly as it is, not as we would like it to be, not interpreting it in a certain temperamental fashion. Then, when we understand something, it isn't that an individual mind has understood it, but rather there is a total awareness of that fact. It would be rather absurd and not quite honest to say to ourselves, "I'm not seeking pleasure." Everyone is.

To understand it, we must not only go into this question of thinking but into the structure of memory. This morning, very early, on the reservoir there was not a breath of air, and there was perfect reflection of all the trees, the light, and the towers, without a movement. It was a beautiful sight, and it has given me great pleasure. The mind has stored that memory as pleasure and wants that pleasure to be repeated, because memory is already a dead thing. The pleasure is in thinking about that light on the water this morning, and the thinking is the response of memory which has been stored up through the experience of this morning. Thought proceeds from that experience to gather more pleasure from what it experienced yesterday, or this morning. You have flattered me; I have enjoyed it, and I want more of it. I think about it. (Laughter)

Please don't laugh it away. Look at it. Go into it. That's why we avoid talking about death. We want to repeat all the experiences of youth. Pleasure comes into being through an experience in which there has been a delight. That experience is gone, but the memory of it remains. Then the memory responds and, through thinking, wants more of it. It is making constant effort. This is simple. Thought, thinking over something which has given pleasure, keeps on thinking about it, as sex, achievement, and so on. Of course it's much more complex than that, but there is not enough time to go into all the complexity of it; one can watch it; one can be aware of it; one can see it for oneself.

The problem then is: Is it possible to experience, and not have that experience leave a memory; and therefore there is no thinking about it? It's over.

Man has lived for so many millennia, thousands upon thousands of years, and he is the residue of all time; he is the result of endless time. Unless he puts an end to time, he is caught in this wheel, the wheel of thought, experience, and pleasure. We can't do anything about it. If we do actually say, "I must end pleasure"—which we won't— we do it out of desire for further pleasure. We must understand and go into this question of action. Here is an issue, a great problem. All religions have tried, and vainly, to say that any form of pleasure is the same. The monasteries are full of these monks who deny, suppress pleasure. Pleasure is related to desire, so these people say, "Be without desire," which is absolutely impossible.

How is it possible for an action to take place with regard to the structure of pleasure, an action which is not taken by the desire for a greater pleasure? Action is the doing, the having done, or future action. All our actions, if you observe very closely, are based on an idea: an idea which has been formulated, and according to that idea, according to that image, according to that authority, experience, I act. To us, idea, the ideal, the prototype is much more important than the action itself. We are always trying to approximate any action according to the pat-

tern. If we want to discover anything new in action, we must be free of the pattern.

The culture in which one lives has imposed certain patterns of behavior, certain patterns of thought, certain patterns of morality. The more ancient that particular culture is, the more conditioned the mind becomes. There is that pattern, and the mind is always imitating, following, adjusting itself to that pattern. This process is called action. If it is purely technological activity, then it's merely copying, repeating, adding some more to what has been. Why do we act with an idea? Why is ideation so terribly important? I have to do something, but why should I have an idea about it? I must find out why I have a formula, why I have an example, an authority. Isn't it because I am incapable, or do not want to face the fact, the *what is?*

I'm in sorrow. Psychologically, I'm terribly disturbed; and I have an idea about it: what I should do, what I should not do, how it should be changed. That idea, that formula, that concept prevents me from looking at the fact of *what is*. Ideation and the formula are escapes from *what is*. There is immediate action when there is great danger. Then you have no idea. You don't formulate an idea and then act according to that idea.

The mind has become lazy, indolent, through a formula which has given it a means of escape from action with regard to *what is*. Seeing for ourselves the whole structure of what has been said, not because it has been pointed out to us, is it possible to face the fact: the fact that we are violent, as an example? We are violent human beings, and we have chosen violence as the way of life— war and all the rest of it. Though we talk everlastingly, especially in the East, of nonviolence, we are not nonviolent people; we are violent people. The idea of nonviolence is an idea, which can be used politically. That's a different meaning, but it is an idea, and not a fact. Because the human being is incapable of meeting the fact of violence, he has invented the ideal of nonviolence, which prevents him from dealing with the fact.

After all, the fact is that I'm violent; I'm angry. What is the need of an idea? It is not the idea of being angry; it's the actual fact of being angry that is important, like the actual fact of being hungry. There's no idea about being hungry. The idea then comes as to what you should eat, and then according to the dictates of pleasure, you eat. There is only action with regard to *what is* when there is no idea of what should be done about that which confronts you, which is *what is*.

There is the question of fear. There are various different forms of fear, which we shan't go into now. There is the actual fact of fear; and I've never met fear. I know what fear is; I have ideas about it: what I should do, how I should treat it, how I should run away from it, but I am never actually in contact with fear. The ideation process is essentially the observer, the censor. I am afraid. Can I deal with it totally so that the mind is free completely of fear, not with regard to a certain aspect of life, but in the total field of existence, so that the mind is completely free? Inevitably the question arises: If I am not afraid, won't I have an accident, physically? We're not talking of physical, self-protective existence, but rather the fear which thought has created with regard to existence. Can the mind face that fact, without the formula of what it should or should not do? And who is the entity who faces that fact?

Let's put the question differently. You're there, and the speaker is sitting on this platform. You are the observer, and the observed is the speaker. You have your own temperament, your own worries, your own tendencies, ambitions, greeds, and fears. That is the observer watching the observed, as you would watch a tree, which is objective. You, the observer, are watching fear. You say,

"I'm afraid." The 'I' is different from the observed. Fear is something outside of you, and you, who are the observer, want to do something about that fear. This is what we are all doing. But is the observer different from the observed? The observer is afraid, and he says, "I am different from the observed." But the observer is the observed. There is no difference between the observer and the observed. He is afraid as well as the observed.

For instance, one is afraid of death; and death is something totally different from the observer. And one never inquires into what is the observer. What is the observer, the 'you'? Who is afraid? Being afraid, of course he has all kinds of neurotic ideas. Who is the observer, with regard to fear? The observer is the known, with his experiences, with his knowledge, with his conditioning, with his pleasures, his memories—all that is the observer. The observer is afraid of death because the observer is going to die. What is the observer? Again, ideas, formulas, memories—already dead. So, the observer is the observed.

This is real meditation, not all the phony stuff that goes under the name of meditation. This requires a great deal of attention; it requires a great deal of energy to discover this—discover it, not be told. When you discover this, you will find that change through will, through effort, through desire, through the fear of sorrow disappears totally because then action takes place, not action through an idea. Action is change, and total action is mutation.

When we are talking about change, we have to understand what pleasure is, not deny it. We also have to understand this whole accumulation of memory, which is always the known. You may take any drug, do any exercise, do anything to escape from the known. The escape is merely a reaction, an avoidance of the known, and therefore you fall into the pattern of another known. That's what is taking place. You may take LSD. They do it remarkably well in the East, much better than you do it here because they have been doing it for centuries, because they think that through that way they are going to escape from this shoddy, miserable existence of life. But I'm afraid you can't do it because the mind is conditioned, and a conditioned mind cannot experience the real under any circumstances, give it whatever chemical you want. It must be free of its conditioning—the conditioning of society, the influence, the urges, the competition, the greed, the desire for power, position, and prestige. A petty, little mind, a shallow, little mind can take a drug—it is called LSD here, another thing in India, and in other parts of the world they have got it by other names—but it still remains a petty, little mind. We are talking about a total change, a mutation in the mind itself.

This is a problem of great awareness, not of some spiritual, absurd, mystical state, but awareness of your words, of your talk, of what you do, of what you think—to be aware of it so that you begin to discover for yourself the whole movement of your mind, and your mind is the mind of every other human being in the world. You don't have to read philosophy or psychology to discover the process of your own mind. It is there; you have to learn how to look, and to look you must be aware, not only of the outward things, but inward movements. The outward is the inward movement; there is no outward and inward. It's a constant movement of interaction. You have to be aware of that, not learn how to be aware by going to a monastery and watching to be aware, but by watching every day when you get into a bus, into a tramcar, or whatever it is. That demands a great deal of attention, and attention means energy. You begin to discover how that energy is dissipated by endless ab-

surd talk, so you begin, through awareness, just to be aware without any choice, any like or dislike, without any condemnation—just to observe, to observe how you walk, how you talk, how you treat people. Without any formula, that very watching brings tremendous energy. You don't have to take drugs to have more energy. You dissipate energy by likes and dislikes. Then you will see for yourself that a mutation has taken place, without your wanting it.

Question: When you use the two words what is, *is it metaphysical, is it something abstract, is it intellectual?*

KRISHNAMURTI: When we say *what is,* we know what it is. When I have a toothache, that is *what is.* When I'm afraid, that's *what is.* When I'm hungry and have a great appetite for many things, that's *what is.* When I'm ambitious, competing with someone and talking about love and brotherhood—which is sheer nonsense when I'm ambitious—the *what is* is the ambition. The idea that there should be peace in the world is an ideation, which has no reality. There is no peace in the world because as a human being I'm aggressive, competitive, ambitious, dividing myself into different groups, sociologically, morally, and spiritually. I belong to this religion, and you belong to that religion. So the *what is* is very simple.

Comment: When the pleasure is not named, what remains is energy.

KRISHNAMURTI: Have you observed your pleasure? Have you observed what the content of your pleasure is, how that pleasure arises, what is implied in that pleasure? Look, sir; make it very simple.

There is the visual perception of a woman, a beautiful car, or something or other. The perception evokes, stimulates sensation, and from that sensation there is desire. I think about that desire, which gives me pleasure. We will find out what remains when we've understood pleasure.

Question: If I see a woman without thought . . .

KRISHNAMURTI: The gentleman wants to know what happens. (Laughter) Go to bed! It is very important to understand the question that we are discussing. Can you observe something without pleasure, without pain? Can you observe anything? And when you do, what takes place? Unless you're blind or paralyzed, you have reactions, surely. You may have controlled those reactions, suppressed them, denied them, avoided them; but there is a reaction. And you must have that reaction; otherwise, you're dead. That reaction becomes desire, and the more you think about that desire, the more it gives you either pain or pleasure. If it is painful, you try to avoid thinking about it, but if it is pleasurable, you think about it. You can't say, "Well, I won't have pleasure." You have to understand the whole machinery of this very complex process, both physiological and psychological. To observe very clearly demands a clear perception.

Sir, have you ever watched a flower?

Question: For a long time I have not been able to be clear about idea and action. If I am hungry and if I don't have the idea of choosing between milk and bread, how can I make that choice?

KRISHNAMURTI: Sir, you have to make a choice of different dentists and different doctors, don't you? There is choice when you choose a coat or a dress. But is there any other choice at all? Is there choice when you

see something very clearly? For instance, when you see nationalism, which is rampant in the world, when you see what it entails, what is involved in it—the limitation, the quarrels, the battles, the pride, and all the ugly business involved, which is poison—then, if you realize that it's poison, it drops away. There is no action; there is no choice. Choice exists only when there is confusion. When the mind is not confused, there is no choice. There is direct perception.

We are using very simple words. There is no jargon behind these words. When we use the word *pleasure*, we mean the ordinary dictionary meaning of that word.

Question: Is it possible to arrive at direct perception and to come to action in the way that you have described?

KRISHNAMURTI: It isn't that I have described action. This is what we do; this is what takes place every day of our lives.

Comment: I didn't hear the question.

KRISHNAMURTI: Let me repeat again something. To ask the right question is very important—not to me, not to the speaker. And to ask the right question there must be a great deal of skepticism, and not the absurd skepticism of an immature mind. To ask the right question, there must be no acceptance, no authority; and to ask the right question is one of the most difficult things to do because we have never asked a right question. We have asked many, many, many questions; but to ask the right question implies that there is no person who is going to answer that question. To ask the right question implies that the mind is free from all authority and comparison; therefore, it is in a position to ask—and in the very asking of that question is the answer.

Question: What is spontaneous action, free from conditioning?

KRISHNAMURTI: First of all, there is no spontaneous action as long as there is conditioning. The moment there is freedom from conditioning—please, sir, you are dealing with this as though it were one of the easiest things to get rid of our conditioning. Good God! (Laughter) You'll find out what is implied if you go into it. Take a person who has been conditioned for ten thousand years as a Hindu, can he just throw it off? To be free of conditioning is not a matter of time. It isn't a gradual process. When you know you are conditioned, and observe it, the very awareness of that fact is the ending of the fact. Then you'll find out that there is no action at all. You're just moving. There is no question of spontaneity. It is only the man in bondage who is always talking about spontaneity.

Comment: At the start of your talk tonight, you asked if it is possible for man to be totally free without returning to his confusion, and I think that you answered yes. At the end of your talk you spoke about moving along the path of discovery, which implies that there will be moments of experiencing what is, and moments of not experiencing what is.

KRISHNAMURTI: Most of us are unaware that we are confused. When we are committed to a particular formula—communist, Catholic, Hindu, or whatever it is—or the latest fashion in thought, we think we are clear of confusion. We are not, and confusion can only cease when there is no movement of the observer. There are moments when we think we are not confused, and we think we are very clear; the next moment we are confused. We think that we have solved a problem completely, and that very same problem arises another day. We are caught in con-

fusion, and out of this confusion we listen; we seek a leader—political, religious, psychological, or whatever it may be. What we choose is born out of confusion, and therefore what we choose is also confused. It is really a quite complex problem, and I hope we can go into it next time.

September 28, 1966

Third Talk in New York

We said that we would talk over together this evening the question of confusion. Before we go into that we should understand what we mean by freedom, whether there is such a thing as freedom, and also what we mean by choice. Freedom from something, which is really a reaction, is not freedom at all. Mere revolt against a certain pattern of thought or a certain structure of society is not freedom. Freedom implies a state of mind in which there is no imitation or conformity, and therefore no fear. We can revolt and yet conform, as is happening in the world now, and this revolt is generally called freedom. But that revolt, whether it is the communist revolution, or any other social revolution, must inevitably create a pattern. There may be a different social order, but it is still a pattern of conformity. When we are talking about freedom, surely we mean a state in which there is no conformity at all, no imitation. Imitation and conformity must exist when there is fear, and fear invariably breeds authority: the authority of the experience of another, the authority of a new drug, or the authority of one's own experience, one's own pattern of thinking.

We should be clear when we talk about freedom. The politicians talk about freedom, and they really don't mean it at all. The religious people throughout the world have talked about freedom from bondage, freedom from sorrow, freedom from all the travails of human anxiety. They have laid down a certain course, a certain pattern of behavior, thought, and action to bring it about. But freedom is denied when there is conformity to a pattern, religious or social. Is there freedom? Is there freedom when there is choice? Choice, it seems to me, is an act of confusion. When I'm bewildered, uncertain, confused, then I choose; and I say to myself, "I choose out of my freedom; I am free to choose." But is not choice the outcome of uncertainty? Out of my confusion, bewilderment, uncertainty, the feeling of being incapable of clarity—out of this I act. I choose a leader; I choose a certain course of action, and I commit myself to a particular activity; but that activity, that pattern of action, the pursuit of a particular mode of thought is the result of my confusion. If I'm not confused, if there is no confusion whatsoever, then there is no choice; I see things as they are. I act not on choice.

A mind capable of choosing is really a very confused mind. Perhaps you may not agree with this, but please, if I may suggest, just listen to the very end of it, neither agreeing nor disagreeing. As we said the other day, we're not doing any propaganda for any particular philosophy, for any particular course of action, and we are not laying down certain principles. All those are the indication of an utter lack of freedom. When we are confused, bewildered, as most people are right throughout the world, out of this confusion we choose a political leader, a religious system, or follow the dictates of the latest craze.

We must go into this question of what clarity is, and whether the mind—which is so confused, uncertain, which thinks that it is incapable of real clarity—can see clearly, since it is so conditioned by various social influences, religious patterns, by the propaganda that goes on incessantly to force us to think this way or that way, conditioned by the innumerable political and religious

leaders that exist in the world, and by the various sects. All these have brought about confusion in the mind. When I am dissatisfied with one particular pattern of activity, or a course of thought, or a particular philosophy or dogma, I move to another series; and so I am always held, always committed. I think that there will be clarity, freedom from confusion, when I'm committed to a particular course of action.

It seems to me that if the mind is confused—and we know the various reasons, religious and political, for this confusion, the philosophies, the theologians with their particular patterns of thinking, telling us what to believe and what not to believe, with their commitments—an ordinary human being is lost, does not know what to do. It seems to me that the first thing is not to be committed to any organization, religious, political, sectarian, or to any latest drug—not to be committed. And that's very difficult because all the pressure around us says that we must be committed. We must do something: do this or do that, take the latest drug, or go to this particular philosophy, or to that particular teacher. Because they assert so clearly, so positively and with such clarity, out of our confusion we accept, hoping that out of this acceptance there will come about a certain clarity of thought, a feeling of certainty. Can the mind be in a state of noncommitment?

As we said the other day, a talk of this kind is only worthwhile if we can go beyond the word, because the explanation and the word are not the thing. There can be a hundred explanations of the reasons for confusion; but a mind that wants, that demands freedom from confusion, is not satisfied with explanations, with words, or with any authority. Can we this evening find out for ourselves whether it is possible for a mind which realizes that it is confused, realizes it is committed to a particular course of action, social or religious, to cease to be committed—not because someone tells it to do so, but through understanding that any commitment to any particular pattern of thought or action engenders more confusion? If a mind demands clarity, demands that it be free from all confusion because it understands the necessity of freedom, that very understanding frees the mind from commitment, and that's one of the most difficult things to do. We are committed because we think that commitment will lead us to a certain clarity, to a certain facility of action. And if we are not committed, we feel lost because all around us people are committed. We go to this group or to that group, to this teacher or to that teacher; we follow a certain leader. Everyone is caught in this, and not to be committed demands the awareness of what is implied in commitment. If we are aware of a danger and see it very clearly, then we don't touch it; we don't go near it. But to see it clearly is very difficult because the mind says, "I must do, act; I can't wait. What am I to do?" Surely, a mind that is confused, uncertain, disturbed, must first realize that it is disturbed, and also understand that any movement of this disturbance only creates further disturbance. Not to be committed implies to stand completely alone, and that demands great understanding of fear. We can see what's happening in the world. No one wants to be alone. I do not mean alone with a radio, with a book, sitting under a tree by yourself, or in a monastery with a different name or a different label. Aloneness implies an awareness of all the different implications of the various forms of commitments of man out of his confusion. When a mature human being demands freedom from confusion, then there is that awareness of the facts of confusion. Out of that there is an aloneness. Then one is alone. Then one is really not afraid.

What are we to do? We see very clearly that any action born of confusion only leads to more confusion. That's very simple and very clear. Then what is right action? We live by action. We cannot but act. The whole process of living is action. We must again go into this question of what action is. We know very clearly the action born of confusion, through which action we hope to achieve certainty, clarity. If we see that, then, not being committed to any course of thought, philosophy, or ideals, what is action? This is a legitimate question after we have said all these things. The only action that we know is the action of conformity. We have had certain experiences, certain pleasures, certain knowledge, and that has set the course of our action. We believe in certain things, and according to that belief we act, conform. We've had certain pleasures in our experience: sexual or nonsexual, ideological, and so on. Pleasure dictates the course of our action. Most of our action, the doing, is always the outcome of the past. Action is never in the present; it is always the result of the past. That action is what we call positive because it's always following what has been, in the present, and creating the future.

Please, we're not talking about any deep philosophy. We're just observing the facts. We can go very, very, very deeply. But first we must clear the field.

The word *action* implies an active present. Action is always action in the present, not "I have acted," or "I will act." Our action is an approximation of an idea, a symbol, an ideology, a philosophy, an experience which we have had, or of our knowledge, accumulated experiences, traditions, and so on. Is there an action which is nonconforming?

Only in freedom do we have passion. I'm not talking of lust. Not that it doesn't have its right place, but I am talking of freedom in which there is intense energy and passion. Otherwise we can't act; otherwise, we're merely repetitive, mechanical machines—machines set up by society, by the particular culture in which we have grown, or by the religious organizational machine. If we see the urgency of freedom, in that seeing there is passion. Passion is always in the present, not something that has passed or that you will have tomorrow, which is the passion created by thought. I have pleasure. Surely there is a difference between the passion of pleasure and the passion which comes when there is complete freedom from confusion, when there is total clarity. That clarity is only possible, with its intensity, with its passion, with its timeless quality, when we understand what action is, and whether action can ever be freed from imitation, from conformity to the dictates of society, of our own fears, or of our own inherent laziness. We like to repeat, repeat, repeat, especially anything that gives us great pleasure: the sexual act and all the rest of it. That becomes much more important when society becomes more and more superficial, which is what is happening in the world. When progress is technological, outward, when prosperity is self-centered, then pleasure becomes of the highest importance, whether it's the pleasure of sex or the pleasure of a religious experience. (Laughter) Please don't laugh, because all these things are much too serious. We are facing a tremendous crisis in life. Some know this crisis, which is not economic or social but a crisis in consciousness itself, and to break through that, to answer that crisis as a challenge demands great seriousness.

We have to go into this question of action because life is a movement in action. We can't just sit still, but that is what we are trying to do. We are in the movement of what has been, and young people say, "We are the new generation," but they're not. To understand all this, we must go into this question of what action in freedom is. Is there such a thing as freedom? Can the mind be free from its conditioning, and the brain cells themselves, which have been so heavily

conditioned for so many million years, which have their own responsive patterns?

What is action? Action according to an idea we know very well, and action according to a formula—either one imposed outwardly on the mind or a formula which the mind creates for itself, according to which it acts: a formula of knowledge, of experience, of tradition, and of fear of what the neighbor says. That's the action we know, but that action is always limited. It always leads to more conditioning.

Is there any other action which is not conditioning? I think inevitably one must ask this question for oneself. Knowing what is taking place in the world—the misery, the wars, the political divisions, the geographical divisions, the divisions created by religions, by beliefs and dogmas—seeing all that, can there be an action which is not of that pattern?

As we have said, to agree or disagree has no meaning. We can turn our backs on the challenge, on the crisis, and amuse ourselves, entertain ourselves in various ways. Each one of us is confronted with a crisis because we are totally responsible for the whole structure of human society. We are responsible for these wars; we are responsible for these national, geographical divisions; we are responsible for the divisions of religion, with their dogmas, with their fears, with their superstitions, because we have committed ourselves to them. We cannot avoid them; there they are. How will we answer?

Is there any action which is not creating its own bondage? I think there is, and I'm going to go into it. Please, again, we're not accepting any authority. The speaker has no authority whatsoever because there is no follower, nor is there any teacher. The follower destroys the teacher, and the teacher destroys the follower. What we are trying to do is to examine, and in the process of examination discover for ourselves what is true. It really is not a process. Process implies time, gradually, step by step. But there is no step by step; there is no gradual process of understanding. When we see something very clearly, we act; and clarity of perception doesn't come about through a gradual process, and time.

As we said, there is positive action, with which we are all familiar. We are trying to find out if there is an action which is not positive at all in the sense which we have understood as positive, which is conformity. To put it differently, we are confused. Of that there is no doubt. In our relationships with each other, in our activities, trying to decide which god to worship, if we worship at all, we are confused. Out of that confusion any action is still confusing. That understanding, if you observe it very carefully— and I hope you are doing it now—brings about a negation of the positive. There is an action which is not positive. The very denying of the positive is negative action.

Let me put it differently. Is there action which is not based on a mechanical process? I'm not talking of spontaneous action. There is no such thing as spontaneous action, except perhaps when one sees some dangerous thing, or when a child is drowning. One does not face something like that every day. One must find this other type of action; otherwise, one is a mere machine, which most human beings are, with the daily routine of going to an office for forty years, with the repetitive action of pleasure, and so on.

We're trying to find out if there is an action which is not at all conforming. To find out, positive action must come to an end. Is it possible for positive action to come to an end without any assertion of the will? If there is any assertion of the will, a decision that all positive action must come to an end, that decision will create a new pattern, which will be an action of conformity.

When I say to myself, "I will not do that," the assertion of will is the outcome of my desire to find something new; but the old pattern, the old activity, is created by desire, by fear, by pleasure; by denying the old pattern through an action of will, I have created the same pattern in a different field. Is this fairly clear, not verbally clear? Explanation is never the thing. The word is not the real; the symbol is never the real. What is real is to see a thing very clearly, and when you see it, then positive action comes to an end. Freedom is total negation of the positive, but the positive is not the opposite of the negative; it is something entirely different, at a different dimension altogether.

Death is the ultimate negation of life, ending. And the ending we resist through positive assertion of the known—"my family," "my house," "my character," "my this," and "my that." We're not going into the immense question of death now. That we'll have to do another evening. What we're trying to find out is whether there is an action in total negation. We have to negate totally all the structure of fear, all the structure that demands security, certainty, because there is no security, no certainty. There is no certainty in Vietnam. A man killed there is a man, is you.

Can we, in the very denying of the total positive fragmentary approach to life, deny that totally, not through any ideal or through any pleasure, but because we see the absurdity of the whole of that structure? Not belonging to any nation, to any group, to any society, to any philosophy, to any activity— completely denying all that because we see that it is the product of a confused mind. In that very denial is the action which is not conforming. That is freedom.

During the five thousand years since recorded history began, man has chosen the way of war: nearly fifteen thousand wars, two and a half wars every year, and we haven't denied wars. We have favorite wars and not-favorite wars. We haven't denied violence, which indicates that man does not want peace. Peace is not something between two wars, or the peace of the politician. Peace is something entirely different. Peace comes when there is freedom from the positive. When we totally deny war, or totally deny the division of the religious absurdities because we understand the whole nature of it all, its structure, not because we don't like this or that—it has nothing to do with like or dislike—in the very denial of that is the negation, and out of that negation is an action which is never conforming.

A confused mind seeking clarity will only further confuse itself because a confused mind can't find clarity. It's confused; what can it do? Any search on its part will only lead to further confusion. I think we don't realize that. When it's confused, one has to stop—stop pursuing any activity. And the very stopping is the beginning of the new, which is the most positive action—positive in a different sense altogether. All this implies that there must be profound self-knowing—to know the whole structure of one's thinking-feeling, the motives, the fears, the anxieties, the guilt, the despair. To know the whole content of one's mind, one has to be aware, aware in the sense of observing, not with resistance or with condemnation, not with approval or disapproval, not with pleasure or nonpleasure, just observing. That observation is the negation of the psychological structure of a society which says, "You must; you must not." Therefore self-knowledge is the beginning of wisdom, and also, self-knowledge is the beginning and the ending of sorrow. Self-knowing is not to be bought in a book, or by going to a psychologist and being examined analytically. Self-knowledge is actually understanding *what is* in oneself—the pains, the anxieties;

seeing them without any distortion. Out of this awareness clarity comes into being.

Question: How can one start to learn to know oneself?

KRISHNAMURTI: I wonder why we make everything so difficult. First of all, we don't know ourselves at all. We are all second-hand people. We are at the mercy of all the analysts, philosophers, teachers. To know ourselves, we must understand what learning is. Learning is something entirely different from accumulating knowledge; learning is always active present. Knowledge is always in the past. A mind that learns a language is accumulating words, storing up. Any technique is the same. From that accumulation the mind acts. Learning is something entirely different. Learning is never accumulating. I have to accumulate if I have to learn a technique, and from that technique, from that skill which I have learned, I operate and add more to the skill. That surely is not learning. Learning is a movement, a flow; and there is no flow the moment there is a static state of knowledge, which is essential when we function technologically. But life isn't technological accumulation; life is a movement, and to learn it and to follow it, one has to learn each moment. To learn, there is no accumulation.

That's the first thing one has to observe. If there is to be self-knowledge, there must be an act of learning each minute—not having learned, I look at myself and then add more to that knowledge after I have looked at myself. In that case the division between the observer and the observed is sustained.

Look, sir, I want to know about myself. First of all, I've been told so many things about myself—that I am the soul, that I am the eternal flame, and God knows what else. There are dozens of philosophies and ideas: the higher self, the lower self, the permanent reality, and so on. I want to learn about myself, so I have to discard all that, obviously. I have to discard by observing how tremendously the mind has been influenced. We are the slaves of propaganda, whether religious, military, or business. We are all that, and to understand it, we can't condemn it. We mustn't say, "This is good, this is bad, this I must keep, this I must not keep." We must observe.

To observe there must be no condemnation, no justification, no acceptance. Then I begin to learn. Learning is not accumulation. Then I watch. I watch to see what I am, not what I should like to be, but *what actually is*. I'm not in misery; I do not say, "How terrible what I am is!" It is so. I neither condemn nor accept. I observe. I see the way, the pattern of my thinking, my feeling, my motives, my fears, my anxieties.

Who is the observer? This is not deep philosophy but just ordinary, daily occurrence. Who is the observer? Who is the 'I' that says, "I look"? The 'I' which is looking is the accumulated experiences, condemnations, observations, knowledge, and so on. It is the center, the observer. He separates himself from the observed. He says, "I am observing my fear, my guilt, my despair." But the observer is the observed. If he is not, he wouldn't recognize his despair.

I know what despair is, what loneliness is, and that memory remains. The next time it arises, I say that I see something different from me. The division into the observer and the observed creates a conflict, and then I go off at a tangent, trying to find out how to resolve that conflict. But the fact is that the observer is the observed. This is not an intellectual concept but a fact. When the observer is the observed, then learning is acting. I don't learn and then act, but this action takes place only when the observer is the observed, and that action is the denial of what has been, the mechanical process.

Question: Is there a state of awareness where the past does not continually reassert itself?

KRISHNAMURTI: "Is there an awareness of the total process of time, the total process, not the fragmentary process of yesterday, today, and tomorrow?" Again, we have to go into the whole question of time, but this is not the moment. If there is a total awareness of time, then there is no continuity as "I am aware," or "I have been aware," or "I will be aware."

When you are completely attentive—giving your mind, your heart, your nerves, your eyes, your ears—when everything is attentive, there is no time at all. You then don't say, "Well, I was attentive yesterday, and I'm not today." Attention is not a continuous momentum of time. Either you are attentive or you are not attentive. Most of us are inattentive, and in that state of inattention we act and create misery for ourselves. If you are totally attentive to what is taking place in the world—the starvation, the wars, the disease, the whole—then the whole division of man against man comes to an end.

Question: There are moments almost like that, but the next day or the next moment it's gone. How am I to keep that memory which I have had?

KRISHNAMURTI: It's a memory, and therefore it's a dead thing. Therefore it's not awareness, not attention. Attention is completely in the present. That's the art of living, sir. When you are inattentive, don't act. That requires a great deal of intelligence, a great deal of self-observation, because it's inattention that breeds mischief and misery. When you are completely attentive with all your being, in that state action is instantaneous.

But the mind remembers that action and wants to repeat it, and then you are lost.

Question: Can you speak about the relation of action, energy, and attention?

KRISHNAMURTI: I am doing it, sir. Inattention is a dissipation of energy, is wasted energy. And we are trained, through education, through all the social and psychological structure of the world, to be inattentive. People think for us; they tell us what to do, what to believe; they tell us how to experience, to use a new drug; and we, like sheep, follow. All that is inattention. When there is self-knowledge, when there is delving deeply into the whole structure, the nature of oneself, then attention becomes a natural thing. There is great beauty in attention.

September 30, 1966

Fourth Talk in New York

I would like to talk over something which seems to me to be extraordinarily important. I think a community or a society that has not understood the problem of time, death, and love will obviously be very superficial; and a society or a community that is superficial must inevitably deteriorate. I mean by that word *superficial* merely to be contented with outward phenomena, with outward success, with prosperity, having a good time and demanding entertainment. Human beings who are part of that society must inevitably deteriorate, whether they go to a church or to football games. These are just the same. People go to them because they need to be entertained, stimulated. Unless we human beings resolve these fundamental questions, inevitably the mind will deteriorate. The problem is: Is it possible to stop this continuous wave of deterioration, not only of the mind and the heart, but also the deterioration which takes place when there is no earnestness, an urgency, a passion? When we talk over this question of time, death, and love, I think it is most important to bear in mind that the word, the explanation, is not the fact. Most of us are so easily satisfied with explanations; we think we have understood. Most of us who have read a great deal or who have experimented with many things are clever enough to explain anything away. We can give an explanation for almost anything, and the explanation seems to satisfy us, but when we discuss something very seriously, mere satisfaction of verbal explanation seems to me utterly futile, immature. Also, if I may go over it again a little briefly, it is very important how we listen because most of us do not really listen at all. We listen either with pleasure, with distaste, or with a formula of ideas, a philosophy which we have cultivated, or have learned. Through these screens we listen, interpreting, translating, putting aside what we don't like, keeping what we like, and the act of listening never takes place.

I do not know if you have ever observed, when you are listening to someone whom you have known for many years, with whom you are fairly intimate, that you hardly listen; you already know what he is going to say. Your mind is already made up; you already have certain conclusions, certain images, which prevent actual listening. To listen is an extraordinarily important act. I feel that if you could listen, not only to what is being said by the speaker, but also to everything about your lives, every day—listen to all the various noises, listen to the incessant chatter of your friend, your wife or your husband, or to the rumblings of your own mind, the soliloquy that goes on, neither condemning nor justifying, but actually listening—then that listening would bring about in itself an action which is totally different from the action of a very calculated, drilled thought.

Perhaps, this evening, you can so listen, which doesn't mean that you must agree or disagree. On the contrary, to listen the mind must be extraordinarily sensitive, eager, critical, aware of its own functioning, which means that it is in a state of attention, and therefore of passion. Only such a mind can actually listen and go beyond verbal images and conclusions, hopes, and fears. Then only is there communication between two people, which is actually—if I may use that word which is so heavily laden and spoiled—love. I hope we can establish that relationship between the speaker and yourselves so that we can discuss informally this question of time and death.

I do not know if you have ever gone into the question of death. Most of us are afraid of this thing called death, which is the unknown. We avoid it, put it away; or we have come to certain conclusions, rationalize death, and are satisfied to live the allotted time. To understand something which we don't know, there must obviously be the end of fear. We must understand fear, not the explanation of fear, not all the psychological structure of fear, but the nature of fear.

Our first concern, it seems to me, when we are dealing with deep subjects and deep realities, should be to approach them with a fresh mind, with a mind that is neither hoping nor in despair, a mind that is capable of observing, facing facts without any tremor, any sense of fear or anxiety. Unless fear is totally resolved, neither suppressing it nor escaping from it, we cannot possibly understand the nature of death. The mind must be completely and entirely free of fear because a mind that is afraid, that is in despair, or has the fantasy of hope, which is always looking to the future—such a mind is a clouded mind, is a confused mind, is incapable of thinking clearly, except along the line of its trained, drilled, technological knowledge; it will function mechanically there. But a mind that is afraid lives in darkness; a mind that is confused, in despair, in anxiety cannot resolve anything apart from the mechanical process of existence, and I'm afraid that most of us are satisfied to live mechanically. We would rather not deal with deeper subjects, deeper issues, deeper challenges.

Is it possible to be free in the whole area of the mind, in what is called the unconscious, as well as in the conscious? As we said the other day, there is no such thing as the unconscious. There is only this field of consciousness. We can be aware of a particular area of the field, and not be aware of the rest of it. If we are not aware of the rest of it, then we don't understand the whole area. Unfortunately it has been divided into the conscious and the unconscious, and we play this game between the conscious and the unconscious all the time. It has become the fashion to inquire into the unconscious. Whereas, if we are at all aware of the whole field, there is no need for the unconscious at all; and therefore there is no need for dreams. It is only the mind that is aware of a particular corner of the field and totally unaware of the rest that begins to dream, and then there are all the interpretations of dreams, and all that stuff. If we are aware during the entire day of every thought, every feeling, every motive, every response—aware, not interpreting it, not condemning it, not justifying it, but just being aware of the whole process—then we will see that there is no need for dreams at all. Then the mind becomes highly sensitive, active, not made dull.

When we inquire into this question of fear, when we examine it—and I hope we'll do it together this evening—we have to cover the whole area, the whole field, not one particular form of fear, not your particular, favorite fear, or the fear which you are avoiding. Fear, surely, exists only in relationship to something. It doesn't exist by itself. I'm afraid of you; I'm afraid of an idea; I'm afraid my belief will be shattered because of a new idea, and so on. It's in relation to something. It doesn't exist per se, by itself. And to understand the total fear, we must look at it nonfragmentarily, not as a particular, neurotic fear which we have. We must look at it as we look at the total map of the world. Then we can go to the particular. Then we can take in detail and look at the particular road, the particular village we're going to. We must have total comprehension, and that's somewhat arduous because we have always been thinking in terms of the particular, in fragments.

To contact fear, total fear, requires total attention. By that word *attention* I do not mean concentration. Concentration is the easiest thing to do, but to attend demands your complete energy. To give your complete attention, everything must be at its highest point—your body, your mind, your heart, your nerves. Only then is there attention. With that attention you can look at fear; in that attention there is no fragmentary, broken concentration on a particular subject; you see the whole of it, the totality of fear, its structure, its meaning, its significance, its inwardness. If you go that far, then you'll see that fear comes to an end, totally, completely, because you are not caught by the word, by the symbol, by the word *fear*, which creates fear also, like the word *death* creates its own fear. You become attentive when problems are urgent, when the challenge is immediate. You feel that challenge instantly, come into contact with it completely.

Ordinarily we are never in contact with a problem, with a challenge, with an issue, because when an issue arises, we already have an answer for it. We already have a conclusion, a verbal, cunning mind which meets that word, that challenge and has already answered the challenge. So there is no contact. To be in contact means to be directly in touch with something, and you cannot come

into touch with something directly if there is an idea between.

To come into contact with fear, one has not only to understand the word which stimulates fear but also to understand how the mind is caught in words, for all our thinking is formulated in words, in symbols. To come directly into contact with fear, one must be free of the verbal structure which the brain, the mind, has created. If one wants to come into contact with that, one has to touch it. To touch it is not the word, is not a conclusion; it's an actual fact. If one is cunning, clever, erudite, full of knowledge and intellection, one doesn't touch it at all; there is no direct contact with it.

If you do listen to what is being said in that direct sense, then you will discover the total area of the mind, and the mind will have understood the nature of the word, how the word creates the feeling, and how the image foreshadows what it is afraid of. The verbal, the symbolic, the process of thinking in terms of words, all have come to an end, and you are able to come directly into contact with that thing which you call fear.

As we were saying the other day, we are never in contact with any other human being: our wife or our husband, our children or whoever it may be, because we have images of the husband, the wife, the boss, and so on. These images have relationships with each other, but there is no actual relationship at all. These images are everlastingly in battle with each other. We also have images about fear, about death, about love, and all the deeper issues of life.

To understand the question of time is very important. I am using the word *understand* in the sense of coming directly into contact with something which the mind through thought cannot possibly comprehend. You cannot comprehend love through words, through ideas, through the experiences which you have had. This question of time is important because to understand death you must understand time, and to understand death and time is to know, to understand, what love is. Without understanding these three things, these fundamental issues, life has very little meaning. You may go to the office and have plenty of money, but it actually has very little meaning. When life loses its deep significance, then you are satisfied with superficial activity which leads to more confusion and to more sorrow. That's what is actually taking place in the world, not only in this country, but in the whole of Europe, in India, and elsewhere.

These questions must be solved by each human being because a human being is part of society. A human being is not separate from society; he is conditioned by society, which he has created. To create a new society or a new community, the fundamental issues of life must be solved.

When we are talking about time, we do not mean chronological time, time by the watch. That time exists, must exist. If you want to catch a bus, if you want to get to a train or meet an appointment tomorrow, you must have chronological time. But is there a tomorrow, psychologically, which is the time of the mind? Is there psychologically tomorrow, actually? Or is the tomorrow created by thought because thought sees the impossibility of change, directly, immediately, and invents this process of gradualness? I see for myself, as a human being, that it is terribly important to bring about a radical revolution in my way of life, thinking, feeling, and in my actions, and I say to myself, "I'll take time over it; I'll be different tomorrow, or in a month's time." That is the time we are talking about: the psychological structure of time, of tomorrow, or the future, and in that time we live. Time is the past, the present, and the future, not by the watch. I was, yesterday; yesterday operates through today and creates the future. That's a fairly simple

thing. I had an experience a year ago that left an imprint on my mind, and the present I translate according to that experience, knowledge, tradition, conditioning, and I create the tomorrow. I'm caught in this circle. This is what we call living; this is what we call time.

Please, I hope you are observing your own minds, and not merely listening to the speaker.

In this process of time, memory is very important: memory of a happy childhood, memory of some deep experience, memory of a pleasure which I've stored up, which I want to repeat tomorrow; and the repetition of the pleasure tomorrow is continued through thought. So thought is time because if I do not think, psychologically, of tomorrow, there is no tomorrow. Please, this is not oversimplification. To understand something very complex, something that needs deep examination and penetration, you must begin very, very simply; and it is the first step that matters, not the last step.

Thought, which is you, with all its memories, conditioning, ideas, hopes, despair, the utter loneliness of existence—all that is this time. The brain is the result of time chronologically—two million years, and more. It has its own reactions of greed, envy, ambition, jealousy, anxiety. And to understand a timeless state, when time has come to a stop, one must inquire whether the mind can be free totally of all experience, which is of time.

I hope I am not making it complicated. Explanations are complicated, but not the actual fact; and if one is aware, attentive, one sees this process. Life is a continuous process of challenge and response, and every response is conditioned by its past. Every challenge is new; otherwise, it is not a challenge, and we're always responding from the past, except on rare occasions which we needn't even discuss. They are so rare that it doesn't much matter. Into the brain every challenge and response as experience is being accumulated, and from that accumulation we act, we think, we feel, we function psychologically, inwardly, inside the skin, as it were, and that is time.

One asks oneself whether it is possible to live so completely that there is neither yesterday, today, nor tomorrow. To understand that and live it, not theoretically but actually, one must examine the structure of memory, of thought. One has to ask oneself what thinking is. What is thinking, and why should one think? I know it's the habit to think, to reason, to judge, to choose. To do this at a mechanical level is absolutely necessary; otherwise, one couldn't function. But is it possible to live from day to day freed from psychological time as yesterday, today, and tomorrow? This doesn't mean that one lives in the moment; that's one of our absurd fallacies. What matters is to live now. The now is the result of yesterday: what one has thought, what one has felt, one's memories, hopes, fears, all that has been stored up. Unless one understands that and dissipates it, one can't live in the now.

There is no such thing as the "now" by itself, for life is a total movement, an endless movement, which we have divided psychologically into yesterday, today, and tomorrow, and hence we have invented the process of gradual achievement for freeing ourselves. It's like a man who smokes or drinks: he'll give it up gradually; he'll take time over it. It's like a man who is violent, but who has the ideal of nonviolence. He is pursuing nonviolence and sowing the seeds of violence in the meantime. That's what we actually are doing, which is called evolution. I'm not a fundamentalist, please!

The mind, the brain, the whole structure can only understand the state of mind which has no time at all when it has understood the nature of memory and thought. Then we can face and begin to understand the nature of death. Death now is something in the distance, over there. We turn our backs on it; we run away from it; we have theories about it; we rationalize it, or we have hopes beyond it. In Asia, in India, they believe in reincarnation, and that's their hope. This doesn't mean that we have understood the whole beauty of death. The speaker is not being sentimental about death when he uses the word *beauty*. The issue involved in a future life is that there is a permanent entity, the soul, something which continues. They have given various names to that in the East and in the West, but in essence it is the same thing—something permanent, something that has a continuity. There is the death of the physical, the organism wearing itself out through strains, stresses, through various misuses, drugs, overindulgence in everything. The mechanism gradually wears out, dies. That's an obvious fact, but hope comes in and says, "There is a continuity. It isn't the end of everything. I've lived, struggled, accumulated, learned, developed a character"—I don't know why one develops a character, which is neither here nor there; character is merely a resistance—"and that permanent entity will continue until it becomes perfect," whatever that may mean.

Is there a permanent entity at all? I know the believers say yes, but the believers are not the speakers of truth. They are merely dogmatists, theologians, or people who are full of fanciful hope. If you examine yourself to find out if there is a thing that is permanent, obviously there is nothing permanent, both outwardly and inwardly. Though each one of us craves security outwardly, we are denying it by our nationalities, by wars. They are denying security, total physical security, in Vietnam, though each side craves security. Is there such a thing as permanent security, except an idea about it? If there is not, and there is no such thing as "there is," then what is it that continues? Is it memory, experiences which are dead, ashes of things that have been? If you believe in reincarnation and its different forms, such as resurrection, then it matters tremendously how you live today, what you believe today, how you act, what you do. Everything matters immensely because in the next life you are going to pay for it, which is just an avoidance of the real fact of what death is. There is the death of the physical organism; and to find out what is beyond that, can the whole psyche, with all the tendencies, pleasures, idiosyncrasies, memories, experiences, die each day, completely, without argument, without restraint—just die?

Have you ever tried to die to a pleasure, something that you want tremendously, that gives you great satisfaction, delight, without any reason, without any motive, without any argument—just to die to it? If you can, you will know what death means: to empty the mind totally of everything of the past. It can be done; it should be done. That's the only way to live, for love is that, isn't it? Love is not thought. Love is not desire, pleasure. Pleasure, desire, continues through thought; and when thought thinks about a particular pleasure, sexual or otherwise, then it seeks to be loved. It's an appetite. An appetite has its own place, but unfortunately there is a great deal of talk about love in the churches, in books, in cinemas.

If we loved there would be no war. We would educate our children entirely differently, not merely condition them to certain technological knowledge. Then the whole world wouldn't be mad about this thing called sex, as though it had discovered something totally new. We only know love as sexual appetite, with its lusts, demands, frustrations, despairs, jealousies, and all the travail of the human mind in what is called love. Love has nothing whatsoever to do with the formula of

thought, and it comes into being only when memory as thought, with all its demands and pleasures, comes to an end psychologically. Then love is something entirely different. We cannot talk about it; we cannot write everlasting books about it. Love of God and love of man—this division doesn't exist, but to come to that, we must not only be free from fear, but also there must be a time ending, and therefore an understanding of life. We can only understand life when we understand death. The thing that we call living is this anxiety, this despair, this sense of guilt, this endless longing, this utter loneliness, this boredom, this constant conflict, this battlefield. In the world of business, in our daily existence at home, on the battlefields all over the world, we are destroying each other—this is what we call living. Actually it is a frightful mess, a deadly affair. When that so-called living comes to an end—and it can only come to an end when one dies to the whole of it, not partially or to certain fragments of it—then one lives. Death and living go together; and for death and life to continue together, there must be dying every day to everything. Then the mind is made fresh, young, innocent. That innocency cannot come through any drug, through any experience. It must be beyond and above all experience. A light to itself does not need any experience.

Question: Why were we put here? Why are we alive?

KRISHNAMURTI: Please, as we said the other day, don't let's ask irrelevant questions. What is relevant is how to live, not why we are put here. Obviously, you know how we have come into being: father-mother. But we are here, and we are dying slowly or rapidly, deteriorating, with our prosperity, with our self-centered activities. Is it possible to live in this world, and not in a monastery, not isolating ourselves in some conclusions, beliefs, and dogmas, or in some nationality, or in good works? Can one live? That's the real issue.

Question: How does one die each day?

KRISHNAMURTI: Is there a method? If there is a method, then the method produces its own end. If I follow a particular method, if you tell me how to die every day and give me a method, step by step, what happens? Do I die actually, or am I practicing a certain method of dying? It is very important to understand this. The means is the end; the two are not separate. If the means is mechanical, the end is mechanical. If the means is a way of assuring pleasure, gain, profit, then the end is also that. The means creates its own end, and one has to completely deny that means, or the total means, which is time. So there is no "how" to die.

Sir, look. You have a certain habit: sexual, or a certain habit of drinking, smoking, talking, mannerisms, temperaments. Can you die, can you completely put away, on the instant, smoking, drinking, pleasure? I know there are the methods of how to give up smoking little by little, one by one. There is no ending to that. Ending means finishing it, completely ending it; and that does take place when death actually comes. You don't argue with it.

Can one live so completely each day, each minute, that there is no yesterday or tomorrow? To do this requires a great deal of meditation and inward awareness. It is not a matter of agreeing or disagreeing, or asking how it is to be done. No one is going to tell one whether one has or has not done it. This demands a great deal of energy, insight, understanding, awareness, and the highest quality of sensitivity, which is intelligence. Drugs, LSD, and all the rest—not that I have taken them—make one sensitive in a par-

ticular corner of that vast field of life. In the rest of the field one is insensitive, dull; and because one becomes highly sensitive in a particular area, seeing colors, visions, and having experiences, one thinks that is the whole substance of life. But to understand the totality of life, one must be totally sensitive, both physiologically and psychologically. One thinks that one can be highly sensitive psychologically, but physically brutal, heavy, and insensitive. Life is not to be divided into fragments, with each fragment in conflict with the others. We only know this conflict, this endless effort until we die. In the family, in the office, even in the quiet moments of our lives, there is never a moment of silence, a state without effort.

Question: The other day you said that the man dying in Vietnam is you. Would you speak further on that?

KRISHNAMURTI: We are not talking of the man dying in Vietnam; we are talking of the man living here, now. The man dying in Vietnam is the result of our life. We do not want peace. We talk about it endlessly, but to have peace, we must live peacefully. That means no competition, no ambition, no division as nationalities, no color prejudice. That's what it means to live peacefully. As we don't live peacefully, we have wars in Vietnam, in India, in Russia, and elsewhere. Really, we educate our children to die, to be killed, whether in the office, in the family, or on a battlefield; and this we call living. We are supposed to be highly civilized, sophisticated people. Too bad! Sorrow is the lot of us, and to end sorrow, we must end time; we must understand the nature of death. Where there is love, there is no sorrow, for the neighbor, for someone beside you, or ahead of you. Where there is love, there is an ending of sorrow, not the worshiping of sorrow.

Comment: Sir, if one is not to make any effort, then it must all be a matter of accident whether anything is understood.

KRISHNAMURTI: Why do we make effort? First let's understand it, and not try to find out if we are not to make effort. We are making effort. From the moment we are born until we die, there is effort, struggle. Why? If we rightly understand this struggle psychologically, inwardly, then outwardly existence will have a totally different meaning. We must understand effort, this constant striving. There is an effort when there is contradiction. There is effort when there is comparison: you are better than I, you are much more clever, you have a better position, you're famous, and I am no one, so I must reach you. That's a fact, not a supposition. That is how we function every day of our lives. We worship success. Every magazine is filled with success stories, and from the moment we start going to school until we die, we are comparing, struggling, in incessant conflict, because there is a division, a contradiction between the one who compares and that which he is compared to. Through comparison we think we understand, but actually we don't.

To live without comparison requires tremendous intelligence and sensitivity because then there is no example, there is no something that should be, no ideal, no hero. We begin with what actually is, and to understand *what is,* there is no need for comparison. When we compare, we destroy *what is.* It's like comparing a boy to his elder brother who is very clever; if you do that, you destroy the younger boy. That's what we are doing all the time. We are struggling, struggling for what, psychologically? To end violence? To have more experience? To end violence is to come directly into contact with it in yourself, and you cannot come into contact with it if there is an ideal, such as non-violence or peace. This opposite creates conflict, but if you can look at that violence completely, with total attention, then there is no conflict, no striving. It comes to an end. It is these absurd, idiotic ideals which destroy the direct contact with reality.

You can live a life without conflict, which doesn't mean that you become a vegetable. On the contrary, the mind then becomes highly aware, intelligent, full of energy, passion. Conflict dissipates this intelligence.

Question: Is there any difference between love and understanding?

KRISHNAMURTI: One word will cover everything, but the danger of one word is that it becomes a jargon. You can use the word *love* or the word *understanding.* It doesn't really matter which word you use because every word is loaded, like *God, death, experience, love*—heavy with the meaning which people have given to the words. When one realizes that the word love is not the actual state, then the word doesn't matter at all.

Comment: The world is so densely populated that I wonder how we can exist without politics and participation in the direction of the community.

KRISHNAMURTI: There is only one political problem, which is the unity of mankind. You cannot have the unity of mankind if there are nationalities, if there are armies, if there is not one government—neither democratic, nor republican, nor labor—until we are concerned with human beings, whether they live in Russia, in India, in China, or in England. We have the means of feeding, sheltering, and clothing all peoples, now, but we don't do it, and you know the reasons: our nationalities, our religious prejudices, and all the rest.

Question: Are not technical knowledge and psychological knowledge tied together? Can they be separated?

KRISHNAMURTI: This is a tremendously important point. How is a human being, living in this utter chaos, how can he live supremely intelligently so that he is a good citizen, not of a particular community, but of the world? The world is not America or Russia or India. How can he live in this world, with such chaos and misery around him? That is the issue. Should he join the communist party, the democratic party, or some other party? There must be action. How shall we act together? With which end shall we begin? Shall we begin from the technological end, or from a totally different end, from an end which is not of time, which is not of class, which is not of any experience? If we can come to grips with that, then we shall solve all our problems.

Question: What's the name?

KRISHNAMURTI: Do you think, sir, that a name will be really satisfactory? Call it X, call it God, call it love—any name. The name is not the real. Will naming it be sufficient? Thousands of people have named it.

Comment: Give us a formula. (Laughter)

KRISHNAMURTI: We have talked about formulas, an ideology. A community based on an ideology is no longer a community. The people battle with each other for position, prestige in that community. We are talking of something entirely different. We said that a new mind is necessary, not a new technique, a new method, a new philosophy, or a new drug; and that new mind cannot come into being unless there is a dying to the old, completely, emptying the mind totally of the past. Then you don't want a name; then you are living it; then you know what bliss is. Living in this world with all the chaos round it, it is only the innocent mind that can answer these problems, not the complicated mind.

October 3, 1966

Fifth Talk in New York

Most of us must have noticed, not only in this country, but also in Europe and in India, that though the mechanical part of the brain is rapidly increasing, there is a deterioration taking place in other fields of life. The general relationship of man to man, morally and ethically, is actually deteriorating. We must, as human beings, not only come to grips with this great problem, but go beyond it, see what we can do, see if it is possible to stop the deterioration, the disintegration of a very capable mind. We have spent many, many years in cultivating the mechanical, technological side of life. The problems that exist there can easily be solved, but we have other problems, and we never seem to resolve them. Throughout life we go on increasing, or running away from, our problems, and we die with them. Is it possible for a mind to be totally free from all problems? It is the problems which remain unsolved that bring about the destruction, the deterioration of the mind.

Is it possible to resolve every problem as it arises, and not give to the problem a root in the mind? We are talking about non-mechanical problems, the psychological, the deeper issues of life. The more we carry these problems with us, the more heavily we are burdened with them, the more obviously the mind and the totality of our human existence become more and more complex, more and more confusing. There are greater strains and greater confusion. Naturally, the brain, as well as the totality of the mind, which is consciousness as a whole, deteriorates. Can a human being, living in this world, with all its influences, resolve his problems?

A problem exists only when there is an inadequate response to the challenge; otherwise, we have no problem. When we are incapable of responding totally to a challenge, whatever that challenge may be, then, out of that inadequacy, we have a problem. These challenges being always new, we respond to them mechanically, or with the accumulation of knowledge or experience, and there is no immediate response.

All over the world this is taking place. Outwardly we are making great progress; outwardly there are great changes taking place, but inwardly, psychologically, there is no change at all, or very little. There is a contradiction between what is going on within, and the vast changes taking place outwardly. Inwardly we are tradition-bound; our responses are animalistic, limited. One of our great problems is how to renew, make new the psyche, the whole of consciousness. Is it possible?

Man has always tried to go beyond his problems, either escaping from them through various methods or inventing beliefs, which he hopes will renew the mind that is always deteriorating. He goes through various experiences, hoping that there will be one experience which will transcend all others and give him a total comprehension of life. He tries so many ways—through drugs, through meditation, through worship, through sex, through knowledge—and yet through all these methods he doesn't seem to be able to solve the central factor that brings about this deterioration. Is it possible to empty the mind totally so that it is fresh every day, so that it is no longer creating problems for itself, so that it is able to meet every challenge so completely, so totally, that it leaves no residue, which becomes another problem? Is

it possible to have every kind of experience that human beings have, and yet at the end of the day not have any residue to be carried over to the next day, except mechanical knowledge? Don't let's confuse the two issues. If this is not possible, the mind then deteriorates, naturally; it can only disintegrate. Our question is: Can the mind, which is the result of time, of experience, of all the influences of the culture, of the social, economic, and climatic conditioning—can it free itself and not have a problem so that it is always fresh, always capable of meeting every challenge as it comes? If we are not capable of this, then we die; a miserable life has come to an end. We haven't resolved our sorrows; we haven't ever satisfied our appetites; we have been caught in fulfillment and frustration; our life has been a constant battlefield.

We must find an answer to this question, not through any philosophy, for of course no philosophy can answer it, although it may give explanations. To answer it is to be free from every problem so that the mind is tremendously sensitive, active. In this very activity, it can throw off every problem that arises.

We understand what we mean by a problem—the inadequate response to a challenge. There are endless challenges going on all the time, consciously or unconsciously. The more alert we are, the more thoughtful we are, the more acute the problems become. Being incapable of resolving them, we invent theories; and the more intellectual we are, the more cunning the mind is in inventing a structure, a belief, an ideology through which it escapes. Life is full of experiences which constantly impinge on the mind. As most of our lives are so utterly empty, lonely, boring—a meaningless, sorrowful existence—we want more and more, wider and deeper experiences. The peculiarity of experience is that it is never new. Experience is what has always been, not actually *what is*. If you have had an experience of any kind, you have recognized it and you say, "That is an experience." Recognition implies that you already know it, that you have already had such an experience, and therefore there is nothing new in experiencing. It is always the known that is capable of recognizing any experience, the past that says, "That experience I've already had," and therefore it is capable of saying it is an experience.

Both in Europe and in this country, LSD is giving new experiences to people, and they are pursuing these new experiences—"taking a trip," as it is called. These experiences are the result of their own conditioning, of their own limited consciousness, and therefore it is not something totally new. If it is something totally new, they would not recognize it as an experience. Can the mind be in such a state of activity that it is free from all experience?

We are the result of time, and during that time, we have cultivated all the human tendencies. Culture, society, religions have conditioned the mind. We are always translating every challenge in terms of our conditioning, and so what happens generally is, if we observe ourselves, that every thought, every movement of the mind, is limited, is conditioned, and thought cannot go beyond itself. If we did not have experience, we would go to sleep. If there were no challenge, however inadequate the response is, with all the problems that it brings, we would go to sleep. That's what is happening to most of us. We respond inadequately; we have problems; the problems become so enormous that we are incapable of solving them, and so these problems make us dull, insufficient, confused. This confusion and this inadequacy increase more and more and more, and we look to experience as a measure for bringing about clarity, bringing about a great, fundamental change.

Can experience of any kind bring about a radical change in the psyche, in consciousness? That is the issue; that is the problem. Our consciousness is the result of the past; we are the past. And a mind functioning within the field of the past cannot at any time resolve any problem. We must have a totally new mind; a revolution must take place in the psyche. Can this revolution come about through experience? That's what we are waiting for; that's what we want. We are looking for an experience that will transform us. That's why we go to church, or take drugs, or sit in meditation—because our craving, longing, intensity, is to bring about a change within ourselves. We see the necessity of it, and we look to some outside authority, or to our own experience.

Can any experience, through any means, bring about this total revolution in the psyche? Can any outside authority, outside agency, such as God, an idea, a belief, bring about this transformation? Will authority as an idea, as grace, as God—will that bring about a change? Will authority transform the human mind? This is very important to understand because to us authority is very important. Though we may revolt against authority, we set up our own authority, and we conform to that authority, like long hair, and so on.

There is the authority of the law, which obviously one must accept. Then there is the psychological authority, the authority of one who knows, as the priest. Nobody bothers about the priest nowadays. The so-called intellectual, fairly clear-thinking people, don't care about the priest, the church, and all their inventions, but they have their own authority, which is the authority of the intellect, reason, or knowledge, and they follow that authority. A man afraid, uncertain, not clear in his activities, in his life, wants some authority to tell him what to do—the authority of the analyst, the book, or the latest fad.

Can the mind be free from authority, which means free from fear, so that it is no longer capable of following? If so, this puts an end to imitation, which becomes mechanical. After all, virtue, ethics, is not a repetition of what is good. The moment it becomes mechanical, it ceases to be virtue. Virtue is something that must be from moment to moment, like humility. Humility cannot be cultivated, and a mind that has no humility is incapable of learning. So virtue has no authority. The social morality is no morality at all; it's immoral because it admits competition, greed, ambition, and therefore society is encouraging immorality. Virtue is something that transcends memory. Without virtue there is no order, and order is not according to a pattern, according to a formula. A mind that follows a formula through disciplining itself to achieve virtue creates for itself the problems of immorality.

An external authority which the mind objectifies, apart from the law, as God, as moral, and so on, becomes destructive when the mind is seeking to understand what real virtue is. We have our own authority as experience, as knowledge, which we are trying to follow. There is this constant repetition, imitation, which we all know. Psychological authority—not the authority of the law, the policeman who keeps order—the psychological authority, which each one has, becomes destructive of virtue because virtue is something that is living, moving. As you cannot possibly cultivate humility, as you cannot possibly cultivate love, so also virtue cannot be cultivated; and there is great beauty in that. Virtue is nonmechanical, and without virtue there is no foundation for clear thinking.

That brings in the problem of discipline. For most of us discipline is suppression, imitation, adjustment, conformity, and therefore there is a conflict all the time; but there is a discipline which is not suppression, which is not control, which is not adjustment. That discipline comes when it becomes imperative to see clearly. We are confused, and out of that confusion we act, which only increases confusion all the more. Realizing that we are confused, to not act demands great discipline in itself.

To see a flower demands a great deal of attention. If you really want to look at a flower, at a tree, at your neighbor, at your wife or your husband, you have to look; and you cannot look if thought interferes with that look. You realize that; you see that fact. The very observation of the fact demands discipline. There is no imposition of a mind that says, "I must be orderly, disciplined, in order to look." There is the psyche that demands authority to guide itself, to follow, to do the right thing. Such an authority ends all virtue, and without virtue you cannot possibly think clearly, live a life of tremendous sensitivity and activity.

We look to experience as a means to bring about this revolution in the psyche. Can any experience bring about a change in consciousness? First of all, why do we need experience? We demand it because our lives are empty. We've had sex; we've been to churches; we have read; we have done hundreds of little things; and we want some supreme experience that will clear away all this mess. What do we mean by experience, and why do we demand it?

This is a very serious question; do go into it with me. Find out for yourselves why you want experience, not only the experiences that LSD gives, but also other forms of experience. Obviously these experiences must be pleasurable, enjoyable; you don't want sorrowful experiences. Why? And who is it that is experiencing? When you are experiencing, in a state of experience, is there an experiencer who says, "I am enjoying it"? All experiences are always in the past, never at the moment, and any experience that you have is recognizable; otherwise, it is not an experience. If you recognize it, it is already known; otherwise, you can't recognize it.

A mind that demands experience as a means to bring about a radical revolution in the psyche is merely asking for a continuity of what has been, and therefore there is nothing new in experience. Most people need experience to keep them awake; otherwise, they would go to sleep. If there were no challenge, if there were no response, if there were no pleasure and pain, we would just become vegetables, cow-like. Experience keeps us awake, through pain, through suffering, through every form of discontent. On one side it acts as a stimulant, and on the other it keeps the mind from having clarity, from having a revolution.

Is it possible to keep totally awake, to be highly active, intelligent, sensitive? If the mind is sensitive, tremendously active, it doesn't need experience. It is only a dull mind, an insensitive mind that is demanding experience, hoping that through experience it will reach greater and greater and greater experiences of enlightenment.

The mind is the result of many centuries, thousands upon thousands of years. It has functioned always within the field of the known. Within that field of the known there is nothing new. All the gods it has invented are from the past, from the known. Can the mind by thought, by intelligence, by reason bring about a transformation?

We need tremendous psychological change, not a neurotic change; and reason, thought, cannot do it. Neither knowledge nor reason, nor all the cunning activities of the intellect will bring about this radical revolution in the psyche. If neither experience nor authority will bring it about, then what will? This is a fundamental question, not a question that can be answered by another; but in examining the question, not in trying to find an answer to the question, we will find the

answer. To put that question, we must be tremendously earnest because if we put the question with a motive, because we want certain results, the motive dictates the answer. Therefore we must put the question without motive, without any profit; and that's an extraordinarily difficult thing to do because all our activities, all our demands, have personal motives, or a personal motive identified with a greater motive, which is still a motive.

If thought, reason, knowledge, experience will not bring about a radical revolution in the psyche, what will? Only that revolution will solve all our problems. I'm examining the question; I'm not *answering* the question, because there is no answer, but in investigating the question itself we will come upon the answer. We must be intense, passionate, highly sensitive and therefore highly intelligent to pursue any investigation, and we cannot be passionate if we have a motive. Then that passion is only the result of wanting to achieve a result, and therefore it becomes a pleasure. Where there is pleasure, there is no passion. The very urgency of putting that question to ourselves brings about the energy to examine.

To examine anything, especially nonobjective things, things inside the skin, there must be freedom, complete freedom to look; and that freedom cannot be when thought as the response of previous experience as knowledge interferes with looking. If you are interested, just go with the speaker a little, not authoritatively; just look at it.

If you would look at a flower, any thought about that flower prevents your looking at it. The words *the rose, the violet, it is this flower, that flower, it is that species* keep you from observing. To look there must be no interference of the word, which is the objectifying of thought. There must be freedom from the word, and to look there must be silence; otherwise, you can't look. If you look at your wife or husband, all the memories that you have had, either of pleasure or of pain, interfere with looking. It is only when you look without the image that there is a relationship. Your verbal image and the verbal image of the other have no relationship at all. They are nonexistent.

May I suggest something? Please listen. Don't take notes. This is not a class. We are taking a journey together into one of the most difficult things, and that demands all your attention. If you take notes, it means that you are going to think about it later, which means that you are not doing it now, and therefore there is no urgency; and a mind that has no urgency about fundamental problems is a dead, dull, stupid mind, although it may be very cunning, very erudite. The urgency of a problem brings about energy and passion to look.

To observe, there must be freedom from the word, the word being the symbol, with all the content of that symbol, which is knowledge, and so on. To look, to observe, there must be silence; otherwise, how can one look at anything? Either that silence is brought about by an object which is so immense that it makes the mind silent or the mind understands that to look at anything it must be quiet. It is like a child who has been given a toy, and the toy absorbs the child. The child becomes completely quiet; so interesting is the toy that he is absorbed by it, but that's not quietness. Take away the object of his absorption, and he becomes again agitated, noisy, playful. To look at anything there must be freedom to look, and freedom implies silence. This very understanding brings about its own discipline. There is no interpretation on the part of the observer of what he's looking at, the observer being all the ideas, memories, experiences, which prevent his looking.

Silence and freedom go together. It is only a mind that is completely silent—not through discipline, not through control, not through demand for greater experience, and all that silly stuff—that can answer this question. When it is silent, it has already answered the question. Only complete silence can bring about a total revolution in the psyche—not effort, not control, not experience or authority. That silence is tremendously active; it is not just static silence. To come upon that silence, you have to go through all this. Either you do it instantly or you take time and analysis, and when you take time through analysis, you have already lost silence. Analysis, which is psychoanalysis, analyzing yourself, does not bring freedom; nor does the analysis which takes time, from today to tomorrow, and so on, gradually.

The mind, which is the result of time, which is the residue of all human experience—your mind and my mind—is the result of our human, endless struggle. Your problems are the problems of the Indian, in India. He goes through immense sorrow, like yourself. This demand to find truth, whether there can be a radical revolution in the mind, can be answered and discovered only when there is complete freedom, and therefore no fear. There is authority only when there is fear. When you have understood fear, authority, and the putting away of all demands for experience—which is really the highest form of maturity—then the mind becomes completely silent. It is only in that silence, which is very active, that you will see, if you have gone that far, that there is a total revolution in the psyche. Only such a mind can create a new society. There must be a new society, a new community of people who, though living in the world, are not of the world. The responsibility for such a community to come into being is yours.

Comment: Earlier you said that we must accept the authority of law. I can understand this with respect to such things as traffic regulations, but the law would have me become a soldier, and that I cannot accept.

KRISHNAMURTI: This is a problem all over the world. Governments demand that you join the army, take some kind of part in war. What are you going to do, especially when you are young? We older people are finished. What happens to the young people? This is a question that is asked everywhere in the world.

Now, there is no authority. I'm not advising what you should do or not do, whether you should join or not join, should kill or not kill. We are examining the question.

In India at one time in the past there was a community within that society which said, "We will not kill." They didn't kill animals for their food. They thought a great deal of not hurting another, speaking kindly, having always a certain respect for virtue. That community existed for many, many centuries. It was especially in the south as the Brahmin. But all that's gone. What are you to do: to help war or not to help? When you buy a stamp, you are helping the war; when you pay a tax, you are helping the war; when you earn money, you are helping the war; when you are working in a factory, you are producing shells for the war; and the way you live, with your competition, ambition, self-centered prosperity, you are producing war. When the government asks that you join the army, either you decide that you must, or must not and face all the consequences. I know a boy in Europe. There every boy must go through the army for a year, or a year and a half, or two years. This boy said, "I don't want to do it. I'm not going to do it." And he said, "I am going to run away." And he ran away, which means that he can never come back to his country. He left his property with the family. He can never see his family again. Whether you decide to join or

not to join becomes a very small affair when there are much larger issues concerned.

The larger issue is how to stop wars altogether, not this particular war or that particular war. You have your favorite war, and I may have my favorite war. Because I may happen to be a British citizen and hate Hitler, therefore I fight him; but I don't fight the Vietnamese because it's not my favorite war; it doesn't pay me politically, or whatever the reasons may be. The larger issue is: Man has chosen the way of war, conflict. Unless you alter that totally, you will be caught in this question in which the questioner is caught. To alter that totally, completely, you must live peacefully, not killing, either by word or by deed. That means no competition, no division of sovereign governments, no army. You say, "It is impossible for me to do it; I can't stop the war; I can't stop the army." But what is important, it seems to me, is that when you see the whole structure of human violence and brutality, which expresses itself ultimately in war, if you see that totally, then in the very act of seeing, you will do the right thing. The right thing may produce all kinds of consequences; it doesn't matter. But to see the totality of this misery, you need great freedom to look; and that very looking is the disciplining of the mind, brings its own discipline. Out of that freedom there comes silence, and you'll have answered your question.

Question: What do you mean when you say that we must accept the authority of law?

KRISHNAMURTI: Like traffic. . .

Comment: Oh.

KRISHNAMURTI: Taxes. . .

Comment: Oh, all that.

KRISHNAMURTI: Don't put me in a position or yourself in a position where I reject, or you reject accepting law. We purposely said the issue is greater than this. Man has lived for five thousand years in war, and can man live peacefully? To live peacefully every day demands an astonishing alertness, an awareness of every issue.

Question: Can an attempt to revolutionize the psyche also be termed expansion of consciousness?

KRISHNAMURTI: To expand consciousness there must be a center which is aware of its expansion. The moment there is a center from which you are expanding, it is no longer expansion because the center always limits its own expansion. If there is a center and I move from that center, though I call it expansion, the center is always fixed. I may expand ten miles, but since the center is always fixed, it is not expansion. It is wrong to use that word *expansion.*

Question: Doesn't revolution also imply a center?

KRISHNAMURTI: No, that's what I carefully explained. Sir, look, let me put it very briefly. You know what space is. When you look at the sky, there is a space, and that space is created by the observer who is looking. There is this object, the microphone, which creates space round itself. Because that object exists, there is space around it. There is this hall, this room. There is space because of the four walls, and there is space outside. We only know space because of the center, which is creating space around himself. Now, he can expand that space by meditation, concentration, and all the rest of it; but the space is always created by the object, like the microphone creates space around itself. As long as there is a center, as the observer, it creates a space round itself; and he may call that space ten thousand miles, or ten steps, but it is still the space restricted by the observer. Expanding consciousness, which is one of the easiest tricks to do, is always within the radius which the center creates. In that space there is no freedom at all because it is like my being free in this room, this hall. I'm not free. There is freedom, and therefore space which is not measurable, only when there is no observer; and the revolution of which we are talking is in the psyche, in the consciousness itself, in which there is now always the center who is talking in terms of 'me' and 'not-me'.

Question: "In the beginning was the word." What does this mean to you?

KRISHNAMURTI: Why should what another says mean anything to you? If you are investigating, looking, observing, then these questions don't arise. Even if it says in the Bible "the word" and all the rest of it, if you understand what authority is, then you can be free of authority to look, and you go beyond the word. To find out that ultimate reality which man has called God for thousands upon thousands of years, you must be free from belief; you must be free from authority. Then only can you find out if there is such a thing as God.

October 5, 1966

Sixth Talk in New York

This evening we will go into something that may be rather abstruse. In explaining things we must bear in mind that the explanation is not the fact. We are easily persuaded by explanations to believe or not to believe, to accept or to deny, but we must neither accept nor disregard the explanations.

When we are talking over together certain psychological facts, we must remember that the word and the explanations become barriers, that they hinder rather than help us to discover for ourselves. We are going together into something that needs a great deal of attention, a sensitivity of careful observation. It seems to me that erudition and being familiar with various philosophies and ideals do not in any way resolve our immense psychological complexities and problems. To understand these problems, one must have a serious intention to examine very closely, not what is being said so much as what actually is taking place when one is listening. As has been said, listening is one of the most difficult things to do—to actually listen, with neither pleasure nor displeasure, not bringing in one's idiosyncrasies, knowledge, and petty, little demands, which actually prevent listening. When one goes to a concert—and I don't know why one goes—one listens with pleasure. One says, "I have heard that music before; I like to hear it again"; there are memories, certain pleasurable experiences that one has had; and these memories prevent the actual fact of listening to a note, or to the silence between two notes. The silence is far more important than the note, but the silence becomes filled with the noise of memory, and therefore one ceases to listen altogether.

To actually listen needs attention, but not a forced, cultivated, drilled attention. Attention, and therefore listening, can only come when there is freedom, not when there is a motive. Motive always projects its own demands, and therefore there is no attention. Attention is not interest, either. If one is interested, then that attention becomes concentration; and concentration, if one observes, is always exclusive, limited. With a limited concentration, one seems to hide every thought and every feeling in order to listen, which prevents the actual act of listening. When one really listens, an actual trans-

formation takes place. If one ever observes oneself, one will see that one never actually listens. It is only when one is forced, cornered, bullied into listening that one listens with a resistance, or with pleasurable anticipation.

As we are going to examine together several issues, we must examine them without the interest which always has a motive behind it. We can examine only a fact— the fact of what is actually taking place. To examine there must be observation—to look and therefore to listen. If we listen, which is an act of total observation, all the interference of thought ceases. Then that very observation is the catalyst. This is important to understand because most of us are so conditioned that we accept what we are told. We want something positive, a directive, a method, a formula, a system; and if we see the whole significance of a system, of a formula, whose pursuit only brings about a mechanical activity, then we can discard this so-called positive method. As we are so heavily conditioned, through propaganda, and also by our own fear and uncertainty, we easily accept. We want to be told what to do, how to think, and what to think about. We are not going to do that at all tonight because this mechanical thinking leads to immaturity, not to freedom at all. Following someone who gives a positive direction has been required for centuries upon centuries by the churches, by every kind of sect, religion, guru, and all the rest of that business. That's too crude, too obvious; and when we see that whole structure and its destructive nature, we discard it totally.

As we are not thinking in terms of formulas, direction, we have to be sensitive and put aside this mechanical approach to life, to action. Perhaps this evening we can look without a positive demand and can observe or listen, not merely to the speaker, but also to our own intimations, to our own movement of thought and feeling, neither accepting nor rejecting, neither being depressed nor being elated by what we see. Without knowing, without observing the total movement of our own selves inwardly, every movement of thought, feeling, word, gesture, and what lies behind the word, behind the thought—this whole structure of the psyche—we have no actual foundation to anything. What we have is merely acceptance of what has been, or what will be, the inevitable. But when we begin to learn about the whole structure, the meaning of ourselves, then we have the foundation deeply laid; then we can move, or not move.

Self-knowing is very important—knowing for yourselves, not what you have been told about yourselves. You have to relearn about yourselves. Learning is not a movement of what has been accumulated as knowledge. Learning can only be in the active present all the time, and not what you have learned through experience, through your previous activity, through memory. If you are merely accumulating, there is no actual fact of learning, no seeing something for yourselves and moving from there. Unless you do this, action then becomes merely an idea; you divide action and idea, and hence the conflict, the approximation of action to the idea.

If this is somewhat clear, not verbally, not as an idea, but as an actual fact, then we can proceed, then we can take the journey together. And we have to take the journey because we are going to delve into something very, very deep and urgent. Most of us do see the utter futility of the meaningless existence that we lead. The intellectuals throughout the world invent a philosophy: how to live, what to think, what kind of world it should be, and so on. That's their amusement. So do the theologians, and of course, inevitably, the priests. But our life, the actual fact, our daily existence is monotonous, utterly meaningless. Not that we

don't have memories, pleasures, and amusements—but that's a very small part of our existence. Deep down, if we can strip off that particular layer, there is this enormous discontent with our lives, with our shoddy little existence; and it breeds despair. Being in despair, we seek; we say there must be something; we want some hope, something by which we can live. So we give, intellectually or emotionally, a significance to our life—which prevents us from actually looking, observing, listening to the whole content of our entity. Being discontented, in despair, we turn to various philosophies, various methods of meditation. We begin to seek; we try this; we try that; we take this special drug, LSD, or another drug, and keep on experimenting, hoping that we will some day discover the key to all this. That's what we are all doing. We want truly religious experiences, something supernatural, something mysterious, because our own lives are so empty, so dull, so meaningless, so utterly petty. We seek because we are discontented; and we don't know where to look because no one believes in any of the things that anyone says any more. The religions have all gone up in smoke; that is not even worth discussing.

Being discontented, eaten up with this absurd triviality of existence which has no meaning whatsoever—except that technologically we must earn a livelihood and have some money; beyond that it has no meaning—there is discontent, a desperate loneliness; and we seek. There is this emptiness, this loneliness, this despair; and to fill that, we are seeking.

Probably you are listening this evening, seeking something to fill that void of nothingness. This search is a terrible thing because it will lead nowhere. You have knocked at many doors in your despair, loneliness, and misery: Eastern philosophies, Zen, this new person to whom you are listening, who is sitting in front of you and talking. You listen to all of them, and you knock at every door. Actually, what takes place is that when you are seeking, you find what you want. So the first thing, it seems to me, is to realize that there must be no seeking at all. That's a hard pill to swallow because most of you have been accustomed, conditioned to seek, psychologically, inwardly. You say, "If I can't seek, if I see there is no meaning in seeking, then what am I to do? I'm lost!" Seeking becomes another escape from the actual fact of what you are.

It is rather crucial that you should understand this. Because any movement of seeking gives the idea that you're actually moving, acting; but actually what takes place is that you're not moving at all. What is taking place when you are seeking is a mental process which you hope will satisfy. Seeking is a static state; it is not an active state. The actual state is this terrible loneliness, emptiness, this incessant demand to be happy, to find a permanent reality. Seeking is done by a mind that is frightened of itself, of what it is. A man who is alive, in the deep sense of that word, completely fearless, is a light to himself; he has no need to seek.

In the midst of this loneliness, this sense of an utterly meaningless existence, can one find out—not through philosophies, not through psychoanalysts, nor through any organized religion—actually for oneself, beyond any shadow of a doubt, if life has a significance at all? And what is that significance, if there is one? Man, historically, has been seeking this thing called God. It is not the fashion nowadays to talk about that entity; He's not worth talking about even, because no one is interested. It has been the monopoly of the organized religions, and the organized religions have gone up in smoke, or in incense. It has no meaning at all any more. Yet man is seeking, wanting to find out, and without finding that out, life has no significance, do what one will—invent every

kind of philosophy, or take the very, very latest drug to give a certain stimulation so that one will have a certain experience because in another corner of the field one has become slightly, extraordinarily sensitive.

If one relies on stimulation of any kind, including the speaker here, that stimulation inevitably leads to dull minds. One has to find out. One has to examine, and through that very examination discover a certain reality. If one projects from one's conditioning, from one's fear, or from one's hopes, then one is back again to the same old circle.

First, we must realize the utter shallowness of our lives, not because someone tells us, but the actual fact of *what is:* the meaninglessness of going to an office for the next forty years; or if we have already been doing it for forty years, struggling, struggling, struggling, and at the end, dying; or filling the odd moments when we are not occupied with earning money, with some philosophy, with some idea; or if we have money, going to certain places and learning meditation and how to be aware. It all becomes so utterly meaningless and childish. But we have to find out; we have to discover if there is a real significance, not invented by the mind. That's very easy. To find out if there is a significance, there must be an end to seeking, and then we face what actually is within ourselves.

Because of our despair and anguish, we have invented a network of escapes, beliefs, dogmas; or we just live for the time being, and die, rationalizing our whole existence. The mind must be free of belief to examine. To examine there must be freedom, obviously; otherwise, we can't examine. To look, to listen, there must be extraordinary freedom from all our conditioning, all our demands, so that we can look at our own demands, at our own fears. It is extraordinarily arduous to have no movement of seeking or achievement, because we want to succeed, we want a quick answer to everything. We take a drug and we think we have answered the whole of existence because we have certain experiences. Those experiences are the shadow of the real, so why play along those lines?

To see all this structure, and not escape either through a conclusion, through a word, or through the movement of seeking an answer demands astonishing attention; and this attention is not to be gained by practicing attention—that becomes mechanical. One realizes for oneself the utter futility of what one is doing, which must be done at a certain level. One realizes that the marvelous escapes which man has invented to run away from himself and so prevent him from looking at himself—concerts, paintings, and so on—are not the whole substance of life. All consciousness is always limited, however much one may expand it through drugs, through the practice of certain disciplines, hoping to expand consciousness. There is always the observer; the observer is the center; and where there is a center, the expansion is always limited.

As we were saying the other day, an object creates space around itself. I have space round me physically because the object is here. This hall, with these four walls, creates this space; and there is space outside the wall. We only know space from the center. When we look at the stars of an evening, a beautiful sunset, we know the space because there is the observer; and that space is always limited. We can expand it through various tricks of memory, drugs of various forms, but it is always limited, and therefore there is no freedom. But there is space in which there is complete freedom when there is no observer, when there is no center.

As we were explaining the other day, the experiencer is the experienced, or the experience. The observer, the thinker, the experiencer is always creating space around himself; and that's the only space he knows. Within that he is doing everything to escape from that prison which the observer has created. But the observer, the experiencer is the experienced, the observed, and therefore his experiences which he is seeking, wanting, longing for, hoping for, are always within the limitation of that space which the observer creates. We can see this for ourselves very simply when we observe ourselves, when we observe a building, a flower by the wayside, or when we have an experience or want an experience; there is always the observer. But the observer is the observed; the two are not separate. It's very important to understand this. Then the observer doesn't create or demand any experience; there is no center from which to observe, to experience, to gather memory from which to move.

When one says one is afraid, there is the observer who says, "I'm afraid," and he wants to do something about that fear. That's irrelevant. But is the fear different from the observer? The observer is the observed. The observer, the center, by his thought, by his memories of pleasure and pain, has bred this fear, which he has put outside of himself. He looks at it and says, "I must get rid of it." There is conflict between the observer, the center which says, "I must be different. I'm angry, and I must get rid of anger," and the observed. There is a separation between the observer and the observed, and hence conflict. A mind in conflict, at any level, even physically in conflict, brings about a certain dullness, weariness. It loses sharpness. It is no longer active in its sensitivity. It is wearing itself out through conflict, and that's all one knows, both outwardly and inwardly.

Outwardly this conflict manifests itself as war, as success, as competition; and inwardly we are doing the same; we are in that state; we want to achieve; we want to become this or that. There is this everlasting struggle, this conflict, and the mind deteriorates. But when the mind realizes, understands the nature of the observer and the observed, conflict comes to an end; and the cessation of conflict is essential because then the mind becomes completely peaceful. Then we can find out what the significance of existence is—not before, not when we are ambitious, greedy, envious, acquisitive, seeking more and more and more experience. All that immature stuff ceases when the observer realizes that what he observes is the observer; the seeker is the sought. If one sees that, then there is a totally different kind of action—not this restless, meaningless activity. The mind has examined, has understood the whole meaning of seeking, and also it is rid of fear. Therefore there is complete quietness, stillness, silence of the mind—which hasn't come into being through drill, through mesmerism, through self-hypnosis. It comes because we have understood all this. Then meditation becomes a tremendous activity. An agitated mind—a mind that has problems, a mind that is everlastingly, restlessly seeking, searching, asking, questioning, being critical and not critical, accepting, and all the things that it goes through—comes to an end when the observer, who is creating this movement, realizes that the experiencer is the experienced, is the experience.

This whole process is a kind of meditation, not a self-hypnosis, because there is no demand, no desire, no seeking, no saying, "I want this; I don't want that." Then only can one come upon that thing which man has sought for centuries upon centuries, which has nothing to do with belief, with organized belief or religion, with all that immature nonsense. To come upon it, there must be, naturally, love. Love is not desire, nor is it pleasure. One has to understand it, not become puritanical about not having desire or pleasure, which merely means suppressing. To understand this unfortunate word *love*, one must also understand the nature of dying, because life is dying. One cannot understand the full depth of life if there is no dying to

the past, and the past is memory, which is the observer. Without understanding this, life has no meaning. One can have more cars, more bathrooms, more prosperity, and more wars; but life has no meaning. One can invent a meaning for it, but actually it has no meaning. To come to that significance, to that immense reality—and there is such a thing as that, not because the speaker says so, but there is, apart from every assertion or nonassertion—to come to it there must be freedom from the animal, the animal which is aggressive, violent, killing, and all the rest of the things one is. Without that, do what one will, go to all the analysts, to all the temples, to all the new philosophies, one's life will still be empty and meaningless.

Comment: The Lord Buddha, I think, did it without killing the animal in him.

KRISHNAMURTI: Sir, one must really be rather careful in this. It is no good quoting authorities. One really does not know what the Buddha said or did, or Christ, and so on. Discard all authority and find out for oneself. I did not say to "kill" the animal in one. Man has tried that. Every monk in the world has done that, either that or indulgence. But one must understand the whole structure of the animal in one, not intellectually, not sentimentally, not verbally, but actually come directly into contact with it: the petty, little jealousies, anxieties, and hopes.

To understand it, to look at it, you need care; and to care, you must have affection for it. You can't care for a child if you have no affection. It may be ugly; it may be silly; it may be whatever it is, but you have to look at it; and to look you have to care—which doesn't mean you destroy something in you, or suppress it, or control it, or run away from it. That's one of your conditionings—that you suppress, or indulge. You must understand the nature of pleasure, which is desire—

understand it, not suppress it, not sublimate it, nor run away from it—and to understand it, you must look at it with care.

Question: If I, the observer, look upon a tree as the thing observed, are the tree and I one and the same thing?

KRISHNAMURTI: You have heard that the observer is the observed. You have heard it; you haven't listened to it. There is a vast difference between hearing and listening. You haven't learned about it; you have heard it, and it has become an idea. Immediately that's what takes place: an idea, and that idea is trying to say, "Is the tree me? I, the observer, look at the tree, and the tree is me." But the tree's not you, obviously.

Have you ever looked at a tree, at a cloud, at the beauty of the sunset—looked at it— and there is no observer at all? Ordinarily when you look at it, what actually takes place? Your memories come pouring in. "Ah, that marvelous sunset I saw the other day in California, that light on the mountain!" Or you are absorbed by the sunset, and for the moment you are silent; and in that silence you remember and say, "By Jove, I'd like to repeat that," like sexual pleasure. That's what you do; it becomes a repetition because you think about it, you want that pleasure repeated, and in that you are caught. But to really look at a tree, its movement, or the folds of a mountain, thought as memory must come to an end. Though you have mechanical knowledge, that knowledge prevents you from looking at that tree. When you do look at the tree without the observer, the tree is not you, and you are not the tree; there is no space between the observer and the observed. Then you don't say, "Am I the tree," or "I shall attempt to identify myself with the tree." All that becomes meaningless.

Question: Does this separation between the observer and the observed exist in the mind of a baby or a small child?

KRISHNAMURTI: I'm afraid we can't go back to childhood. Actually we are discussing what takes place with grown-up people, with you—what takes place when you look. You always have a space between you and your wife or your husband, between you and your neighbor. In this space all conflict exists, all separation exists—not only between the black skin and the white skin, the brown skin and the yellow skin, but also there are the images you have built through memory, through fear, through flattery, through insult; and therefore there is a separation. Separation is an indication of a lack of love. A lumberman, looking at a tree, looks at it with a different eye from that of a scientist. The sentimentalist looks at it differently; so does the artist. But you never actually look because you look through space which is created by the observer; there is quite a different relationship if there is no observer, when the observer realizes that the thing he observes is the observer.

When you know that you love, when you know it as an observer, as an entity loving something—a tree, a woman, a man, a child—is that love? We have divided love into divine and mundane, sexual and nonsexual, something sublime and something absurd. We live in fragments. Our fragmentary existence is the curse of our life. Life is a total movement, not a fragmentary movement in conflict with another fragment. To understand this total movement, the maker of fragments must come to an end.

Question: When you see a thing the way you say, is it not attention?

KRISHNAMURTI: The questioner asks, "What is total attention?" Why do you ask?

Not that you shouldn't ask, but why do you ask? Can't you find out for yourself what total attention is?

Let's begin with a very simple thing: to be aware. What does it mean? I'm aware of the size of this hall, the lights in it, the shape of it, the height of it; and I'm aware also of the colors worn by the people sitting here, their faces, how they look, how they smile, with their glasses, and so on and so on. I'm aware. Then I begin to say, "I like; I don't like; this is nice; this is not nice." I'm aware with choice. I say, "This is a nice hall, or a not nice hall; that's a nice color, or a not nice color." Choice begins, and where there is choice, there is confusion. That's a fact that is going on all the time, not only outwardly, but also inwardly. Can I look, be aware, without choice, without choice of any kind? Of course I have to choose between this coat and that coat, or something else, physically; but inwardly, why should I have a choice? Can I look at anything, be aware of anything, without choice?

When you put that question, no one can answer it. You have to do it! And if you do it, you will find out that there is an awareness without choice. When there is that awareness with choice, go into it deeper; then you will begin to discover what concentration is. Concentration is a form of resistance, exclusion, either with a motive of pleasure, profit, or fear. If you go into it still deeper, you will see that there is attention in which there is no effort at all because there is no motive which makes you attend. When you are totally attentive, which means with your nerves, with your body, with your ears, with your heart, with your brain, with your mind—completely attentive, in which there is no success, no motive, nothing, completely attentive—you will find that there is no observer at all. To be so attentive is its own discipline, not the discipline of compulsion, imitation, fear, adjustment to a pattern.

Comment: I've experienced these states of choiceless awareness, and I have longed to get back to them, but I wonder very much if they are really meaningful.

KRISHNAMURTI: Choiceless awareness has a meaning, and you can examine only in that state—examine what the politician says, what the priest says, what propaganda says, what your wife or your husband says, or what your own memory, your promptings, your intimations, your dreams, everything says. It has tremendous meaning if you're aware choicelessly because then your thinking becomes highly clear. You are no longer persuaded or influenced by your own motives, or the motives of society. Then you can look and not distort what you're looking at. You do this when you're really in a crisis. When you're shocked, your whole attention is there; you're watching. Of course, if the shock is too great, you are paralyzed. That's different. The questioner says further that he has had this experience of choiceless awareness, and he wants to go back to it.

Comment: I know choiceless awareness is meaningful, but I wonder if the whole life process is meaningful.

KRISHNAMURTI: Sir, I have explained all this evening that the whole life has a meaning, significance, when that thing that man has been seeking is found. Otherwise it has no meaning. That thing cannot be found if the mind is confused, is at war with itself. And the questioner would like to go back to that state of choiceless awareness. If you are aware of this demand to go back, or to gain again that state of choiceless awareness, then you are not in a choiceless state of attention. The moment you say, "I want something repeated," what you want repeated is something that you have had, that is a memory, that is not actual. The pleasure of that experience remains and you want that pleasure repeated. The repetition of any pleasure becomes mechanical, and choiceless awareness is not at all mechanical. On the contrary, it is attention from moment to moment. When there is no attention, there is inattention; and in inattention all our misery comes.

Question: What effect does a revolution in the mind of a single person have on the whole human race?

KRISHNAMURTI: As we explained before, the individual is the local entity, the American, the Russian, the Indian—the local, conditioned, modern entity. The human being is much older. You are asking, if there is a mutation in the human mind, whether it will affect the whole consciousness, not only of the individual, but of man.

There are several things involved in this question: first, how to change society. You see that society must be changed, but how? And is it possible? Realizing the vested interests of the politicians, of the army, of the priests, of the businessmen, is it possible? You are society, psychologically. You have created this society; you are part of it. The psychological structure of society is what you have psychologically created. It is not something different from you. You have conflict; your life, your daily existence is a battlefield; and the battlefield in Vietnam is the extension of your daily life. You say, ''I want to change all that.'' Can it be changed, or should you be concerned with the total human being, the human being who is ten thousand or two million or whatever years old? If there can be mutation there, then everything will come out right. Merely changing a local entity, the individual, is not going to affect it a very great deal. Cultivating your backyard isn't going to do very much. But when you are concerned with the total man, then in that mutation of the psyche, perhaps the mutation will affect society.

Question: Is it not true that in modern society one must have accumulated knowledge, technological knowledge, and this brings about inattention?

KRISHNAMURTI: No, sir. I have very carefully explained that you must have technological knowledge. You must have knowledge of where you're going tonight, where your home is, what your name is.

Comment: You have said that we must have this basic technological knowledge, but that we must also have complete attention.

KRISHNAMURTI: You must have knowledge, and also you must be free from the known; otherwise, you're merely continuing in the known. You may take a drug, hoping to go beyond the known, but you can't. Those are all cheap tricks.

Question: Why are the sunset and the tree easier to observe as an observer identified with the object?

KRISHNAMURTI: That's very simple. The tree and the sunset do not interfere with your life. (Laughter) I can look at the tree, but I can't look at my wife or husband, my neighbor. (Laughter) I know it's quite funny, but do look at it sometime; look at yourself, at your wife or husband, at your neighbor. Look. Do not identify yourself with what you see, but look, and you will see a great miracle there. Then you are looking at life totally anew; you are looking at the tree, at the person for the first time as though you had never looked at anything before.

Question: I understand that to observe oneself brings clarity. When the body dies, is the clarity lost also?

KRISHNAMURTI: Death is a most complex thing. You can't answer a question like this in two minutes, and then go to the next subject. It's like understanding life. Life is an immense thing, with all the pain, the despair, the anxiety, the pleasure, the joy. It is a tremendous thing, and to understand living, you must care for living; you must listen to the whole movement of living. When you understand this thing, this enormous movement of life, then this movement is part of dying.

Question: Doesn't the child have more choiceless awareness than the adult, and less prejudice?

KRISHNAMURTI: It depends on the child. (Laughter) And it depends on the adult.

Comment: I am speaking of the condition of childhood. I'm not speaking of any particular child.

KRISHNAMURTI: The child is conditioned by the parents, by society, by the culture in which he lives, by the school he goes to, and by the children around him. He is conditioned, and this conditioning increases as he grows older. The walls thicken by his own ambition, by his own greed. He becomes more and more nonobservant, noncurious, nonaware. This is what takes place in modern education. Technologically the child is trained, and practically the whole of life is neglected.

Question: Are you saying that when one has technological knowledge, in that moment one cannot possibly be aware?

KRISHNAMURTI: Quite the contrary, sir! Of course it is possible to be choicelessly aware when you are being trained technologically. The more nonmechanistic you become, even technologically, the more active you are, the more you produce. If you give a workman the same layout day after day, he gets bored with it, and produces less. If you give him the same work and help him to learn about it, he'll produce more. That's what they are all doing in factories. That's one of the gadgets, the tricks they are playing. I divide technological knowledge and awareness only because the inevitable question arises: What shall we do if we destroy all that? To prevent that, I divided it, and also went into it and said that the thing cannot be divided. Life cannot be divided into fragments.

Comment: Sir, so many millions of people are caught up in confusion and in a materialistic type of life that it seems to me almost hopeless to think that there will ever be enough people with enough clarity to do any good.

KRISHNAMURTI: Why are you so concerned about the multitude? Are you one of the do-gooders, and not really concerned about yourself and your relationship with the world?

We have produced this world by our thought, by our feelings. The total human being, which is each one of us, must change, must bring about the mutation we talked about. Leave the others alone. We have done enough propaganda, and propaganda is never the truth; it's a lie. When there is love we will know for ourselves what relationship is between man and man. Without that, we want to bring about a change in society; we want to change man; we want to do good; we want to put up the various flags. When we love, then there is no problem; then, do what we will, there is no harm.

October 7, 1966

Ojai, California, 1966

✳

First Talk in The Oak Grove

I do not know how you regard these meetings. It is really quite a serious gathering, not an afternoon picnic, nor have we gathered to have an amusing time here. Presumably we have come together to talk over the many problems that every human being throughout the world is faced with. And as we are going to go into it, not only in detail if there is time, but also to go into it seriously, with a deliberate intention, one must come to these talks and discussions not in any sense of being entertained intellectually, or emotionally excited, but rather to go into the many human problems seriously, with a great deal of hesitation and understanding. Then perhaps these meetings will be worthwhile.

First of all, I think we should be clear that we are not discussing any particular philosophy. The speaker does not belong to the Orient or to the Occident. He has no particular philosophy, nor formulated ideas which one must accept or reject. But what is, it seems to me, necessary is that we should together examine the very complex problems of our lives, the very urgency of these problems. Most of us try to run away from them because we do not understand, or escape has become such a habit that we easily slip, without thought, without any intention, into this network of escapes that man has cultivated through centuries upon centuries.

What is necessary is to examine unemotionally, not merely intellectually. Because the intellect doesn't solve any problem; it can only invent a lot of ideas, theories. Nor can emotion dissipate the urgency of the problems that one has to face and resolve. What is necessary, it seems to me, is a mind that is capable of examination. To examine there must be freedom from personal views, with a mind that is not guided by one's own temperament, inclination, nor is compelled by circumstances. And that's quite a difficult task because we are accustomed to examine everything from a personal point of view of like or dislike, to certain commitments, to certain philosophies, to certain formulas. And therefore we're always translating these problems according to our particular limitation; but if we would translate or understand these problems deeply and fully, it seems to me that one must look at them, not as an individual, but as a human being. I think there is a vast difference between the two. The individual is the local entity, the American, the man who lives on the West Coast or the East Coast, or in the Midwest. The individual is the Indian, far away, with his outlook, with his limitations, with his superstitions, with his innumerable religions and doctrines and beliefs. The individual is caught in his nationalities, by the division of the sectarian spirit, whether it be Catholic or Protestant, or the various nationalistic divisions with their Democratic, Republican political parties, and so on and on and on. In that frame the individual exists. But I think the human being supersedes the individual. Whether they live in Russia, China, India, America or in any other part of the world, human beings have the same common factor of sorrow, of joy, of unresolved miseries, despairs, the immense loneliness of modern existence, the utter meaninglessness of life as it is lived now throughout the world—the wars, the continuation of hatred, the national divisions, the utter despair of life. At that level is the human being, though the individual does partake of all that; but if we merely consider the individual, we shall not inquire much, very deeply. It is like cultivating one's own little backyard, and to cultivate that little backyard is necessary. But that little land is in relation to the whole of the earth upon which man lives as a human being in travail, in despair, in agony—this endless sorrow, this fleeting love, and the ending of life.

So if we could consider these problems as human beings, not as an American unrelated to the rest of the world, unrelated to the vast hungry East, but rather as a human being with all the innumerable problems, then perhaps we can intelligently, with care, resolve our problems. And into that we are going together, taking a journey together. When we take a journey, both of us give attention to every step that we take. It isn't that you are listening this evening to a speaker, but rather sharing together the whole of life's problems. And to share together, the responsibility is yours as well as the speaker's. You can't just sit there and be told what to do or not to do, what to believe and what not to believe, or what to follow, and so on—which becomes rather immature and rather childish—but to share together any problem, both of us must, both the speaker and you must be alert, attentive, see the urgency of the problems, and

give one's mind and heart, everything that one has, to find out, to inquire. Because what we are going to do in all these talks and discussions is to inquire, to examine, and thereby find out for oneself. Because there is no guide, no philosopher, no teacher; no one can lead you, because all that has been tried. There have been teachers; there have been gurus; there have been systems, saviors, priests, little sectarian leaders with their particular idiosyncrasies and philosophies; but all these priests, leaders, teachers, saviors have not solved the human problems of war, of our daily misery, of our despair, our innermost agonies and loneliness. They have helped to escape, to bring about some kind of narcotic which will give us some vague hope, or gives visions of a new life; but actually the change does not take place. It is like those people who take LSD, hoping thereby to escape into some reality of a life of a great vision, but actually these innumerable drugs, or many drugs, do not fundamentally, radically alter the human mind.

So, what we are going to attempt to do is to explore, and to explore there must be freedom. That's the first thing: freedom to inquire, which obviously means freedom from any commitment, intellectual or otherwise, from any philosophy, from any dogma, so that the mind can look. And a mind can only look, explore, when it is not caught, for the time being at least, in its own problems, or in its own hopes. It is not committed to any philosophy, to any dogma, to any church. And this, it seems to me, is one of the most difficult things to do. To look attentively at our own problems as human beings demands not only freedom but attention. To attend implies, surely, doesn't it, to give your mind and heart to it, totally—with your nerves, with your ears, with your eyes, with your heart, with your mind—to give totally to understand something. And to give so attentively, totally, there needs to be no motive, no persuasion. You do it naturally because the urgency of the problem is so great that it must be solved. But if we have a motive—and all our urgency generally is based on some limited motive—our problems continue.

The task for the listener, for you, is very great, because most of us don't want to solve these problems—the problems of love, death, and how to live. And that's what we're going to discuss; that's what we're going to inquire into: whether it is at all possible for human beings to be totally rid of all despair, which means to be totally free of all fear, and therefore to lead a life, not in the future, but a life that is not limited by time as yesterday, today, and tomorrow; and whether it is at all possible to free the mind from all the centuries upon centuries of conditioning by the propaganda of churches, religions, by the propaganda of society, the whisper of the neighbor, of the magazines, of the newspapers, of the politicians, of the priests, so that the mind is free. Otherwise man will live everlastingly in pain, misery, and sorrow.

We are asking ourselves whether it is at all possible for human beings, living in this world—not running away into a monastery or to some peculiar philosophy, or taking drugs—to change radically. Because the more intelligent you are, the more aware you are of the world's problems, the more there is despair, there is no meaning, and so drugs are a way of escape. By escape we think we are going to resolve the problems. On the contrary. So, can we bring about a radical change in our way of thinking, living, feeling?

Obviously, considering what the world is, the more aware one is of these extraordinarily complex problems, the more one wants a change; one wants a deep, revolutionary change—not at the economic or social level because they never do really solve any human problem, as the communist revolution has proved. After killing millions and millions of people, they've come back to the same pattern. But what we are talking about is a revolution at a totally different level, a revolution in the psyche, in the mind itself; and whether it is at all possible to bring about that change, that revolution, not guided by our inclination, by our temperament, or compelled by circumstances, society.

One can see that one does change a certain amount, to a certain degree, by circumstances, by influence, through some form of compulsion, an invention. That's going on all the time in our life. Some environmental compulsion makes us, whether we are willing or not willing to change, modify; but such modification doesn't alter the fundamental issues of life. First, one of the fundamental issues of life is freedom, and it requires tremendous inquiry, intelligence, sensitivity to find out what it is to be free. Revolt is not freedom. Revolt against the present structure of society, which is completely bourgeois, middle-class, the revolt against prosperity—going about with long hair, dirty, and all the rest of it—that's not freedom, surely. And we always, it seems to me, regard freedom as from something—from despair, from psychological states. We always regard freedom as going from one state to another state; this we call freedom. If we examine it a little closely, such freedom is merely a reaction; and a reaction invariably produces other reactions; and in that one is caught, and therefore it is not freedom at all. Therefore freedom is not from something but per se, in itself. One is aware of the utter meaninglessness of life. One may have money, property, live in a comfortable house, with three meals a day, and all the rest of it, but through all that runs a thread of utter hopelessness—the utter meaninglessness of going to an office every day for the next forty years, or spending the rest of the years cooking, cooking, cooking, and washing dishes. I know one does it automatically, or one is compelled to do it, or one says, "That's part of life and one has to go through with it." At the end of it all, life has no meaning, except that one has had pleasure, sexual or otherwise—pleasure looking at the blue sky, the light through the leaves, the stars of an evening, and the movement of water in the moonlight. There is great delight in all that. But that soon passes away and becomes a memory, an ash, ashes. One wants to be free from this utter boredom of life, and therefore that freedom is translated into revolt, saying that there are the young and the old, that the old do not understand the younger generation, and so on, and all the rest of that business.

Freedom comes not through revolt. It comes naturally when there is the intention, when there is the urgency and attention in examining the social, psychological structure of what we are, examining as human beings what we are. Because we are the result of a social structure. The society is you, and you are the society. You have built this society according to your particular idiosyncrasies, greed, and all the rest of it. The psychological structure of what we are is the result of thousands of years of society, of communities, with their beliefs, dogmas, superstitions, with their hopes, with their gods, and all the rest of it. It is that one has to understand, and one has to go very deeply to be free from the turmoil of the social structure, this psychological structure of what we are. You may run away, take to drink, start new religions, take LSD, and all the rest of it; but unless you are free of this psychological structure, there will be no escape. There can be understanding only when there is tremendous urgency. And when there is an urgency, there is attention; and out of that comes freedom. Then you can look. Then you can go much further. Then you can begin to inquire if there is any truth. There is something far beyond that which thought has put together. Man, throughout the historical

process, has always inquired into the something beyond this everyday, monotonous, routine life. And when he inquired, it was an escape from the daily existence, with all its despairs, miseries, and conflicts. When he inquired it was an invention, a projection of his own desires, hopes. And it's only a free mind, and therefore a new mind, that can discover something far beyond that which man, out of his fear, despair, and boredom created, something which man calls God.

Our task, during these talks here, is not to be stimulated to inquire. If you are relying on being stimulated in order to inquire, then you depend on another. You are already committed, and therefore you cease to examine. One inquires because of the urgency. Know what is happening in the world. There's a war; people are killing each other. And there are those who say, "This is not my war, my favorite war; I like another war." There are those who justify killing. And this has been going on for five thousand years. An archaeologist said that in Babylon, on a brick, a man had written that he hoped this would be the last war—five thousand years ago. And man, until now, has chosen war as the way of life—not only war outwardly, but inwardly. Our life is a battlefield of resentment, hate, conflict, struggle, endless competition. We may deny the outward war—intelligent people generally do; and when they do, they do not belong to any religion, to any class, to any group, to any nationality, to any system of thought. We may reject outward war, but inwardly we are in battle with ourselves and with another; and that's our life. And that we are incapable of facing and understanding and going into and being utterly free of. We are afraid to understand it, go into it, because it may produce a totally different kind of revolution from that which we want. So we avoid, and hence we continue with war; and that's our way of life. And one may talk of love, talk about it, go to church, and all that immature, idiotic stuff, but we continue to live in a way that produces wars. To live without war means to live peacefully, without competition, without envy, without resentment. People store resentment and carry on for years.

So, if we would bring about a different world—and we must; that's man's only hope—we must have a different mind, a mind that has observed all this, observed how man has divided the world into nationalities, into races, into colors, into religions. Observing all these inventions, putting them all aside completely, then only can one live peacefully. Then only can there perhaps be a world where there will be no wars, where there will be no envy. In this country there is immense prosperity. And in the East there is nothing at all. There is hunger, misery. Naturally they are envious, and the self-centered prosperity will only lead to further wars, further misery. There is only one political problem, which is the unity of mankind—not according to the democratic, or the communist, or this or that policy, but actual unity of mankind. All this is not possible when thought is guided by personal inclination and temperament, or compelled by circumstances. What will bring about a radical revolution in the mind? A radical, fundamental mutation of the mind is only possible when we are capable of examining, not something else, but ourselves, not through a psychologist or analyst—that will lead nowhere; it may temporarily alleviate the problems of certain types of people who are neurotic, and so on, but even then that's another problem. To resolve anything one has to watch without time, to see the thing immediately, and thereby bring about a total mutation in oneself.

I think I've talked enough for this afternoon. Perhaps you'll ask questions.

Question: If you had to choose between the church within and the war, which way would you go?

KRISHNAMURTI: The questioner says: "The church within, between that church and war, what would you choose?"

First of all, we must understand this word *choice*. I'm not quibbling, please. Where there is choice, there is confusion. It's only the confused mind that chooses. A clear mind that sees things clearly has no choice. (Laughter) No, sir, please, don't pass it off by laughing and being amused by a statement. Most of us are very much confused because we have been told so many different things by so many experts, specialists, by the priests, by the books, by religions, by propaganda; everything is contradictory, and we are the result of all that contradiction. So out of that contradiction, out of that confusion we say, "I must choose between this and that, between this inward church"—follow it, sir, right to the end, follow it, sir— "and the war." Before I choose I must inquire, surely, what the element is, the factor that chooses. Who is the chooser? The chooser is the center who says, "I will" and "I will not," "I will do this, I will join the war," or "I won't join the war." And can a confused mind choose? And when it does choose, will not its choice always be confused? Please do listen to this a little. Please listen to it; I'm not asking you to agree with me.

You know, one of the most difficult things to do is to listen. Because, after all, sir, you have your own opinion; you have your "This is right." But we are not trying to convince you of anything; we are just examining. We said that when a mind is confused—and most minds are confused—out of that confusion to choose only produces more chaos, more confusion. Whereas, if one is capable of looking, if one looks very clearly, with a clear mind, with a mind that is not burdened with personal views—and that's very difficult, to be free of personal views—with a mind that is capable of giving its whole attention, then there is no choice. Then you don't choose between this church inside and the war outside. Then there is only one action, and that action comes when there is no choice at all.

Question: You say it is necessary for people to think clearly. How is it possible for them to think clearly when they are not very healthy, and they are continually getting sicker every day all over the world, especially in this country?

KRISHNAMURTI: Sir, I have to repeat the question, so would you mind making the question short?

Question: Yes. The people in this country, and all over the world, are sick and getting sicker. How can they think clearly when they are sick?

KRISHNAMURTI: Obviously not. Obviously, physical sickness does confuse the issue. But to be physically healthy, you also have to be psychologically very healthy. Mere physical health doesn't solve the problem. You cannot separate physical health from psychological health.

Question: You spoke of urgency when speaking of freedom. Would you explain further what you meant by urgency?

KRISHNAMURTI: When we are in acute physical pain, there is an urgency, and you act. There is not all the tremendous intellectual, complex motivation, and all the rest of it. You act. And the psychological urgency—and that urgency is much more important than the physical urgency—we neglect; we

postpone the urgency of a man who is frightened, the urgency to resolve it and to find out if it is at all possible, psychologically, to be totally free from fear. And that is the urgency: to inquire into this whole question of fear, whether it is possible to examine, to find out what is involved in the question of fear. There is not only fear, which we shan't go into now because it's a very complex problem. In that problem is involved the whole process, the machinery of thinking—what brings on fear, whether it's thought, or purely physical danger. So, to inquire into it and to resolve it demands urgency, and that's what we mean by that word *urgent*.

Question: Krishnaji, historically there is an urgency at this time. Historically we are coming to the end of an age, the Judeo-Christian age, and we will be entering a new age of man. Now, do you see this mutation that you speak of coming about rather automatically, if we just don't stand in the way of it?

KRISHNAMURTI: First of all, I don't quite see how this historical thing is coming to an end because the churches have tremendous vested interest—vested interest in property and also in each one of us. If we disregard a particular church, or a particular group of beliefs, we'll invent our own because we are frightened people. A mind, if it is not free from fear, may see the futility of a particular organization of churches, but because it is afraid, because it seeks comfort, because it seeks various answers for its despair, it will invent another. This has happened historically. Our concern, surely, is not whether certain forms of religious activities come to an end but rather whether man, the human being, can be free from fear, totally, right through his being. To go into that—perhaps we shall do it the next time we meet here—

requires a great deal of understanding, a great deal of open inquiry, not personal prejudice of fear and hope.

Question: When there is urgency, fear, or some other kind, it demands action, and at that moment, how can there be awareness?

KRISHNAMURTI: Again, those two words *action* and *awareness* need a great deal of inquiry. What is action? And what is it to be aware? To be aware implies to be aware of the trees, of the colors, of the people, and so on and so on and so on, all that; externally, objectively to be aware; and also inwardly to be aware of what is going on: one's own prejudices, one's own inclinations, tendencies, compulsions, all the rest of it—to be aware both outwardly and inwardly. It is not that I'm aware outwardly and totally unaware inwardly. If I am outwardly aware and not inwardly aware, there is a contradiction; and that contradiction obviously leads to confusion, and so on. This requires a great deal of not only verbal exposition but also actual experimentation, because awareness implies choicelessness. To be aware of a tree, you can be aware of it botanically, with knowledge, with thought, aware of it; but with that awareness you don't see the whole tree; you are never in contact with that tree. You are in contact with the image that you have created about that tree, or the person you have created in your relationships, and so on. One may be aware of that person, but actually you are aware of the image which you have created about that person. Again, to go into awareness one has to spend a little time. And also action; again, that's a tremendous word, so heavily loaded. Most of our action is based on an idea, on a formula. I have an idea of what I should do or should not do, or an action based upon a technique which I have learned, and so on and so on. So there is the formula, the idea, and action

corresponding to that idea. There is a division between the idea and action, and to find out what action is, one must ask: Is idea necessary at all?

Sir, just a minute; I haven't finished yet. I've not finished this particular question. Sir, please, if you would kindly listen. One question rightly asked will answer all the rest of the questions. And also, please, if I may request you, don't take photographs and all the rest of it. This isn't a circus. We are supposed to be serious people.

You know, sirs, to ask a question is very easy. And one must ask questions, endlessly, because questioning implies a certain skepticism. There must be skepticism, not accepting—which doesn't mean that you deny everything. To ask a right question is one of the most difficult things; and in asking the right question, in the very asking of it is the answer. But we never ask fundamental questions; we never ask a fundamental question and remain with that question, not easily finding an answer. Nobody, no one on earth or in heaven can answer a fundamental question except yourself, and to ask a right question demands a great deal of intelligence and sensitivity—which doesn't mean that the speaker is preventing you from asking questions.

We're asking just now: What is awareness and what is action? The action that we know is always based on this formula: first the idea, the concept, the 'what should be', 'what has been', and from that, act in approximation to that. This is our life. We are violent—that's an obvious fact—and we have an idea of nonviolence. And we're always approximating violence in terms of nonviolence. Whereas, the idea is idiotic, is unreal. Nonviolence is unreal to a man who is violent. The understanding of that violence is urgent, immediate, and the action of a mind that is pursuing nonviolence and yet is violent is merely sowing violence all the time.

What is essential is the understanding of violence, and the understanding of violence is not through nonviolence. You have to face it; you have to look at it. And when you know, when you are aware of the whole implication of violence, then it comes to an end immediately—which means inquiry into the whole question of time, because we use time as a means of solving our problems, and so on. This is not the time to go into it.

Question: Would you like to enlarge your thoughts of love, that you mentioned several times before?

KRISHNAMURTI: We'll go into it perhaps during the next few talks, but I would have thought that most of us would ask, "I see the urgency of change, radical revolution, mutation in the mind. I see it. It is necessary. How is one to do it?" I should have thought that would be the most urgent question, wouldn't you? Is it possible for a human being who is so heavily conditioned, either as a communist or a capitalist or a Catholic or whatever you will, to break down that conditioning completely, not at some future date, but immediately? Is it at all possible? It is only possible if you understand, first, what the nature and the structure of this conditioning is, the meaning of it. Then one also has to inquire into time, and what the entity is that is going to bring about this change, and so on. These are the problems involved in this.

I think we had better stop. We have gone over an hour. Perhaps we'll continue tomorrow morning at eleven o'clock.

October 29, 1966

Second Talk in The Oak Grove

California has one of the most beautiful climates in the world, perhaps rather hot, especially in the south; and it seems to me it should produce a marvelous society, a society which is totally different from that which it is now; a society which is highly disciplined—I am using that word with great care, and we shall go into the meaning of the word presently—a society that's not wholly materialistic, as it is now; a society that is not self-centered in its progressive acquisitiveness; a society that has deep inward life, not everlastingly seeking entertainment, amusement, and various forms of thrills. It seems to me, as I've been all over the world, except behind the Red Curtain and all the rest of that, the world is looking and more or less copying America, trying to bring about prosperity. The world of cinema, the world of entertainment, football, and all the rest of those things are being imitated all over the world. And one asks oneself, if one is at all serious, as those who live in this climate must have asked themselves, this real question: What is America producing, apart from cars, going to the moon, technological advancement, prosperity, great concerts, museums, and all the rest of that; what is it actually giving? Apart from literature, which is a form of entertainment, apart from new sectarian dogmatism, or experimentation in the field of narcotics and LSD and all the rest of those things, what actually is this country bringing about? Shouldn't we know, shouldn't we ask, shouldn't we demand, not only of ourselves, but also of those people who are attempting to create a different world, a different society, especially the politician? And the politician, obviously, will never create a new world, nor the priests. One has to ask oneself, it seems to me, and ask oneself not out of curiosity but out of some deep despair and anxiety, ask oneself what it is all about. Where are human beings going? We have asked this question of some very prominent people, Americans, and unfortunately they have no answer; nor have they an answer in the East, either. They have some speculative formula, a hope; but you cannot build a society on hope, or on a formula. A society can only be built by a small group of people, a dedicated people who are not persuaded by ambition, greed, by the principle of pleasure. And so, as you are going to listen to these talks and discussions, unfortunately, I wonder what your own answer is—not a speculative answer, not an answer based on hope, on some fantastic myth.

If you examine the world, not only in this country, in Europe, in Asia, but in Russia where also there are great changes taking place, where they are leaning more and more to the right, when you look at all this, surely one asks oneself where the new seed is taking place—a new culture, a new society, a new mind, not fashioned in the mold of the old pattern, not belonging to any particular religion, group, class, sect, nor doing all the immature things that one does. I do not know if one has asked that question; one is, maybe, too occupied with one's own problems; or one is caught up in the trap, going round and round, having no time, no leisure, no mind to investigate. Of course they cannot answer this question. But of those who have perhaps put this question to themselves seriously, especially in a climate like this, where there is a great deal of leisure, where you can sit under a tree and look at the blue sky, where the climate is gentle, where there is plenty of food, clothing, great prosperity; what is the outcome of this? Is it lost? Is this country already on the decline, never having matured? And that's a difficult word also, maturity. And who is going to answer this question? Some philosopher? Some scientist? Someone who has studied history deeply and has all the information, what this society should be, what it will become? Or shall one turn to some clairvoyant, some visionary, some phony individual with some ideas? Who is going to answer this? And it seems to me, we human beings right through the world have no faith in anything any more, neither in the gods that man has invented out of his fear nor in the scientist, nor in the politicians, nor in the books and the theologians with their conditioned thoughts. As one cannot possibly put faith in any of these people, and having no fundamental faith in oneself because one is so uncertain, confused, torn by innumerable desires; as one cannot possibly allow oneself to be led by another, or follow another, one has to find an answer for oneself as a human being. If you answer it as an individual—please do pay a little attention to this—if you answer it as an individual, then you are answering it from a personal point of view, from an inclination, from a temperament, from a conditioned, narrow little individual experience, a narrow little hope; and your answer will invariably be rather infantile, immature; it has no meaning at all because the problem is much greater than the individual mind that is tackling it. The challenge is immense, and to meet that challenge one has to meet it with the understanding of the whole of the human world: the wars, the starvation, the underdeveloped countries, the overpopulation, the extravagance of the rich and the difference of the poor class, and so on and so on—the world, what is going on in the world actually at the present time. If one can look at it totally, not partially as an individual, as an American, as a Catholic, as a Hindu, as a Buddhist or a communist, and all that, but look at the whole phenomenon totally, then I think we shall find the answer—which may not be according to your like and dislike, what you want it to be. Otherwise, if one doesn't find a real, significant answer to this, our lives become rather shoddy, meaningless.

To understand this thing—I mean by that word *understand* not an intellectual comprehension; that's fairly easy, intellectually to see why all the civilizations, cultures have ended, and from that study come to a conclusion and say, "America should be this," or "The world should be that." That's not understanding; that's merely an intellectual analysis of what should be. Nor does understanding come into being with an emotional, sentimental, hopeful outlook. Understanding has nothing whatsoever to do either with the intellect or the emotions; and as most people are rather emotional, their response is sentimental, rather cruel, thoughtless.

We are using that word understanding. This takes place only when the crisis is great and you have no answer to it, and therefore your mind becomes completely silent; and in that silence there is an understanding. This must have happened to all of us. When you are faced with something to which you cannot possibly find an answer, you try everything; you consult, you talk it over, you inquire, you go through all the analyses, and so on, and yet there is no answer. Suddenly, when you have put it aside, as it were, there is an understanding, there is clarity, because the mind at a certain moment has become extraordinarily quiet with regard to that problem, and it is only then that there is an understanding.

But to answer this question, which is a tremendous challenge that's going on right through the world, you have no answer. You can pretend you have an answer, or answer according to the Catholic or the Protestant ideas; then we are back again with the same old issue. But to understand this immense problem, to bring about that complete quiescence of the mind so that it can observe, not from a particular individualistic point of view, demands a great discipline. We are using that word *discipline* not in the military sense, nor in the orthodox religious sense.

Generally that word implies conformity, cultivating certain habits, suppressing, forcing, adjusting; and all that is implied in that word discipline, generally, but we are using that word quite differently. The root meaning of that word discipline is to learn, and you cannot possibly learn if you are merely conforming or suppressing or controlling. So one has to understand again the meaning of the word *learning*. Because if there is no right discipline, the mind cannot possibly find an answer to this, the answer in which is implied the meaning, the structure, the whole of life.

To understand there must be discipline. Please follow this a little bit; give your attention. Understanding is not the outcome of the intellect, or of emotion, of sentiment. As we said, understanding comes when the mind is really very, very quiet, has no movement at all in any direction. When you observe a tree, if you have ever done it, when you look at a tree, your mind never observes the tree; it observes the image it has created about a tree; and that image is always moving; it is never quiet. It is being added to and taken away from. It is only when the mind is very quiet, really observant, without any movement, that it observes the actual fact of the tree.

Any problem, especially this problem that is confronting us, the crisis in the whole consciousness of man, can only be understood, and therefore answered radically, when that understanding is the outcome of discipline; and by discipline we do not mean drill, conformity, enforcement, adjustment through fear, through punishment, all that. Discipline comes naturally when there is learning. So, one has to go into this question of what learning is. Learning, surely, is always in the active present. I am always learning, always in the present, active. That active present of learning ceases when it has become the past: I *have* learned.

Please do follow this, if you will, because we are going to go into something which will be rather difficult if you don't understand this first thing.

What we generally do is, having learned, having accumulated knowledge, a technology and so on, with that we act; or in that acting after we have learned, we learn more, and add more to what we have already known. Right? This is what we are doing all the time. I learn from an experience and store that experience as memory, as knowledge, and a further experience is translated according to what I have accumulated, and so I'm always adding and therefore never learning. Learning is an active present, an action, a process always in the present; and therefore learning is action—not having learned, act. Then action has a totally different meaning. Then you are always learning; therefore, life is always new; therefore, there is never a moment of having learned and acting from that past, and therefore conflict with the present or with the future.

That demands great attention, great awareness. It's very easy for most of us, having gathered information, experience, storing that up, which we call knowledge, and from that knowledge to act. That's mechanical. That doesn't need great energy. That doesn't need great attention, awareness, intensity. But if one understands the meaning of that word learning, then it is an actual movement in the present all the time, and therefore never a moment of accumulated knowledge, and acting from that.

To learn is to be extraordinarily aware, not aware of what you already know, which becomes—please follow all this—the so-called unconscious. You are following this? Is this all rather a puzzle? Bien. To me there is no unconscious. The unconscious is one of the fashionable things nowadays—to investigate it, to go into it, to analyze it, to examine it, examine your dreams; you know all

that circus that goes on. There is only consciousness. It's like a field. Either you take the whole field into view, into observation, or you take one corner of it and call that the unconscious, this the conscious, this action, that something else, which we'll go into.

Learning becomes extraordinarily vital, and it brings great energy because in that there is no conflict. You follow? Because now our energy is dissipated, lost between what has been accumulated through learning, through experience, through information, and so on, and the action; and hence there is a contradiction—the action approximating itself to the knowledge. Where there is a contradiction, there is a waste of energy; and our life is a contradiction, and therefore it is a constant dissipation of energy.

Please, I hope you are not merely listening to the words, but rather observing your own activity of your own mind. Because it will be utterly meaningless to listen to these talks, just hearing the words, going away either appreciating it or saying, "Well, that's old stuff." But if you are aware, not only of what the speaker is saying, but also aware of yourself in relation to what is being said, then the act of listening has great significance; then you are discovering for yourself actually what is taking place. It is of great importance also to find out how to listen. We hardly ever listen. Either we are too occupied with our own problems, with our own point of view, with our own amusements, with guarding ourselves, protecting ourselves—the "ourselves" being the image that we have built about ourselves—or, when we do listen, we are interpreting, agreeing or disagreeing, coming to a conclusion, or comparing with what we already know. So actually you're never in the act of listening. If you are aware of all this, that very awareness is discipline. As we said, the word discipline implies learning—never having learned. That's what modern education is doing—

having learned, apply. But learning, as we said, demands a great deal of awareness—awareness of the machinery of your own thought and feeling; awareness without choice, obviously. The moment you choose, or say, "This I like; this I don't like," you are introducing a factor of choice. Whereas, if you are merely aware of your own machinery of thought, feeling, pleasure, displeasure, experience, knowledge, and all the rest of it, just to be aware without any choice, then you are in a state of learning; and in that learning there is not a dissipation of energy. On the contrary, your mind becomes astonishingly alert, alive, and therefore very sensitive; and such a mind that is alive, sensitive, learning, and so energetic, needs no drug of any kind, no stimulation, because then learning is a challenge itself, and the response to that challenge is the act of learning.

Such a mind can answer this question, this challenge: Is there actual significance to living, not an invented significance, either of the existentialists, of the Catholics, or of the drug fiends, and so on and so on, but an actual, deep significance which you have found out for yourself? Then out of that a different society can come into being.

Our society, as it is, has no meaning—three meals a day, a house, comforts, and all the rest of it. If you would go further into this, one has to understand this whole principle of pleasure.

Would you like to ask questions, or shall I go on?

Audience: Go on; go on.

KRISHNAMURTI: It's very easy for you to tell me to go on. (Laughter) All that you will do is just to hear. But if you were actually working, working together, going step by step into it, then you wouldn't ask me to go on. Then you'd be asking questions to find

out. You know, we are so used to being entertained: on the football field, in the cinema, in the churches, in the magazines, and so on, entertained. That's what you want. But to actually work hard, one has to be serious; and that's why one has to go into this question of pleasure, which cannot be discussed in ten minutes, which we'll perhaps go into on another occasion. Without understanding pleasure, learning, discipline, and the whole structure and meaning of all this, we'll never find out as a human being the real issue, the right response. So perhaps now we can ask questions bearing on what we have talked about this morning, and through questions go into the problems.

Question: If it's a question of the individual learning for himself, doing for himself, by learning what the necessary thing is in the moment as it arises, if he's busy, occupied in that, how can he be going out to life to form a society?

KRISHNAMURTI: The gentleman asks: "If the individual is occupied in the observation of learning, and therefore learning, how can he go out and form a society?"

Comment: Going after life.

KRISHNAMURTI: Going after life?

Comment: This is forming society.

KRISHNAMURTI: Sir, life is learning, isn't it? Life is a movement, an endless movement. It's like a vast river of great depth, with a great volume of water, moving endlessly. And to learn about it is to observe it choicelessly, to be with it endlessly; and that movement of being with it is the creation of a new society. You don't have to learn, and then go out. You see, sirs, one does not actually—I'm not criticizing you as a personal criticism at all, but one does not actually observe what one is thinking, feeling, one's motives. When one is aware of all that, if there is an awareness, and if it is a discriminative awareness, then it ceases to be awareness. Awareness is to be aware of everything: to be aware of the people sitting here, the colors, the trees, the light on the leaf, the noise, to see the mountains, the movement of wind among the leaves. Awareness is not concentration. Again we can't go into all that now. But to separate life and the individual, and to learn about the individual, is to create a chasm of contradiction and misery. The individual, the human being is life, is you and me. Unfortunately that life has been divided into nationalities, into groups, into sects, into beliefs, into this and into that.

To learn about the whole movement of existence is to be aware of this vast field. The question is not a division between life and action, learning and creating, but rather how to look at this whole field of life. You understand, sirs? I hope my question is clear. Just a minute, sir. I know you're full of questions and responses.

Comment: It's the same question; I wanted to word it differently.

KRISHNAMURTI: I'm answering the same question, sir. You know, to look at the whole world, whether in Vietnam, in Russia, the Chinese brutality, and so on, to look at all this world as a whole, not as America, as an individual, or as a Christian, as a Catholic, as a Hindu, as a Buddhist, and so on, but to see this whole enormous movement—which is the human movement, the agony, the despair, the love, the tragedies, the jealousies, oh, all the travail of human anxiety—just to see the whole of that, that is the real problem. Is it possible to see the whole of it, not intellec-

tually? If you see the whole of it at one look, with one glance, then you'll have the answer. Then you are no longer looking at the world as an individual; then you are no longer thinking of the world in terms of East and West, communist and noncommunist, and so on and so on.

The question is: Is it possible for us to look at this whole thing, this whole division, contradiction, this misery, this battle as a whole? If you are capable of looking at it as a whole, totally, then the answer will be total, not particular. And it's only that answer that's going to solve any problem, whether it's an individual problem, or a political, economic problem—but to see the whole of it demands your complete attention.

When you are really very attentive—we mean by that word when you are giving your mind, your heart, your nerves, your ears, your eyes, your brain, your mind, everything—in that attention there is no observer at all, and therefore the observer is the observed. There is only attention. Again, we'll go into that on a different occasion.

Question: Is it ever possible to change, to create a new society if you use force? Is not force the outcome of fear?

KRISHNAMURTI: The questioner asks: "Is it ever possible to create a new society out of force, out of compulsion, out of threat and punishment, for all that is based on fear?" Obviously you can't create a new thing—

Question: I have burned my ego, so I would like to ask—I, not the small, but I the capital—how do you make this world so desperate that they receive the transformation of the mind? And the second question would be. . .

KRISHNAMURTI: Oh, sir; one question! (Laughter) The questioner asks: "How is it possible to bring about a total transformation of a society?''

Question: No. How do you make this world so desperate that they receive the transformation of the mind?

KRISHNAMURTI: Who is going to give this transformation? The priests have tried it; the theologians have tried it, for centuries upon centuries, as though you were going to receive this transformation from an outside agency. This transformation—they have threatened with hell and heaven to bring it about; they haven't succeeded, and nobody believes that somebody else is going to transform you. That's all too immature; that's gone, finished. One has to transform oneself.

Question: You said, and I quote you: "To me there is no unconscious." Now, my question to you is: For me there is an unconscious, this bubbling up that comes up from within for most of us. My question is: How can we reach this point of awareness so it is only consciousness, without the unconscious?

KRISHNAMURTI: Sir, what is the unconscious? Not according to Freud and Jung and all the analysts and so on, but actually, what is your unconscious? Have you ever gone into it? And the question is also: How will you find out what your unconscious is, not have somebody tell you what it is? You understand the difference? If somebody tells me I'm hungry, that's quite a different state from being really hungry, isn't it? So can I find out what my unconscious is, and what is the instrument that's going to find out, the censor, the observer, the analyzer, the thinker; and is the thinker different from the analyzed? When one looks into the so-called unconscious, what is it, and why is it so tremendously important? It is as trivial, as

petty, as shoddy as the conscious mind. Why do we give it such extraordinary importance? The question is: "How to analyze the unconscious, first of all"—wait, sir, I'm coming to that—"and having observed it, transform it completely into the conscious?" Right, sir?

Comment: Yes.

KRISHNAMURTI: That's it. First one has to look at this very carefully. How will you examine the unknown? You understand my question? We say the unconscious is buried deep down. People say that, and you want to examine it. How will you examine it? Through dreams? Through various intimations that it projects, intimations, hints? And why do you dream at all? Why should you? One has to find out, first, how to meet the unconscious, how to look at it. Is it possible for the conscious mind to look at the unconscious? Please follow this, sir. When the conscious mind looks at the unconscious, the conscious mind is already conditioned, already has its own desires, its own purposes, its own motives, its own anxieties, securities, and with that it looks; and what it looks at is its own self. Therefore the question is, then: Is it possible to look at something which is hidden, which cannot be perceived by a conscious mind? You understand my question? Look, sir, there is something hidden which we call the unconscious. How am I to know about it? That is, how am I actually to come into contact with it, not through ideas, not through what people have said, but actually come into contact with it? To come into contact with something actually, immediately, there must be complete quietness of the conscious mind. Right? Obviously! And then, when the conscious mind is completely still, is there the unconscious?

Question: How is this achieved? How? The word how *is the most important part of my question.*

KRISHNAMURTI: First see, sir, what has taken place, if you have followed. The moment the conscious mind is completely quiet, without any movement of pleasure, experience, knowledge, and all the rest of it, then there is no unconscious. Now, the questioner says, how is this to be achieved? The "how" is the most mischievous question because in asking how, you want a method, a system. And the moment you follow a system, a method, a practice, you're already caught in that practice, system, method, and therefore you never discover. You're caught. But if you see the thing actually, if you see that only the completely quiet mind can observe, if you understand that, if you see the truth of that immediately, then the unconscious is not. But if you said, "Tell me the path along which I must go in order to achieve it," it's like going to college to become intelligent. (Laughter)

Question: I would like to know, along with the quiet, still mind, what happens to the body?

KRISHNAMURTI: The body is also quiet. We divide the body, the mind, the brain, the heart, the feeling and thought—you follow? You know, sir, this is really a very complex question. You can still the body by doing various kinds of tricks: by tranquilizers, pills, or your own particular inward tranquilizer, by thought, repetition of words and sitting in a certain posture, breathing in a certain way; you can absolutely bring about a quietness of the body. That has been done, but the mind remains at the end of it equally petty and shoddy. We are concerned with the whole process, not just one part of it.

Question: What is the place of memory in education?

KRISHNAMURTI: I'm afraid we have talked for an hour and a quarter. I think that will be enough, won't it? We'll take up that question, perhaps, if you'll be good enough to ask it next time.

October 30, 1966

Third Talk in The Oak Grove

Shall we continue with what we were talking about when we met here last Saturday and Sunday? We were saying how very important it is to bring about in the human mind a radical revolution. The crisis—and there are always crises in the world, especially now—it seems to me, is a crisis in consciousness, a crisis that cannot any more accept the old norms, the old patterns, the ancient traditions, a particular way of life, whether it is the American way, the European way, or the Asiatic way. And considering what the world is now, with all the misery, conflict, destructive brutality, aggression, the tremendous advancement in technology, and so on, it seems to me, though man has cultivated the external world and has more or less mastered it, inwardly he is still as he was—a great deal of animal in him; he is still brutal, violent, aggressive, acquisitive, competitive, and he has built a society along these lines. The more one observes—and I think almost everyone sees it, unless he is totally blind, deaf, and dumb—the more one is aware of the extraordinary contradictions of human beings, and of the great demands, intellectual as well as a demand at a different level—a demand which is not emotional, not built on enthusiasm, not sentimental, but factual. And to understand the factual, which is neither intellectual nor emotional, there must be a great deal of passion.

For most of us, passion is merely mental or physical gratification, which soon fades and has to be renewed. All passions generally are evoked by external circumstances, or by our own particular temperament, idiosyncrasy, and appetite. Such passion soon withers away. Any passion with a motive is bound to come to an end. And to understand this extraordinary, complex problem of existence, one must have tremendous passion, which cannot possibly be supplied by the intellect, or by casual sentiment or emotionalism; or the passion aroused by committing oneself to a particular course of action, or belonging to a particular political or religious group. That does give a certain quality of intensity, a certain élan, a certain drive. But we are talking about a passion that is not easily come by, because any passion for any action must be without motive. Most of us seek gratification—intellectual, emotional, physical—and various forms of comfort; ideologically or psychologically we demand this gratification, and as long as this gratification is fulfilled, that arouses a certain quality of intensity. But that intensity soon fades away, and it has to be renewed, stimulated, pushed, driven; and hence we are always seeking a certain perpetuated purpose, a certain continuity of passion. A life without this intense drive, passion, has no meaning at all. Generally one seeks an idea, a concept, a formula, to which one can give oneself over, and from that there is a certain intensity, a certain passion. But through it all there is the demand for gratification, for pleasure. And it seems to me that society, of which we are a part, as human beings—and society is not different from the human being; psychologically they are one—the whole structure of society, with its morality, with its gods, with its culture, with its entertainment, is based on pleasure. There may be a rare occasion when mind functions without a motive, and without the demand for gratification, but most of our life and our conduct is based on the demand and the search for the continuity of pleasure.

I hope when one is listening to this talk, or to the various other talks that are coming, that one does more than hear a lot of words; hearing many words is not listening. It is like a noise among the leaves. It soon passes away. When we hear, we either accept or reject; or we translate what we hear according to our knowledge, our background; or we compare what is being said with what is already known; or we oppose one idea by another. All these characteristics of hearing deny the act of listening. The act of listening is entirely different. When one listens, there is no comparison; there is no acceptance or rejection. The quality of listening is attention, and when you attend totally with your whole mind, with your heart, with your nerves, with your eyes and ears completely, in that state of attention there is the act of listening. And that act of listening puts away anything that is not true, when you give your whole attention to something, that is, when you are completely listening. You listen to the totality of the thing. When you attend, there are no borders of inattention. When you so intensely listen, you are listening to the birds, to the wind, to the breeze among the leaves; you listen to the slightest whisper that's about you. In the same way, when you listen, that very act of listening brings about a total attention in which you see the totality and the whole significance and structure of what is being said; not only what the speaker is saying, but also when you are listening to your wife, to your husband, to your children, to the politician, to the priest, to everything about you. Then there is no choice. Then there is only clarity. There is no confusion, but right perception.

We hope that you will so listen to what is being said, not hear a lot of words, a lot of ideas, because ideas and words are not the fact. Ideas and words never bring about a radical revolution, a mutation in the mind. I'm not dealing with ideas and opinions and judgment. What we are concerned with is bringing about a radical revolution in the mind, and that revolution must take place without effort because all effort has behind it a motive; and a revolution with a motive is not a revolution at all, a change. It becomes merely a modified continuity when there is a motive. But a mutation, a radical transformation of the mind, can only take place when there is no motive, and when we begin to understand the psychological structure of society, of which we are, which is part of us; and to understand it, there must be the act of listening—not listening to the speaker, but listening to what is actually taking place in ourselves.

How you listen is a responsibility, if I may use that word, on the part of the listener, because we are taking a journey together. We are taking a journey together into the whole psychological structure of man because in understanding that structure, and its meaning, we can perhaps bring about a change in society. And society, God knows, needs a total change, a total revolution.

As we were saying earlier, our whole concept, action, and urges are based on pleasure; and until one understands the nature and the structure of pleasure, there will always be fear—fear, not only in our relationships with each other, but fear of all life, the totality of existence. So without understanding pleasure, there can be no freedom from fear. We are not denying pleasure; we are not advocating a puritanical way of life, a suppression of pleasure, or a substitution for pleasure; or denying that thing that we call great satisfaction. We are examining it, and in examination there must be freedom from opinion; otherwise, you can't examine. You can't say, "Well, how will I live if there is no pleasure?" When you are certain that one

cannot, or can, live without pleasure, you are already blocking all examination, and therefore all discovery, all understanding of something, understanding of the problem totally anew. We are examining pleasure; we are not condemning it. And without really, radically, seriously understanding that pleasure principle in man, as in the animal, we shall live within the borders of fear always—which is fairly obvious.

First of all, pleasure is an extraordinary thing to understand. It needs a great deal of attention, a swiftness of mind, a subtle perception. There is pleasure in aggression. There is pleasure in violence. There is pleasure in ambition, in self-fulfillment, in domination, in asserting, in pursuing any gratification. There are various forms of pleasure which we don't have to go into in detail, but one can see that the totality of our deep thinking, feeling, is based on this extraordinary principle of pleasure. Our relationships are based on it, and our morality; and the gods that the mind through fear has invented, the saviors, the Masters, the leaders, and so on are essentially based on that pleasure which gives gratification. The assertion of will is part of that pleasure; and denial, sacrifice, is also based on pleasure. So one has to understand it, and to understand it there must be neither withholding nor denying that quality, that principle of pleasure. And that's very difficult to do because we are so heavily conditioned to accept and to function with the motive of pleasure, with gratification; and therefore we are always limiting our total attention. We look at life in fragments—as a businessman, as an artist, as a psychologist, as a scientist, as a politician, as a priest, as a housewife, as a professor, and so on and so on and so on. All in fragments—and we try to relate one fragment to the totality of other fragments, which is called identification. As long as the particular fragment exists, one cannot possibly see the total. If one says, "I must have a certain pleasure, and I am going to hold on to it at any price,'' then we will not comprehend or see the total pattern of pleasure. We are concerned with seeing the totality of pleasure, what is involved in it: the pain, the frustration, the agony, the remorse, the ache of loneliness when all pleasure is denied; and naturally we try to escape from all that through various forms, which again is the continuation of pleasure. A mind that is caught, that is conditioned by this principle of pleasure, obviously cannot see what is true; it cannot think clearly, and therefore it has no passion. It translates passion as sexual, or achieving some fragmentary activity and fulfillment in that fragment. Where there is no understanding of pleasure, there is only enthusiasm, sentimentality, which evokes brutality and callousness, and all the rest of it.

So, what is pleasure? Because, without understanding pleasure, there is no love. Love is not pleasure; love is not desire; love is not memory. And pleasure denies love. Therefore, it seems to me, it is important to understand this principle. Surely pleasure is desire—desire, which comes into being very naturally when you see something which gives you a stimulation, a sensation, and from that sensation there is desire; and the continuation of that desire is pleasure; and that pleasure is sustained by thought. I see something, and in that contact with it, there is a sensation; the sensation is the desire sustained by thought. Please, you can see this in yourself. You are not listening to something extraordinary. This is an obvious, daily fact. You see a beautiful car, a nice house, a beautiful face, and there is the sensation, there is contact: contact, sensation, and desire. Then thought comes in because thought is the response of memory; that memory is based on other experiences of pleasure and pain, and thought gives to that desire the sustenance, the quality of pursuit and fulfill-

ment. One can see this in oneself very simply. One doesn't have to read psychological books about all this. I don't know why one reads psychological books anyhow, or goes to analysts, and so on. If one observes, it's all there in front of you; and the quality of observation cannot be taught by another. If you are taught how to observe, you cease to observe. Then you have merely the technique of observation, which prevents you from actually seeing.

This whole concept of going to somebody to be taught, to be analyzed, to be psychologically informed about yourself, seems to me to be so utterly immature. I know what we are saying goes contrary to all the present fashion, but if one observes, not somebody else, but yourself—for 'yourself' is the whole of mankind, with all the aches and the miseries, with the solitude and loneliness, despair, the utter loneliness of existence, the meaninglessness of it all—in that observation you are so anxious to resolve everything quickly. We haven't the patience nor the intention to observe clearly; and when you do so observe, it unfolds endlessly, which is life itself. Then you are not dependent on anybody, on any psychologist, on any theologian, on any priest, on any dogma. Then you are looking at this movement of life, which is yourself. But unfortunately we cannot look with clarity because we are driven by this principle of pleasure.

To understand pleasure one has to understand the structure of thinking because it is thought that gives continuity to pleasure. I had the experience of pleasure yesterday, of different kinds, and thought thinks about that pleasure and demands its continuity. The memory of that pleasure of yesterday is reacting, demanding that it be renewed through thought, and thought is time.

I hope all this is not becoming too difficult and abstract. I don't think it is abstract, but it may be rather complex. But it's not even that, really, if you're actually following, not so much what the speaker is saying, but what is actually taking place in yourself. After all, what the speaker is saying is a mirror in which you are looking at yourself. And when you do look, you see that pleasure is sustained by thought. There is thinking about the past pleasure, past gratification, yesterday's delight and enjoyment; and that thought demands its continuity now. Thought projects tomorrow's pleasure, and thought creates the past, the present, and the future, which is time. There is time by the clock, chronological time. We're not concerned with that. If you have to keep an appointment, and so on, you must have the chronological time of yesterday, today, and tomorrow. But we're talking about the psychological time which thought has bred; and that time is the product of thought. I have had that pleasure; I am going to have it; and I shall have it. This time quality is created by thought, bred, put together by thought; and thought is time, and it is time that creates fear. And without probing into this time, pleasure, thought, we are always bound by time; and therefore time has never a stop. It is only when there is an end to time that there is something totally new; otherwise, it is merely a continuity of what has been, modified through the present, and conditioned by the future.

As one can observe, love is not of time. It has nothing to do with memory. And pleasure denies love. Where there is love you can do what you will; it's only pleasure that is destructive.

For a human being to be free of fear, fear about the future, fear about—there are dozens of fears that human beings have, conscious or undiscovered: fear of the neighbor, fear of death, fear of being lonely, insecure, uncertain, fear of being confused, fear of being stupid and trying to become very clever—you know, fear. Fear is always in relation to something; it doesn't exist by itself. To be totally free of fear, not partially, not free of a fragment of that totality of what is considered fear, but psychologically to be totally, completely free of fear, one must understand thought, time, and pleasure. And this understanding is not intellectual or emotional. Understanding can only come when there is total attention, when you give your complete attention to pleasure—how it comes into being—what time is, time which thought has created. I was, I am, I will be. I must change this into that. This idea of a gradual process, this idea of the gradual psychological evolution of man is very gratifying; we'll gradually, all of us, become extraordinarily kindly; we shall gradually lose all our violence, aggression. We'll all be brotherly at some time, much later. This gradual concept, which psychologically is generally called evolution, seems to me so utterly false. We are not offering an opinion. This is a fact, because when you give your attention to something completely, there is no time at all. You don't say, "I'll be it tomorrow." In that state of attention there is neither yesterday, today, nor tomorrow; therefore, time has come to an end. But that ending of time cannot possibly be when there is the center as the principle of pleasure. Pleasure has in it pain. The two things cannot be separated. Pleasure is pain, if you have observed.

So you cannot possibly psychologically avoid pain if you are psychologically pursuing pleasure. We want the one, and we don't want the other. The demand for the continuation of a certain pleasure is the center from which we think, function, and act—call it the ego, the 'me', the personality; it doesn't matter what you call it. Where there is a center, there is always the space round the center in which there is action of fear and pleasure. Right?

I hope we are somewhat following all this. If not, it doesn't matter. (Laughter) Because probably most in us have not given total attention—not for ten minutes or half an hour, but for a long period of time. We function emotionally, in want and not want; when deep issues, fundamental problems are concerned, to give your mind totally to them is rather difficult when all your life has been dissipated—dissipated in fragmentary action. When we do act totally, we only do it when there is a crisis. Then you wake up and give your whole attention. And this is a crisis. A talk of this kind is a crisis, is a challenge. You can't just push it aside. And therefore it may be rather difficult, may be perhaps arduous, to follow all this, but it won't be arduous if you are following your own state of mind. You know, it's like sitting on the bank of a river and watching the river waters go by; and when you so watch there is neither the observer nor the observed. There is only a movement. But to observe that, there must be no fear, no time, no sense of pleasure and no demand for gratification. In that state you can observe the whole movement of life, which is agony, despair, the ache of meaningless existence, the routine, the boredom, the great fears, as of death, which we'll talk about another day. You can watch all this, and when you so observe, the observer is that which he is observing; and then you can go beyond all this. The mutation can only take place in the mind when time, pleasure, and fear have come to an end, and therefore there is a certain dimension or quality which cannot be approached through thought.

Perhaps you can ask some questions about what we have been discussing, and we will see if we can't go into these questions. Please, would you mind making the question short.

Comment: I'm confused about what you said about pleasure because I don't see the distinction between pleasure and the desire for gratification. I would like to know what the sensation is that you get when you look at a painting, because I would define that as pleasure without desire, and that's a good kind of pleasure. Pleasure is good.

KRISHNAMURTI: The questioner says that pleasure is good, when you look at a picture, when you look at a sunset, when you look at a beautiful face with a lovely smile. Pleasure, the questioner says, is gratification. I don't see the difference between gratification and pleasure.

Comment: I said your distinction.

KRISHNAMURTI: What?

Comment: I'm sorry. I didn't see your distinction between the two. I thought you were equating the two of them, and I was saying that desire for gratification is something very different from pleasure.

KRISHNAMURTI: Yes, that's right. The questioner says that pleasure and gratification are two different things, not disagreeing with what the speaker has said. Isn't that it?

Comment: No.

KRISHNAMURTI: Oh, I beg your pardon. (Laughter)

Comment: Pleasure is love.

KRISHNAMURTI: What?

Comment: That kind of pleasure brings love.

KRISHNAMURTI: When we are examining something of this kind, don't come to any conclusion. Don't say, "Pleasure is love," or "not love." We are examining. And if you have a conclusion, or if you have come to a conclusion and start to examine the question from a conclusion, then that question is already answered by your conclusion.

Comment: I beg your pardon, sir.

KRISHNAMURTI: Not beg my pardon, please. What we are trying to do is to examine, and to examine there must be freedom from any conclusion, from any knowledge, from any demand. Otherwise you can't look; you can't examine. And that's one of the most difficult things in life to do because we all have opinions, dozens of them; and we are so willing to offer opinions. You know, it's only fools who offer opinions. The wise man has no opinions.

It's a very difficult problem to answer this question. When you look at a sunset, it gives you great pleasure, a delight. That delight at that moment is intense, and your mind and your whole being are absorbed by the beauty of it. Then that experience remains stored up, and the next evening you demand that same experience to be repeated. It's like taking that drug, LSD; it gives you an extraordinary experience, and that experience is a great delight; but when that is gone, you're back to yourself with your tawdry little mind; and you take another dose, and so keep that going, until you become cuckoo. (Laughter) No, no, don't laugh, please. Just a minute. We'll go into that at another time.

So, there is the cultivation of memory, which is sustained by thought—or, thought sustains itself. Like yesterday I saw a beautiful sunset, marvelous colors, the extraordinary tranquillity that comes of an evening at the time of sunset; the light is entirely different, and all that I've retained. The mind has taken it in, and next day, in an office or in a school, or in the kitchen, or when I'm by myself, I look to that delight. It comes up in me naturally, and I look out of the window, hoping to see that again. But it never happens again because the mind looks at the new sunset with the old mind, with old memories. But if you can die to the sunset of yesterday, totally, then you can look at the new sunset. Then it is no longer this cloying gratification of pleasure.

Question: I'm confused about the difference between pleasure and joy. Would you speak about joy, and tell us how it is like and unlike pleasure?

KRISHNAMURTI: What's the difference between pleasure and joy? Don't we know it? Pleasure has a continuity; joy has not. When we say, "I am joyful," it's already finished, but pleasure you can continue. Therefore pleasure is a continuity of that which was, which gave you gratification or pleasure yesterday, which, through thought, you can continue today, tomorrow and sustain it. Whereas joy is something that comes immediately, naturally, and goes away naturally; but if you cling to it, it has already become a memory, a pleasure. It's finished.

Question: Isn't life painful in any case?

KRISHNAMURTI: It all depends. If you have a bad liver, it is. If you have pain, continuous physical pain, it is. If you have psychological pains from being hurt, being lonely, having no fulfillment, being unloved, and so on and so on and so on, life does become a torture. Going to an office daily for the next ten years, forty years, is a dreadful torture. (Laughter) But that you put up with because that brings you money, comfort, and so on and so on. That you don't call torture.

Comment: But not going to the office is also. . .

KRISHNAMURTI: One moment, sir; we have not finished that question yet. (Laughter) Sirs, please; this is not an entertainment.

Question: Well, how do you fit. . .

RISHNAMURTI: Wait a minute, madame. Wait a minute; I'm trying to answer. You know, if we understand one question rightly, all questions are answered. But we don't know how to ask the right question. To ask the right question demands a great deal of intelligence and sensitivity. Here is a question, a fundamental question: "Is life a torture?" It is, as it is; and man has lived in this torture centuries upon centuries, from ancient history to the present day, in agony, in despair, in sorrow; and he doesn't find a way out of it. Therefore he invents gods, churches, all the rituals, and all that nonsense, or he escapes in different ways. What we are trying to do, during all these discussions and talks here, is to see if we cannot radically bring about a transformation of the mind, not accept things as they are, nor revolt against them. Revolt doesn't answer a thing. You must understand it, go into it, examine it, give your heart and your mind, with everything that you have, to find out a way of living differently. That depends on you, and not on someone else, because in this there is no teacher, no pupil; there is no leader; there is no guru; there is no Master, no savior. You yourself are the teacher and the pupil; you are the Master; you are the guru; you are the leader; you are everything. And to understand is to transform *what is.*

I think that will be enough, won't it?

November 5, 1966

Fourth Talk in The Oak Grove

This morning I would like to go into several problems, and to really grapple with them. To go very deeply and extensively in comprehension about them, one needs a great deal of energy—not only physical energy, but psychological energy. Generally one has, if one is fairly healthy, sufficient physical energy, impetus, to investigate; but it's much more difficult, it seems to me, to have psychological energy, the energy that will pursue the issue to its very end, and not be distracted on its way. To have this energy in abundance, one must understand the nature of conflict and effort. One is so much used to this conditioning of effort. All our life, from childhood until we die, we are making constant effort, struggle; and where there is struggle, obviously, there is distortion; where there is effort, there is no clarity of examination. Where there is effort there is a strain; there is a desire to achieve an end, which precludes every form of investigation, every form of understanding, delving deeply. As we said yesterday, the desire to achieve is essentially based on comfort, pleasure, satisfaction, gratification. What we are going to deal with this morning does not need any kind of effort at all; effort exists only when there is contradiction—contradiction within, though there is contradiction without which can be understood, tolerated, and perhaps gone beyond. But there is this inward contradiction of various competing, contradictory desires; and it is these contradictory desires that bring about conflict—the wanting and not-wanting, *what is* and 'what should be'; the *what is* trying to conform to a pattern of 'what should be', and so there is always conflict. Apparently that's part of our daily existence, from getting up in the morning, going to the office, struggling until we go back to bed; and from the moment we are born until we die, there is this constant effort and battle;

and to make effort to get rid of effort is still further effort.

Please, as we said yesterday, it's no good merely hearing a lot of word and ideas. What we are concerned with is the understanding of the whole process of life, with all its complexity, with its aggressions and miseries, with its sorrows and confusions and agonies. To understand this vast field of life, which is a constant movement, one must not only hear the words but also go beyond the words because words, the explanations, are not the fact. But most of us are caught in words. To us, words are extraordinarily important. Like the word *socialist* is something extraordinary to an American, or to a communist. The word has become so extraordinarily important that we see the word first, and then the fact afterwards. What is actual is *what is,* not the word; and to go beyond the word, one must also realize, it seems to me, how slavish the mind is to words. Thought is expressed in words. Without words, is there thinking? And without the word, is there comprehension? To understand something totally, to see the whole process of life, one must be free of the word—the word, the symbol, the idea, the conclusion. Then one can look; then one can listen, and that act of listening is really a miracle. Perhaps it's the greatest miracle when one can listen totally, without any defense, without any barrier, neither agreeing nor disagreeing—which doesn't mean that the mind is open. On the contrary. The mind is extraordinarily alert then.

As we were saying, the word is not the fact, and that's a very difficult thing to realize. The symbol is never the reality. The things that we are going to discuss this morning, as I said, need no effort at all. What is needed is a total perception of the whole process of life, and to perceive this whole phenomenon of life, one needs energy. That energy is denied when there is this drive, this effort to achieve something.

It's only when the cup is empty that it can be filled. It is only when the mind and heart are totally empty that they can comprehend; then they can live. But to be so completely empty is not a negative phenomenon. On the contrary, it is the highest form of intelligence. It is the highest form of love to be so completely empty that there is not a scratch of memory, not a word, not a conclusion that distorts perception. What we are going to discuss or talk over together this morning demands a quality of mind that has no fear of any kind. So one has first to understand fear because what we are going to discuss, talk over together, is this problem of death. But to understand it, to go very deeply into it, the mind must be extraordinarily subtle, sensitive, alert, full of attention. And to understand this enormous problem which has faced man from the beginning of time, one has to be free of fear.

There are so many forms of fear: fear of darkness, fear of what somebody says, fear of being hurt, fear of insecurity, fear of loneliness, and the ultimate fear, which is death. And fear, as we said, is always in relation to something; it doesn't exist by itself. I'm afraid of you, or you're afraid of me; or I'm afraid of an idea; or I have committed myself to a certain activity in which I find great comfort and security, and I'm frightened that that security should be destroyed, that comfort should be taken away—that comfort in relationship, in a job, or in ideals.

There are many forms of fear, and fear is essentially the result of time. One is not afraid of the immediate; one is afraid of what will happen, or what has happened. Please examine what is being said. Not that you must agree with the speaker, which would be rather absurd, but rather use what the speaker is saying to inform yourself of your conditioning, of your ways of thought and your ways of thinking.

Fear is the product of thought. Fear in every form is thought in action with regard to the past through the present and to the future. I am afraid of what will happen, and I'm afraid of something which I have done in the past which I want to cover up. So thought, fear, is the movement of time; and it's very important, if we would be free of fear, to understand this movement of time, which is essentially the process of thinking. The now, the actual, living present is the result of yesterday and a thousand yesterdays; so there is no actual now, or the moment. But the moment, the actuality, the *what is,* is the result of yesterday; and that yesterday is the result of many, many, many yesterdays; and the now is the product of yesterday, which is going to move to the future, to tomorrow. And fear is this movement of time, which is the product of thought. When I am confronted with something dangerous immediately, there is no fear. I act, perhaps foolishly, ignorantly, but there is action. But give time, an interval—then thought comes into operation; then I'm afraid.

Look, this is not a mass psychoanalysis. We're not analyzing each other, but I'm sure each one of us has various kinds of fears. Take one of them; bring it out into the open—don't please, don't confess it to me!— bring it out into the open and look at it. And how you look at it matters immensely. We are going to go into it step by step.

As I said, how you look at it is very important. First, do you look at it as though it were something outside of you, a something which is not you, but something which is placed outside? There is the observer, and fear is something outside of you. Right? There is this duality, this contradiction: I am not afraid, but there is fear, which I must overcome. I must do something about that

thing which I call fear. So the observer is different from the thing observed, and is there a difference? There is no difference, if you examine. The observer is the observed. Please follow this step by step. The observer who has fear says there is fear. That fear is something external to the observer. But for the observer to recognize that it is fear, he must have already known it; and therefore the observer is the observed. I don't want to go much more into it because that's enough for the time being.

Hence, as the observer, the thinker, is the thought and the observed, any form of effort to be rid of fear is the creation of another observer. Right? And therefore he's caught in that vicious circle. I hope we are going together!

The observer is the center of accumulated memory, experience, knowledge, information—the censor, and so on. He, or it, is aware outside of himself of something which he calls fear; and he is making constant effort to run away, or translate, or transcend, or suppress, that fear. The more the tension between the observer and the fact of fear, the greater the effort, the greater the desire to escape, to run away, to cover up; and if one cannot run away, one becomes neurotic because the tension becomes so intense; and to live in that intense darkness of fear is a state of neurosis. But, as we said, when the observer is the observed, not an idea but the fact, then there is no effort at all because then there is no contradiction. I am fear. And what can I do? Please follow this. The observer has always acted as though the observed is something different from himself; then he could act. But when he realizes that the observer is the observed, all action ceases on his part, and therefore all effort; and therefore there is no fear at all.

This requires a great deal of inward inquiry, inward observation, step by step without coming to any conclusion. Therefore the mind must be extraordinarily alert and sensitive and swift. And when there is no fear because the observer is the thing which he has externalized as fear, which he is himself, then there is no longer this action which was positive, that is, doing something about fear. Then the observer is the observed. In that state there is complete inaction, and that complete inaction is the highest form of action.

So there is no effort at all. It is only the dull mind, the mind that's committed, the mind that is "achieving, not-achieving," that is in constant battle, struggle, that makes an effort; and this effort, the struggle, is considered the positive way of life. It is the most mischievous way of life. And in this total inaction, when the observer realizes that he is the observed, then in that total inaction there is an action which is not of effort. Let's leave it there for the moment. I hope you understand some of it.

Then let's proceed to examine this question of what death is. There are three things one has to understand: living, love, and death. They all go together. You cannot separate death from love and living. To us, living as it is is a torture, a misery, a meaningless existence. The more clever, the more sensitive, the more intellectually, emotionally one is alive, the more it has no meaning at all. And seeing that it has no meaning, we invent a meaning, we project a meaning, and according to that meaning, try to live—which is not living at all. So one has to understand what living is. Living is not this battle between human beings; it is not this battle of competition, of races, of ambition, and all the rest of it. I don't have to go into all the details of it. We all know what life is, the torture, the sorrow, the endless misery and confusion; and that's what we call living. And love, as we know, is hedged about with jealousy, with suspicion, aggression, violence; and so we don't know what that is, either. And

obviously we don't know what death is because we are frightened of it; we don't talk about it. We talk a great deal about living, a great deal about love, but death is something to be avoided, to be put away. Don't talk about it. And if we do talk about it, we rationalize it; or, out of our fears we invent beliefs that give us comfort, such as resurrection, reincarnation, and innumerable forms of escape from that enormous and mysterious fact which we call death. Various religions throughout the world have given hope—really, essentially a false hope to man. People in the ancient civilizations lived to die. To them death was far more important than living. But this present generation, this present civilization is concerned with living, and not with the other; and this living is a torture, with an occasional bright spot of affection, love, and beauty. So, without understanding living, and without understanding love, there is no possibility of understanding what death is. To understand it, not intellectually, not emotionally, nor escape from this fact that must really be, is the most immense thing because it is something that has to be understood, felt. Now, we are going to go into that.

Again, the word is not the thing; the explanation which we are going into is not—if it doesn't happen, if you don't do it actually, then it has no meaning at all. If you merely treat it as an idea, then it has no value. There are so many ideas, so many books published every week, thousands and thousands. Don't add another idea to what you already have. As we said, it is only the mind that is empty that can see, that can act totally.

First of all, there is the fact of physical death. The body, by constant usage and strain, and so on, gives up, dies, comes to an end—through accident, through disease, through modern life. And one may physically find various medicines, or diets, and so on, that can give it another fifty years more; but there is the inevitable end. Like all organisms, it must come to an end; and it would be good to keep it healthy as long as possible, if you can. But there is a much deeper fact, deeper issue involved in death, and that is the psychological ending. The 'me', the accumulated experience as a human being, with all the knowledge, with all the accumulated information, every form of memory, treasured, cherished, and despised, put away—all that is the center which is the 'me', the ego, the person, and it is that center, the psychological center, that one is afraid of losing.

I don't know if you have ever examined what that center is; not only what we have said about tradition, racial inheritance, education, and all the rest of it. That center is nothing divine, and all the rest of the things man has invented through the centuries, as the atma, the higher self, the soul—all those are a repetition in different words of an idea that there is something supreme in each one of us. And the communists would say, "What tommyrot all that is!" Those who believe in all that hold on to it tremendously, as though it were something everlasting. When you examine it, it is just an idea, a thought, a memory, a bundle of experiences with all its reactions.

Please, we are going into it very slowly. Don't say I am an atheist, or this, or that—all that silly stuff. We are just examining it.

That center is the result of time, and that center creates the space round itself, like all centers do. This microphone exists in space, and it creates a space round itself, which is fairly simple. And there is the center as the 'me', which has created a space round itself. That space can extend widely, can be expanded, but still, where there is a center there is always a frontier; and within that frontier there can be no freedom at all. Though one can expand this consciousness with a center through various forms of mental tricks and drugs and so on, in that space created by the center there is no freedom. Death to most of us is the losing of that center, isn't it?—losing the things that I have known: my family, my friends, all the things that I have accumulated, which is the known. The center is the known, and death is something which I don't know at all. What I'm frightened of is losing the known—not the unknown. And losing the known means that I'm completely lonely; I'm completely alone, in a void; and that's what I am afraid of. That's what each one is afraid of. And being afraid of that, we take to various forms of escape, a whole network of escapes; and the more romantically spiritual you are—I don't know whatever that word *spiritual* means—the more romantically spiritual you are, the more fantastic your ideas.

Now, is it possible to end that center each day; not having accumulated, then giving it up, but to die to that center every day, every minute? That is, that center is the accumulation of experience, knowledge; and life is a process of experience, a challenge and a response; and the more inadequate that response, the greater the conflict. Unless one is highly enlightened, intelligent, and sensitive, one is kept awake through experience, through challenge. And you must receive every experience and not retain a shadow of it afterwards. Am I making myself clear? You have an experience, a pleasant or an unpleasant experience, dangerous or pleasurable; and you must receive that experience, understand it, and die to it immediately so that there is no memory as a center which retains that experience. We often do this naturally. But to be aware so intensely, without any choice, that every experience is totally assimilated, understood, and dissolved, requires a great deal of energy, which means attention—to die every day to every pleasure, to every thought, to every form of accumulation, so that with the dying the mind is made fresh and the heart renews itself, so that life doesn't become a torture.

Dying every day to everything that we know is to love; otherwise, one cannot love. Love is not something to be cultivated. Like humility—the moment you cultivate humility, it's a cloak of vanity. And it's only when you die to everything—to every experience that you have had—that you are living. Then living is a movement, fresh, new, innocent, every minute of the day fresh; and to die to the past is to live totally in altogether a different dimension.

Perhaps, if you are interested, we might by questioning go more deeply into it, or one can put into words in a different way what we have discussed or talked over together this morning.

Question: What then is the faculty which has the power to observe the mind?

KRISHNAMURTI: Sir, first of all, if one realizes that the observer is the observed—which is one of the most extraordinary things when you realize it—then in that state of attention there is no observer at all, or the observed. Now, let me go into it a little bit.

Look at that oak tree; actually look at it. You are the observer, and the oak is the observed. There is a space between you and the thing, which is the tree. In that interval of space is time. Right? The time that has to be covered to see that object. And that object is always static; and what is static, when observed, is time.

Now, the observer is watching the tree; and in that interval of space there are all kinds of ideas: "It's an oak tree: I like, I don't like; I wish it were in my garden, I wish it were this or that," and ten different things, which actually prevent me from seeing the fact of that tree, the totality of it, because my attention is distracted by the words, by the name, by the botanical knowledge of that tree which I have. That distraction prevents me from actually looking at the tree. When you no longer name,

when thought is no longer functioning as knowledge about that tree, then is there a space between you and the tree? Then, if you go into it very deeply and observe all this, the observer is the observed—which is not that the observer identifies himself with the tree. Of course, the identification of the observer with the tree is absolutely silly; it is not a fact. You don't become the tree.

Question: Don't you observe the vacuum?

KRISHNAMURTI: Sir, sir, sir, do examine it, sir; don't ask; examine this fact. Look at a flower. Have you ever looked at a flower? Or have you looked at it, given it a name, and passed it by? Or you say, "How beautiful; let me smell it." All these are distractive actions which prevent you from looking at that flower. Like human beings who have known each other never look; they have the images of each other, and these images are in relationship. And, to observe very closely—and that is one of the most arduous things—that doesn't need effort at all; just to sit of an afternoon, whenever you have time and leisure to look at anything, to look at a flower, to look at yourself, to look at all the movement of your thought and your feelings and your reactions; just to observe without any choice, which is the beginning of self-knowing. And without self-knowing, man is caught everlastingly in confusion and misery. When the observer is the observed—that can only be when there is total attention, not fragmentary attention. And that attention may be for a second, or a minute; but the urge to maintain that attention becomes inattention.

To ask who is the observer, or what that state of mind is when there is no observer—when the observer is the observed—to put it into words what that state is, is to deny that state. One cannot communicate with another about something the other has not known, has not found. And if it is possible to communicate, and if it is communicated—which is *not* possible—then you want to achieve it; and then you say, "Tell me the method to get at it"; and then you are lost.

Question: Sir, what prevents me from seeing the tree is 'me', and I feel I have to be willing to give up the 'me', give it up, let it go, before there's the tree. Isn't that what you're saying?

KRISHNAMURTI: Who is the thing that's going to give it up?

Comment: The 'me'.

KRISHNAMURTI: Sir, the 'me' cannot give itself up. All that it can do is to be quiet, and it cannot be quiet without understanding the whole structure and the meaning of the 'me'. Either that structure and the meaning can be understood totally, immediately, or not at all; and that's the only way; there is no other way. If you say, "I will practice; I will gradually work at it until the 'me' dies," then you have fallen into a different kind of trap, which is the same 'me'.

Comment: If I attend to a tree in the way that you described, so that the observer is the observed, the tree is still there.

KRISHNAMURTI: Of course, sir.

Question: If I attend to my fear in the same way, won't my fear also still be there?

KRISHNAMURTI: No, you see first of all, I don't want to get rid of my fear; I want to understand it. To understand something, I must care for it, I must love it, I must be careful with it; and if I say, "I must get rid of it," I've already acted most foolishly. Be-

cause I have to understand the structure and the nature of fear, and to understand it, I must look at it; and I cannot look at it if I say I must, if I want to get rid of it, or suppress it, or sublimate it. I must actually look at it, come into contact with it, not through a word, but with the fact, with what actually is.

Question: You said that when the mind is empty and the heart is empty, you can really understand. But how to make the heart empty?

KRISHNAMURTI: How can the mind, which is so crowded, so everlastingly chattering, how can that mind be emptied? I'm afraid there is no way. Any method is the most impractical way. I know we think that by following a method, it will help us to clarify the mind. On the contrary. The method produces its own results but does not free the mind from its own accumulated traditions, knowledge. That's why, sir, we said at the beginning that what is important is to listen. And to listen needs attention, care, a certain quality of affection in which there is communion; and then you will find that without an effort it has come into being.

Question: In aloneness sometimes there is clarity, but in living with people, chaos. Can you tell me something about this?

KRISHNAMURTI: "When one is alone at times there is clarity. It is only when one gets together with people that one becomes confused," the questioner says.

I'm afraid one cannot always live by oneself, and to live by oneself requires the greatest form of intelligence. To live by oneself is comparatively easy. There you can develop your particular idiosyncrasies, characteristics, tendencies, and crystallize and become rather heavy in all that. But to live alone requires immense sensitivity and intelligence. Sensitivity—to be very sensitive is to be intelligent, and in that state there is clarity. "And is it not possible," the questioner asks, "to live in this world with people, in the office, and so on, with that aloneness, with that clarity?" Obviously it is possible. But you see, you want someone to give it all to you; take a pill, and the thing is solved. So you see, sir, we are so used to being told what to do that we worship authority, and we have lost all capacity in the world, all intention to find things for ourselves. In what we are talking about there is no teacher, there is no method, there is no practice; there is only perception of *what is;* and when there is that perception, then the problem is resolved.

Question: Of what significance is hope and faith to living?

KRISHNAMURTI: I hope you won't think me harsh if I say there is no significance at all. We have had hope; we have had faith—faith in church, faith in politics, faith in leaders, faith in gurus—because we have wanted to achieve a state of bliss, of happiness, and so on. And hope has nourished this faith. And when one observes through history, through our life, all that hope and faith have no meaning at all because what is important is what we are, actually what we are—not what we think we are, or what we think we should be, but actually *what is.* If we know how to look at *what is,* that will bring about a tremendous transformation.

Question: If one is able at times to have clarity, yet live in the family, how does one keep one's sons from each other's throats? There must be a way of helping the young to live at peace, the same with nations.

KRISHNAMURTI: The questioner says, "How is one to educate children?" The educator must first be educated. And modern education gives such terrific importance to technology, to acquiring knowledge, and neglecting the whole field of life; cultivating one tiny little part—and that's what's called education—and neglecting the whole field of love and thought and death and anxiety. Is it possible to educate in a different way so that one is concerned with the whole of life? That's only possible when the educator is also concerned; such an educator is a rare entity, in the family or in the school.

I think that's enough, isn't it?

November 6, 1966

Fifth Talk in the Oak Grove

I should think one of our greatest problems in life must be, surely, knowing that our minds deteriorate, decline as one grows older, or deteriorate even when one is quite young; being a specialist along a certain line, and being unaware totally of the whole complex area of life, it must be a great problem to find out whether it is at all possible to stop this deterioration so that the mind is always fresh, young, clear, decisive. Is it at all possible to end this decline?

This evening, if I may, I would like to go into that. Because to me, meditation is freeing the mind from the known; and to inquire into this question—which is really very, very important—one must, it seems to me, know or be aware of the whole machinery of the formation of the image which each one has about himself, or about another, and not only be aware of the machinery that makes these images but also how we add to those images that we have about ourselves. Because it is these images that gradually begin to crystallize, become hard. The whole of life is a constant movement, a constant flow, and this crystallization, this process of the hardening of the image, is the central fact of deterioration.

One notices, obviously, as one grows older, that one is burdened with innumerable experiences, hurts, many strains, conflicts, despair, the competitive process of life. All these and other factors bring about a lack of sensitivity in the brain cells themselves. That one sees as one grows older. And one sees also, when one is quite young, that a mind trained along a special line, completely concentrated on that line and avoiding the whole area of this extraordinary life, makes its brain cells also very narrow, very small—being unaware of the whole total movement of life, which is modern education, which is the modern way of living. Not only with the young, but also, as one grows or advances in years, one notices this: The sharpness, the clarity, the precision, the capacity to think impersonally, to look at life not only from one center, declines. Whether that center is noble or ignoble is irrelevant; it is a self-appointed center, and from that gradually comes the crystallization of all the brain cells. The whole mental process declines, and one is then ready for the grave.

The question then arises: Is it at all possible to end this decaying process of the brain, as well as of the mind—the whole, total entity? And also, is it possible to keep the physique, the body, extraordinarily alive, alert, energetic, and so on? That seems to me to be a great issue, and therefore a great challenge to find out.

Now, the inquiry into this—not only verbally, but nonverbally—the inquiry, the examination into this is meditation. That word itself is so misused; there are so many methods of meditation, especially coming out of Asia: the Zen form of meditation, the Hindu, and the dozens of ways of meditation. If we understand one, we shall understand the total of the systems and the ways of meditation. But the central issue that we are going to talk over together this evening is whether the mind can ever rejuvenate itself, whether it can become fresh, young, unafraid. And if one asserts that it is not possible, one is then actually blocking oneself. All examination ceases when you say it is not possible, or when you say it is possible. Either the positive denial of saying that it is not possible, or saying, "Well, it is possible"—both, it seems to me, are irrelevant and they block all examination. But the fact remains that as one grows older, the mind does decline. It declines because one sees that the whole process of thinking, the structure of the brain, and the totality of the whole process which is the mind is a way of conflict, struggle, and constant strain, a self-contradictory process.

If I may point out here, I think it would be well to find out how you are listening to what is being said, because we are not concerned with ideas. One can go on with innumerable ideas, adding them, writing about them, reading about them. There are volumes upon volumes about thought and what the process is, and so on and so on; and there are all these psychologists who have theories about all this, or statistical facts, and so on. Are we listening to a series of words or phrases or ideas? Or are we listening, observing the actual state of our own mind? I think that's very important, especially when we are talking about something which is beyond argumentation, opinions, personal inclinations, or personal outlook. The fact is that there is deterioration; and if one looks at it and translates that deterioration, or tries to transcend it, or go beyond it in terms of personal inclination, temperament, and so on, it becomes a very shoddy affair. But if one observes it as you would a tree, a sunset, the light on the water, the outlines of a blue hill, just observes it—just observes the process of what is actually taking place in each one of us—then we will go on together. If you cannot do this, there will be gaps, and we'll not be able to take the road together.

Also this requires a sustained attention, not for two minutes or three minutes, but for this whole hour. If one can be so alert, attentive, not only to what is being said, but also to relate what is being said to your own activity inside of yourself, then such listening has an extraordinary action. But if you merely listen to ideas, or words, then you can have this idea or that idea; you can accept this opinion or that opinion. We're not dealing with opinions. That only leads to dialectical approach. But what we are talking about is something entirely different. We are concerned with the whole total process of living; and this total process of living, as one observes, is always creating an image about ourselves, about others—image through experience, image through conflict. This image is added to or taken away from, but the central factor of that energy which creates that image is always constant. Is it at all possible to go beyond it? And are we aware that there is an image in each one of us about ourselves, conscious or unconscious? I mean that one might have an image about oneself as superior, or as not having capacity, or as aggressive, prideful—all kinds of nuances, subtleties which build up this image. Surely, each one has this image about oneself. And, as one grows older—it might be that age really has nothing to do with it; one has an image when one is very, very young, and that image begins to be more and more strong, and more and more crystallized, and then there is the end to it all.

Is one aware of it? And if one is aware of it, who is the entity that is aware of the image? You understand the issue? Is the image different from the image-maker? Or are the image-making and the image the same? Because unless one understands this

factor very clearly, what we are going into will not be clear.

You understand? I can see that I have an image about myself: I am this and that; I am a great man or a little man; or my name is known, not known—you know, all the verbal structure about oneself, and the nonverbal structure about oneself, conscious or hidden. I realize that image exists, if I become at all aware, watchful. I know this image is being formed all the time. And the observer who is aware of that image feels himself different from the image. Isn't that what is taking place? Right? I hope we are making this clear. And the observer then begins to say to himself that this image is the factor that brings about a deterioration; therefore, he must destroy the image in order to achieve a greater result, to make the mind young, fresh, and all the rest of it, because he realizes that this image is the central factor of deterioration; and therefore he makes an effort to get rid of that image. Right? Are we going along together? He struggles, he explains, he justifies, or adds; strives to alter it to a better image; moves it to a different dimension, or to a different part of that field which he calls life. The observer then is concerned either with the destruction of that image, or adding to that image, or going beyond that image. This is what we are doing all the time. And one has never stopped to inquire whether the observer is not the image-maker, and therefore the observer is the image. Right? Therefore, when this factor is very clearly understood, which is nonverbal but actual, that the observer is the maker of the image, and whatever the observer does, he not only destroys the present image he has about himself but also creates another image and so keeps this making of images all the time going—struggling, compelling, controlling, suppressing, altering, adjusting—when one sees this observer is the observed, then all effort ceases to change the image, or go beyond the image.

This demands a great deal of penetration and attention; it isn't just that you accept an explanation. Because the explanation, the word, is not the fact. And to realize this, to realize the central fact, eliminates all effort. This is very important to understand. Effort, struggle in different ways—either physically or psychologically, as competition, as ambition, aggression, violence, pride, accumulated resentments, and so on—is one of the factors of deterioration. So when one realizes that the observer is the image-maker, then our whole process of thinking undergoes a tremendous change. And so the image is the known, isn't it? You may not be aware of it; you may not be aware of the content of the image, the shape of it, the peculiar nuances, the subtleties of that image; but that image, whether one is conscious of it or not, is in the field of the known. Right?

Perhaps we can discuss and answer this question afterwards. For the moment we'll go on with what we are talking about. As long as the whole mind—which is the mind, the brain, and the body—functions within the field of the image, which is the known, of which one may be conscious or not, in that field is the factor of deterioration. Right? Please, don't accept it as an idea which you'll think about when you go home. You won't, anyhow. But here we are doing it, taking the thing together; therefore, you must do it now, not when you go home and say, "Well, I've taken notes, and I've understood it; I'll think about it." Don't take notes, because that doesn't help at all.

The problem then is whether the mind—which is the result of time, psychological and chronological, which is the result of a thousand experiences, which is the result of so many stresses and strains, of technological knowledge, of hope, of despair, all that a human being goes through, the innumerable

forms of fear—whether that mind functions always within that field, which is the field of the known. I am using that word, the *known*, to include what may be there, but which you have not looked at; still, it is the known.

That is the field in which the mind functions, always within the field of the known; and the known is the image, whether created by the intellect, or by lots of sentimental, emotional, or romantic thought. As long as its activity, its thoughts, its movements, are within the field of the known, which is the making of the image, there must be deterioration, do what you will. So the question arises: Is it possible to empty the mind of the known? You understand? Am I making myself clear? It doesn't matter!

One must have asked this question—whether it's possible to go beyond—vaguely, or with a purpose, because one suffers, one has anxieties, or one has vague hints of it. Now we are asking it as a question which must be answered, as a challenge which must be responded to; and this challenge is not an outward challenge but a psychological, inward challenge. And we are going to find out whether it is possible to empty the mind of the known. I've explained what we mean by the known.

Now as to this process of emptying the mind—this emptying of the mind is meditation; and one must go into this question of meditation, explain it a little bit. All the Asiatic people are conditioned by this word; the so-called religious, serious people are conditioned by this word because through meditation they hope to find something which is not, something which is beyond mere daily existence. And to find it they have various systems, very, very subtle, or very crude, like the Zen: the discipline, the forcing, the beating; or watching, being tremendously aware of the toe, and then to see how it moves, to be conscious of it all, and so on and on and on in different ways.

Also in that so-called meditative system is concentration, fixing the mind on one idea, or one thought, or one symbol, and so on. Every schoolboy does this when he reads a book, when he is forced to read; and there's not much difference between the student in the school and the very deep thinker who tries tremendously to concentrate on one idea or one image, and who tries to discover some reality out of that.

Also there are various forms of stimulation, forcing oneself, stimulating oneself to reach a point from which one sees life totally differently; and that means to expand consciousness more and more through will, through effort, through concentration, through determination to force, force, force; and by extending this consciousness one hopes to arrive at a different state, or a different dimension, or reach a point which the conscious mind cannot. Or one takes many, many drugs, including the latest, LSD, and so on and so on. That gives for the moment tremendous stimulation to the whole system, and in that state one experiences extraordinary things—extraordinary things through stimulation, through concentration, through discipline, through starvation, through fasting. If one fasts for some days, one has peculiar—obviously peculiar—things happening. And one takes drugs, and that for the moment makes the body extraordinarily sensitive; you see colors which are most extraordinary, which you have never seen before. You see everything so clearly; there is no space between you and that thing which you see. And this goes on in various forms throughout the world: the repetition of words, like in the Catholic church, or in those prayers, which all make the mind a little calm, quiet, obviously, which is a trick. If you keep on repeating, repeating, repeating, you get so dull, obviously, that you go to sleep, and you think that's a very quiet mind. (Laughter) Please!

There are very many systems, both in Asia, which includes India, and in Europe, to quieten the mind. One goes through extraordinary tortures to still the mind. But the mind can be stilled very simply by taking a tranquilizer, a pill that will make you seemingly awake but quiet. But that's not meditation. One can brush all that aside; even though one is committed to it, we can throw all of that out of the window; and as you are listening I hope you will throw it out because we are going into something much deeper than these inventions of a very clever mind which has had a peculiar experience, the other experience, and so on and so on. Having examined, not in too much detail, but sufficiently, one can really put all that aside. Because the more one practices a discipline, the more the mind becomes dull, mechanized; and that mechanizing, routine process makes the mind somewhat quiet, but it is not the quietness of tremendous energy, understanding.

Having brushed those aside as immature, utterly nonsensical, though they produce extraordinary results, then we can proceed to inquire whether it is at all possible to free the mind from the known—not only the known of a thousand years, but also of yesterday, which is memory; which doesn't mean that I forget the road, the way to the house I live in, or technology. That obviously one must have. That's essential; otherwise, we can't live. But we are talking of something at a much deeper level—the deeper level where the image is always active; where the image, which is the known, is functioning all the time; and whether that image, and the maker of the image, which is the observer—whether it is possible to empty the mind of that. And the emptying of that, of the known, is meditation. We are going to go into that a little bit. I don't know if you have the energy or the sustained attention to go into it so far.

One sees very clearly that there is an understanding there, an action, only when the mind is completely quiet. Right? That is, I say I understand something, or I see something very clearly, when the mind is totally silent. Right? You tell me something, and you're telling me something which I don't like, or like. If I like, I pay a little attention; if I don't like, I don't pay any attention at all. Or I listen to what you're saying and translate it according to my idiosyncrasy, to my inclination, and so on and so on and so on, justifying, and so on and so on. I don't listen at all. Or I oppose what you're saying because I have an image about myself, and that image reacts. Please, I hope you are doing all this!

And so I don't listen; I don't hear. I object; I dissent; I'm aggressive. But all that obviously prevents me from understanding. I want to understand you. I can only understand you when I have no image about you. And if you're a total stranger, I don't care; I don't even want to understand you because you are totally outside the field of my image, and I have no relationship with you. But if you are a friend, a relation, and so on, husband, wife, and all the rest of it, I have an image; and the image which you have about me and I have about you, those images have a relationship. All our relationship is based on that. One sees very clearly that only when the image doesn't interfere—image as knowledge, thought, emotion, all the rest of it—only then can I look, can I hear, can I understand. It has happened to all of us. When suddenly, after you discuss, argue, point out, and so on, suddenly your mind becomes quiet and you see that, and you say, "By Jove, I've understood." That understanding is an action, not an idea. Right?

So there is understanding, action in a different sense than the action that we know, which is the action of the image, of the known. We are talking of an understanding which is an action when the mind is completely quiet, in which understanding as action takes place. Right? There is understanding and action only when the mind is completely quiet, and that quiet, still mind is not induced by any discipline, by any effort. Obviously if there is an effort, it is the effort of the image to go beyond itself and create another image. You know all the tricks of that. One sees that there is an understanding action only when the mind is quiet, and that quietness is not induced, is not projected, is not brought about by careful, cunning thought. And meditation—which one can do when one is sitting in a bus, walking the street, or washing dishes, and God knows what else—meditation has nothing whatsoever to do with breathing and all that, or taking postures. We've brushed all that aside long ago, all that childish stuff.

When the observer is the image, and therefore there is no effort to change the image, or to accept the image, but only the fact of *what is,* the observation of that fact of *what is* brings about a radical change in the fact itself. And that can only take place when the observer is the observed. There is nothing mysterious about it. The mystery of life is beyond all this—beyond the image, beyond effort, beyond the centralized, egotistic, subjective, self-centered activity. There is a vast field of something which can never be found through the known. And the emptying of the mind can only take place nonverbally, only when there is no observer and the observed. All this demands tremendous attention and awareness—an awareness which is not concentration.

You know, concentration is effort: focusing upon a particular page, an idea, image, symbol, and so on and so on. Concentration is a process of exclusion. You tell a student, "Don't look out of the window; pay attention to the book." He wants to look out, but he forces himself to look, look at the page;

so there is a conflict. This constant effort to concentrate is a process of exclusion, which has nothing to do with awareness. Awareness takes place when one observes—you can do it; everybody can do it—observes not only what is the outer, the tree, what people say, what one thinks, and so on, outwardly, but also inwardly to be aware without choice; just to observe without choosing. For when you choose, when choice takes place, only then is there confusion, not when there is clarity.

Awareness takes place only when there is no choice, or when you are aware of all the conflicting choices, conflicting desires, the strain—when you just observe all this movement of contradiction. Knowing that the observer is the observed, in that process there is no choice at all, but only watching *what is*, and that's entirely different from concentration. That awareness brings a quality of attention in which there is neither the observer nor the observed. When you really attend, if you have ever done it—we all do sometimes—when you completely attend, like you are doing now, if you are really listening, there is neither the listener nor the speaker. In that state of attention is silence, and that state of attention brings about an extraordinary freshness, youth—not "youth"; in America they use that word terribly—an extraordinary sense of freshness, a quality of newness, to the mind. This emptying of the mind of all the experiences it has had is meditation. Though one has had a thousand experiences—and we are the result of millions of experiences—all the experiences can be emptied only when one becomes aware of each experience, sees the whole content of it without choice; therefore, it goes, it passes by; there is no mark of that experience as a wound, as something to remember, to recognize and keep.

Meditation is a very strenuous process; it's not just a thing to do, for old ladies or men who have nothing to do. This demands tremendous attention right through. Then you will find for yourself—no, there is no question of experience, there is no finding. When the mind is completely quiet, without any form of suggestion, hypnotism, or following a method, when the mind is completely quiet, then there is a quality and a different dimension which thought can never possibly imagine or experience. Then it's beyond all search; there is then no seeking. A mind that is full of light does not seek. It is only the dull, confused mind that's always seeking and hoping to find. What it finds is the result of its own confusion.

Is it worthwhile talking about all this, questioning, asking?

Audience: Yes, yes.

KRISHNAMURTI: All right; go ahead.

Question: Has not deterioration two factors: not only the image-making factor, but also the wrong way of living, wrong food, and so on?

KRISHNAMURTI: Obviously. It's clear, isn't it? All this demands such extraordinary sensitivity, both of the body and of the mind, not that the two are separate. There is a separateness which one cannot possibly understand unless one goes into this question of the observer and the observed. Obviously it matters how one lives, what one thinks, what one's daily activities are, anger, and all the rest of it.

Question: Krishnaji, the image is the known, as you say. Would it be fitting for us to examine together here, now, the nonimage, or the unknown, or the unconscious?

KRISHNAMURTI: As we said the other day, actually there is no such state as the unconscious. Sorry! (Laughter) I mean, one has dreams. One never asks oneself: Why does one have dreams at all? One has dreams if one has overeaten, all that. That's all right. That's clear. But all those dreams which need interpretation, all the fuss they make about dreams! Why do you dream at all? Is it possible not to dream so that when you wake up, the mind is fresh, clear, innocent? One dreams because during the day you have not paid attention, you have not watched what you have said, what you have thought, what you have felt, how you have talked to another. You have not watched the beauty of the sky, the trees. And so, all this field which has not been examined, watched, looked at, naturally projects, in that state of the mind when it is half-asleep, an image or an idea or a scene; and that becomes the dream, which has to be interpreted, and so on and so on and so on.

When one is aware, watching all things, choicelessly, looking, not interpreting, then you will find for yourself that you don't dream at all because you have understood everything as you are going along.

Wait; I have not finished, madame. Look, please. If you understand one question, you have understood all the questions. This question which we are taking, which has been asked, is whether the conscious mind can examine the unconscious, can look into something which is hidden, whether it can analyze; and it can, obviously. It can see the motives, the reactions in relationship, and so on. It obviously can analyze, and the process is analyzing part of the whole field. That part is a corner of that field, which is called the unconscious, which we make so much ado about; that can be examined very quietly without analysis by just watching the whole field. And the whole field is the conscious. The whole field is limited, the whole area is limited because there is always the center, the observer, the censor, the watcher, the thinker. You can observe the whole field, what is called the unconscious and the conscious, which are on that field, only when there is no observer at all, when there is no attempt to change *what is*, when you are totally attentive, completely attentive of the whole field. Then you will find out for yourself that there is no such thing as the unconscious, and there is nothing to be examined. It is there to be looked at, only we don't know how to look, and we don't want to look. When we do look, we want to change it to our pleasure, to our idiosyncrasies, to our inclinations, which becomes terribly personal, and that's what interests most of us: to be personal.

Question: What is the state of the quiet mind that makes discoveries? Are these discoveries to be treated any differently from the rest of the field?

KRISHNAMURTI: Obviously not, sir. A quiet mind, a still mind, never experiences. It is only the observer that experiences. Therefore it is not a still mind.

Comment: To see the false as the false, and to realize that this is not true is very difficult.

KRISHNAMURTI: Yes, sir. As long as you have concepts, you never see what is true.

Comment: My main trouble is that I can't stay aware for a long enough period of time, maybe a few seconds, a few minutes, and I fall asleep; and this has been going on for years.

KRISHNAMURTI: To be attentive at the moment of awareness, attentive at that moment when you are aware, is enough. But when you say, ''I must extend it, keep it going,'' then the trouble begins. Then you want it as a pleasure. Behind this question lies the desire to have something permanent—a permanent awareness, a permanent state of attention. What is important is to be aware, to be completely attentive at that moment. It may last one second; you are completely aware for one second, and the next second you may be inattentive. But know also you are inattentive. Don't say, ''Inattention must become attention''; thereby, you introduce conflict, and in that conflict awareness and attention completely end.

Question: Sir, if there is no such thing as the unconscious mind, unconscious thinking, how do you explain phenomena such as post-hypnotic suggestion?

KRISHNAMURTI: When I said there is no such thing as the unconscious, I have been saying, ''Don't accept what is being said.'' Look into this, neither accepting nor denying. Your question, sir, ''What happens after hypnosis, and so on, through hypnosis?'' is very explainable, all still within the field of the known, the conscious.

What is important to understand in all this, in asking questions and getting answers, or explanations, is that the explanation has no value at all. What has value is how you ask the question, and what you're expecting out of that question. If you are attentive to what you are asking, you will see that the question is answered without any difficulty. Therefore there is no teacher. You are everything yourself, both the teacher and the pupil, everything. That gives you tremendous freedom to inquire. Right, sirs?

November 12, 1966

Sixth Talk in the Oak Grove

This is the last talk. It's a lovely morning. The sunlight is clear on the mountains, the new grass is coming up, and you see very clearly the beauty of the land. As one looks at all this extraordinary beauty and color and light, there is a joy, there is a sense of freedom; and naturally one asks: What is beauty? Is it something that is the outcome of some stimulation, an appreciation of an object, of a movement of light among the leaves? And does it depend on one's mood, on one's education, or on one's state of mind?

Is beauty awakened by an object, or is beauty something entirely different? Is there a state of mind which is awakened to beauty without the object, not the appreciation of a man-made thing or of nature, but is there beauty without the object? Is there a sense of beauty, not only physical, but much more deeply psychological, inward? Without these mountains, without the light, without that clarity which exists especially in California— is there beauty beyond all that? That sense of beauty can come only when the mind is completely at rest, quiet, undisturbed, and is not provoked or induced by circumstances, by social environment, and education. And is that beauty personal? Is not beauty something that comes when there is freedom, total freedom? Without freedom, obviously, there is no peace. Peace is not something that you buy, or that state between two conflicts, outward or inward, but that comes when the mind is no longer harassed, no longer driven by any impulse, is not concerned with its own peculiar self-centered activity; then there is that freedom, and that freedom is very difficult to come by. Unless that freedom exists, there is everlasting searching, asking questions, gathering information, knowledge and experience, piling up memory endlessly; and this search that one indulges in—searching for truth, searching for love, searching for companionship, searching for happiness, searching for something beyond all this—surely exists only when the mind, out of its immense dissatisfaction, is seeking satisfaction.

As we said, during these talks please listen, not to the words—I hope you don't mind—not to the words or to the phrases or to the cunning thought cleverly developed, but rather listen to discover for yourself a state of mind that is no longer seeking, hunted, driven, perpetually after something. Unless one discovers that, a state where there is no longer search but intense aliveness, intense alertness, intense penetration of clarity—unless one discovers that, one is caught, not only in this deep discontent, but also in this ever time-binding quality of seeking. Most of us right through the world are very, very disturbed and discontented. In the East it takes one form: first food, clothing, and shelter, for there is immense poverty and overpopulation. In the West it takes the form of having been well-fed from womb to tomb, secure, greatly at ease, with leisure, prosperity, and being dissatisfied, wanting more prosperity, more things, more books, more amusement. But there is deeper discontent, which is not satisfied by the external acquisitiveness. Then one haunts, one pursues the inward acquisition, the inward mind that is demanding complete satisfaction from this endless discontent. We seek something that is enduring, satisfying; we call it by different names: God, truth, bliss, happiness. The things that one invents, the symbols that one has, the pictures, the paintings, the music, the museums, the endless forms of outward expression which will be satisfactory, sexually, psychologically, intellectually—that's what most of us are seeking. Man is always seeking, and the search is brought about by his deep inward discontent, dissatisfaction, frustration, despair; and the very seeking brings about its own conclusion. We seek and find something in a group, in a com-

munity, in social welfare, in politics, or in innumerable sects of religion: the Catholic, the Protestant, and I don't know how many there are in this little village. The earth is broken up, not only geographically, nationally, but also it's broken up in the name of God, in the name of peace, in the name of love, by various religions, by various sects, with all their vested interests, exploiting people, and so on. Few find satisfaction in these man-made things: in books, going to concert after concert, talking endlessly about them, comparing who is the best musician, who is the best painter, and so on and on and on and on.

Behind all these intellectual, literary, artistic activities, or going to an office endlessly for over thirty, forty years, the utter boredom of it all, everyone wants to find something that will be utterly, completely, wholly satisfactory and gratifying; and religions throughout the world have offered this. They have offered gods, beliefs, dogmas, rituals, and in these there is great pleasure, there is great gratification; and, having found that gratification, we stay there, and we don't want to be disturbed; we don't want to be questioned. We have built a house which we hope will be permanent, lasting, and we are afraid of any storm, of any movement of life that will be disturbing, that will be destructive, that will be revolutionary. And this we call seeking reality, God, happiness, and so on.

First one must understand this discontent. There is the obvious discontent of wanting a better car, a better house, and so on. We won't go into that. We will go into this question psychologically, which is much more vital, much more real, more penetrating. Why are we psychologically discontented? Because without finding out this discontent and ending it, or giving it such vitality that it is not satisfied in any way—a flame that burns without motive, without a purpose, but alive—without understanding discontent, the search has no meaning; and most of us, I presume, have come here this morning, or go to church, or do anything, because our life is so monotonous, so lonely, so utterly meaningless; and we want to find something that will be deeply gratifying, that will bring about deep content.

It is important, it seems to me, to find out why we seek at all, and what we are seeking, and from what depth this search comes into being. First of all, seeking is so utterly false, because the psychological process of it is very simple. I seek because I am dissatisfied, I am confused; and out of my confusion, out of my misery, out of my endless agony and suffering, I am seeking, seeking, seeking. What I am seeking really is already predestined, is already established, is already found, because I have projected what I want already, and therefore it is no longer seeking. It is really a movement of escape from *what is,* and this movement towards what is already known is called seeking.

Do please listen to this a little bit. This movement from *what is* to 'what should be', or this movement of seeking, is a movement which is essentially static; it's not a movement at all. And yet we're caught in this. I join this, I don't find satisfaction, and I discard it; I go from one trap to another, from one teacher to another, from one book, one system, one philosophy, one psychologist, one analyst, and one bishop to another; move, move, move, move; and this movement is what we call seeking. If you look at that movement very closely, you haven't moved at all. You are where you were, and you are always going to be there, only one deceives oneself; one hypnotizes oneself by thinking that this movement of so-called seeking gives a certain vitality, a certain inquiry, a certain movement from *what is* to what you want to discover, which is already fixed. It is not a movement at all; it is static. What is a movement is *what is.* That you

don't have to seek. Am I making myself clear?

Audience: Yes.

KRISHNAMURTI: Good. Please do observe yourself. These words are merely a mirror to see what actually is, to see in that mirror what is actually taking place in yourself. Otherwise what you hear will have little value; otherwise, it becomes merely an idea. Then you will interpret that idea and ask how it should be put into action. Whereas, if one discovers that the fact is *what is,* and the movement away from that, which we call seeking, is static, has no vitality, and if one is aware of *what is,* there is no seeking at all. Then the movement of *what is* is entirely different; then the seeking comes to a complete end. Then you have the energy to look at *what is.* Right?

So, being discontented, being dissatisfied, unhappy, miserable, deeply wounded, deeply anxious, deeply driven by some personal anguish—which is a fact, which is *what is—* being discontented with that, we go through all these processes of experiencing, of seeking, of learning, of putting aside. Why are we discontented, and with what? Please answer this question to yourselves. The speaker will go into it, but you have to answer it for yourself.

We are discontented through comparison; we are discontented because we want to bring about a change in *what is;* and we are discontented because we don't know what to do with *what is.* Being discontented with *what is,* we develop the idea of 'what should be', the ideal, the utopia, the gods, heaven, and so on and on and on. Our action then is based on an idea, and the approximation to that idea is action, isn't it? I am discontented with *what is,* and I want to be something different from *what is,* the idea being rational or irrational, thought put together as an idea or an ideal, and I have that ideal, and according to that ideal I live, which is called action. And there is conflict between *what is* and 'what should be', and in that conflict we are caught; all our questions, demands, searching is that: between *what is* and 'what should be'. And the greater the tension between *what is* and 'what should be', the greater the neurosis; and also, if one has the capacity, the greater the urge to express that conflict verbally: in the theater, in music, in art, in literature, in so many ways. And being discontented with *what is,* we invent gods, which become our religion. That is the escape we have from *what is.* And is it impossible to radically change *what is?* That is the real search, not the other. The other is no search at all. Is it possible to totally bring about a mutation in *what is?* To go into that, to go into this question of bringing about a total revolution in *what is,* one must have an extraordinary sense of awareness. You know what it means to be aware—to be aware of the trees, of the blue sky through the trees, of those hills beyond, of that noise of a motor, of the colors that are there in front—just to be aware; and to be aware so choicelessly that you know very well that you can't change it. You can't change the mountain, except with a bulldozer; you can't change the beauty of that sky. But when we are aware of *what is,* we want to transform it; we are endlessly active about it; and there begins sorrow. Because with the ending of sorrow is the beginning of wisdom, and the ending of sorrow is the understanding of *what is.* And the understanding of *what is* can only come when you observe, when you are aware, when the mind is incapable of wanting to change *what is*—which doesn't mean it is satisfied with *what is.*

So, one has freed the mind, or the mind has freed itself from this everlasting search—that's finished, and that means a tremendous burden off one's shoulders. Then, being free, you can look; and to look you need great energy, and that energy comes only when there is awareness without conflict—this awareness in which there is no conflict of any kind, just observation. And there is a conflict only as long as there is the observer and the observed, which is *what is.* But *what is* is the observer.

Please don't learn phrases but see the actual fact. Then you will find that where there is the observer, the center, the censor, the experiencer, the entity that is always creating the division between the observed and the observer—as long as there is an observer, there is no freedom.

Every object, like this microphone, creates a space around itself, and is in space, isn't it? Not only the object outwardly, but an object inwardly, as the 'me', as the experiencer, as the 'I', as the thinker—that center creates a space in consciousness. This space in consciousness is always limited because there is always the center. Right? One may expand this space from the center, but however much you may expand, it will always have a border, a frontier; and therefore, that space is always psychologically limited, and therefore there is no freedom in that space. That center, that observer is obviously memory: memory of what has been, whether of yesterday, or a thousand years. That center is the tradition, is a conditioned state which has been put together by time, both chronologically and psychologically. That center is the accumulation of knowledge, of experience. That center is always the past; therefore, that center is not a living thing; it is a dead memory of what has been. And when it creates its space—as most of us do—whether it is very, very, very small round itself, or is concerned with itself endlessly, with its activities, its propositions, its ideas, it's a shabby, little thing round itself. That can expand, but however much it may expand through various tricks of thought, of compulsion, of drugs, it is always within this space which the center has created, and therefore there is no freedom; and therefore there is no peace at all. When one observes, one sees that only when there is space is there freedom; and that space cannot possibly exist, psychologically, as long as there is an observer. Right? And one must have space, as one must have beauty—beauty which is not man-made, or nature, which is not stimulated, which is not the product of thought—as love. Without that space, and having no freedom, man is everlastingly seeking, searching, wanting, hoping—thereby living in endless sorrow and misery. This is a fact; you can observe it psychologically if you watch it, see yourself in a mirror, a psychological mirror. If you observe very, very, very closely, this is what's going on.

And so one asks oneself: Is it possible to end that center? Not through time, you understand? Not through gradually getting rid of it, chipping away little by little, until there is nothing left—that involves time. When there is time, there is no space. Time is between the observer and that thing which he observes; that interval is time, and that interval is always static.

Is it possible, then, if there is no time at all, to end *what is,* to end the observer, and therefore to look without the interval of time? You understand the question?

Time is the space between the observer and that tree. The observer is static, and the tree is static, psychologically; and to cover the distance between the observer and the tree takes time; and that distance, which has been created by the observer and the observed, is always static, is always stationary. When one thinks of using time, or having time to bring about a change in the observer, you're only being caught in this static state. When you discover that, then you ask if it is possible to change instantly *what is.* We are using the word *understand* not verbally, not

intellectually, but as meaning actually to see what is taking place, step by step.

So one asks: Is it possible to end the observer who creates a space round himself and the object, and the movement towards that object—to change it, sublimate it? Whatever it is, it is static and therefore utterly useless. Then how does one bring about a revolution in *what is?* The center is violence—I'm taking that as an example. It isn't really an example; it is a fact. One is violent. That's a fact. And the movement towards non-violence is a static movement; it's no movement at all; I explained that previously. Our question then is: Is it possible to end violence, not through time, but immediately? Because, if there is an observer, he's always limiting the space, and therefore there is no freedom. Therefore, as long as the observer exists, every form of attempt to transcend it, to go beyond it, is still a waste of time. Our question then is: Is it possible to end the observer, not *what is?* When there is no observer, there is no *what is.* It is the observer that creates *what is.* So, how is it possible to end the violence, the aggression, the immense hatred that one has stored up, the resentment—how is it possible to end it so that one is completely, totally free of it?

Probably one has never asked this question. One puts up with it, gets used to it, and carries on. But if you put that question, either you put it casually or you put it with the intention to find out; therefore, you become very serious. And when you put that question because you are serious, because you are intent, then you are aware of the whole process of the observer; which means that you are totally attentive, completely attentive, and in that attention there is no border created by the center. When there is complete attention, there is no observer.

When you look over at those mountains behind the speaker, they're blue—the line, the straight lines, and the valley, and so on—

when you give your complete attention to look, is there an observer? The observer comes into being only when, in that look, there is inattention, which is distraction. So, only total attention brings about the cessation of the observer. And when there is the ending of the observer, there is the ending of the thing which he has created as *what is* because, as we said, the observer is the observed.

Now, we have in this way eliminated all conflict of search. We have eliminated all conflict between *what is* and 'what should be'. We have put away the observer, and therefore there is attention—even if it lasts a second, that's good enough. Don't be greedy to have more. In that greed to have more, you have already created the center, and then you're caught. In that attention there is no seeking at all, and therefore there is no effort, so the mind becomes extraordinarily alert, active, silent. It is not the silence brought about through conformity, suppression, control. That's not silence at all. It is not a state which is the result of some absorption in something, like a boy, like a child being absorbed by a toy. And then only can the mind be in a state of no experience; and this is important to understand.

We all depend on experience—experience being to go through something. We all depend on experience to keep us awake—a challenge, a question, an external impetus, an influence. Naturally for the moment that challenge, that external force, keeps us awake for a few minutes; and then one goes back to sleep. One depends constantly on experience to keep awake. When one realizes that, one rejects all outward stimulus, all outward or inward experience. Then one can ask: Can the mind—I am making it very quick because I must go through it—can the mind be so intensely alert without experience? If it is made alert through experience, it is not alert, obviously. If an experience makes me love, then it is not love. Behind it there is a motive. So, such a mind is the religious mind—no longer seeking, no longer demanding experiences; it is not caught in visions. Such a mind has an activity totally different, at a different dimension, which thought can never possibly reach. Thought has a place, a very small place; but when one realizes that, thought has no place at all—which doesn't mean that you live on ugly little sentiments, emotions.

So one can function normally, healthily, sanely in this world, with a mind that is not cluttered up by thought; and it is only such a mind, the religious mind, that can know something beyond all the imaginations and structure of man's hope.

Do we ask any questions?

Question: You speak often of beauty in nature. Would you please speak a little of beauty in human relationship.

KRISHNAMURTI: What is relationship? Relationship is between the two images—I must be quick; otherwise, it can drag on—between the images that I have about you, and you have about me. The images have relationship. You have hurt me; you have wounded me; you have dominated me; I've had pleasure; this and that—that is the image, and equally you have an image about me; and these two images are constantly meeting, and that we call relationship. In that there is no beauty, obviously. To be free of that image is to be free of the observer.

Comment: If you become aware of what is, and beyond that, it would seem that one could also reflect sort of human emotions, even though he was aware of what is; and that to reflect these human emotions could not be avoided.

KRISHNAMURTI: I don't know quite what you mean, sir, by saying "human emotions." Human emotions are aggression, which is part of the animal emotion. You mean to say you shouldn't avoid aggression, violence?

Comment: Yes, as they are part of an animal, or of a child, so they are part of a human being.

KRISHNAMURTI: Therefore they should not be avoided?

Comment: Yes.

KRISHNAMURTI: You know, sirs, there is no end to talking, to words, to attending meetings, and reading. But attending meetings, reading, discussing, have very little value, if attending meetings, discussions, and all the rest of it are merely a stimulus; then you are dependent, as people are dependent on LSD, on music, on pictures, on doing something; and as long as one is dependent, one is in conflict, one is in despair. And one has to come, not through reading, to discover the whole process of knowing oneself; for the knowing of oneself is the beginning and the end of all misery.

November 13, 1966

New Delhi, India, 1966

✱

First Talk in New Delhi

I think it is necessary to consider what is actually taking place in the world, not only in this country, but in different parts of the world—the grave incidents. Deep questions are being asked and I think we should, from the beginning, consider most objectively what is actually taking place. There is general deterioration: of that there is no question. Morally, religiously, the old values have completely gone. There is a great disturbance and discontent in every part of the world. They are questioning the purpose of education, the purpose of man's existence altogether, not only in a very limited manner, as it is being done in this country, but also extensively, deeply.

And one can see both in the West and in this country that this questioning, this challenge is not being adequately met. In this country, you know as well as I do—probably better, because I am an alien resident, I come occasionally every year for three or four months and I observe—there is a rapid decline; people are willing to burn themselves over very trivial questions about whether you should have two governors or one governor. And you are willing to fast over some idiotic little question; the holy men are ready to attack people, and so on and on and on—a tribal approach to a tremendous problem. And I do not think we are aware of this im-

mense problem. This country has dissipated its energy in various trivial things, responding to the pressure of circumstances without having a large, wide outlook; it has approached nationalistically every problem, including the problem of starvation. There is no consideration of man as a whole, but only consideration of the limitation of a particular tribe, a particularly narrow, religious, sectarian outlook. We all know this, and apparently the government and the people are incapable of stopping all this. They are caught in utter inefficiency, deep distrust, wide discontent, unable to respond totally, deeply, to the whole issue. And you will see in Europe and in America as well as in Russia and China, there is tremendous discontent, and again that discontent is being answered very narrowly.

There is war, and people treat wars as a favorite war or not a favorite war, a war that is righteous, or a war that is not politically right. You take sides when you have preached nonviolence for forty years and more; you are ready to battle, to kill, to become violent at the throw of a hat. You see all this, and when you consider all this—not only what is taking place in the West but in India—the problem is so great. And I do not think any of the politicians, any of the religious leaders throughout the world, see the problem as a whole. They see it according to their limited, political, religious point of view, or according to their particular economic demand or social demand. No one apparently takes the problem entirely as a whole and deals with it as a total thing, not fragmentarily, not as a Sikh, not as a Hindu, a Muslim, a Christian, a Catholic, a communist, or a socialist. And because they are not dealing with the problem as a whole, people are trying to escape in different ways; they are taking the drug LSD that gives them tremendous experience. They are going off at tangents, responding to a minor, infantile, immature challenge and responding equally immaturely.

So we are all concerned with the problem—every one of us must be. There is starvation, there is war; religion has totally failed and has no meaning any more, except for some people. Organized belief is losing its power, though propaganda in the name of religion, in the name of God, in the name of peace is everlastingly being trumpeted in newspapers and everywhere. So education, religion, and politics have completely failed to answer the problem, and science has not answered it either. And it is no good looking to those things any more, or to any leader or to any teacher, because man has lost faith in all this. And because he has lost faith, he is afraid, and therefore he is violent. Not only in this country but all the world over, people are violent—the riots that are going on in America between the white and the black, the appalling things that are taking place in this country. Essentially man has lost faith not only in those beliefs, in those ideals, in the values which have been set up for him, but also in himself. He has completely lost faith. He does not know where to turn, in what direction to look for any light. And because he has lost faith, he is afraid; and because he is afraid, his only answer to fear is violence. This is what is taking place.

So we have to be serious, dreadfully earnest, not according to some belief, not according to some pattern, but serious to find out so that we can begin again to discover the source which has dried up.

I do not know if you have observed that in yourself, as a human being—not as a fragmentary being in a world of fragments. A human being—whether he is an Indian, a Hindu, a Muslim, a Sikh, a Christian, a communist, or a socialist—has no nationality; and you, as a human being, do not belong to any religion, or to any political party or ideology. If you have observed yourself as a human being, you will see in yourself—and therefore you will see in others—that the source of our being, of our existence, the meaning of our life, the struggle that we are making all day long, these have no meaning anymore. And therefore we have to find for ourselves that source which has dried up and also if it is possible to find the waters of that immense reality again, and from that reality to act. And that exact source is what we are going to discover for ourselves during all these talks here.

You understand the problem, sirs? Religions, leaders, whether political or religious, the books, the propaganda, the beliefs, the doctrines, the saviors—all have lost their meaning. To any really serious intellectual man totally aware of all these problems, all those things upon which we have relied have lost totally their meaning. You are no longer the religious people that you pretend to be. You are no longer a human being because you have lost the purpose, the meaning, the significance of your existence. You can go to the office for the next forty years as a routine, earn a livelihood, but that is no answer either.

So to discover this whole thing, to understand this immense problem, we have to look at it anew, not with the eyes of a Christian, a Hindu, a Muslim, or a communist. We have to look at it totally anew—which means first we must not be driven by circumstances, nor respond to the immediate problem—we have to act to the immediate problem, but not act as though that was the only thing in life. We must be aware of the circumstances and not be compelled by them to act.

You understand the issue? Because in this country you are quarreling over little pieces of land, and you are ready to burn and kill each other because you happen to be a Sikh, a Muslim, or a Hindu, or God knows what else. And compulsion of the environment, of circumstances, is so strong that you react.

Therefore one has to be aware of the circumstances and what is implied in those circumstances, and act as little as possible depending on those circumstances. Then one has to be aware of one's temperament and not be guided by one's temperament, nor has one to act according to one's inclination. These three things are essentially important when you are facing an immense problem. Not to be guided by your inclination, however pleasurable, however demanding, not to act according to your personal inclination—that is the first thing to realize. Then not to allow your activity, your life to be shaped by your temperament, whether you are intellectual or emotional, or whether you have various forms of idiosyncrasies. Then not to be compelled by circumstances. If we can understand these things fully, these three things, then we shall be able to meet this immense challenge, this immense problem—which is that the human being is at stake. You understand? To consider an issue of some land, a governor—all that is too immature, too childish, too appalling.

So, what we have to do, if we are at all serious—and it is absolutely necessary to be serious because the house is burning, not only the house that is called India, but the world is burning—is to respond to it totally, not bring a little bucket of sand and hope to put the fire out. We have to be enormously serious. And I am afraid we have not been serious; we have dissipated our energies because we have responded to circumstances which are so trivial and wasted our energies in all these directions. You became followers of Gandhiji. You became followers of someone else and so on and on. So having dissipated your energy, when an immense problem is put before you, you are incapable of responding to it totally.

Therefore one has to understand this immense problem of man, that man is at stake, the human being is at stake—not any particular individual but the whole human being is at stake. And to understand that immense problem you have first not to be guided by your inclination, not by your pleasure or dislike; you have to look at the problem. And you cannot look at the problem if you are depending on your personal inclination, or being guided by your temperament. You know, most of us are very clever people because we have read a great deal, we have passed many examinations. Our mind, our intellect is very cunning, deceptive, hypocritical, and our temperament has this capacity to deceive itself, to assert itself, to function along a particular line, according to its particular demand. And, of course, when you are driven by circumstances, compelled to act according to circumstances, you cannot possibly be concerned with a total human being.

So those are the first things of which one has to be aware: inclination, temperament, and circumstances. When you have understood those, then you can face the immense problem of man. Your personal inclination, whether you believe in a god or do not believe in a god—that is a personal prejudice. It has no value at all. When you approach a problem intellectually, or emotionally, or sentimentally, that is your particular temperament. And one can go much more deeply into the question of temperament, but that is not important now. So any particular approach to this immense problem indicates either you are being guided by your inclination or compelled by circumstances, or you are acting according to your narrow, little temperament.

So, if that is very clear—that we cannot possibly act according to these—we will then be able to look at the problem entirely differently. And there is an immense problem because man, that is, the human being has lost—if he ever had it—the source, the fountain, the depth, the vitality of living anew; he has become a lonely human being, frightened, anxious, caught in despair, discontented, unhappy, in tremendous sorrow. You may not be aware of all this because nobody wants to look at oneself very clearly. To look at oneself clearly is very difficult because we want to escape from ourselves. And when we do look at ourselves, we do not know what to do with ourselves.

And so our problem is: As the source of our being, the source of our existence, is drying up, has lost its meaning, we have now to find out for ourselves what it all means. You know what is happening in the West? Young men have passed brilliant examinations; they see war, they see great business corporations; they become executives and so on; and they say, "What is the point of it all, what is the point of a war, what is the point of becoming very clever, having a lot of money when life itself has no more any meaning?" So they take various forms of drugs that give them a tremendous sense of new experience, and they are satisfied with that. They are not stupid people who take these things—they are very intelligent, very sensitive, highly trained people.

Because life has no longer any meaning, you can invent a meaning, you can invent a purpose, you can invent a significance. But these inventions are purely the acts of an intellectual mind and therefore have no

validity. Nor has faith validity anymore; whether you believe or do not believe has no meaning at all because you will believe according to your circumstances. If you are born in this country, you will be a Hindu, or a Sikh, or a Muslim, a Christian—God knows what not. According to circumstances you are forced to believe or not to believe. So belief, an invented purpose of life, a significance carefully put together by the intellect—these have no meaning anymore.

I do not think you see the seriousness of this: Man has come to the end of his invention, his beliefs, his dogmas, his gods, his hopes, his fears; he has come to an absolute end. You may not be aware of it, you may still be hiding behind the walls of your belief, of your hopes. But they are illusions; they have no validity at all when you are faced with this crisis.

So, having realized this—if one is at all capable of realizing this—one must proceed to begin to find out how to renew the mind, to renew the total being. You understand? I hope I am making my question very clear. Look, sirs, human beings for over five thousand years and more have struggled, have had to face their own immense sorrow, their wars and disillusionment, the utter hopelessness of life without any meaning, always inventing their gods, always inventing a heaven and a hell to keep themselves righteous, always surrounded with ideas, ideals, hopes. But all that has gone. Your Ramas and Sitas, your Upanishads, your great gods—everything has gone in smoke, and you are faced with yourself as a human being, and you have to answer. Therefore your responsibility as a human being becomes extraordinarily great.

So our question then is: How is a mind that has been so heavily conditioned for so many centuries, through so many agonies, how is such a mind to be made new so that it can function totally differently, think entirely differently? You understand the question? The communists and the totalitarians say, "We will shape the mind. We will make the mind, break the mind, and recondition it." You are following all this? The Catholics, the Protestants, the Hindus, the Muslims, people all over the world have done this over and over again. And each human being is so heavily conditioned, conditioned in one way and reconditioned in another way by the politicians, by propaganda, by the priests, by commissars, by socialists, by communists—endlessly reshaped and again reshaped. And when you realize that absolute fact—the absolute truth, not according to me or according to you—then you ask yourself whether it is at all possible to break this conditioning and not enter into another conditioning, but be free so that the mind can be a new thing: sensitive, alive, aware, intense, capable. So that is our problem. There is no other problem. Because when the mind is made new, it can tackle any problem, whether it is a scientific problem or the problem of starvation or corruption; then it is capable of dealing with any circumstance.

So that is our main issue: whether it is possible for a mind that has been so heavily conditioned for so many centuries to uncondition itself and not fall into another conditioning, and therefore to be free, capable, intensely alive, new, fresh, so that it can meet any problem. As I said, that is the only question which we, as human beings, have to face and to find the answer for. And you cannot depend on anybody to tell you what to do. You understand? You cannot depend on anybody to tell you how to uncondition yourself; and if you do depend on that person, you are conditioning yourself according to his ideas; therefore, you are caught again.

So, see the immense problem that is in front of you. There is no leader, no savior, no guru, no authority anymore. Because, all they have done is to condition one as a Hindu, a Muslim, a Christian, or a communist, and all that. They have not answered the problem. They have found no solution to human misery, to human anxiety, to human despair. They have given you escapes, and escapes are not the answer. When you have got cancer, you cannot run away from it; you have to face it.

So that is the first thing to realize: that you cannot possibly rely on anybody to uncondition you. When you realize that, either you get frightened because you cannot rely on anybody, but you are left to yourself—that is a very frightening thing—or you are no longer frightened, and you see that you have to work because nobody can help you, and therefore you have vitality, you have energy, you have the drive. And you can only have the drive, the energy, the vitality when you are no longer depending on anybody and no longer afraid. Then you are no longer following anybody. Then you are your own master, your own pupil; you are learning, you are discovering.

So, our question being very clear, how do we proceed? You understand the question? You understand the problem? The problem must be very clear; otherwise, you cannot answer it. The question can be put in ten different ways, but the essence of the problem is always the same: that human minds are shaped by circumstances, by environmental influences, by one's own temperament and inclination which shape the mind, which condition the mind. And a mind that is conditioned, a mind that is molded by a particular belief, by a particular dogma, by a particular experience or tendency—such a mind cannot possibly answer this question: Is it possible for the mind which has been made so dull, heavy, stupid, so heavily conditioned by circumstances, by environment, and so on, to free itself and therefore meet every problem of life anew?

I say that it can, and I am going to go into it, show you whether it is possible or not. But I am not your teacher, nor are you my followers; God forbid, because the moment you follow someone, you have destroyed the truth. If you have a leader, you are destroying the truth. So all that we can do is to consider together, take the journey together—not I lead you along a path or show you, but together we partake—share together this question and discover together the issues and the way out.

So to share does not mean merely stretching your hand out and receiving something. To share means that you must be capable of sharing, which means that you must be extraordinarily alive, keen to find out; otherwise, you cannot share. Somebody can give you a most beautiful jewel, but if you do not know that is the most precious thing, you will throw it away, and you cannot share it. And to journey together, you must be capable of walking together. And the capacity to walk, to share, to observe, depends on your earnestness. And that earnestness, that seriousness comes into being when you see the immensity of the problem. It is the problem that makes you serious, not that you become serious. You understand the difference? We say we are serious and tackle the problem; that is not at all so. The problem itself is so great, and that very greatness makes you serious. Then that seriousness has vitality, that seriousness has a pliability and enormous strength and vitality, and one can go to the very end of it. So we are taking the journey together; therefore, we are sharing the thing together. Therefore you are no longer a listener, you are no longer just hearing a few words, a few ideas which either you accept or reject—say, "I like this and I do not like that." Because we have gone beyond all that which is mere inclination.

So our first question is: Is it possible for a human mind that has been so heavily conditioned to break through the conditioning? You cannot possibly break through it if you are not aware of your conditioning. That is an obvious fact, isn't it? You cannot say, "I am conditioned and I must break through it." That has no meaning. But if you are aware of how you are conditioned, what are the factors of your conditioning, what are the circumstances, then being aware of this conditioning, you can do something. But if you are not aware of it, then you cannot do a thing. So the first thing is to be aware of your conditioning—conditioning, how you think, how you feel, what are the motives behind that thinking, feeling.

You may say, "Well, this is all too complicated; I want a simple pill which I can take very quickly and the whole problem is solved." There is no such pill. Life is a very complex process, and you cannot solve it by some kind of trick. You have to see the complexity of it, and you can only see the complexity of it if you are completely simple. You understand, sirs? If you are really simple, then you can see how extraordinarily complex you are, and all your conditioning. But to be simple is one of the most difficult things. Simplicity is not wearing a loincloth, or having one meal a day, or walking around the earth preaching some idiotic nonsense. Simplicity is not obedience. Please do listen to all this. Simplicity is not following an ideal. Simplicity is not imitation—just to be simple so that you can look. You know you can only look at a tree, or a flower, or the beauty of an evening when your eyes are not clouded, when your mind is not somewhere else, when you are not tortured by your own particular little problem. Then, you can look at the tree; then the evening has a beauty; then out of that simplicity you can observe.

And as I said, to be simple is one of the most difficult and arduous things—to be simple. But, you see, that word has been loaded by all the saints with all their pretentions, with their dogmas; and therefore the saints are not simple people at all. A simple mind means a mind that can see very clearly. And the moment you see anything with clarity, the problem is over. That's why to look at our conditioning needs clarity. And you can only have clarity when you do not say, "I like or I don't like." Do you understand, sirs? I want to see myself as a human being, actually *what is,* not what I pretend and all that rubbish. To see very clearly, there must be light, and there is no light if what I see I translate in terms of like or dislike. You understand? It is simple, sir, when you go into it—very, very simple. That is, to see anything there must be light, and to have light there must be care, and with clarity and care you can observe. But that clarity and care are denied when you condemn what you see, or justify what you are. Therefore, when you want to see very clearly, like and dislike, judgment and condemnation disappear. Am I making myself clear? This is a very serious thing. Then you will find that you are your own guide, then you are your own light which nobody can put out. In that way one begins to discover for oneself the source of all life, that source which has dried up, that man has been seeking everlastingly.

You may have great prosperity as they have in the West and in America. You may be hungry, miserable; but a mere solution of these is not the answer because our being, the human being is at stake. Your house, which is yourself, is burning. And to find an answer you must be able to look clearly. And therefore when you look clearly, you can reason clearly. And reason becomes insanity when there is obscurity. You understand, sirs? The politicians, because they are obscure, are breeding inefficiency, hatred, division among men. And also the priests, whether in the West or in the East, are contributing to this darkness. Religion, after all, is not a matter of belief, not what you

believe or what you don't believe. Religion is the way of life. It does not depend on any belief, or any dogma, or any ritual. Only the religious mind which lives peacefully can find that ultimate reality.

Perhaps some of you would like to ask questions, and if this is the occasion for asking questions, we will answer them. If not, perhaps at the next meeting there will be time to ask questions. You know, to ask is not to find the answer necessarily. To ask a right question is one of the most difficult things. When you ask a right question, in that question itself is the answer. But to ask the right question demands great intelligence, not cleverness, not erudition. So to ask the right question needs great sensitivity, intelligence, a great awareness of one's own problem. And then when you do ask the right question, the right answer comes. Because you have been so intelligent, so sensitive, so aware of your problem, and because out of that awareness you ask the right question, the right question is the right answer. So I hope next time we meet here there will be an occasion for us to ask questions and perhaps find the right answers.

December 15, 1966

Second Talk in New Delhi

If we may, we will continue with what we were talking about the other day when we met here. We were saying how urgently it is important that a total revolution in consciousness should take place. And we pointed out how throughout the world there is a general decline, a deterioration—a moral, ethical, religious decline. It is observable; this is not a matter of personal opinion because we are not dealing with opinions but with facts. And these facts cannot possibly be understood if we approach them through any sense of personal inclination or temperament or responding immediately to environmental influences.

We said that there must be a radical transformation, a mutation in the mind, because man has tried every method, both outwardly and inwardly, to transform himself. He has gone to temples, churches, mosques; he has tried various political systems, economic order; there is great prosperity and yet there is great poverty. Man in every way—through education, through science, through religion—has tried to bring about a radical mutation in himself. He has gone to a monastery, has given up the world, he has meditated endlessly, repeating prayers, sacrificing, following ideals, pursuing teachers, belonging to various sects. He has tried, if one observes through history, everything he can possibly try to find a way out of this confusion, this misery, this sorrow, this endless conflict. And he has invented a heaven. And in order to avoid hell, which is punishment, he has done also various forms of mental gymnastics, various forms of control; he has tried drugs, sex, innumerable ways that a very clever mind has thought out. And yet man throughout the world has remained as he was. Man has inherited animal instincts, and most of us have still the inherited animal instincts of greed, proprietorial rights, sexual rights, and so on and on. We are the result of the animal. And we have tried to escape from it, consciously or unconsciously. And yet we remain what we were, slightly modified through pressure, through environmental influences, through threats, through necessity; we have somewhat changed here and there, but essentially we remain what we were. Deep down we are aggressive, violent, greedy, envious, brutal, violent—which is being shown throughout the world. And what is taking place in this country after years of preaching the philosophy of nonviolence? Man is violent and the ideal of nonviolence is only an im-

mature approach to violence. What is important is to face the violence, understand it, and go beyond it, and not invent an escape, an ideal called nonviolence which has no reality whatsoever, which is being shown in this country and elsewhere.

So we see objectively, clearly, the necessity for man's total change. I think everybody intellectually is agreed on this point. Any serious man with deep intentions who is earnest, honest, not deceiving himself by theories or dogmas, is concerned with this: Is it possible for a human being, whether he lives in Russia, America, here, or elsewhere, to bring about a total mutation so that he lives differently, not like an animal everlastingly struggling, destroying one another, in conflict, in misery, in sorrow, always fearful, uncertain, always waiting for death with all the pain, anxiety, guilt, and all the rest of it? And people have invented various philosophies. And the psychologists with their analysis have helped a little bit here and there, but the problem still remains. Is it possible to uncondition man totally so that he lives in joy, in clarity, without confusion, without conflict?

Now, having stated the basic problem, which I think is clear, what can one do actually? One sees the problem of man's conflict—his brutality, his anxiety, his jealousies, his ambitions, his desire to hurt others, creating enmity. Is it possible to change this consciousness into something that is entirely different, that is not an ideal, that cannot be foreseen, that is not a premeditated result? You understand? Because if this mind which is confused, which is brutal, which is ugly— if this mind can project an ideal, a future, it will be according to its own pattern, only modified; and therefore the ideal, the purpose, the ultimate change in terms of *what is,* is still *what is.* Is it not?

You see the problem: if I am confused and out of that confusion I imagine clarity or create an ideal of clarity, it is still the result of confusion and therefore that so-called clarity, the so-called ideal, the so-called ultimate purpose will be the result of a confused mind and therefore will still be confused. Please see the importance of this. Because we are caught in this cage, in this trap of so-called civilization, we are always projecting an idea of 'what should be', a philosophy, a doctrine, and we are pursuing that, each of us according to his conditioning, according to his belief, according to his religion, according to the climate, circumstances, inclinations, and so on. So, out of this he creates a future. And that future has its roots in the present, the present being the past. So, as long as the mind is capable of creating a formula for itself for the future, that formula is the result of the past—past experience, past knowledge, past information—and therefore the future, the ideal, is still the condition, is still the result of what has been. And so to change from *what is* to 'what should be' is still *what is,* though modified.

Please do see and understand this extraordinarily clearly, not only verbally, but actually. And that is where listening comes in. Because one can communicate verbally, as we do just now. You all, I hope, understand English, and we are communicating verbally. You are translating what I say into your own language, or you are hearing the words. But hearing the words is not actually listening. When you actually listen, not only do you listen to the words, but your whole attention is there; otherwise, you cannot listen. And when you give your whole attention to any problem, there is not only efficiency, clarity, a reasoned-out outlook, but you go beyond it. And that is what we are doing now. We are not only hearing, not only communicating verbally, but also together we are listening to what is true, not according to anybody. Truth is not Christian, Hindu, yours, or mine. It is the fact. And to observe that fact, you have

not only to listen intently to that fact but to prevent all translation of that fact. Because, if you translate, you are translating it according to your conditioning, according to your memories, according to your inclination, to your tendency, according to the pressure of circumstances. Therefore in that state you are not listening. And I hope this evening you are listening actually to facts, not to opinions, not to any conclusions.

As we were saying, there must be a radical revolution, a mutation of the mind, because man has lived two million years and more—according to the biologists and the archaeologists—in misery, in sorrow, in conflict, killing each other, destroying each other, creating enmity. Religions have said, "Don't kill." Religions have said, "Love one another, be kind, be generous." And religions have cultivated belief, organized propaganda of belief, dogma, ritual; they are not actually concerned with man's behavior. But what we are concerned with is man's actual behavior from day to day, because man must live in peace; otherwise, he cannot do anything. In his laboratory he is at peace, and therefore he can invent, he can look. He may go to the moon, but he is not at peace either at home or in the office, outwardly or inwardly, and therefore he is confused, he is frightened. And so this radical change is essential, as we said, not according to a pattern, not according to some future ideal or some utopia, which are the inventions of a mind that is being conditioned and, wishing to free itself from its conditioning, invents a philosophy, an ideal, a purpose—which are the result of its own confusion and conditioning. That is clear. Also, that radical change must take place immediately.

We have divided time as the immediate and the ultimate. Please, I am not going to go into details because it is too complex and I have not the time. But one can see what we have done. We all see the immediate necessity of change. We see that. And we say it is not possible to change immediately; we need to have time, we need days to bring about this change. Put it round the other way. There are the immediate problems of this country: starvation, disorder, inefficiency, corruption, and the immature quarrels over a piece of land, burning each other or burning oneself, and so on. And to the immediate everyone reacts. We say, "We must do something about the immediate. It is all right to talk about the ultimate, but the ultimate is not so important as the immediate." And with that conception, with that formula that the immediate is far more important than the ultimate, we live. Isn't that so? You put it in different ways, but that is what is happening. The politician is concerned with the immediate, and so also the reformer and the so-called social worker. Everybody is concerned with the immediate, not with that thing which he calls the ultimate; for him the ultimate may be all right, but the immediate matters. So he has divided time as the immediate and the future. But the ultimate contains the immediate. The immediate does not contain the ultimate. So a man who is concerned with the immediate—he is the real mischief-maker, whether he be a politician, a religious man, or a reformer. But if we have understood the ultimate, in the ultimate is immediate action.

So as long as we divide time as yesterday, today, and tomorrow, as long as we think in terms of the immediate which is the environment, the circumstances to which we must answer immediately—as the politicians and all the people throughout the world are doing—then what takes place? I hope you are following all this.

You know, one is not used to giving one's attention for a long period. You give perhaps your attention for two or three minutes, and the rest of the time you just casually listen. Therefore you don't take it in. And we are

discussing a very serious problem. To understand it, to go with it, to flow with it, you must give your whole attention all the time that you are here—not for a period, a minute or two, and then wander off. What we are dealing with demands a total receptivity, a total attention.

When you divide time as the immediate and the ultimate, you are not only creating conflict between *what is* and 'what should be'—but also creating an environment, circumstances which will be in contradiction to 'what should be'. Time is a movement, which man has divided into yesterday, today, and tomorrow. It is a movement, and as long as you divide it, you must be in conflict.

Please, this is important to understand. Because, if you do not follow this, I am afraid, you won't be able to follow what comes after. We are concerned with change, with total mutation in the whole of consciousness. And consciousness is conditioned to think in terms of yesterday, today, and tomorrow; and it thinks in terms of change as *what is* and 'what should be', and therefore 'what should be' demands further time. So change never takes place. Do you understand, sirs? When we think that we are changing from this to that, that movement is static; it is not a movement at all. "I want to change from this to that"—that is projected by a mind that is caught in *what is,* and that has, out of that confusion, out of that misery, out of that pain, created the future. So the future is already known. And therefore when the mind moves from *what is* to 'what should be', that movement is static; it is not a movement at all; therefore, it is not a change at all.

Man is violent. About that there is no question. He is violent in so many different ways, and that is a fact. He may occasionally be nonviolent, but his whole psychological structure is based on violence, ambition, desire for power, position, domination, assertion, attachment to that thing which he calls ownership, sex, and so on. His whole structure is based on violence, and that is a fact. Then he invents nonviolence, an idea, a theory, which is nonfactual. And he says, "I am violent and I will move to nonviolence. I will change from this to that." That change, that movement towards the ideal, is no movement at all; it is just static, it is merely an idea. What is actual is violence. So when he pursues the ideal he is avoiding the actual. And what he calls the ideal, the pursuit of the ideal, the practice and the discipline—all that is merely the activity of a mind that has become static, that has become dull, that is not living. What is living is violence in different forms.

So the ideal has no importance whatsoever. And this is a very difficult pill to swallow for most people because we have lived on ideals, we have been fed on ideals, we are conditioned to think in terms of ideals, in terms of purpose and significance and so on. So there is only the fact, and nonviolence is not a fact. And when he says he will ultimately become nonviolent, what he actually is doing is sowing the seeds of violence, thinking that ultimately he will be peaceful. But he will not. That is fairly clear, fairly obvious. So as long as one thinks in terms of the future, of bringing about a change in terms of an ideal, in terms of what should be, he is merely continuing to live in violence; and therefore that movement has no value whatsoever.

Therefore, the problem arises: How is a mind to change totally, that is violent, greedy, or whatever it is? Greed, envy, ambition, competition, aggressiveness, and also the so-called discipline which is imposed, which is conformity—all this is a part of that violence; how is that violence to be totally changed so that it is no longer violent, not in terms of time, not in terms of a future ideal? You understand the question now? My mind is no longer distracted or taken away, wasting its energy on ideals—what should be, what should not be. It is completely attentive to that one problem in which many other problems are involved. So there is no ultimate or the immediate. There is only that problem—right? Like a man having cancer, he has to decide immediately, and the immediate decision does not depend upon his fancy, on his environment, on his family, on what people say or do not say. It is an immediate urgency, and therefore when it is immediate, there is an immediate decision, not a decision in terms of a mind wanting to act upon the fact.

So time as the means of overcoming or destroying, or going beyond the fact has come to an end. You understand? Time as a means of change has come to an end. Therefore time as will comes to an end. Will is time, isn't it? "I will do this"—the will is the result of determination, inclination, desire; all that is involved in that one word. And when I say, "I will become peaceful," the very assertion "I will" implies time. And when I assert "I will become," the movement to become is static, it is not alive, it is something dead. So, will and time have been put aside. Please see the importance of this. We are used to assertions, we are used to saying, "I will do this, I must do this, I should do this"—all that implies time. Doesn't it? Obviously, the "will be," the "should be," the "must be" is the future tense of the word "to be." But the word "to be" is always the active present. And therefore when a man asserts he will do that, what is taking place is that he is using time as a means of achieving it, and the means and the end are projected by the mind that is conditioned, and therefore the end is still *what is*. Right? Sorry if it gives you a headache. It is really quite simple.

Man has lived by will and time, and we see that will and time have not changed man at all. That has been his favorite game of escape: He invents the future and all the rest of it and so remains what he is. You may believe in reincarnation, as probably most of you do. And if you believe in reincarnation, what matters is how you live now, not what you are going to do tomorrow. But you don't believe in it to that extent, it is just a theory, a convenient hope, a pleasant idea, and therefore has no value at all. So when you have eliminated time as will, you have only this problem. Then you are full of energy to tackle this problem, come to grips with this problem—which is a total revolution in the mind. And that is total revolution which is not ultimate but which is immediate. And when there is no time as a means of achievement and no will as a way to that achievement, then you have only the central issue: How can the mind which is so conditioned change, bring about a complete mutation? That means a mind that is no longer struggling to become something. It is what it is— greedy, envious, ambitious, full of hate and all the animal things that have been cultivated and prolonged throughout the centuries. That is what actually is, and any effort to bring about a change in that structure of the human mind is still part of time and therefore is ineffective.

So what happens to your mind that is no longer thinking in terms of time, of the will to achieve? The speaker can explain what takes place, but it will be mere words. But if you do it yourself, you will see what an extraordinary action takes place when you have abolished time—that means no longer yielding to circumstances, no longer concerned with personal inclination or tendency, no longer using will as a means of operation. If you do it, not theorize about it, if you actually do it as you would do when there is an urgency of disease or of a threat, you act immediately. Then there is no action of will, no time operating. Then there will be total action, not the fragmentary action of will and time; and a total action contains the immediate action to circumstances.

Look sir! There is starvation in this country, overpopulation, total inefficiency of the government. And that starvation each politician, each group, wants to solve according to his own pet theory. The communist, the socialist, the congress, etc.—they have theories on how to solve that problem. They will take this side or that side, they will go to America or to Russia according to their theory; but in the meantime people are starving. Right? You may not be starving, but there are people starving; probably, we have all known what it is, not having enough food. The problem of starvation is not to be solved by politicians; never has it been. It is a world problem, and the world is divided by politicians, by the tribes which they represent—the American tribe, the Hindu tribe, the Muslim tribe, the African tribe. We are all tribes, we all belong to tribes—which is again a fact. So as long as the mind thinks in terms of tribes, in terms of formulas, starvation will go on. Please see this simple fact, sir. As long as you are a Hindu with your nationality, with your separate government, and all the rest of it, you are going to have starvation because each group wants to solve it in its own way and will not cooperate with another. The communist is not concerned with the starvation of the people, nor the congress, nor the democrat, nor the republican—they are not concerned; they want to be in power, in position. To solve the problem of starvation, we must be concerned only with how to feed the people, not who is going to feed the people, what is the system that is going to feed the people, and so on. But nobody is concerned with solving the problem.

So when you are concerned with solving the problem, you are not concerned with the system at all. In the same way when you are concerned with the problem of a total change, you are not concerned with how to change it. You never will ask how because the "how" is the method, and the method implies time, practice, and the end result is already known towards which you are practicing, and therefore it is not a change at all. So all that one can do is to be totally aware of the function of will and of time, and be totally indifferent to it, not battle against it, but see the falseness of it. Then one will be only concerned with the central issue: How is one to bring about a total revolution? And when you are tremendously concerned with it, you will find that it is taking place without your wanting it.

Perhaps, if there is time, you will ask questions. You can discuss this. And if you are going to ask questions, please be brief because I have to repeat them. Don't make long speeches.

Question: Sir, is that state possible?

KRISHNAMURTI: A gentleman asks: "Is that state possible?" The state which I have been talking about—is that right, sir? When you ask that question, "Is it possible?" are you asking out of curiosity?

Comment: No.

KRISHNAMURTI: Please, just listen. Are you asking out of curiosity, or are you asking it because you doubt it, or because in your own mind there is a feeling that it is not possible? If you say it is not possible, then you are blocking yourself, you are preventing investigation. If you say it is possible, that also will prevent you from investigation. Naturally, because you are already biased. So to find out if it is possible or not, you have to work, you have to investigate, you have to examine; and to examine, you must be free. If you are biased, if you are inclined, if you are

this or that, you are not free to investigate, to go into it. But to go into it is not a matter of time. You must give to it your whole mind and heart and your nerves, everything you have. But, you see, you are not so eager, intense. To go into it you need tremendous energy; and you can only have energy if there are no distractions, which the mind has invented in order not to face the fact, the fact being what you actually are. Your violence, your greed, your envy, your competition, your brutality, your wanting to achieve, to become somebody, and all the rest of it—that is the fact; and to face that fact demands complete energy. And to face that, you have to put aside time and will, and you have to look.

That is why, sir, it is very important to know how to look, how to observe. Probably you have never observed a tree. Probably you have never observed your wife, or your husband, or your daughter. You have observed through the image you have built of your wife, and the wife looks at you through the image she has built of you, the image being memory. As you look at each other through the image that each one has created of the other, there is no observation at all. When you look at a tree, you have an idea, an image, a symbol, a meaning about the tree; and therefore the meaning, the symbol, the idea interferes with your observation of that tree. To look, there must be freedom from the image. And when you are free, you look, not with the intellect, not with emotion, but with love, with clarity, with something totally new. When you look at your children, your wife, and your husband without the image, you will then be in real relationship. Real relationship is affection, love. Without that, do what you will, there will be misery, there will be sorrow.

Question: Sir, what is the role of memory and the state that you are talking about?

KRISHNAMURTI: "What is the role of memory and the state we are talking about?" Again this is a rather complex problem. All human problems are complex; they are not mechanical; therefore, one has to think about them anew.

What is the function of memory? And how does memory come into being? Before one can discuss what is the function of memory, one must find out how memory is built up. Have you ever noticed that when you respond to something totally, there is very little memory? Have you? When you respond with your heart, with your mind, with all your being, there is very little memory. Haven't you noticed it? It is only when you do not respond to a challenge completely that there is a conflict; then there is a pain, then there is a confusion, then there is a struggle. The struggle, the confusion, the pain or the pleasure builds memory. This is simple. You can observe this in your daily life. You develop memory through a technique. You go to college and learn a certain technique because that technique gives you a job. And that cultivates a memory because that memory is necessary to function efficiently in a particular job. That memory you must have, obviously; otherwise, you cannot function. But I have psychological memory: what you have said to me, how you have hurt me, you have flattered me, you have insulted me. And you also have psychological memory. Therefore there are the images which I have built up of you and you have built up of me. Those memories remain. And those memories are added to, all the time. And it is those memories that will respond. Therefore, thought which is the result of memory is always old, never new, and therefore never free. There is no such thing as freedom of thought—which is sheer nonsense.

Your memory has a place when you are functioning efficiently, and efficiency is necessary. Memory is necessary at a certain level. But when that memory becomes a mere mechanical action in human relationship, then it becomes a danger, then it creates mischief. All the tribal instincts are part of that memory. You are a Hindu, you are a Muslim, you are a Christian; you know the machinery of conditioning. There it is deadly. Because life is a movement; life is not something that you carve out for yourself in a little backyard; life is a total movement, an endless movement, not an evolutionary movement. It is one of your pet theories that, eventually, man is going to become perfect and that in the meantime he can sow hatred, in the meantime he can create havoc. So memory has a place and when you function there naturally, it has to be efficient, reasoned, impersonal, clear, and all the rest of it. But there is the state of mind where memory has very little place. When we are talking now, we are using the English language. The usage of English language is memory, obviously. But the state of mind that is using it is silent, it is not crippled by memory, and that is real freedom.

Question: Sir, where does the soul go after death?

KRISHNAMURTI: Wait, sir.

Comment: You have talked about the unconditioned mind and simplicity of mind. And I doubt if there is any way that we could get simplicity of mind and an unconditioned mind.

KRISHNAMURTI: The gentleman asks: "You have talked about the unconditioned mind; is there a way, a method to achieve that unconditioned mind?"

Comment: Without talking about it.

KRISHNAMURTI: "Without talking about it." I don't know what that means. Is there a way to uncondition the mind?

Now there are two states. First of all one must be very sensitive to words—sensitive, alive—you must feel the words. If you are not, then you use any word and it has no meaning. When you use the words *conditioned* and *a way*, have you understood the word conditioned? Is the understanding merely verbal and therefore not real? Mere intellectual understanding of that word—which means to free the mind from its conditioning—is the dictionary meaning. And if you use that word in a dictionary meaning, there is no depth to that word at all. But if you say, "Look, I have found I am conditioned, I have discovered it, I see it. I was aware this morning, for a minute, how conditioned I am. I think in terms of a Hindu, or I think in terms of hate or jealousy." Then, when you use that word conditioned, it has a vitality, a depth, a perfume, a quality. And when you use the word way, what is implied in that word, a way? From this to that—a path, a method, a system, which by practicing you will be able to uncondition yourself, to arrive at a state of nonconditioning. See the question! Is a method going to uncondition you? There is no method to uncondition you. We have played with these words, we have done all these things for centuries—the gurus, the monasteries, Zen, this or that method—with the result you are caught, you are a slave to the method, aren't you, and therefore you are not free. The method will produce the result, but the result is the outcome of your confusion, of your conditioning, and therefore it will still be conditioned. So, when you put that question, you have already answered it.

That is why I said the other day: To ask a question is very simple, but to ask the right question is one of the most difficult things. And you must ask questions all your life, but they must always be the right questions. And if you ask a right question, you have the right answer; you don't have to ask anybody.

Question: One question, sir. The nonviolence which Gandhiji tried to practice by himself, is that also to be denounced?

KRISHNAMURTI: Sir, do you remember what I said? Any practice of nonviolence is violence.

Comment: That is a statement which has to be proved.

KRISHNAMURTI: To be proved by whom?

Sir, you have asked a question; you must have the courtesy also to listen to the answer.

Comment: I asked a question.

KRISHNAMURTI: Yes, we are all so impatient.

Comment: The rest of the question I am not asking.

KRISHNAMURTI: Yes, sir, I know.

Can you practice nonviolence when you are violent? Violence means not only physical violence but also psychological violence. When I discipline myself according to a pattern which I have established as the ideal, I am violent. You don't take all that into account. Discipline, as is practiced by most people, is a suppression, is conformity, is a control of an idea, a pattern; that is violence, distorting the mind. This does not mean that there is not a discipline which has nothing whatsoever to do with control, suppression, conformity. That real discipline comes when you are confronted with the problem, and you are completely concerned with the problem.

Sir, look. Discipline, the right discipline, the real discipline, the only discipline that matters—not all the others—that comes in the very action of learning. When you are learning, not acquiring—when you are learning about anything, that very act of learning demands discipline. For instance, I am learning a language, and it is tremendously interesting to learn a language, and that very interest is its discipline. Now man is violent. To understand the problem of violence, really to understand it, to go with it to the very end of it, to inquire into it very deeply—that very inquiry is the beginning of discipline. You don't have to have any of the so-called discipline which man has practiced and thereby destroyed himself and tortured his mind by imitating, by conforming to a form, a pattern.

Question: Where does the soul go after death?

KRISHNAMURTI: "Where does the soul go after death?" Sir, it is a very important question. Perhaps we will deal with that question the next time that we meet because it requires a great deal of going into, because the word *soul*, or the *atma*, or whatever word you use, is still part of your tradition. You repeat that word endlessly. You have not inquired if there is such a thing as the soul—which means there is a permanent entity in you which, when you die, goes somewhere. Is there something permanent in you? Have you found out anything permanent in you?

Comment: Sir.

KRISHNAMURTI: Yes? Sir, do be clear. Is there a permanent thing in you? You are changing, your body changes, unless you are dead. Everything is in a movement, but you refuse to accept that movement. And to say there is a soul, an atma, means that thought has thought about it, or has invented it. If thought can think about it, it is still within the field of thought, and therefore it is part of the old, it is nothing new. As I said, thought is always old. Therefore, soul is a word that you use without understanding, or going into. It is the result of thought because man is frightened of death. As he is frightened of life, so he is frightened of death. Please sir, leave that question, you are not paying attention.

Comment: Conditioning. . .

KRISHNAMURTI: Wait a minute, sir. Wait. I think that is enough, sir, for this evening.

Look, sir. You have asked questions; each person is concerned with his question, and he will not listen to another question. In answering the one question, if you have listened to it, your questions also will be answered; but we are so impatient—which means what? Each one is concerned with his own little problem, and the little problem does not contain the big problem. When you understand the big problem—in that problem is the little problem—the little problem will be answered, and it will be answered rightly. As I said, it is very easy to ask questions. And one must always ask questions, one must always have a spot of skepticism about everything, including about what the speaker is saying. But to ask the right question demands a great deal of intelligence, sensitivity to words, and awareness of one's own conditioning. Then out of that when you ask a question, it is full of light and delight.

December 18, 1966

Third Talk in New Delhi

Shall we continue with what we were talking about the other day? We were saying that a radical revolution in the way of living, in our whole outlook, in our activity, in our state of consciousness is absolutely necessary. And we pointed out the reasons for it. Considering what the world is like now—the utter confusion, the misery, the wars, the corruption, a life in which there is nothing new, a mind that is not renewing itself totally each day, fresh, young, innocent—a complete mutation of the mind is necessary. Our minds are the result of centuries upon centuries of propaganda. We have been shaped by circumstances, by our own inclinations and tendencies. We are the result of time, time in which the mind has matured, has grown, has—if you like to use that word—evolved from the animal to the present state.

And our present life as it is actually now—not theoretically, not idealistically, not as one would wish it to be, but the actual fact of what it is today—is a life of sorrow, is a life of frustration, deep anxiety, a sense of guilt, a groping after something other than *what is,* a life in which there is a constant battle, not only outwardly, but also inwardly. Our life is a battlefield for endless, meaningless struggle. There are those who struggle for power, as most of us do. Power gives one a certain sense of being—politically, economically, or inwardly. One can dominate people through propaganda; you can dominate your neighbor, your wife, your husband—all that implies a sense of power. And it also implies a life of constant competition normally, a better life outwardly, better conditions, and so on—ambition, competition, a sense of meaningless pursuit, a terribly lonely life, a despairing life, though one may not be aware of all this. But one generally is not aware because one is too frightened by the observation of all this. But that is a fact.

This is our daily life, in which there is no affection, no love; there is a sense of insecurity always seeking security, a life in which there is always the end, which is death. And this is what we call living. Being

frightened, we invent our gods, we invent theories intellectually, theologically, religiously. We have ideas, formulas about what we should be. And we function according to formulas—which is called an intellectual way. And we are very proud of that intellect; the more one is clever, the more is one ruthless, brutal—and generally the intellect is always that. And that is our life. Whether we like or don't like it, that is a fact which we seem to be incapable of changing. And especially in the modern world life is becoming more and more mechanical—going to the office every day for the next forty or fifty years, and being bullied, insulted by the superior, and so on.

And we said: Is it at all possible to bring about a radical revolution in this life? Of course we do change a little bit here and there, but compelled by circumstances; a new invention will alter outwardly the way of our life and so on. So we see actually what is taking place in our consciousness, in our life every day. I think anybody who is at all aware, not only of himself, but of the world's affairs, sees this taking place, that we are the result of circumstances and their influences, we are the result of enormous propaganda—religious, political, commercial, and so on. I do not know if you have noticed, or if you have read that one of the Russian generals very high up, a field marshal, said in his report to the high authorities that through hypnotism they are teaching soldiers.

You understand? They are teaching soldiers through hypnotism new techniques, which means teaching them how to kill more cleverly, how to protect oneself through killing another. I do not know if you realize the implications of all this, that through hypnosis you can learn a great many things—a new language, a new way of thinking, and so on. Hypnosis is, after all, propaganda. You have been told every day of your life to believe in God, and you believe in God. Or if you are told there is no such thing as God, that also you believe. You believe in an atma, because that is the popular thing, and it has been handed down through centuries; and you also like to believe that there is something very superior in you, which is permanent, which is divine, and so on—which is all an intellectual concept and does not actually alter the ways of your life. And politically it is so obvious what is going on in this country. Religiously, politically, and inwardly we are the result of what has been and what people have said. And the more clever, the more cunning, the more psychologically able one is to persuade you, you believe him; and that is your life. You are a Hindu because you have been told you are a Hindu, and circumstances have forced you—or a Muslim, a Christian, and so on and on.

And in this field the human being lives, whether in America or in Russia or wherever it is. And we are asking whether it is at all possible for a human being to throw away all this and completely bring about a mutation, not intellectually, but actually. That is the problem, it seems to me, that each human being has to face, because we can go on for another thousand years and more just as we are, battling with each other, deep in sorrow, calling ourselves by this name or that name, belonging to this nationality or that nationality, to this religion or that—which is all so utterly immature and has no meaning any more. And all that is the result of propaganda, whether the propaganda of the Gita or the Bible or the Koran, or of Marx-Lenin theories. You understand? That is what we are, nothing original, nothing which is true; we are but secondhand human beings. Again this is a fact and that is our life. And through it all there is a sense of deep, abiding fear, from which comes violence, imagining ways of escaping from that deep fear. And we have developed a network of escapes from that extraordinary fear that human

beings have. As I said, most of us are aware of this fact.

Now, what can one do to bring about a tremendous mutation in this state? You understand my question? After we have talked a little this evening, perhaps you will be good enough to ask questions, as you did the last time that we met here.

So that is our problem. How am I, who am the result of time, of an endless series of circumstances which have compelled me to act, think, feel in a way which has so conditioned my mind—how am I to bring about a total revolution? We are using the word *mind* to cover the total being—the physical, the emotional, the neurological, the brain, and so on—the totality of consciousness which is the mind. And how is it possible for a human being to bring about a total revolution in this? I do not know if you have ever asked yourself that question—probably not. You may have to change a little bit here and there, and according to your pleasure and pain. Especially when it gives pleasure, when it promises to give delight, you try to change a little, or you want the continuance of a particular delight or a particular pleasure. But what we are asking ourselves is something entirely different.

As a human being is it possible for me to change completely—not change to something, because the something is a formula, an ideal, from Marx, Lenin, or your own particular ideal and so on. Do you understand? The change from *what is* to 'what should be' is no change at all, as we explained last time. And we are deceived by this movement because *what is* is the fact and 'what should be' is not the fact. Because in that time interval between *what is* and 'what should be' there are various forms of influences, environmental stresses and strains, and there is always change going on. But if one formulates 'what should be' and tries to change according to that, the change gives one a certain feeling. A certain sense of moving towards 'what should be' gives one a vitality. What actually has taken place psychologically is that the mind has formulated a pattern according to which it is going to live, and that pattern is projected from the past. And so it is a movement of the past and therefore a movement of the dead; it is not a living thing at all. If you observe this in yourself, you will see this very clearly.

So, how is it possible for a human being like you and me to make the mind young, fresh, innocent, tremendously alive? Our whole life is a process of challenge and response; otherwise, life becomes dead—most of us are dead anyhow. Actually life is a process of challenge, a demand and a response—whether that demand, that challenge, is outward or inward, it does not matter. And as long as that response is not totally adequate, totally complete to the challenge, there is friction, there is a battle, there is a strain, there is suffering, and so on—obviously. As long as I do not respond totally to any issue, I must live in conflict. Do you understand, sir?

And life now demands—unless we want to live very superficially, casually, and therefore live a life that has no meaning whatsoever—that we bring about a revolution in ourselves. So we have to find out for ourselves if it is possible to bring about this mutation. That means, is it possible to die totally to the past, die totally to what has been, so that the mind is renewed, made fresh? Because, as we said the other day, thought is always old. You understand? Thought is the response of memory. If you had no memory, you would not be able to think. So that memory is the result of accumulated experience. Whether it is the accumulated experience of a community or of society, or it is your own particular individual accumulation of memories, it is still memory. So the whole of consciousness, whether you call it high or low, is memory. You understand?

And in that field which is consciousness, there is nothing new. You can say, "Well, there is God who is totally new, there is atma that is always fresh"; but it is still within the field of that consciousness and therefore within the range of thought. And thought is memory, whether it is your memory or the memory of the propaganda of a thousand years. You follow? Thought can never bring about this revolution.

And the problem arises then if you go into it very deeply: As thought cannot bring about this mutation, what is the function of thought at all? I must use thought in the office; in doing things, in cooking and washing dishes, in using a language—as we are now doing—thought must exist. If you were asked where you live, your response would be immediate because you are very familiar with the place where you live. Therefore there is very little gap, there is hardly any gap between the question and the answer. Obviously, sirs. And if a deeper question is asked, the time interval you take between the question and the answer will be greater; and in that interval you are looking, you are searching, you are asking, you are expecting, you are waiting for somebody to tell you. The whole of that is still the field of consciousness which is memory, and from that memory we hope to bring about a change. Right? And that memory from which springs thought will always be old, so there is nothing new in thought. Thought can invent new things, new ideas, new purposes, a new way of electioneering, a new way of political thinking, and so on. But it is still based on memory, knowledge, experience—which is the past. So, thought, however clever, however cunning, however erudite, cannot bring about this complete revolution in the mind. And that revolution, that mutation is absolutely necessary if we are to live a different kind of life. So, is it possible to die to thought? Do you understand the problem? Though we must have thought and use it most efficiently without any personal inclination, tendencies, use it carefully with tremendous reason, care, with great honesty and without any self-deception, thought cannot possibly create the new. Right?

So from that arises the problem: What is death? For most of us death is something to be avoided, something of which we are frightened, something that is to be put away in the distance. And we know that death exists, death of the physical organism; but also we think of death as an end. If you believe in reincarnation and so on, then you don't actually face the fact. Then you are avoiding the issue. There is a challenge which says, "You are going to die." Don't avoid it, but look at it, go into it, find out all that you can about it. But to do that there must be no fear whatsoever. But fear is created by thought—you have noticed that, perhaps. That thought projects itself in time as "tomorrow or in fifty years' time I am going to die," or "I am going to be happy," or "I am going to heaven," or whatever it is, and thought creates fear. You must have noticed all this. Have you? And this fear prevents you from looking, from observing. So the fear is the observer, isn't it? The fear is the one entity, the center, the censor, the observer, the thinker, the experiencer, the center from which you look, you think, you act. The fear is the observer, the thinker who creates time between himself as the observer and the thing observed. You understand all this, sirs?

Look, sir, make it very simple. Have you ever looked at a tree? I doubt it very much. You know, we have no sense of beauty. There is the sky, a flower, a reflection of the sunset on water, the flight of a bird, a beautiful face, a lovely smile; but we never look. When we do look, there is space between the observer and the observed. Right? There is space between you and the tree. And in that space you have your thoughts about the tree,

the image about the tree. You have also your ideas, your hopes, your fears, and the image about yourself. You have the image about yourself and your fears. Those images are looking at the tree. And therefore you never look at the tree. But when you have no image of the tree, or of yourself, then the distance between the observer and the observed does not exist at all—the observer is the observed. Please, if one understands this thing, it is a tremendous revolution in itself—that there is no observer separate from the observed.

Look, sir, make it much more familiar to yourself. Have you ever looked at your wife, or your husband, or your children, or your neighbor, or your boss, or at any of the politicians? I doubt it. All the world over politicians are mischievous because they are dealing with the immediate. And the person who deals with the immediate, and does not take the whole, deals with confusion, mischief, and war. Have you ever looked at these people? If you have, what is seen? The image you have about a person, the image you have about your politicians, the prime minister, your god, your wife, your children—that image is being looked at. And that image has been created through your relationship, or through your fears, or through your hopes. The sexual and other pleasures you have had with your wife, your husband, the anger, the flattery, the comfort, and all the things that your family life brings—a deadly life it is—have created an image about your wife or husband. With that image you look. Similarly, your wife or husband has an image about you. So the relationship between you and your wife or husband, between you and the politician is really the relationship between these two images. Right? That is a fact. How can two images which are the result of thought, of pleasure, and so on, have any affection or love?

So the relationship between two individuals, very close together or very far, is a relationship of images, symbols, memories. And in that, how can there be real love? Do you understand the question?

So we never look, not only at life, but also at death. We have never looked at life. We have looked at it as something ugly, something dreadful, or as a life of constant battle which we have had, struggle, struggle—monetary struggle, emotional struggle, intellectual struggle, and so on. We have accepted it as inevitable. And having accepted it, we invent a theory that perhaps in some future life, next life, or whatever it is, we shall be rewarded. That is the way we live, and each religion throughout the world has invented some hope—reincarnation, resurrection, and so on; we are not going into all the details of it because this is not the occasion and there won't be time.

So to understand something, even your wife, your husband, or your politicians, you must observe. And to observe, there must be no barrier between the observer and the observed. Right? Otherwise you cannot see. If I want to understand you as a human being, I must get rid of all my prejudices, my impressions, my tendencies, the circumstantial pressures, and so on; I must get rid of them totally and then look. Then I begin to understand it because I have freed myself from fear. Right? As long as there is the observer and the thing observed, the thinker and the thing thought about, there must be fear, uncertainty, confusion.

To observe death is to observe life. You understand, sirs? We have neither observed living nor are we capable of observing death. When you know how to observe living with all its complexities, with all its fears, despairs, agonies, aching sorrow, loneliness, boredom, when you know how to look at it—not whether you like it or dislike it, whether it gives you pleasure or no pleasure,

but just to observe—then you will be capable of observing death. Because then there is no fear. So to die is to live. But we do not know how to die to everything every day, to all the things that we have learned, to all the things that we have gathered as character, and so on. In something that continues in time, there is nothing new. It is only when there is an ending that there is something new. But, you see, we are frightened to end everything that we know. Have you ever tried to die to one of your pleasures? That is good enough to begin with. To end without reason, without argument—that is what is going to happen when death comes to you; there is no argumentation with death. In the same way if you know how to die to one of your pleasures, to the smallest and to the greatest, then you will know what it means to die. Because death is a most extraordinary thing. Death means a renewal, a total mutation, in which thought does not function at all because thought is the old. But when there is death, there is something totally new.

You know, sirs, when the mind is empty, the mind is silent, not endlessly chattering about something or the other. When the mind is completely empty, being silent, it is capable of renewing itself entirely without any outside pressures, circumstances; then it is something clear, pristine, and there is a joy which is not pleasure.

Perhaps now you would ask some questions.

Question: My last question which I put at the last meeting—where does the soul go after death?

KRISHNAMURTI: That gentleman asks the same question as he did the last time. He wants to know what happens to the soul when he is dead. How do you know there is a soul? Do you know, or is it an idea which has been handed down to you, as it is being done in Russia that there is no such thing as a soul. You understand, sirs? You are repeating a question that you have been told. You have not found out for yourself if there is a soul. Is there one? Which means what? Look at it first—not with your fears, with your hopes, with your memory, but just look. What is implied in "soul"? There is something permanent, continuous, which is beyond thought, something not created by thought. Right? That is generally what we call the atma, the soul, and so on—something not within the field of time and thought. But if thought can think about it, it is in the field of thought; therefore, it is not permanent. Right, sirs?

I am not being logical; logic can deceive you very easily. But when you observe very closely, then you need no logic; you just observe and see fact after fact.

There is no such thing as permanency in your own life. Sirs, have you observed there is nothing permanent? Even your government, your ministers, your own self, your own ideas, your own anxiety—nothing in life is permanent. But thought, the observer, says, "There is something permanent. I must have something permanent; otherwise, life is a movement without meaning." So it invents the Marx-Lenin theory, it invents a god, soul, and so on; it creates a permanency out of its own fear, which is the intellectual form of deception. So there is nothing permanent, not even your house, your family, your relationship. You know to discover that nothing is permanent is one of the most important things. Only then is your mind free—then you can look, you can see the sunset; and in that there is great joy.

You know the difference between pleasure and joy? Pleasure is the result of thought. I have had pleasure from the sunset, looking at a face, and so on. At that moment of looking there is neither pleasure nor displeasure. I just observe that sunset. A second later thought comes in and says how lovely that was, and thought then thinks about that loveliness more and more; from that comes pleasure. If you observe this for yourself, you will see this. You have had sexual pleasure and you think about it; the more you think about it, the more pleasurable it is, and this goes on. But joy is an immediate thing, and you can make that joy into pleasure by thinking about it.

Most people are frightened of death. One of our problems then is how to be totally free of fear, not of death. Because death must be extraordinary, like life. When you know how to live, then it becomes extraordinary. But as we do not know how to live, we do not know what is death. We are frightened of living and we are frightened of death, and out of that fear we invent all theories. So the question is: Is it possible to be free completely of fear? This means one has to investigate into the whole problem of thinking. Because it is thought that creates fear, it is thought that creates pleasure. And can one observe fear silently without any image, observe fear, but not merely the word that creates fear. Because death is a word, and that word creates fear. So one has not only to be aware of the word but also to be aware of a death which might happen to you through disease, accident, or in a natural way; to see what is implied, and to observe without any image about fear. And that requires tremendous attention, not concentration. Concentration is too immature, and any boy, any of you can do it. In your office you concentrate—that's nothing, that is too immature. But you have to be tremendously attentive. And you cannot be attentive as long as there is the observer who has his own images created by circumstances, tendencies, inclinations, and so on. As long as those images exist from which springs thought, thought must always create fear.

Question: How do emotions form, and what is their role in the state of mind about which you are talking?

KRISHNAMURTI: How do emotions come into being? Very simple. They come into being through stimuli, through the nerves. You put a pin into me, I jump; you flatter me and I am delighted; you insult me and I don't like it. Through our senses emotions come into being. And most of us function through our emotion of pleasure; obviously, sir. You like to be recognized as a Hindu. Then you belong to a group, to a community, to a tradition, however old; and you like that, with the Gita, the Upanishads, and the old traditions, mountain high. And the Muslim likes his and so on. Our emotions have come into being through stimuli, through environment, and so on. It is fairly obvious.

What role has emotion in life? Is emotion life? You understand? Is pleasure love? Is desire love? If emotion is love, there is something that changes all the time. Right? Don't you know all that?

Comment: Sir, just a minute.

KRISHNAMURTI: Sir, I have not answered that gentleman's question. As I said the other day, we are so eager with our own questions that we do not listen to anybody else, and we are guided by our emotions or we are guided by intellectual ideas which are destructive. Whether you are guided by your emotions or guided by your intellect, it leads to despair because it leads nowhere. But you realize that love is not pleasure, love is not desire.

You know what pleasure is, sir? When you look at something or when you have a feeling, to think about that feeling, to dwell constantly upon that feeling gives you pleasure, and that pleasure you want and you repeat that pleasure over and over again. When a man is very ambitious or a little am-

bitious, that gives him pleasure. When a man is seeking power, position, prestige in the name of the country, in the name of an idea, and all the rest of it, that gives him pleasure. He has no love at all, and therefore he creates mischief in the world. He brings about war within and without.

So one has to realize that emotions, sentiment, enthusiasm, the feeling of being good, and all that have nothing whatsoever to do with real affection, compassion. All sentiment, emotions have to do with thought and therefore lead to pleasure and pain. Love has no pain, no sorrow, because it is not the outcome of pleasure or desire.

Question: Sir, you have just observed that in total observation there is neither the observer nor thought, nor fear, and that one observes that the observer is the observed. My question is, who is the observer who observes in that state?

KRISHNAMURTI: I will explain the question; if I am not repeating the question correctly, please correct me.

The questioner asks: "Who is the observer when there is no observer and the observed?" The speaker said that when there is total, complete attention, there is neither the observer nor the observed. So one must understand what one means by that word *attention*. There is no attention when there is any kind of endeavor, effort. Right? If I am making an effort to attend, my energy is gone in making the effort. So the first thing I have to realize is what it means to attend. And there is no attention if there is any form of trying to shape the attention, trying to limit it, trying to enforce it in a particular direction. And there is no attention if there is thought functioning according to inclination, pleasure, desire, or temperament, or compelled by circumstances—which is, if there is any form of image, there is no attention.

Sir, all this means meditation, not the meditation that some of you may practice, which is the repetition of Ram, Ram, Sita, or whatever the name is. Such repetition of words makes the mind dull. And the mind which is made dull can be very silent, but it is still a dull mind.

So there is attention when there is no image, when there is no time. Time is a process of thinking within the field of consciousness, and all consciousness is the result of time and thought; and in that boundary of consciousness attention is not possible. And coming to this attention is the easiest thing. Because attention comes when there is an awareness of every action, feeling, thought that you have. That is, attention comes into being when there is self-knowing, not according to some philosophy or some psychologist and so on, but actually knowing yourself as you are—your thoughts, your gestures, the way you talk to your wife, to your husband, to your boss—just to be aware of your reaction, not to condemn it, not to justify it, not to translate it into something, but just to observe, to be aware choicelessly. From that comes this extraordinary attention in which there is neither image nor time nor thought. And in that state of attention—which is meditation—there is neither the observer nor the observed. Sir, try it, do it; don't ask me who is the observer when there is no observer or the observed; do it.

Question: Sir. . .

KRISHNAMURTI: Wait, sir, just a minute. You know it is good to ask questions, but you must ask the right question. But the right question implies a very high quality of mind, a mind that is really serious, really earnest, wanting to find out—not a mind that just asks a flippant question and does not even pay attention to the answer. You see, most of us. . . .

Question: I wanted to ask—

KRISHNAMURTI: Sir, that gentleman asked a question: "When there is no observer, does the observed exist?" That is the first thing. When there is no observer, does that thing observed exist? Of course, it exists. It exists as it is, not as you would like it to exist. Observe a tree, observe it. If you have no symbol about that tree—symbol being the image, the botanical knowledge, the species, and so on—but merely look at that tree, you give your whole attention to that looking. And to look with attention means to look with your nerves, your body, your ears, your eyes, your heart, everything that you have; and therefore it means energy. And that energy is dissipated when you have an image about the object. Then, if you do this, you will find out for yourself that a mind which is so completely attentive is an empty mind. And from that emptiness and silence there is action even with regard to the most ordinary thing.

Question: Are thought and fear permanent in all living beings, or do they come from somewhere else?

KRISHNAMURTI: "Is fear permanent in a human being?"

Sir, what is fear? Fear cannot exist by itself, obviously. It exists in relation to something. I am frightened of my wife, I am frightened of my boss, I am frightened of death, I am frightened I might get ill; The boss can kick me out, if he has power—bosses generally have power these days—and I am psychologically afraid of it. So fear is in relation to actuality, which is danger. And also psychologically, inwardly, I am afraid. I am afraid I might get ill because I have had pain, and that pain is a memory, and the memory says I must be careful not to get ill; I might be frightened of the dark and so on. So fear exists, as always, in relation to something—it does not exist by itself—and I can change that relationship. But if that relationship is based on pleasure and pain, it will always create fear. Therefore there is nothing inherent in human beings. We are the result of time, we are the outcome of the animal, and the animal is still with us.

Comment: Sir,

KRISHNAMURTI: Yes, sir.

Question: With regard to the total mutation in the mind, how are we to get that total. . .

KRISHNAMURTI: What? Sir, repeat.

Question: If we accept that the total mutation in the mind is sufficient to solve all the problems, how are we going to bring about that total mutation in the mind?

KRISHNAMURTI: Please correct me, sir, if I don't repeat the question properly. The gentleman asks: "If we accept mutation as a necessity, how are we going to bring about that mutation?" Is that right, sir?

Now, why do you want to accept it? If you accept it, you could also reject it, can't you? Right? And so I am asking you: Why do you accept such things? Don't you, for yourself, realize the necessity when you observe what extraordinary misery there is in yourself and in the world? Don't you want to change, not accept some idiotic idea from somebody else? So, there is no question of acceptance; first there is only a question of fact. You can reject the fact, saying that man cannot change, that man has been dumb for ten thousand years and he will always be stupid. And that is the end of it. But the moment you observe what is taking place in yourself and the utter despair of man, of

which you must be aware—if you see that, then you must demand, then you inevitably ask the right question, which is: Can man totally change? Sir, you know what I mean?

It is the third time that poor chap has got up to ask. Sir, you will ask the next time as soon as I finish this question.

Sir, the questioner asked: "How is it possible to bring about mutation?" Now when you ask "how," you want to know the method. Don't you? The "how" implies a method, a system, a way. Right? The "how" is always that. I do not know mathematics and I say, "How am I to learn it?" You are told there is a way, there is a method, there is a system, there is a formula, and you follow that and learn mathematics. Now, just listen to the word and the feeling of the word. Is there a system to help you to change? If there is a system, then you become a slave to that system and what it promises. Therefore it is not mutation. There are people who say that there is a method for meditating by which you will reach the highest—there is a method even in madness, but it is still madness. You understand? There is no method, sir. There is only attention, observation, beginning with yourself, because you are the result of the whole of human endeavor, human misery, human sorrow: You are the result of the past, whether the past is of the community or the past is of the race. And by merely asking "how," you are pursuing the past which is the mechanized process of thinking. So there is no "how," but you have only to observe yourself, to observe what you say, to observe and to be aware of what you think and the motives behind it, how you treat another, how you eat, how you walk, how you look at a woman, or how you look at a man, how you look at the stars or see the beauty of the sunset—to be aware of all that choicelessly. And out of that, if you can pursue it to the very end, you will find that the mutation comes without your knowing. Yes, sir.

Question: Sir, there is a saying of Shankaracharya...

KRISHNAMURTI: The gentleman's question is: There is a saying of Shankaracharya that the world is an illusion. What do you say?

You know, I do not personally read any of these books—Shankaracharya, Gita, Upanishads, or any religious book, or any philosophical book, or any psychological book. And when you repeat what Shankaracharya or somebody says, I say, "Don't listen to them. Don't follow anybody. Don't accept any authority." Because they might be all wrong and they generally are, the moment they become an authority. Technologically there must be authority: how to run a machine, a computer. But if you have any psychological authority, it is death, it leads to darkness. This country is full of this kind of authority—the authority of the family, the authority of the teacher, Shankaracharya, the Buddha, this, or that; in the West it is Christ and so on. There are the professors, the philosophers, the Shankaracharyas who are burning themselves or who are fasting, the saints and all the rest of it. Don't follow anybody, including the speaker. Please, sir, I am saying this most earnestly. Don't laugh it off. You cannot see for yourself, or think for yourself originally—that has been the poison. To think for yourself means to revolt. You are not capable of revolting; you are frightened because you might lose your job, you might go wrong. And so you accept tradition. Tradition is always dead, and you follow the dead things, and therefore you are dying.

So a wise man—a man who is really honest, earnest—has no authority.

Question: Sir, one thing. You explained attention, but....

KRISHNAMURTI: I will explain, sir. The questioner asks: "You said that in attention there is no memory; how am I to be free of memory?" Right, sir?

Sir, when you know the machinery, the significance, and the structure of anything, then you begin to understand it. Then you can put it aside. Then you are really free of it. You understand?

I must stop, sir. It is seven o'clock. This is the last question.

The questioner says that a human being is burdened with memory. To understand memory you must first see the structure of memory, how it comes into being, and what its place is, and also where it must not interfere. You know how memory comes, sir? Do you know the beginning of memory? I see a beautiful face; there is perception, sensation, contact, and desire. You follow this, sir? This is the process, isn't it? I see something—a sunset, a face, a tree—and there is visual perception; from that there is sensation; then the desire to touch it, sensation; then thought comes in and says, "That gives me pleasure, I must have more of it." Right?

So thought generated by sensation, desire, prolongs the pleasure principle. Where there is pleasure, there is pain, and the battle is on. And so memory becomes thicker and thicker; the older, the more traditional it is, the more heavy it becomes. And then you say, "How am I to get rid of it?" You cannot. All that you can do is to observe in the minutest detail how it comes, how it begins. And to discover how it begins, your mind must observe silently. You understand, sir? To discover anything you must look; and to look, your look must be silent. Sir, if you look at your husband, your wife, or child, if you have any ideas about that child, or about the image of your wife or your husband, then you are not silently looking; your mind is cluttered up with all these things, and therefore you cannot look. So, to look, your mind must be silent, and the very urgency of looking makes the mind silent. Not that you first have a silent mind and then look, but rather the very necessity of looking at the world's problem and therefore at your problem—that very urgency of looking makes the mind quiet, silent. That very look makes the mind silent, and then you can look at your memory and the beginning of the memory. The demand to look at your memory and to find out how it begins—that very demand makes the mind silent. Then you can look at the beginning of every movement of memory.

December 22, 1966

Fourth Talk in New Delhi

I believe this is the last talk, at least for this year. There is no end to collecting ideas, to multiplying words, to gathering knowledge and information. But to act seems to be one of the most difficult things to do—to act sanely, healthily, without any conflict, with a certain quality of mind that is total, that is not distorted by conditioning, by the environment in which one lives, by all the strains and stresses that human beings are heir to. Apparently, it is much more easy to discuss ideas, theories, rather than to live a rich, full day without any problem, without disturbance, without misery and sorrow.

It seems to be one of the most difficult things in life to live completely, totally—not fragmentarily, but as a total human being—whether you are in your office or in your home, or whether you are walking in a wood. It is only complete action that brings about intelligence. Total action is intelligence. But we live in fragments, as a family man opposed to the rest of the world, as a religious man, if one is at all religious, having peculiar theories, ideas, separate beliefs and dogmas. And one is always struggling to achieve a status, a position, a prestige, whether that status is worldly or saintly. One is always striving, striving. There is never a moment when the mind is completely empty and therefore silent. And out of silence action takes place. We are no longer original; we are the result, as we have said over and over again, of our environments, of circumstances, of the culture, the tradition in which we live, and we accept that. And to change always demands a great deal of energy.

It is very easy to discuss ideas—that does not demand much energy. Theories, quoting somebody or other—all that does not demand much energy, interest, drive. But to bring about a total revolution in oneself—that demands tremendous energy. And to have that energy, man has tried several things; he has become a monk, shutting out all the temptations of the world, withdrawing, isolating himself from the world. But inwardly he is still tortured, inwardly he is still burning with his desires, with his ideas, opinions, what somebody has said or not said. So outwardly you may withdraw, but inwardly there is always conflict, a striving. So this strife, this struggle, wastes energy. So, one must have tremendous energy to change. That is fairly obvious. Even to stop smoking, if you are so inclined, you must have a certain energy. To observe why you smoke, what is the process of it, and so on—that demands a certain energy. To give it up also demands energy, as it demands energy to get into the habit of smoking. Perhaps it demands greater energy to give it up.

But we have to understand this whole process of living which is very complex. We live very superficially; outwardly we may perhaps lead a very simple life, but inwardly, inside the skin as it were, we are very complex human beings. The motives, the ambitions, the greed, the frustration, the fears, the competition, and the everlasting fear and sorrow—all that is going on inwardly. Now to bring about a radical transformation in all that demands a great energy, which is obvious. Now, is it possible to have this energy without any conflict? Because, we have considered that the gathering of energy is through effort; that is, one thinks that the more effort one makes, the more energy one has. Isn't it?

Please, as we said, don't merely listen to words or to the ideas. Listen with your heart and mind, neither taking sides nor opposing, nor offering your own particular opinion; just listen. The speaker is doing all the work when he talks. All that you have to do is to listen. And if you know how to listen, then you are also working with the speaker. But if you are merely listening—hearing words and translating those words into opinions, or opposing those words with your own ideas, or comparing those words with what has been said by previous teachers, and so on—then you are not sharing; then you are wasting your energy. Whereas you have to listen—as you would to a bird in the morning, as you would listen to all the various notes—neither rejecting nor opposing, but just listen with intensity, with affection, with a tremendous enjoyment. Because it is only when we listen with our heart and mind totally that that very listening is an end in itself. Then you don't have to do anything. Because then the seed has taken its place, and the seed, if it is vital, will bring its own fruit. But if you merely oppose because you are a Sikh, a Hindu, a Muslim, or God knows what else, or if you are tortured by a particular problem and you want that particular problem to be resolved, then you are listening with a fragmentary mind, listening partially. This partial listening, this inattention is the very essence of waste of energy. Either you listen completely or don't listen at all.

You have to give your whole attention to your sorrow and all the things involved in it—the loneliness, the lack of companionship, the frustration, the misery, the endless annoyance. You will not give your whole attention to it if you want your sorrow to be solved in a particular way, according to a particular pattern; then that demand that it should be solved in a particular way is a waste of energy. But, if you only listen with care, watching every movement of thought, without stopping, watching it with great, minute attention, then you will see for yourself that the problem which loomed large no longer matters at all. Because that very attention is the energy which resolves the problem.

This evening, if we may, we are going to consider the gathering of this energy to tackle all human problems. We have many problems, not a single problem; and every problem is related to another problem. If one can solve one problem completely—it does not matter what it is—then you will see that you will be able to meet other problems easily and dissolve them. It is inattention that breeds mischief, not attention. And to know when you are inattentive is to be attentive. You understand? To know I am lazy, to be aware I am lazy is already to be active. But when I am not aware that I am lazy, when I am not aware that I am inattentive, then begins the mischief and the misery of the problem. Do listen to this, please, because we are talking about your life, your daily anxiety, your daily misery, your daily conflict, the insults, and so on. And to resolve all that, not partially, but totally, demands great energy.

And we are going to find out this evening if we can communicate to each other this energy. And to communicate about anything, there must be contact. To communicate about any problem, there must be contact with the word and the meaning of the word—not translate the word as you wish it to be. This means when there is communication, both the people must be in a state of attention. If I am telling you something, you must be attentive, you must be interested, you must care. But if you are not attentive, if you are merely waiting to be stimulated, or waiting to be told what to do, then communication ceases. Because we are not going to tell you what to do. For generations upon generations you have been told what to do. Your teachers, your gurus, your politicians, your books, and everything have told you what to do, what to think—not how to think, but what to think—and that pattern, that tradition, has been established. And you are waiting to be told what to do. But we are not concerned with such a triviality as what you should or should not do—that will come to you when you give attention. Then you will find out for yourself, out of your own mind, out of your own heart.

So, we are going to consider, this evening, the gathering of this energy that is not generated through stimulation. Please listen to all this carefully. Most of us depend on stimulation. Either you take hashish or LSD, or this or that, for stimulation. There are different forms of stimulation, both outward and inward. The outward we know, which is fairly simple: a ritual, a repetition of a phrase, reading a book, depending on something external which gives one a certain stimulation. Or inwardly you derive stimulation through your desire, through your pleasure, through an idea which is very stimulating. But we are talking of energy which is not dependent on stimulation. Because the moment you are dependent on something, you are already wasting your energy. You understand all this, sirs? You know, most of us depend—and we must depend—on food, clothes, and shelter; that is obvious. Don't let us mix the two. You must have food, you must have clothes, you must have shelter. We depend upon the

postman, the milkman, the railway, our bureaucracy, and so on and so on. But we also depend on others inwardly. Inwardly we are desperately lonely. And out of the fear of that loneliness, of that emptiness, inwardly we depend on people, and the people then become the stimulus. And the moment there is a stimulant, whether it is a psychological stimulant or an outward stimulant, that stimulant dulls the mind. Do you understand? You drink coffee, tea, or alcohol; when you keep on drinking it, you will need more and more, which makes the mind more and more dull—not sensitive, alert, awake. So when one realizes that any form of outward or inward stimulation breeds inevitably a sort of indifference and dullness, and when one sees the truth of it, the stimulation naturally will drop away. In that there is no conflict; it is conflict that wastes energy. You understand, sirs?

Our life is a conflict from the days of the school—where we compete with another, try to get better marks in an examination—to the days of the college, the university. And then in getting a job, there is conflict for getting a better job, competing with another for arriving at a certain position, a certain status, and then demanding more status and so on. From the beginning to the end we are perpetually in conflict, striving, striving, emotionally as well as intellectually. And this effort, like all effort which is friction, does not make the mind subtle and capable of functioning freely. Every effort is a distortion. I hope you are following all this.

It is only when effort ceases that you have an unbounding energy inwardly, so that your mind remains crystal clear and can tackle any human problem. So, for this energy to come into being totally, one must understand effort—not ask the speaker: How am I to live without effort? That would be too silly. Because then if I would be foolish enough to tell you how to do it, then you would try to follow that system. In the very following of that system you are making an effort and therefore destroying the very thing that you want to bring about. But if you understand the nature and the structure of effort, then you will have energy to deal with the problem, or do what you have to do, much more efficiently. You understand, sirs?

The world is divided socially: the high, the middle, and the low. Isn't it? The high have all the prestige, the position, the wealth, the power, and they want to hold it. That is what is happening in this country—one political party has the power, position, prestige, and what not, and wants to hold it; and it is going to make tremendous effort to hold it. The middle wants to come to the top and push the high away. This is called revolution. And the middle becomes the high and then holds on to power until again the low comes and pushes it away. This pattern is repeated over and over again.

Now, man in society is seeking prestige, status, through function. Right? You make a tremendous difference between the prime minister and the cook. Not only outwardly, but psychologically, inwardly, to you status matters much more than function. Because with the function, you have identified status. And hence when status becomes so tremendously important, as it does throughout the world, then function becomes less and less efficient. Then you are not attentive to function; your eyes are on status. Right? So conflict between function and status—the struggle to achieve status through function—becomes the purpose of existence. This is what is actually taking place. And hence we are all the time increasing conflict. The saints do this; only in their own way they want to achieve heaven, break the record for fasting, or burn themselves, and so on. And to them status matters very much, not what actually they are. How petty, how silly human beings are!

And so, we have to bring about a change in the shallow mind because most of us have very shallow, petty, little minds—whether it is the saint or the chief minister or God knows who else. And these minds are everlastingly making effort to become something different. You follow all this? But the moment you are attentive to your shallow mind, the moment you are aware that you are shallow, narrow, limited, petty, you will see in that state of attention you are no longer petty. If once you understand this principle—understand it, not repeat it, not quote it—what the speaker is saying has no importance at all. The speaker is not at all important. What is important is that you listen and see if it is true and carry it out with all your heart and mind.

So we need energy, and that energy is wasted when there is conflict. Please listen very carefully to what is going to be said. Conflict will continue as long as you are seeking pleasure. Because most of us want pleasure. That is the thing we live by: sexual pleasure, appetite of various kinds, pleasure that you derive from status, from position, from prestige, out of your capacity, out of your knowledge. And pleasure arises, comes into being, is put together, through thought. That is fairly simple, isn't it? Thought creates pleasure. I think about something that has given me pleasure for a moment, and the more I think about it, the more I give strength to that pleasure. It is fairly simple, how pleasure begins. And as long as the mind is seeking pleasure, there is always the fear of not having it. And as long as there is fear, there is effort to run away from it, to resolve it, to do something—which is a waste of energy. You understand? One has to see the structure, the meaning of pleasure, just to understand it, not intellectually.

You know the word *understanding* is so misused. We say we understand intellectually—which is sheer nonsense. You don't understand anything intellectually. What you mean when you say, "I understand intellectually," is "I understand the words that you are using and I understand the meaning of those words, but not the content of the whole thing." You can only understand something totally when you are listening to it silently and completely. You understand? This happens to all of us. You understand something completely when you are quiet. Out of silence there is understanding, not out of your chattering.

So, you have to understand the nature of pleasure, its structure, how it begins very unexpectedly, very slowly, without your knowing. You see a beautiful sunset, a lovely face, or have some kind of sexual or other experience, and you want to repeat it. The repetition is a process of thinking about it. And the more you repeat, the more mechanical it becomes. You can go every evening to look at the sunset, but you will never see it because out of that sunset you are deriving a pleasure. You are not looking at the sunset. You want the pleasure which that sunset gave you two days ago. So, as long as there is any demand for pleasure, there must be conflict. But we are not talking of puritanical banishment of pleasure. On the contrary, if you understand the whole structure of pleasure, then you will have tremendous joy in life. Because joy is entirely different from pleasure. You cannot think about joy, but you can think about pleasure. Have you not noticed it?

So one has to understand not only effort but the whole meaning and the significance of pleasure, not cut away pleasure, which monks have tried in their monasteries, which the sannyasis also have tried—they will never look at a woman because they are so frightened and so on. Because to them pleasure is something very wrong. They consider it a sin. And therefore they have destroyed the vitality of understanding. Be-

cause they have said this is wrong, they have never examined the whole structure of pleasure. So one has to understand not only effort but also pleasure, because in pleasure there is fear and therefore pain. You understand? Where there is a search for pleasure, there is fear; and it is this fear that creates pain. So if you are willing to put up with pleasure, with fear and pain, go to it; but know all the implications of it, don't just slip into it. But if you give your whole attention to it, then you will find that you can look at a sunset and not let pleasure creep in—which means no thought of wanting the repetition of it. Therefore when you look at a sunset, or at a face—or anything, at a bird, or the beauty of water, a sheet of water shimmering in the sun—look at it without thought, there is in that tremendous joy; therefore, there is no pain, no fear, and therefore there is an end to effort.

And we also make an effort when we are trying to become something. Schoolboys trying to pass an examination are becoming, are making an effort. This is not the occasion to talk about the whole business of education. We touched it for the moment. Inwardly we want to be something. I do not know if you have noticed ever in yourself how you are craving to be somebody, famous, full of knowledge. You know all the things that one imagines. Why do we do this? Why do we want to be somebody? Why do we want to be a hero, like somebody else? Most of you do, why?

Again, one has to understand this. Because inwardly we are empty, we are shallow human beings, shoddy, little human beings. I do not know if you have ever seen a horse galloping at full speed and a little man riding on top of it; the horse is much more useful, has more beauty, is full of power and joy. And the man who owns that horse is a very small man, with a little mind, frightened. And that is what we are. We want to be outwardly something, but inwardly we are utterly empty, full of memories, full of knowledge—which is of the past, the dead ashes of something which we have lived or remembered or experienced. And because we are empty, we are frightened of that, and therefore we are trying everlastingly to become something. But if you give complete attention to that emptiness, not trying to alter it, not trying to say that you will do something about it, when you are completely attentive of that emptiness, you will see you can go beyond it. And then there is no attempt to be anything. Then you will know what it is to be without a demand. Then it is a light to itself.

So we waste energy through constant effort of different kinds—inwardly of course. Most of us are indolent, lazy, and we are always trying not to be lazy. Someone disciplines himself to get up at a certain time every day punctually, and makes tremendous effort, because he is lazy in himself. But he does not inquire why he is lazy. You understand? He is concentrated on becoming, on being not lazy, and therefore he never looks at the structure, the meaning of laziness.

Why is one lazy? Probably you are not eating rightly, you have worked too much, walked too much, talked too much, done so many things; and naturally the body, when it gets up in the morning, is lazy. Because you have not spent an intelligent day, the body is tired the next day. And it's no good disciplining the body. Whereas if you are attentive at the moment of your talking, when you are in your office—if you are completely attentive even for five minutes, that is enough. When you are eating, be attentive and do not eat fast, nor stuff yourself with all kinds of food. Then you will see that your body becomes, of itself, intelligent. You don't have to force it to be intelligent; it becomes intelligent, and that intelligence will tell it to get up or not to get up. So you begin to discover

that one can live a life of going to the office and all the rest of it without this constant battle, because one has not wasted energy, but is using it totally all the time—and that is meditation.

You understand? Meditation is not what is done all the world over: repetition of words, sitting in a certain posture, breathing in a certain way, repeating some *sloka* or mantra over and over again. Naturally that makes the mind stupid, dull; and out of that stupidity, dullness, the mind becomes silent and you think you have got silence. That kind of meditation is merely self-hypnosis. It is not meditation at all. It is the most destructive way of meditating. But there is meditation which demands that you attend—attend to what you are saying to your wife, to your husband, to your children, how you talk to your servants if you have any, how you talk to your boss—be attentive at that moment, do not concentrate. Because concentration is something which is very ugly. Every schoolboy can do it because he is forced to do it. And you think that by forcing yourself to concentrate, you will get some peace. You won't. You will not have what you call "peace of mind"—you will have a piece of mind, which is not peace of mind. Concentration is an exclusion. When you want to concentrate on something, you are excluding, you are resisting, you are putting away things which you don't want. Whereas if you are attentive, then you can look at every thought, every movement; then there is no such thing as distraction, and then you can meditate. Then such meditation is a marvelous thing because it brings clarity. Meditation is clarity. Meditation then is silence, and that very silence is the disciplining process of life, not your disciplining yourself in order to achieve silence. But when you are attentive to every word, to every gesture, to all the things you are saying, feeling, to your motives, not correcting them, then out of that comes silence, and from that silence there is discipline. Then in that there is no effort; there is a movement which is not of time at all. And such a human being is a joyous person; he does not create enmity, he does not bring unhappiness.

There are some questions which have been handed to me. Perhaps you would ask first, before I answer these questions.

Question: Who should rule, the philosopher or the politician?

KRISHNAMURTI: I hope neither. Don't laugh, you don't see the implication when you laugh so quickly. Why should anybody rule the world? The politician and the philosopher have made such a howling mess. Why should they rule you? Why don't you rule yourself? Why do you want somebody else to rule you? For God's sake, what are we, monkeys? Why should anybody tell us what to do? You know what is going to happen: the computers are going to take over, not the philosophers, not the politicians. Their day will soon be over, I hope. The computers which are completely impersonal will tell you what to do. You know, I was told that during the Korean war, the computers decided whether to attack China or not, not the generals, but the computers decided. They knew the strength of both and said, "Don't do it." The computers cannot be made corrupt, but the politician and philosopher can be, and are. So what is important is not whether the world is governed by them but whether you can govern yourself. Then you don't want governments. But please do this: govern yourself. And that is one of the most difficult things because to govern yourself you have to know yourself, not invent that you are atma, this, or that. You have to learn about yourself, you have to look at yourself as you would look at your face in a mirror, without distortion. You have

to look at yourself: the way you talk, the way you walk, the way you say, the way you think—everything. Then out of that attention, out of that looking, you will know how to act. And then you will know how to govern yourself and therefore govern. Then man needs no government at all. You know, one of the communist theories was to end all government; but there is not going to be an end of government because the communists want a certain pattern repeated, a certain ideology, and the moment the high hold the power, they are not going to let go. So a wise man, a man who is really humble, who has great affection and love, does not want anybody to guide him or rule him.

Question: Sir, I have two questions. Is it possible to communicate joy, and is it possible to have that joy?

KRISHNAMURTI: "Is it possible to communicate joy, and is it possible to have it? Is it possible to have joy and to communicate it to others?"

First of all, to understand what joy is, you must understand what pleasure is. That is what I have been talking about a little earlier. When there is joy, why do you want to communicate it? What for? To tell somebody that you have got it, you put it in a book, in a painting. See, sir, we are so concerned to communicate, when we have nothing to communicate. When you are full of something, you are not bothered whether you communicate or do not communicate.

Question: Sir, I have two questions: one is on love, and the other is on meditation. My question is, sir, would you explain what that love is about which you have been talking. That is a question on love. And the other is on meditation. Meditation, as you have defined

*today, is complete attention. Now what is the
thing we may reject or accept. . .?*

KRISHNAMURTI: *Sir, be brief.*

*Question: Let me finish it, sir. If the con-
ception of your meditation is essential, why
bring in words which have been used by so
many other people?*

KRISHNAMURTI: Right, sir.
The gentleman asks, "Would you define
what love is." And also he suggests that I
should not use the word *meditation* because
it is heavily loaded, but I shall use the word
attention.
All right. But I do not think words matter
very much if one knows the meaning of
words. If you can brush aside the weight, the
load which that word meditation has been
given, then one can use that word meditation
as well as attention. And we are not defining.
A dictionary will give you a very good
definition of what meditation is, what attention is, what love is. Is that what we are talking about? To define, to have a formula
about what love is? Then with that formula
you will go, compare it with what Shankara,
Buddha, X, Y, Z said, and at the end of it
will you know what love is, and will you
then love? Dialectically or through explanation will you know what love is? Sir, how do
you come by love? Not according to any
concept. We have been saying right through
this talk, "no concept." Concepts are merely
the result of thought, put together as concepts, formulas. A man who lives by formulas is a dead human being. And that is
what is happening in this country. You have
dozens of formulas, according to Shankara,
Buddha, and God knows what else, and
where are you? So we are not talking of concepts. We said love is not pleasure, love is
not desire, love is not jealousy, love is not

possession or domination. If you can
eliminate these, then you will find out. When
you eliminate these—and eliminate them
rightly, not force them—then you will find
out for yourself what kindliness is, what
courtesy is, what gentleness is. Then perhaps
you will come upon this strange flower
which man always hungers after.

*Question: Sir, the problem of relationship
you were discussing the other day: When you
are face to face with two persons with two
different ideas which both of them hold to be
right, and when you have to put up with
them, is there not the problem of your
relationship with them?*

KRISHNAMURTI: If you have to put up
with a person who thinks he is right, the
questioner asks what relationship have you
with that person? A person who insists he is
right obviously is a neurotic person. And
what relationship have you with an unbalanced person who says, "I am right about
everything"?
Sir, first you make a problem. You don't
examine the question of those people who
say, "I am right." You know, sir, truth is
something entirely different from being right.
Truth is something which is not personal,
which has nothing to do with any religion,
with any group, with any individual; it is not
to be found in any church, in any organized
religion. And right and wrong are things of
thought. And without understanding the
whole machinery of thought, there is no
meaning in merely submitting to another who
thinks he is right—like these gentlemen who
are going to burn themselves about nothing;
they consider themselves tremendously right,
and they are going to create havoc, mischief,
which has nothing to do with truth. To find
that strange thing one must be free. And to
be free means to be without fear, to investigate, to look, to observe. Right, sir?

Question: Is not some effort necessary in order to be attentive?

KRISHNAMURTI: "Must not one make conscious effort to be attentive? Is not some kind of effort necessary in being attentive to what one does?"

First of all, most of us are trained, educated to do something which we don't like at all. Right? Most of us are going to the office for the next forty years, and don't like it. It is a horrible business, endlessly getting up every morning and trotting to the office; it is a rat race, and you are forced to do it. So what does one do? Look at it. I hear somebody saying, "Don't make effort. It has no meaning." And he explains the nature of it. I think I have grasped the meaning of it. And here I am next morning; I have to do something which I don't like. What am I to do? I either put up with it and do the very best possible or I walk out. I cannot walk out because I am married, I have children, I have responsibilities; so I am stuck there. Being stuck there, what happens? I am old, there is self-pity, I compare myself with somebody who has a better job, I am all the time grumbling about it. Don't I have a bad leg! No doctor can cure it. There it is. Or, I say I put up with it. I don't everlastingly complain, complain. Now the way I put up with it demands attention, whether I put up with it, because I understand the whole meaning of it, and therefore it is no longer a problem. But if I resent it, if I am incapable of dealing with it, or if I want to deal with it in a certain way because I want this and that, then I multiply the problem through self-pity, through comparison, through various forms of ambition. Whereas if I am aware of all that, then I put up with it and go beyond it.

Question: Sir, I wanted one simple question to put to your good self. The question is:

What place has altruism in defining human life?

KRISHNAMURTI: "What place has altruism in life?" You mean by altruism, unselfishness?

Comment: Yes.

KRISHNAMURTI: Unselfishness, doing social work, is that it, sir? What place has unselfishness in life, is that it?

Comment: Yes, sir.

KRISHNAMURTI: What do you think? Why do you ask me? When it becomes an ideal that I must be unselfish in order to save somebody, then it is no longer unselfishness. When you give up—rather, when you do social work—it is an escape from yourself, do you understand? Because you are miserable, because you are frustrated—of which you may not be conscious—you go and do social work, you help a vast number of people; then, that leads to mischief because reformation needs always further reformation. A total revolution never needs reformation. It is only these petty, little saints with their petty, little issues and resolutions and plans—they are the real mischief-makers. Whereas when there is a total understanding of the whole process of life, out of that comes a mutation; and that is beyond those words of altruism and social work and all the rest of it.

Comment: The employers and employees are in conflict everywhere, whether in government or public and private undertakings. They are undergoing a great deal of conflict.

KRISHNAMURTI: The difference between the employer and the employed, the divergence, the division between them is growing greater and greater; the relations between these two, of course.

Question: And they are in conflict. Can there be an understanding between these two?

KRISHNAMURTI: Sir, you know that nationalism—it is not my job talking about all this—sometimes succeeds, sometimes doesn't. It has been shown right through the world. And they have experimented in Russia, in China, and in different parts of the totalitarian states where there is dictatorship, where there are no strikes, where the state is the employer; and it is said that the difference between the state, which is the managerial party—the top dogs, the high people—and the low people is equally marked, and there is constant battle between the two. The capitalists have done this too. Only there the worker can buy shares in the company; he can join the company.

So what is involved in this, sir? There is work that has to be done. Labor is going to be done more and more by automation. Great factories can be run, and probably will be run, by half a dozen people. And that is going to come, and labor will have little to do; you and I will be lazy, you and I will have leisure. And then the problem is relationship between man and man in leisure, not in function. Relationship becomes a conflict when there is status and no function. This is simple, sir. When the employer seeks status and so on, everything in life becomes a conflict. So the problem is not that we cannot deal with problems in the immediate, but we must take the problem—as we pointed out earlier in the talks—in the total process of time. Man is going to have a great deal of leisure, and what is he going to do? That is the real issue which you have got to face when you are dealing with the employer and the employed. So leisure is going to be exploited by the entertainer, whether the entertainer is television, the radio, football, or the priest, or the sectarian leader, or the political party, and so on. So leisure becomes a very important issue: Are you going to be completely entertained, to be entertained always, or are you going to enter into a different world where you become true human beings not kept entertained by circus and parade? You understand? Then we shall have right relationship with the employer and the employee or the employed. Until then there will always be conflict.

That is enough, sir. There is a question. Do you want me to answer this question?—because it is nearly 7 o'clock.

The questioner says he is shy to ask this question and therefore he has written it, and the question is: "I am very sexually inclined; education, culture, music, literature have just slightly modified it, but basically it is deep-rooted; I suffer a lot from this; what am I to do?" You have understood the question?

The questioner says music, art, literature, and so on have slightly modified the central issue, which is the drive, the urge, the demand for sex. You know, it is one of the most complicated problems, like every human problem that is bedeviling the world. You understand? Right through the world there is this problem. Why? It is as though for the first time human beings have discovered sex as though it were a very strange thing, and they want to have complete enjoyment and make a tremendous issue of it. Why? Now let us examine it. I am not telling you what to do. That would be so utterly immature, childish, and would reduce you to be immature and childish. So we are going to examine it. To examine you must be free to look. You understand? You cannot have prejudices: Oh, sex is sin, sex must be controlled, this and that. To look, you must be free from your prejudice and opinion, not only with regard to this, but with regard to every issue in life, with regard to your politician, with regard to the scientist, with regard to your newspaper, with regard to your sacred books, everything. To observe, to learn, there must be freedom.

Now why has it become a problem? Are you listening to this, sirs? Are you waiting for me to tell you? Why has it become a problem to you? Look, first of all, intellectually you function within a pattern. Intellectually you have drawn a line, a boundary, and within that you function; and within that boundary, the space is very small. Right? You dare not question your leaders, political or religious; intellectually you don't doubt, you don't say, "What do you mean by this?" but you have accepted them as authorities, and you function intellectually in that little frame. Therefore, what has happened? You have blocked yourself off. Haven't you? Intellectually you have cut yourself off, you have cut away, you dare not think in freedom—not that there is any freethinking; there is no such thing—but intellectually you are crippled. Look at what is happening through the world. Here in this country, art, music, and literature are at a very low ebb because you have accepted tradition and you repeat, repeat. So intellectually you have made yourself small, narrow. So you have no release through the intellect. By release, I don't mean right release through fulfillment, but I mean to think clearly, not to be afraid to say what you want to say even though society may threaten you, may put you in prison, or burn you, to stand by what you think. And that you don't do.

Have you noticed, sir, those people, those holy men, Shankaracharya and those gentlemen in the Punjab, who are burning themselves over some trivial matter? But then not one of the people in this country burned himself when there was a war between Pakistan and you, though you

professed pacifism, though you professed nonviolence; you never stood up and burned yourself, or even fasted.

Intellectually you are dead. This is a fact. You may function a little bit after learning a new technology, become a marvelous administrator, a marvelous engineer; but that is not being active, it is merely repetition. So intellectually you have cut the flow of the mind. Then, emotionally what is happening? To be sensitive, to be alive to trees, to poverty, to dirt, to squalor—you don't even notice all that. You are not sensitive to beauty: to look at the stars, to feel a leaf, to look at poverty, to see a poor child with a fat tummy. You don't look, you don't feel, you don't cry, you have become callous. And this is right through the world, not only here. And when you do feel, you become sentimental, you become devotional to some idiotic picture or a statue, you rush to a temple when you have got a headache, give away your jewels. So emotionally too you are starved, empty. Physically look at yourselves: what you have made of yourselves by overeating, overindulging, not having enough exercise, and all the rest of it; physically one has become flabby.

So when you shut off the movement of the mind, when you throttle down, destroy, become callous inwardly, when emotionally you have no feeling, no consideration, no kindliness—you talk about it, but you never stand for it; you never treat your servants or your children with consideration, with kindness—what happens? You have only one thing left which is sex, and nothing else; and that you have indulged in, though all your saints have said, "Don't, don't, don't look at a woman, she is your sister, she is your mother, and so on." You go on playing with sex, and it becomes a terrific problem. All around, you have become insensitive. Please see this for yourself. Then you will do something, then sex will be no longer a problem. And also at that moment probably you would have noticed that there is the total absence of yourself, and you want the repetition of that state of mind when there is no worry, no problem, when you are totally unaware of yourself—that is what sex gives you for the time being, and then you are back again with your turmoil.

So when you shut off all the movement of life, all affection, all kindliness, consideration, looking at nature, looking at trees, flowers, thinking clearly, when you have none of these things, you have only one thing left—like a peasant in a village. What has he? He has no beauty, he has nothing but work and the everlasting sun burning his body and his soul away. What has he left? He has got one thing left, sex, and therefore he has dozens of children. That is his only pleasure, and that too you deny him through your sacred books and the examples of these shallow, empty sannyasis who have run away from life.

Sir, to renounce the world is to understand the world, not to run away from it. To understand it you must look, you must see very clearly. And when you see clearly, you love. You have no love in your heart at all, though you may talk about it. When there is no love in your heart, you have only one thing left, which is pleasure; and that pleasure is sex, and therefore it becomes a mountainous problem. To resolve it, you have to understand it. When you understand it, you begin to face the mind; don't be afraid, you are human beings, not driven cattle. Then out of that freedom comes a beauty in everything, and nothing becomes a problem.

December 25, 1966

Madras, India, 1967

✳

First Talk in Madras

I think everybody must be aware of the extraordinary discontent in the world. That discontent takes different forms in different countries. Here, the students go on a strike; and some holy man fasts to save some cows while thousands upon thousands of cows are dying, I believe, in Bihar; somebody is willing to burn himself over some political issue. And in Europe, where there is great prosperity, discontent is shown through extensive traveling, seeking entertainment, either religious or on the football field or in the cinemas. And in America it takes the form of an antiwar campaign about Vietnam, taking LSD or a new kind of drug—if you know anything about it—and general antisocial activity of every kind, violence—not that there is no violence in this country. Violence is the common factor of all human beings, whether they live in Russia, here, or in America, or in China. I think one is aware of all the vast, frustrating, unrelated, isolated activities and fragmentary issues, which become extraordinarily important. This is happening right through the world.

And as one observes, one is always asking—not only the world at large, but for oneself—if one is at all serious and wants to do something about this chaotic, contradictory, almost insane world. One asks: What is right action? What is a human being to do

when he is confronted with such confusion, with such misery, with actions that are fragmentary, unrelated, with actions that have no meaning whatsoever—like saving an animal and killing human beings? And strangely, when this country was at war, nobody fasted for peace, nobody burned himself in order to stop the war, though they had talked endlessly about nonviolence!

So, one sees all this extraordinary confusion and deep, abiding misery, and a frustration that has no end. Whether in a marriage, or in religious activity, or in going to the moon, or in whatever man does, there is this extraordinary sense of deep, abiding frustration. Being aware of all this, I think most people who know what is taking place in the world must be conscious of this, not only outwardly, but inwardly, inside the skin of each one of us—of this sense of utter meaningless, the utter despair, the hopeless misery of man. And watching all this, seeing all this, both outwardly and inwardly, what is a human being to do?

I think there is a difference between a human being and an individual. The individual is a local entity, living in a particular country, belonging to a particular culture, a particular society, a particular religion, and so on. A human being is not a local entity, whether he is in America, in Russia, in China, or here. And I think we

131

should bear that in mind while we are talking during these discussions. Then what is a human being to do? Because if the human being understands the totality of this problem and acts, then the individual has a relationship to that totality. But if the individual merely acts in a particular corner of the vast field of life, then his activity is totally unrelated to the whole. So one has to bear in mind that we are talking of the whole and not of the part, of the whole of the human being—in Africa, in France, in Germany, here and elsewhere. Because in the greater is the lesser, but in the lesser the greater is not. And we are talking about the individual, and the individual is the little—conditioned, miserable, frustrated, endlessly discontented, satisfied with the little things, with his little gods, with his little traditions, and so on. Whereas a human being is concerned with the total welfare, with the total misery, with the total confusion. And when we are clear on that issue, I think we can then ask: What is a human being to do?

Seeing this enormous confusion, this revolt, this brutality, wars, the endless divisions of religion, nationalities, and so on, what is a human being to do when confronted with all this? I wonder if one has asked this question at all? Or, is one only concerned with one's own particular little problem?—not that it is not important. But that problem, however little, however immediate, however urgent, relates to the whole existence of man. One cannot separate the individual's little problem from the totality of the human problems of life. And as all problems—the family problem, the social problem, the religious problem, the problem of poverty—are related, to concentrate on any one particular problem seems to me to be utterly meaningless.

So we have to consider man as a whole. And when he is faced with this tremendous challenge, not only outwardly, but in his con-

sciousness, the crisis is not only for the world outside the skin but also within the consciousness itself. The two really are not separate. I think it would be foolish to divide the world as the outer and the inner; they are both interrelated and therefore cannot be divided. But to understand this whole movement, this unitary process, one has objectively to understand not only the outward events, the various crises that we go through, but also the inward crises, the inward challenges within the field of consciousness. And when we are, as we are, faced with this issue, I am sure one must have asked, ''What is this all about?''

This is rather a lovely evening—isn't it? The sun is on the leaves. There is a nice light on the leaves, and there is the gentle movement of the branches, and the light of the setting sun is coming through the leaves and through these woods. And somehow all that beauty is unrelated to our daily living; we pass it by, we are hardly aware of it; and if we are, we just glance at it and go on with our particular problem, our endless search about nothing! And we are incapable of looking either at that light on those leaves or of hearing the birds, or of seeing clearly for ourselves nonfragmentarily, not in isolation, the totality of this issue of human existence. I hope you don't think I am becoming romantic when I look at those lights! But you know, without passion, without feeling, you cannot do anything in life. If you feel strongly about the poverty, the dirt, the squalor, the decay in this country, the corruption, the inefficiency, the appalling callousness that is going on round you, of which one is totally unaware; if you have a burning passion, an intensity about all that, and also if you have the passion to look at the flowers and the trees and the sun through the leaves—you will find that the two are not separate. If you cannot see that light on those leaves and take delight in it and be passionate in that delight, then I am afraid you will not be passionate in action either. Because action is necessary, not endless theories, endless discussions.

When you are confronted with this enormous and very complex problem of human discontent, human search, human longing for something beyond the structure of thought, you must have passion to find out. And passion is not put together by thought. Passion is something new every minute. It is a living, vital, energizing thing; whereas thought is old, dead, something derived from the past. There is no new thought, for thought is the outcome of memory, experience, knowledge, which all belong to time, which is the past. And from the past, or by going to the past, there is no passion. You cannot revive a dead thing and be passionate about that dead thing.

So, we are concerned as human beings with this problem: What is it all about? The wars, the dictatorships, the political activities, the religious fragmentation of the world as the Hindu, the Muslim, the Christian, the Protestant, the Buddhist, the Zen, this and that—what is it all about? What are we all trying to do? And where is the answer? Go back to the Upanishads, to the Gita, to the guru—you know all that—to find the answer? Or join a new cult, a new sect, a new tamasha, a new circus? Or wait for science to tell you what to do? Or escape beyond all this—go to the moon, take a drug, enjoy yourself completely, sexually, in every possible way that is being done in Europe and America without any limit? Or, enter the political field, social reform, trying to do little reforms here and there like saving the cow? You know what is going on!

So, what is one to do? And who is going to answer this question? You understand? Man has always asked this question: What is it all about; has life any meaning whatever? Because, more and more, man is becoming mechanical. And when he has leisure—and

prosperity is going to give him great leisure—how will he utilize it? And when we ask this question, where do we find the answer? Because we must ask questions, and we must always ask the right and fundamental questions. And when we do ask, we wait for somebody else to answer it—some book, some prophet, some crank with a peculiar kink in his mind. And we wait until we die, never having found the answer. Or we think we have found the answer when somebody tells us what is the purpose of life, and we like it! That is, we are guided by our inclination, by our temperament, or are compelled by circumstances; and according to circumstances, temperament, inclination, pleasure—which we think is essential—we find the answer.

So we have to banish all those superficial, rather infantile, immature answers, whether given by the politician or by the religious books or by the local guru; we have to put all that away because they are all based on authority. And more and more in the world, the generation that is coming is rejecting authority altogether. Your gods, your politics, your communism—all that has no value at all, except for the old people. And the old people generally have made an awful mess of the world, and they are the people who are going away. And they have not given the right answer either; on the contrary, they have created a dreadful world with all these things: this double talk, double thinking, double standards, and deep inward hypocrisy.

And so, when one is serious enough and has time enough to inquire into this question, how will one find the answer? And we must find the answer because there is nobody that is going to answer us. Because all organized religions have totally failed. Your superstitions, your books, your gurus, your traditions, your family—everything has failed; and you can no longer have faith in all that. And one has really no faith in all this; one pretends, but actually when it comes to daily life, all those cease to exist.

So how are you going to find out? And as the speaker has no authority whatsoever, you and I are going to take a journey together to find out. You are not going to be merely a listener, taking what you like and discarding what you don't want, accepting or rejecting. Then we do not share; then we do not travel together.

And to inquire deeply, the first thing is freedom; otherwise, you cannot possibly inquire. There must be freedom from your nationality, freedom from your religion, from your sects, from your books, from your family; otherwise, you cannot discover. It does not mean that you become a sannyasi or a monk—these poor individuals are tortured enough; they have tortured themselves in their minds, and they cannot see straight.

So really, profoundly, to inquire with all earnestness, with passion, with deep, profound interest, there must be freedom: freedom to observe, to listen, to ask, freedom to doubt everything. Because the house is burning, and there is nobody that can save that house except through a right approach to build a different society, a different culture, a different movement of life.

So, as we said, to take a journey together, which is to share together, there must be freedom—freedom not from anything particularly, but the sense of being free. I think there is a difference between the two—the feeling of freedom and the revolt from something or revolt against something. Revolt is not freedom because when you revolt, it is a reaction. And that reaction sets its own pattern, and one becomes caught in that pattern. And that pattern one thinks is a new pattern, but it is not; it is the old in a different mold. You understand? There are beatniks, the long-haired people, the LSD people who take this peculiar drug which has not come into India—probably it will come presently; you

have your own drugs anyhow. Don't laugh, sirs, we are talking about deadly serious things—and of such people as are in revolt against society or against the culture in which they live. Such revolt is a reaction which sets its own pattern, and you conform to that pattern: everybody must have long hair, go about somewhat dirty, take this or that. So this revolt, like any political or social revolt—as one has observed—will inevitably bring about another pattern which is the old pattern in a different line. Like the Russian revolution: you see, after killing thousands or millions of people, torturing them for an ideology, they are coming back to the good old bourgeois mentality.

So revolt is never freedom. Freedom is something entirely different. And freedom comes only when you see and act, not through reaction. The seeing is the acting and, therefore, it is instantaneous; when you see danger, there is no mentation; there is no discussion, there is no hesitation: there is immediate action; the danger itself compels the act. And therefore to see is to act and to be free. Therefore seeing is acting, and acting is the very essence of freedom—not revolt.

So we are taking a journey together. And to learn, to act, to listen, one must have a different quality of mind—surely! Because the old mind, the traditional mind, the mind that is Indian, lives in India, has a particular cultural inheritance—all that is the old mind, the traditional mind. And the traditional mind, whether it is Indian or American—not that there is much tradition in America, as yet; there is a great deal of it in England and so on—cannot see anything new; it will always answer according to its conditioning, according to its culture—culture being society, religion, education, food, climate, and all the rest of it.

So our problem when we are taking a journey together is to see the whole of this confusion, this misery, this anxiety, this discontent, the enormous sorrow of man—to see it totally, differently. And it is only when you see it differently, freely, that you have the right answer; then you act rightly; then that seeing is the acting.

Sirs, if you look at the whole problem of man, whether he is in America or elsewhere, from an Indian point of view, your answer will always be fragmentary. Or if you answer it from an ideological point of view, that ideological concept is derived from your inclination, from your pleasure, from your conditioning, from your temperament, from society, from the culture in which you live. Isn't it? So if you answer the total issue from a fragmentary point of view, then it will be contradictory, it will be immature. It is like answering a world problem by talking about the cow! You understand? And that is how you are answering war. You talk about saving the cow, which shows utter immaturity—and people get so terribly excited, because it is very popular. But those very same people will never stand up and say, "Let us burn ourselves to prevent war." They have never done it; they have never said, "Look, there is so much starvation in this country; let us do something, let us act." But they won't because that would entail a great deal of unpopularity and so on.

So our issue is: Can a brain which has been so conditioned for centuries upon centuries, which is the result of time—time being many, many, many centuries, a million years—a brain which is conditioned by the society in which it lives, by tradition, by the books, by the Upanishads, by the Bible, by the Koran, by the society in which it has been brought up, by the education, however rotten it may be, through which it has been— can that brain see something totally new? And you must see the new to find an answer, to respond to this challenge. Am I making myself clear? My old brain cannot possibly answer this question. My old brain is Indian,

Brahminical, or non-Brahmin hating Brahmins, or Catholic hating Protestants, or Jews hating Christians, this and that—that old mind cannot answer this enormous problem. Right?

Therefore is it possible to bring about a complete mutation in the brain cells themselves? You understand the issue? The brain cells are the result of the animal—animal instincts, animal demands, animal pursuits, animal fears, fears of wanting security, and so on and so on—reconditioned by society in which one has lived. Can those very brain cells, which are the storehouse of memory, be made completely quiet so that they can see something new? You understand the issue? Otherwise you will always answer a challenge in terms of the past. And when you answer a challenge in terms of the past, the challenge being always new, your answers will be totally inadequate. But your answers must be completely new. If they are not new and they are inadequate, there is contradiction, there is conflict, there is pain, there is misery, there is sorrow—even logically, do you understand? Even if you are intellectual—I hope you are not, because the intellect is as petty as the little brain—even intellectually, even logically, you must see that fact—the fact, not whether you wish it or you don't wish it. It is a fact because thought is matter. I am sorry, I will go into it very quickly, and we will discuss it another time. Thought is matter, thought is energy; and that energy has created thought, which has become the matter in the very brain cells themselves. You can observe all this yourself; you don't have to read books about it. You can watch it.

So the quality of the brain projects thought when confronted with a problem, with an issue; that thought is the result of memory, the past, the old. So thought is never new. And therefore thought is never free. So when you examine the problem, the issue, the challenge, as a process of thinking, then you are meeting it with the old. And therefore you will never be able to solve it. Right? Is it clear so far? You may not go directly so far, but if you do not, I am sorry; I will have to go into it.

So, our problem arises when we are confronted first with war—war outwardly or inwardly. There have been wars for five thousand and more years. There have been thousands and thousands of reforms and never a mutation, never a complete change. Man has tried various forms of social structure: a classless society, a collective society, and so on, tried dictatorships. He has tried various disciplines. He has joined monasteries, he has become a sannyasi. He has rejected all that and accepted to live merely for the day, never thinking about tomorrow, saying, "I will enjoy myself completely now; it does not matter what happens tomorrow." He has been through all this. You may not have done it as an individual; but man has, a human being has, and he has not found the answer. He has sought, and seeking is born out of this vast discontent. And seeking, searching, he will find according to his inclination and temperament and be compelled by circumstances. Therefore his search invariably ends in a little god, in a little church, in a little savior.

So we have this world problem: whether the brain cells themselves can be so totally quiet that they respond when demanded. You understand? You know, we are dealing with something that demands very close attention on your part. Probably you have never thought about this. And if you have, you have not been able to quieten the brain. Because you have not found a way to quietness; you have found a way to discipline thought, to control thought, to suppress thought. Thought is the response of memory, thought is matter; that, you have transformed or controlled or reshaped. But we are asking some-

thing entirely different, which is, thought—however clever, however cunning, however erudite—can never answer this problem. Whatever the structure thought creates—through science, through electronic brains, through the compulsion of environment, necessity, and so on—it must be the result of the old because thought is never new, as I explained. And therefore thought can never find an answer to this tremendous question.

So our question is whether thought, which is matter, which is in the brain cells themselves as greed, envy, ambition, security—the inheritance of the animal, which is all that is called evolution in time—whether those brain cells themselves, without any compulsion, can be still so that they can see something new. Right? Is this all rather too difficult?

Now I am going to go into it. You have heard this. You have heard this statement that thought is old—like the statement that time is sorrow. You hear it. And thought begins to analyze it. Thought begins to investigate itself. If you have heard this statement, this is what has happened. You have heard these two statements—time is sorrow, and thought is old—and you begin to think about them. Having heard them, having understood English, thought is beginning to interpret it, translate it. But its interpretation, its translation, is based on yesterday's experience, knowledge, thought. So it will invariably translate it according to its conditioning. That is what is taking place when you hear a statement of that kind.

Now, to hear that statement first—the English, the meaning of it—then to listen to it completely is: having heard, you have moved away to listen. You understand? You have heard that statement and the brain cells become active and begin to translate. When they don't translate, but you have merely heard the statement, then you can listen without interpretation; then the brain cells are quiet because you are giving complete attention. Attention is not concentration. When you give complete attention—with your nerves, with your ears, with your bodies, with your eyes, with the totality of your being—when you so listen completely, you will find there is neither the listener nor the thing listened to. There is only a state of complete attention in which there is neither the observer nor the observed—this is not a philosophical thing; we don't go off into some mystical affair, but we are dealing with actual facts. Then you will see, if you have gone that far on the journey, that you will respond to the challenge totally anew, not with the old brain.

Sirs, that demands tremendous discipline, not the discipline of suppression, imitation, conformity through fear, and so on. To be aware of this process, how the brain acts; to realize that thought is the response of memory accumulated in time and is therefore old; to see that thought is quiet, not compelled, not forced, because you understand that the old cannot possibly create the new or understand the new—to understand all that is itself tremendous discipline, which has nothing whatsoever to do with conformity, which is that of a soldier.

So, when you are earnest, not carried away by a flippant, sectarian outlook, then the very necessity and the urgency of the crisis, that very problem, makes you tremendously serious. And when one becomes so earnestly serious, then one can begin to observe the whole process of thinking, one can observe the individual as the human being, one can see how the individual, the local entity, destroys the total perception. Whereas the perception of the total includes the particular, and when the particular is related to the whole, its action will be harmonious with the total. The total is not an ideology. To be aware of the total process of human existence is not an ideology—the ideology of Marx, Lenin, or your particular ideology of Shankara, atma, and all the rest of it.

Ideologies have no place whatsoever because you are dealing with facts. You cannot put out a fire consuming a house with ideology, with theology; but you have to act. And to act one has to have a totally different mind. And that means really a mind that is completely quiet, that can look at the whole problem out of silence. And silence is always now because thought does not enter into silence at all.

Do you want to ask any questions? Would this be the right occasion, or would you like to wait until Tuesday morning? Would that not be better?

You know it is fairly easy to ask questions. Anybody can ask questions. But to ask the right question is very difficult because the right question demands that there be intelligence behind it, that there be sensitivity. The right question is not a momentary issue, but it implies that one has gone into it tremendously. Then if you can ask the right question, in the very asking of that right question is the right answer. Then you don't have to ask anybody. To put the right question demands an awareness of the total relationship of every problem; then the question about a particular problem—however urgent, however important—becomes unanswerable; and if it is answered, it only leads to more conflict. But when one is aware of the problem of man—his sorrows, his despair, his utter loneliness, and the tremendous boredom, which are not covered over by ideologies, by books, by belonging to some little sect—then one will put the right question. And when one puts the right question, we can then discuss, go into it freely and easily, with great affection and care.

January 15, 1967

Second Talk in Madras

Shall we continue with what we were talking about the other day? We were saying that human beings now are confronted with extraordinarily complex problems; and to meet them adequately there must be a total revolution in the very field of consciousness itself, in the very structure and cells of the brain itself. We were saying also that freedom is necessary. And that word is so loaded and can be interpreted in so many ways that we must, I think, use it very carefully.

We see that there must be a change, not a mere economic or social change, but in the very structure of our thought process. And to bring about that change, we must understand the nature of the energy that will bring that about. Because energy is necessary for everything; to do anything, to talk, to do, to function at any level, energy is necessary. We can compel that energy to function along a particular pattern, a particular ideology, whether it is Marx, Lenin, the Catholic, the Christian, the Hindu, the Muslim, or the Buddhist. And most of us function with ideologies, with formulas, with concepts; that is, first we conceive an idea, a belief, an ideology, and then, according to that, function. This functioning according to a pattern is called action. And we see in the world, not theoretically, but actually, that is how human beings function all the time.

And we also see that freedom has been thoroughly misused. Society demands order, and it is afraid of freedom because it thinks it is disorder. In nature all species of animals live according to their pattern of order—this has been established by study and so on. We, human beings, who have inherited the consciousness of the animal, though modified and refined—we also demand order. Society is based on that structure. And anybody that revolts against that structure of society is called disorderly. This is what is going on; that is, anybody who challenges the authority in power brings about a certain disorder, and society does not want disorder. Again, this is an everyday observance; and you can see this for yourself, without reading historical books and sociology.

And our problem is to have freedom and yet have a relationship within society that is not conforming. Society tries to force a human being, an individual, to conform to its pattern, and therefore the struggle begins between the human, the individual, and the structure of the society into which he fits; and society—though it is modified, though it changes—is always there to control, to shape, to mold opinion. And again one can observe this purpose going on throughout the world. That is, the "high" holds the power, and there is the "middle" that wants to usurp that power. And so there is always conflict between the middle and the high, the top.

This conflict within the pattern of society is still orderly—at least it calls it orderly—until the middle becomes so strong that it can topple the high, and that is called revolution. This process we are seeing throughout our lifetime. Historically also this is going on, and this is what has taken place also in recent years. When the middle takes over the power from the high, then it holds on to it through psychology, through propaganda, through compulsive, tortuous methods, liquidation, and so on, and establishes an ideology according to which society must function. Again you will observe, in the Russian Revolution and in other forms of revolution, that the more powerful the group on top, the more insistent, the more clever, the more brutal it is. And they deny freedom, though they may call it democratic; there is double thinking, a double way of looking—which is the denial of freedom.

On the other hand, we have in Europe—as in this country—freedom to function within that society which European culture and religion have established. Again the same formula has gone on. That is, organized religion, which is part of the culture, has established an ideology: the savior, "you must pray this way, you must think that way." And they have seen to it that every heretic is burned or liquidated, as the other side, the left, did—only now they dare not do it. So there is a battle going on, the battle of ideology on the right side and ideology on the left side, and there is a similarity of patterns in each. The organized religions throughout the world are facing this at the present moment. Because they are based on the authority of the few who represent on the one side God or Christ or Krishna or whoever it is, and on the other a social structure based on the authority of an ideology—Marx, Lenin, and so on.

So, though outwardly there is freedom in the so-called democratic society, inwardly they are so heavily conditioned that it is difficult for them to break through. In India, for example, or in the Muslim world, or in the Catholic world, there has been brainwashing for thousands of years because of the pattern which has been set as tradition, as moral values, and so on. And to break away from that becomes almost impossible because society is so big. That is, if you do break away, you might lose your job, you might not be able to get your daughter married. So it is really a matter of ideology, one on the left side and one on the right.

So man, his consciousness, has been conditioned by ideologies based on the animal inheritance and refined by greed, envy, power, prestige, competition, and so on. And there are those people who deny that, who take to *sannyasa*, who become religious, who outwardly recognize no authority but inwardly are bound hand and foot to authority. They both deny freedom. And without freedom you cannot have abundance of energy. And if you have not complete abundance of energy, you cannot bring about a change.

So, as we were saying the other day, the brain cells themselves, whether the people are living in Russia or in India or in America, have been conditioned through centuries, through time. And thought is the response of that conditioning. So thought is always old, there is nothing new; thought cannot bring about a change at all. And a revolution at a totally different level is necessary—at the level of consciousness, at the level of a mind that is conditioned and breaks through that conditioning. Of course, one can go much more into detail, but I think it is sufficiently clear that the human brain is conditioned according to some ideology, and all action takes place according to that ideology, according to that formula. So, there is a division between the ideology and the action, the action always approximating the ideology. The people who are in power see that the action does approximate the ideology—that is what is going on in China. Here, fortunately, this country is not sufficiently organized, is not so clever at propaganda, because we are more human, a little more clever, and we say, "That is propaganda."

So our issue is, our problem is: Can there be action without any ideology? Because if there is no action without an existing ideology or a new ideology, action can never be free but always frustrating and therefore always limiting; and therefore energy is wasted in friction. Please see this point clearly. We need energy to do anything and, especially, we need tremendous energy to bring about a mutation in the very brain cells themselves. Because, as we said the other day, the brain cells—through experience, through thought, through knowledge—have been so conditioned that thought is the response of that conditioning, and thought is that matter. Thought is matter. And energy has created this conditioned thinking for its own greed, for its own security, power, prestige, position, safety, and so on. It is necessary to liberate that energy from the very structure which it has created, so that it may break it.

So, our problem is whether there can be action without the limitation of an ideology, without a formula. The formula, or the ideology, and action are two different things. When we are approximating action to the formula, to the ideology, there is friction. And that friction is a waste of energy. So, action in relation to the formula, to the ideology, is a waste of energy, of time. There is the ideology given to us through propaganda, through compulsion, through various forms of traditional culture, and all the rest of it. And according to that norm we act. And the action is divided from the ideology; the division is time. Isn't it?

Sirs, we are not talking any deep philosophy, we are not giving any philosophical ideas about time. You just see what is factual. To see what is factual is very difficult because we always see the fact through an ideology. I cannot look at that tree without the ideology, the image of that tree. You cannot look at your wife, or your husband, or your political leader, or your religious leader without the ideology, the image that you have created of that person; and that person who is looking at you has an ideology about you, his image about you; and therefore the relationship between the two is a relationship of two images, two ideologies.

So, one asks oneself: Is there freedom when time interferes with action? That is, "I will do, I should, I must, I will be"—these are all activities of the past, not of the future; these are the activities which are the result of a past conditioning. Surely, I hope I am making myself clear. If not, we will discuss it on Friday morning or perhaps, if you have time, after I talk a little. So, as long as time interferes with action, there is no freedom. That is, as long as my mind is caught-in an ideology, left or right or center, or an ideology supposed to be a religious condition-

ing—which belongs to neither, but is still the outcome of all this, thought being the result of this conditioning—there is a division between ideology and action. To that we have been conditioned, and we think in these terms: "Gradually I will do this; there must be that; I will become that." So, this involvement of time postpones action. You understand? But that postponement of action never takes place if there is a danger in front of you; there is immediate action if you see a precipice, a snake, a dangerous animal, poison, and so on; there is not an ideology and then the act, which has an interval of time. Right? One has to go into it much more deeply than this. We will do so, perhaps, on another occasion.

Is there an action in which time and ideology are not involved at all? That is: seeing is doing. That is what the world is demanding. The man who has nothing—no food, no clothes—who is tortured, is not going to wait for some evolutionary process to come into being, and for his being fed according to that ideology. He says, "Feed me now, not tomorrow." Right through the world, there is a whole group of people, especially the young, who are saying that there must be action now, not tomorrow. Now is much more important than tomorrow; the present generation is far more important than the generation to come.

So, is there action without time and ideology? And that is the only revolution—which is, I see something as dangerous, and the very seeing is the acting. I see that nationalism—I am taking that as a very superficial example—is poison because it divides people and so on. I see that as poison and drop the whole cultivation of nationalism completely and immediately. And immediacy of action is freedom.

Sir, look, take a very stupid example. If you smoke and if you know what effect it has—that it will give you lung disease, and the doctors have threatened you with all that—and yet there is the desire, the pleasure of something to do with your hands, which is involved in smoking, can you act immediately and drop it? Because there the very seeing is the acting. Now, take a deeper pleasure, because most of us are guided by inclination, which means pleasure. We are guided by the principle of pleasure: "I like this and I don't like that; this is profitable, that is not profitable," and so on. It is much more complex than that, but that is the basis of our action inwardly, psychologically, and also outwardly. Take any pleasure and see what is involved in that pleasure. Don't take time—time for examination, time for analysis. See immediately what is involved in it: frustration, pain, sorrow, a thought process which is the continuity of an experience which has been dead and which you want to continue, which will give you pleasure as sex or something else.

One has to be aware of this pleasure principle and act immediately. That is, seeing what is involved and, not admitting time, acting—that requires a great deal of attention, a great deal of awareness of the whole problem of the nature and the structure of an ideology, how we develop an ideology. You may reject an outward ideology, but inwardly you have your own ideology. You have to be aware of all that—not through a process of analysis, because that admits time. The process of analysis is to think about this a little more carefully and examine it very closely. We are used to this analytical process, finding out the cause; and we think that by finding out the cause, we can drop the effect. But that is not always so, and that takes time. It may take time—two minutes or six months or more to examine the whole process, layer after layer. Analyzing everything, bit by bit, takes time; and when you admit time, there are other complications coming into that

field: postponement, conflict, friction, the authority of the past as memory, and so on.

So, is it possible to see something so directly that that very seeing is the action, now? You are probably sitting in front of a tree, watching that tree. There is a distance between you and that tree—distance in time as well as in space. To go from where you are to that tree takes time: one second, two seconds. Therefore between you the observer and the thing observed there is a time interval. Why does this time interval exist at all? It exists because you are looking at that tree with thought, with memory, with knowledge, with experience, with botanical information. So actually you are not looking at the tree, but the thought is looking at that tree. Right? So, the relationship between you and the tree is the relationship of your image about that tree, and therefore you are not in contact with that tree at all. Only when you are in contact, you are in relationship; and you can only have that relationship when there is no image—which means no ideology, and therefore there is action.

So, can you look at that tree without this time-space interval? That is, can you look at your wife or your husband or your political leaders, religious leaders, and so on, without the time interval? If you can look at that tree without that time interval, then your relationship to that tree is entirely different. You are directly in contact, therefore directly capable of action. And by taking the drug LSD—not that we have taken it—it is said that this time interval disappears. I believe bhang, hashish, and other forms of drugs remove this time interval. Therefore the experience of seeing that tree without the time interval is something extraordinary because for the first time you are acting—not secondhand, not through an ideology which compels you to act in a different manner. Right?

So, freedom is this action which springs immediately from seeing. Now, seeing is also listening—that is, to listen without the time interval. It is very simple if you know how to do it. And you must know. Otherwise your mind becomes stale, dull, caught and conditioned by an ideology, and therefore the mind can never be fresh, young, innocent, alive. As we said, as long as there is a time interval between the observer and the observed, that time interval creates friction, and therefore it is a waste of energy; that energy is gathered to its highest point when the observer is the observed, in which there is no time interval. You hear that statement. But you have not listened to it. There is a difference between "hearing" and "listening." You can hear words, thinking you understand those words intellectually. Then you will ask, "How am I who have heard the words to put those words into action?" You cannot put words into action! So you translate the words into thought, into an ideology; and then you have got the pattern, and according to that pattern you are going to act. Now, listening is not to have that time interval at all. So listening, as seeing, is acting.

We have inherited violence from the animal. But the animal has not invented nonviolence, the ideology; human beings have invented it. The violence is there, and ideology is nonfactual. What is factual is violence. But we think that by having an ideology about violence we are going to get rid of violence—which is sheer nonsense, as it has been proved in this country. You have preached nonviolence for forty years, and when the time comes for violence, you all jump into it! So the fact is one thing and ideology is another. We are violent; we have inherited it through the animal. The animal in us has two rights, property rights and sexual rights. And violence is based on them. It is a fact that we are violent. Now, you hear the fact, and the hearing becomes merely intellectual, and you say, "How can I live without violence when Pakistan, China, or some other country is going to destroy me? I must protect myself." And you have innumerable arguments against and for, and so you are still violent at the end of it.

So can you see the fact of violence—the fact not only outside of you but also inside you—and not have any time interval between listening and acting? This means by the very act of listening you are free from violence. You are totally free from violence because you have not admitted time, an ideology through which you can get rid of violence. This requires very deep meditation, not just a verbal agreement or disagreement. We never listen to anything; our minds, our brain cells are so conditioned to an ideology about violence that we never look at the fact of violence. We look at the fact of violence through an ideology, and the looking at violence through an ideology creates a time interval. And when you admit time, there is no end to violence; you go on showing violence, preaching nonviolence.

Now, you have merely heard a series of statements; you have not listened. Because your mind, your way of life, the whole structure of society denies it, prevents you from looking at a fact and from being entirely free from it immediately. So thought says, "I will think about it; I will see whether it is profitable to be without violence." That is, you are admitting the time interval while the house is burning. The house is burning—which is the result of this violence throughout the world. And you say, "Let us think about it and find out which ideology is the best for putting out the fire." That is exactly what is happening with regard to starvation in this country. The communists, the socialists, the capitalists, the congress, and so on—they all have ideologies upon which they are going to feed the people; and ideologies will never feed the people. What will feed the people is not to be concerned with the ways of feeding them but getting together and feeding them, which means no personal prestige, no party, no system, no leader. Because then we are concerned with feeding, organizing together the world in which we have to live.

So, our concern then is that we see that immediate mutation is necessary. Mutation is total revolution, something totally new. We have tried all the other ways—the democratic way, the communist way, the religious way, forming different societies, plans, and so on—and they have not succeeded at all; man remains in perpetual misery, in great anxiety, in great uncertainty. And to bring about a radical revolution in that is the only issue, as the only political issue is the unity of mankind—not whether you have Kerala different from the rest of the country, thus breaking up this unfortunate country into linguistic and little parcels of land. The one problem for the politician—if there should be a politician at all—is to bring about the unity, the economic and social unity of mankind, not divided by nationalities, by sovereign governments. It is only then that we can live happily, peacefully in this world. That is the function of the organizer. And probably the computers, the electronic brains, will take that over; not the little narrow-minded, ideological politicians!

And the other issue is whether we human beings can change completely, immediately, so that there is no tomorrow. You understand, sirs? Because tomorrow is an idea. A man who is completely attentive now, completely watching, listening, seeing—for him there is no time. Because in that watching, listening, seeing, the observer is not creating time through which he can escape into some form of pleasure.

Sirs, look at the problem. Most of us have this problem of fear: the problem of uncertainty, the problem of death, of the unknown, the problem of losing a job, the fear of not being loved, the fear of being lonely, and the fear of living in a world that is like death. There is this fear. Again a great deal of it has been inherited from the animal, to which we have added psychological fears. We are talking about psychological fears. When we understand the deep fears, then we will be able to meet the animal fears. But first to be concerned with the animal fears will never help you to understand the psychological fears.

So most of us have these deep-rooted psychological fears—fear of tomorrow, fear of what is going to happen tomorrow. Have you ever examined how this fear comes into being? Here I am today, fairly well, having food, clothes, and shelter; and I am afraid of tomorrow! How does that fear come into being? Thought comes. Please listen. Thought, because it is secure today, thinks about tomorrow and says, "I may be uncertain tomorrow." So, thinking about tomorrow creates the fear. You understand, sirs? There is death, which we will all have to face one day or the other, and we are afraid of that thing which is unknown. I am living, I go to my office for the next forty years—which is a terrible idea—I think automatically, inefficiently, I carry on in the field I have known, and I am afraid of something I don't know—death. Thought is the very essence of the known, is the result of the known, and therefore thought can never free the mind from the known. So thought thinks about that thing called death, and the very thinking about it is the beginning of fear.

So is it possible to live completely today, because I know the whole machinery of thinking? The issue is not how to end thought, because the thought that says, "I must end thought," is still thought. Therefore it is not ending thought at all, but it is to find out if we can live so completely that there is no tomorrow for thought to think about. Only then is there freedom in action. You understand, sirs? Then freedom is not an ideology, it is not something that you are going to cultivate and gain ultimately.

So the relationship of man, the human being, to the world in which he is living—which is society—must radically change. Any observant person knows that. You cannot go back to your old gods or your old books. That is silly; they have gone and are finished. And we have to live in the world that is changing so completely technologically, the outward change being much more than the inward change; and the inward change is absolutely necessary for man to live peacefully. And that peace is not a matter of time, not a matter of tomorrow. That peace can only be now. And there is that peace when this time interval totally disappears, when you deny. That is, when you look at that tree so attentively that thought disappears altogether, you are really in contact with that tree; then the observer is the observed. And hence there is no conflict at all, and therefore there is that extraordinary energy. And it is that energy that is going to bring about a different society in the world.

You want to ask any questions with regard to what we have been talking about?

Question: Will you kindly tell us how thought is matter?

KRISHNAMURTI: The questioner asks how thought is matter. Have you looked at that sunset? Please do look at it. The tree against that light, the golden light of the setting sun—see the beauty of it nonverbally. You understand, sir, "nonverbally"? The moment you use the word "how beautiful," that very word is thought, which is matter. Right? So you can find out for yourself how thought is matter-energy. Must I go through that again? We will keep it for another day, sir.

But what is important is to look at that tree against that light. Because in most of our lives there is no beauty at all. We never look

at a tree. We are never aware of the squalor and the dirt on the road. And without beauty there is no love. You cannot see that sunset and that marvelous tree against that light if you have no love. And love is not pleasure. Love is not desire. Love is that act of seeing that beauty, that extraordinary light. And to see it is to love it; and that is love. And without it you cannot do anything.

And in this barren, desert world, there is no love at all. There is a great deal of pleasure; there is a great deal of desire. And when desire and pleasure play the greatest role in the world, the world becomes a desert. That is, your life becomes a desert. Your everyday life has no meaning because it is only when there is love that life becomes something entirely different. And you cannot have love if there is no beauty. And beauty is not something you see: a beautiful tree, a beautiful woman, a beautiful man, a light on the water, the moon, or a beautiful building. Beauty is not in a building. There is beauty only when your heart and mind know what love is.

January 18, 1967

Third Talk in Madras

We have been talking about the necessity of a total revolution, not a financial or social or merely economic, outward revolution, but rather a mutation, a complete change in the whole structure of consciousness. If I may, I would like to go this evening into the question of whether it is at all possible for a human being, placed as he is and living in this present world with all the complications, to bring about this radical change. That implies, doesn't it, a real rejuvenation of the mind, a renewal. And the brain, as well as the totality of the mind, is by usage, by habit, by custom, like any other machine and wears itself out through constant friction. Any machine, if it is to run smoothly, lastingly, must have no friction at all. And the moment there is friction, there is waste of energy. We all know this, at least theoretically.

And one asks oneself, first, whether it is possible for one to be free of all friction; and, secondly, whether in this freedom the mind which has been used, as well as the brain cells which have functioned, worked in a certain pattern, can transform themselves. We see the human mind, the human brain, is constantly in friction in all its relationships with regard to things—which is property— with regard to people, and with regard to ideas and ideology. There is always friction, and this friction in relationship must naturally wear down the brain cells themselves. And also one asks oneself whether it is possible to end this friction, this constant struggle, this effort, without creating another series of norms, patterns, which in turn become the cause of friction; that is, whether a man can live first without any friction in this world at all, and whether a brain that has been mechanically functioning, mechanically following a particular routine, a particular habit, either technological or psychological, that has used itself from childhood through friction and therefore is wearing itself out constantly, can become rejuvenated, can become quite young and fresh. That is one of the problems.

We can see in the world everything is declining; there is birth and there is gradual decay which is death—death being not only the ending of the organism but also psychological ending and the fear of not being able to continue.

And one sees in nature, as well as in oneself, that what has continuity has no beginning. It is only something that ends that has a new beginning. Like in those climates where the seasons are very marked—winter, spring, summer, and autumn—you see how the tree rejuvenates itself in springtime, puts forth fresh leaves, new flowers, new perfume; and in the winter it dies, to be reborn again, to resurrect itself. The problem is whether it is possible for the brain cells themselves to be reborn—cells which have been functioning almost mechanically in all relationships.

Now, to understand this and to go into it totally, one has to consider the whole of consciousness, what we mean by that word *consciousness*—not philosophically, not theoretically, hypothetically, but actually—and to discover for oneself what this consciousness is. We use that word very easily. But we have never asked ourselves what it is. If one asks oneself what it is, then one discovers for oneself, without being told by another, that it is the totality of thinking, feeling, and acting. It is the total field in which thought functions, or relationship exists. All motives, intentions, desires, pleasures, passing happiness and fears, inspiration, longing, hope, despair, anxiety, guilt, fear—all that is in that field. And we have never been aware of the totality of it. One has to be totally aware of one's consciousness, not at the periphery, not on the outside at the edges, but right from the inside to the out and from the outside in.

And we have divided this consciousness as the active and the dormant, the higher and the lower. The upper level of consciousness relates to everyday activity—like going to the office—all that takes place outwardly, learning a new technique. And below that is the so-called unconscious, the thing with which we are not totally familiar, which expresses itself occasionally through certain intimations, hints, or through dreams.

So we have divided this consciousness, which is a whole field, into the conscious, a little corner, and the rest, the unconscious. Please just follow this, neither agreeing nor disagreeing. We are stating certain facts, and about facts there is neither agreement nor disagreement. It is so. How you interpret a fact, how you translate it, depends on your opinion, your condition, your desires, your pleasures; and from that arises opinion. If you say this is not a microphone but a telephone, if you have a fixed opinion about that and I have fixed opinion about this, then you and I never contact. But if we stick to facts, a tree is a tree—a fact, both outwardly and inwardly, inside the skin.

So we are dealing with facts and not with opinions—not Shankara's or Buddha's opinions; not the opinions of what they said or did not say; not the opinions of the philosophers, of the modern psychologists, and so on. We are dealing with facts, and you and I can discover them as facts, and therefore we can put aside altogether this question of agreement and disagreement.

As we have said, we have divided this consciousness as the conscious and the unconscious. We are occupied with a little corner of it, which is most of our life; and of the rest we are unconscious, we don't even know how to go into it. We know it only when there is a crisis, when there is a certain urgent demand, a certain immediate challenge, which has to be responded to immediately; only then do we act as total entities. Having divided consciousness into the conscious and the unconscious, we look from the conscious—which is only a small part of it—at the whole of consciousness.

Now the speaker is asking: Is there such a thing as the unconscious at all? Is there something that is hidden, which has to be interpreted through dreams, through examination, analysis, and so on, which we have called the unconscious? Or is it only that, because you have paid so much attention to the little corner of this field which you call the conscious and have not paid total attention to the whole field, you are not aware of the whole content of the field? To go into this very carefully, you have to look at your own consciousness; you cannot just agree with me, accept a few words with a shake of your head! Because if you don't follow this, you will not be able to follow what is coming. I do not know what is coming. I have not prepared the talk, but I am moving, examining; and therefore, if you are not able to follow the examination closely, you will not be able to proceed further.

So is it possible to be totally aware of this whole field of consciousness and not merely a segment, a part, a fragment of it? If one is able to be aware of the totality, then one is functioning all the time with one's total attention and not with a divided attention, a partial attention. This is important to understand because that way we are totally aware of the whole field of consciousness, and there is no friction. It is only when you divide consciousness as the peripheral, the edges and the center, the superficial and the deeper, that you break it up. And when there is a functioning of the totality of consciousness—which is thought, feeling, and action, totally—then there is no friction at all. That is, when you are totally attentive to anything, there is no division. If you are totally attentive to that sunset, to that tree, or to the color of the sari or dress, in that, there is no division as the observer and the observed. It is only when there is a division that there is friction.

Now, is it possible for a brain which has broken up its own functioning, its own thinking, in terms of fragments, to be aware totally of the whole field? You understand my question? Am I making myself clear? Please, as I said, I have not prepared the talk, I am not reeling off. So I must go step by step as I talk. I am asking whether it is possible to be totally aware of this fragmentary process of life, which is consciousness—which is thought, feeling, and action—in which there is fear, despair, ambition, competition, agony, guilt, enormous sorrow. Is it possible for the brain cells, which have produced this consciousness, to renew themselves? It is only when there is total renewal that you are capable of looking at it totally. Sir, look, let us put it differently.

As we said at the beginning, it is only when there is an ending, there is a new beginning. It is only when time comes to an end that there is a new way of living. Now, these brain cells are used to a continuity through habit, through tradition, through their own demands to be secure, to be certain. If one examines one's thought, one will find that the brain, caught in an ideology which will always be perpetual, though modified, has functioned that way. Can one die to that? The brain which has functioned in its mechanical, reactionary way, the brain cells which are the inheritance of the animal, greed, domination, and all such thoughts and feelings—can all that, which is the memory of yesterday, die? The memory of yesterday, the memory of a thousand yesterdays, from which thoughts spring, which is today, those thoughts creating the tomorrow—can that memory completely come to an end? We are not talking of ending the technological, scientific, economic knowledge which man has accumulated through centuries—that, one must not end. But we are talking of dying to yesterday's memory which the brain cells have gathered, which has become the matter. From that there is thinking which becomes energy, which again reshapes the matter and again conditions future thought.

Have you ever tried to die to a pleasure without conflict, without suppressing it, without controlling it—just to let it go? Have you ever done it? Have you ever tried to die actually to a pleasure without argument—without saying, "Is it worthwhile? Should it be? Should it not be?"—without all the mentation that goes on in sustaining that pleasure, to end that pleasure instantly? I am afraid not! If you have tried it, you will see that in that there is no friction, no effort involved at all. It is an ending of something which has given you pleasure, not because somebody asks you to give up the pleasure, but because you see the whole structure of pleasure and its meaning. The very seeing, as we said last time we met here, is the action, and therefore the action is the ending.

You know how pleasure comes into being? We must go into it fairly quickly because there is much more to talk over together this evening. Please, one can see that pleasure comes through desire. And how does desire come into being? Again factually—not theoretically, not hypothetically because somebody has said something about it which you have read, remembered, repeated, and that has become part of your knowledge, and you express that knowledge as though it were your own. You think you have understood it, but actually you are merely repeating something which you have heard, and that has no value at all. But if you discover it for yourself, it has an extraordinary, immediate impact.

How does desire come? You see something; there is first seeing—that sunset, that tree, that face, that car. And when you look at it, there is a sensation, a contact, a relationship: "How delightful that is! What a beautiful face! What a lovely car!" So through observation, seeing, there is sensation; from sensation there is contact, either actual contact or contact with the thing itself as expressed in possession, as sensation; and from that sensation there is desire. That is very simple. Then when that desire has arisen by looking at that sunset, thought comes in and says, "How marvelous! How beautiful!" Thought sustains that desire. Then this thought sustaining that desire becomes pleasure. You see this? Not because I say so, but this is an actual fact, if you observe. You have seen a beautiful car—unfortunately not many in India—the lines, the color, the power behind it. And you have a desire. The desire then is to possess it. And the thought about that car, about having it, going about in it, showing yourself off in it—all that gives pleasure. So through desire, thought produces, sustains pleasure. This is very simple. Sexual memory and the continuous thinking about it, the image, the picturization, and so on—all that is a process of thinking; out of that there arises a pleasure, a repetition of that. And there is the same process with regard to fear, with regard to sorrow. Thinking about something constantly creates either pleasure or fear. Pleasure implies, the whole structure of pleasure is involved in fear, sorrow, frustration, pain. And to end pleasure you have to see totally the whole structure of pleasure. To see the whole structure totally is to be totally attentive to pleasure. And when you are totally attentive to pleasure, there is not the observer who says, "I must keep it," or "I must discard it"; so there is a total ending.

So a mind, a brain, which has accumulated pleasure through the memory of a particular incident, and projects out of that memory and thinks about that incident, can end pleasure totally when there is complete attention to the structure of pleasure. As we are talking now, please look, if you can, at that tree with complete attention. Attention is not concentration—concentration is a silly thing to worry about. In attention there is no thought, there is no sense of enforcement. When you completely attend to that tree, in that state of attention there is no verbalization, there is no compulsion, there is no imitation; you are merely observing that tree with all your being—with your body, with your nerves, with your eyes, with your ears, with your mind, with the totality of your energy. And when you do that, there is no observer at all; there is only attention. It is only when there is inattention that there is the observer and the observed.

Now, can you give total attention to this field of consciousness, as you gave total attention to that tree? Total attention to the tree is nonverbalization of that tree, the nonnaming of that tree. When you say, "I like that tree, I don't like it," you are not attentive. So attention comes into being only when you have understood the nature of friction and effort. You cannot force yourself to be attentive by practicing attention day by day—which is sheer nonsense. You can, by practicing day after day, gain concentration, which is a process of exclusion. But in attention there is no practice at all; there is instant attention. It may last a second, it may last an hour, but it is instantaneous. And that instantaneous attention comes into being when you have understood the nature of pleasure, the nature of friction, the nature of concentration.

So, when there is total attention to yesterday's psychological memory, then that memory comes to an end; the brain cells and the mind then are free. That is, to put it differently, life is a process of experience, which is challenge and response, the response being according to the conditioning of the brain cells. Surely! That is, you are conditioned as a Hindu, a Muslim, or God knows what. And when you are challenged, you naturally respond according to your conditioning. This response being inadequate, the experience then is also inadequate. The inadequacy of anything leaves a memory. Are you following all this? If you have lived through something totally, it leaves no mark. The marking is memory. But if you live partially, not completely, if you have not gone through it to the very end, then the partial, inadequate response leaves a mark which is memory, and from that memory you respond again to tomorrow's challenge, which again strengthens the memory and so on.

So in dying to yesterday, the today is new. But most of us are afraid to die to it. Because we say, "I do not know what is going to happen tomorrow.'' And death is inevitable. Now death implies not only the end of the organism but also psychological ending. If you have lived completely, you are dying every day; therefore, there is no fear. In dying to everything that psychologically you have held on to—namely your memories, your hopes, your despairs, self-pity—there is a resurrection; such dying is a rebirth.

Now, most of us know there is death, but we do not know how to face it; and therefore we invent various theories like reincarnation—that is, there is a permanent entity as you, the soul, the atma, whatever you like to call it, which is going to continue in the next life. And the next life will be the result of the present life, which means the next life will depend on how you live the present life, how you behave, how you think, how you feel, the totality of your life, not just your going to the office and back home. If you believe in reincarnation—that is, you are going to be reborn in the next life—then that life will be conditioned by your present life. Obviously!

So, if you believe in reincarnation, what matters is how you live today. But you don't believe in it because that is just a theory. But if you really believe in it, you are something vital, urgent; your everyday behavior will be totally different. That belief is merely a cover to escape from the fear of death, not how to live!

And there is another problem involved, which is whether thought is identified with a particular entity as the 'me', and whether that thought will continue as thought, not as the soul. Because the soul, the atma, is still the invention of thought; whether Shankara said it or somebody else said it, it is just an invention of thought and therefore has no validity at all. But what has validity is the fact that you have lived these 20, 40, 50, 80 years functioning within a very narrow field, within a field of anxiety, hope, despair, sorrow, misery, conflict, and the agony of existence. And the problem is whether that thought has any continuity, not a permanent thought—there is no such thing as a permanent thought. There is no such thing as a new thought. Thought is always old because it is the response of yesterday's memory.

So, when we talk about continuity, what is continuous is the known, and the known is the thought. And we have to find out whether the known as the 'me' is undergoing constant change. Organically, the organism, the body, is changing all the time. But psychologically we do not change all the time. We have a fixed center—which is memory—from which all thoughts spring, and we want that center, which is the memory of yesterday, to continue. And whether that thought has a continuity is another problem which we will not go into at all now, because that is immaterial and because I know what the mind does—immediately you place your hope in that continuity of thought. Before, you had hope in a permanent entity, the soul, the atma, and all the rest of it. And you have placed your hope in it because you have never understood what it is to die psychologically. But if thought has continuity, that thought is modifying itself all the time. And if that is not completely understood, you will place hope in that, instead of in the atma. That is, you hope your own particular, shoddy little thought will continue!

So what we are talking about is an ending which has a new beginning, an ending to something that ends and therefore begins anew. Consciousness is thought, feeling, and action. Memory, despairs, agonies, sorrows, ambition, power, prestige—all that is within that field which you call consciousness. We are asking whether the totality of consciousness can end totally so that there is a new field, a new dimension altogether. And that can only come into being when you know how to die, when there is dying to yesterday.

We are asking whether the brain cells, with their memories, can end. The brain cells have their own technological continuity, and we are not talking about the ending of that but about the ending of the accumulation of memories, tradition, fears. And you will notice that it can end when you give total attention to whatever you are doing.

You know what meditation is? Meditation is a very difficult word because it is loaded. There are systems of meditation; there are people who practice, day after day, certain forms of repetition of words and so on; they concentrate, they learn a definite method—all that is called meditation. But it is really not meditation at all; it is learning a new technique to achieve a certain result. As you learn how to run a machine, you learn how to run a certain psychological machine so that you will attain a certain bliss which you have already established as the original, the final bliss; for that, you practice. And that practice day after day, hoping to arrive at that ultimate bliss or whatever you like to call it, is called meditation. In that there is friction, there is suppression, separation, concentration, exclusion; there is no attention. And the meditation we are talking about is not the meditation which is loaded with words, which you know.

Meditation is the awareness of the totality of the field of consciousness, which means the totality of the whole thought process—not only the thought processes in learning technology, such as when you learn a language, or when you learn how to run a machine, how to run a computer, and so on, but also those in learning about the totality of the thinking, feeling organism. To be choicelessly aware of all that is to be in a state of meditation. In that state of meditation the totality of the brain cells is utterly quiet, not projecting any thought, any hope, any desire, any pleasure—which are all the responses of the past. The brain cells can be completely

quiet only when there is total attention of the whole of consciousness—which is thought, feeling, and action. Then you will see, if you have gone that far, that there is a state of attention in which there is still movement of the brain cells without the reaction.

What a lovely sunset! Look at it! We do not know what silence is. We only know silence when noise stops, and we are partially aware of the noise of consciousness. But we don't know what silence is, apart from the noise of consciousness. We are talking of a silence which is not the ending of a noise—like beauty, like love, which is not the ending of something. Love is not the ending of hate or the ending of desire. Love is something utterly different from desire, from hate. You don't come to love by suppressing desire, as you have been taught through literature, through the saints, and all the rest of it.

You end a noise because you want silence. But the silence which comes into being when noise ceases is not silence at all. Last night there was a wedding going on next door. It began at about half past five, kept up until ten, began again this morning at half past four, stopped around about nine, and again began this afternoon. And they were making a hideous noise which they called music! I am not criticizing the people who listened to it, who enjoyed it. And when that noise stopped, there was an extraordinary silence. And that is all we know—the silence when noise stops, the silence when thought stops. But that is not silence at all.

Silence is something entirely different— like beauty, like love. And this silence is not the product of a quiet mind, not the product of the brain cells which have understood the whole structure, and which say, "For God's sake, let me be quiet." Then the brain cells themselves produce that silence, but that is not silence. Silence is something entirely different. Silence is not the outcome of attention in which the observer is the observed and there is no friction—that can produce another form of silence, but that is not silence. Silence you cannot describe. You are waiting for the speaker to describe it so that you can compare it, interpret it, carry it home and bury it! Silence cannot be described. What can be described is the known; and the freedom from the known can only come into being when there is a dying every day to the known—to the hurts, to the flatteries, to the image that you have built about your wife, your husband, your society, your political leader, your religious leader—so that the brain cells themselves become fresh, young, innocent. But that innocence, that freshness, that quality of tenderness, gentleness, does not produce love. That is not the quality of beauty or silence. Unless the mind has become aware of that, our life becomes rather shallow, empty, and meaningless.

But that silence which is not the ending of a noise is only a small beginning. It is like going through a small hole to an enormous, wide, expansive ocean, to an immeasurable, timeless state. But that state one cannot understand verbally. You have to understand the whole structure of consciousness and the meaning of it—the pleasure, the despair, the whole of that—and the brain cells have to become quiet. Then perhaps you may come upon that mystery which nobody can give, nor can anybody describe.

January 22, 1967

Fourth Talk in Madras

This is the last talk, isn't it, at least for this year.

We have been considering during these past three talks various problems that each one of us has to face. The outward decay and the inward deterioration of man, the extraordinary progress in science and, inwardly, a dead center—a center which is the result of many centuries of conditioning, of many centuries of conformity, fear, imitation, obedience; a center which feels lonely, empty, guilty, deeply frustrated, everlastingly seeking something. We have been over all these things, perhaps not in great detail, but we have considered somewhat those issues.

And this evening, I think we ought to consider, if we may, why we seek at all? Why this human endeavor to find, to seek something beyond all sensuous, material welfare? Why are we not satisfied with the things of the senses but are always attempting to go beyond them? Why is each one of us, deep down in our hearts, trying to find a god, a truth, a peace, a state of mind that will not be disturbed, a thing that is not transient, which is not made up of time, which is not the result of clever, cunning, theological thinking? I think it will be worthwhile if we could go into it a little bit this evening.

Apparently, throughout the past ages, man has always sought something beyond himself—God—sought some permanent state and called it by ten thousand names! And not being able to find it, he has relied on others—on saints, on saviors, on those who assert they know. Or, he has resorted to the worship of symbols—a tree, a particular river, a particular idea, an ideology, a particular image made by the hand or by the mind. And he worships that according to his inclination—which is really according to his pleasure, though he may call it by a different name—and according to his temperament, or compelled by circumstances, as most people are. Most people believe because they have been brought up to believe—or they do not believe because they have also been brought up not to believe—a belief in a particular doctrine, a particular prophet, a particular saint, or a deity which they themselves have projected out of their own background. And each one of us, I am sure, has done that. And even that does not satisfy, even that does not give sufficient assurance, sufficient certainty; it is not a guide in life. Because we know very well that what we project from our own background, from our own conditioning, is a part of our thinking, which is the result of our own memories, experiences, and knowledge, and therefore time-bound, and therefore not valid at all. Deep down, most of us know this. And outwardly we pretend, using the word *God* when it suits us, or having a particular ideology, or denying the whole works as nonintellectual, bourgeois, stupid, and so on.

So, we are always seeking. I wonder why you are all here! What is it each one of us is seeking? And what do we mean by that word *seeking?* Because that search is related to our daily life. We are not seeking something apart from our daily existence. If we are, then we live in two different contradictory worlds, and that leads to extraordinary misery and confusion. You believe one thing, and you do something else! You worship, or at least pretend to worship, a deity. And your own life is shoddy, petty, narrow, afraid, without much significance; or, if it has not much significance, you try to give significance to it by inventing a theory! So we are always after something!

I wonder why we seek at all? It has been stated throughout religious history that if you do certain things—conform to certain patterns, torture your mind, suppress your desires, control your thoughts, not indulge sexually, put a limit to your appetites—after sufficient torture, after sufficient distortion of the spirit and the mind and the body, you are assured that you will find something beyond! And that is what mankind has done, either in isolation by going off into the desert or to the mountain or to a cave, or wandering from village to village alone, or joining a monastery, forcing the mind to conform to a pattern that has been established, and which

guarantees that if you will do certain things, you will find. A tortured mind, a mind that is distorted, a mind that is broken, made dull through disciplines, through conformity—obviously such a mind, however much it may seek, will find what it wants to find, will find according to its own tortured form.

So to find out actually if there is, or if there is not, something which the mind has sought throughout time, surely a different approach, a different demand is necessary. Because obviously if man had found, or if a few human beings had found, that real thing, then life would be entirely different; life would not be a tortured, despairing, anxious, guilty, fearful, competitive existence. Those people would have asserted what it was and so on.

So, it seems to me that one has to find a different approach altogether. We approach from the periphery, from the outer border; and slowly, through time, through practice, through renunciation, through denial, through control, through obedience, through innumerable deceptions, and so on, we gradually come to the center. That is, we work from the periphery, from the outside, towards the inside. That is what we have done. At least that is what man has been instructed to do: Begin with the control of the senses; control your thoughts, concentrate, hold them tight, don't let them wander away; don't be carried by lust; don't become emotional, turn that emotion into devotion, sublimate it; do everything to make the mind narrow, little, petty, shoddy; and from the outward gradually you will come to that inner flower, inner beauty, love, and so on. That has been the traditional approach: Begin from the outer and work inward; peel off little by little; take time; next life will do or tomorrow will do, but peel off, take off, until you come to the very center. And when you come to that center, you generally find that there is nothing at all! Because your mind is incapable; it is made dull, insensitive. The mind that has lived in insecurity, in fear, is hoping to find security and a state in which there is no fear—that has been the accepted norm of all religions.

And also they have said: Behave righteously, help another, love another, be kind. And they—the organized religions especially—have always emphasized: Don't be sexual; do anything else, but don't do that; be competitive, be ruthless, go to war, fight each other, destroy each other, be greedy, assert, dominate, be brutal; but don't do that one thing.

So, if one has observed this process throughout the world and throughout the religious history of mankind, one asks oneself if there is not a different approach altogether. One sees this is too immature, too childish, too infantile. At least if one has understood all that, one rejects all that. Is there not a different approach altogether? That is, burst from the center, explode from the center, not from the periphery. That is, act, be, feel, think, live from a different world altogether—not a world or a dimension invented by the mind, which only leads to a neurotic state, an unbalanced existence. First see the difficulty involved in it.

Human beings have been taught to approach something which is not measurable by the mind, by forcing the mind to accept certain patterns of behavior or dogma, to perform certain rituals, and gradually come to that. That has been the norm, the tradition. And you can go on that way indefinitely for the rest of your life or for many lives; and you will never get it because obviously your mind is a mind that has been made dull, insensitive, that has no appreciation of what is beauty, that knows no love, that can repeat phrases out of the Gita, the Bible, and so on. Such a tortured mind—what can it find? Nothing whatsoever except an idea, a concept. And that idea, that concept, has been projected by a mind which is afraid, which is guilty, which is lonely, which wants to escape from all turmoil, which has denied the outer world altogether. Though such a mind lives in the outer world and is tortured, it denies that world. So, what can such a mind find? Obviously it finds its own projection, and therefore it can reject that.

Now, you are good enough to listen to, or hear, what is being said. But to go much deeper into the issue, you have to reject it, not intellectually but actually, completely; no ceremonies, no organized religions, no dogmas, no rituals—you have completely to deny all that. This means you are already standing alone. Because the world follows, accepts the traditional approach, and you deny totally that approach; and therefore you are already in much deeper conflict with society, with your parents, with your neighbors, with your world. And you must be in conflict; otherwise, you become a respectable human being, and a respectable human being cannot possibly come near that infinite, immeasurable reality.

So, you have started by denying something utterly false—not as a reaction; if it is a reaction, you will create a pattern into which you will be trapped. You deny because you understand the futility, the stupidity of a mind that has been tortured. And because you deny the way which religions have asserted, you may be called irreligious. But that is the path of true religion: to deny completely the false. You have to do it. If you pretend intellectually that it is a very good idea and do not do it, then you cannot go any further. When you do it, you do it with tremendous intelligence because you are free, not because you are frightened. Therefore you create a great disturbance in yourself and around you. Therefore you step out of the trap of respectability.

Then you are no longer seeking. That is the first thing to realize: no seeking at all.

Because when you seek, what are you seeking? Go into it. When you seek, you are really window-shopping—one deity after another, the Christian, the Catholic, the Protestant, the Hindu, the various divisions and subdivisions of Hinduism, Buddhism, and so on. What is the urge to seek? And what are you going to find? Obviously, when you seek, you are seeking away from the actual fact to something which will give you greater pleasure. Do listen to all this. One seeks because one is dissatisfied with the normal, shallow, narrow, cunning existence. You are dissatisfied with it; it has no meaning. The long boring hours in an office, the long hours in a kitchen, the routine, the habit—all that becomes most extraordinarily excruciating and painful, and you want to avoid and escape from all that. And so you follow. When you don't follow because you have rejected authority—every sensible, intelligent man rejects all religious authority, including that of the speaker—then what are you seeking? What is the motive of your search? In the laboratory of a scientist, the scientist knows exactly what he seeks, he knows what his motive is. But here, as a human being, what are you seeking? That search has a tremendous meaning to our relationship to society. Please listen to this. The search that each one of us is indulging in has a direct relationship to society because we are escaping from society, the society which each one of us has created. Follow this. Each one of us has created the structure of modern society. Having created that structure, one is trying to escape from that structure, escape from its ambitions, from its greed, from its fears, from its absurd activities. Without denying the very thing which one has created, mere escaping from it brings about a relationship which has no validity at all with one and the society.

I do not know if you are getting the meaning of this. I cannot possibly escape from something which I have created, and from my relationship to that thing which I have created. I can only leave it when I deny the structure of that thing which I have created. That is, when I no longer agree with it, when I no longer accept any religious authority or ritual, I deny the structure of society. And when I deny it and not escape from it, then I am out of the structure of that society for which I am responsible. Unless each one of us does this, you can pretend as much as you like that you are finding reality, seeking reality—you can seek bosses, you can follow saints—all that has no meaning whatsoever.

One can find out what one is seeking. You understand? Until then your search is merely a furtherance of your own pleasure, dictated by your tendencies or by the circumstances in which you are placed. If you can go that far, then you can ask what you are seeking. Most of us want greater experiences—experiences that are not of the everyday kind, greater, wider, more significant experiences. And that is why LSD, the latest kind of drug, is prevalent in America and is spreading into Europe and probably will come here, if it has not already come. It gives one a tremendous experience. It is a chemical which alters the structure of the brain cells, of thought, and brings about a great sensitivity, heightened perception; and that experience may alter the course of your life, give you a semblance of some reality. But it is better than nothing because to go every day to the office, to join the army, to become a clerk, to become a business manager is very boring! At least this will give you some new delight, a new experience, and perhaps alter the way of your life!

And so most human beings are seeking experiences, and they want those experiences to be permanent, lasting. Have you ever looked into this whole structure and the meaning of experience? To experience—what does it mean? First, it means to recognize.

To recognize, as it is, a new experience. Recognition is necessary; otherwise, it is not an experience. There is a challenge and there is a response, and out of that challenge and response, if there is not an experiencing which is recognizable, it is no longer experience. This is fairly simple. Therefore recognition is essential for experience—which means the mind must have experienced before; otherwise, it cannot recognize. Therefore there is no new experience at all. Please go into it; you will see it for yourself. Any experience, however great, however sublime, however idiotic, however silly, is called an experience when it is recognizable. And recognition is always born out of past memory. Therefore that experience belongs to the past; it is not a new experience at all because you have recognized it. Therefore one must doubt all experience.

Sirs, if you have an experience which you think is most marvelous, divine, lovely, super, and hold on to that—as most saints do, as most religious leaders do—then such an experience not only becomes destructive but brings about a division among people, such as the prophet, the savior, the Shankaras, and so on.

So seeking is to experience; otherwise, you would not seek. Therefore experience is merely a modified continuity of what has been. And a mind that is wanting experience is a mind that is not capable of perceiving what is true. Please follow this. When a mind recognizes this whole process of experience, it is no longer seeking experience—which does not mean that the mind becomes dull. Most of us, if we are not challenged, generally go to sleep! Therefore, to most minds the challenge and the response are necessary; otherwise, one becomes lazy, lethargic, inefficient, as is happening in this country—there is no challenge, nobody pushes you; and corruption goes on! For a dull mind to keep awake, challenges are necessary. But when you recognize that, your mind is already awakened to this whole problem of experience and then you begin to inquire whether the mind can keep awake without any kind of experience at all, without any kind of challenge.

Are you following all this? Not verbally, please don't; then you will be going home with ashes! But if you are actually proceeding, traveling, moving together, sharing together what the speaker is saying—sharing, not following, not imitating, not repeating, not remembering and then conforming—then you are not listening verbally, you are actually doing it, because in the doing is the learning, not having learned, you do. Therefore we are learning, and in the very act of learning there is doing.

So the mind demands whether it needs any experience, any challenge—whether created outwardly or created inwardly—to keep it awake. And we have thought of keeping it awake through ritual, through the repetition of words, through conformity, through ritualistic habits, ritualistic ways of life; that way, we hope to keep the mind extraordinarily supple, alive, clean, full of light and delight. But we see that when we depend upon something, the mind becomes dull. So can the mind keep awake without any challenge—which means without any question, doubt, search, movement?

We act because behind that action there is a motive. And when there is a motive, that motive can create a passion—passion to do things, passion to serve, passion to reform, passion to be a leader. Because there is the motive behind it—to do good, to become powerful, to reform, to convert—that motive gives a certain passion; this can be observed factually throughout the world. And is there a passion without a motive? That passion without a motive comes into being when there is no seeking any more, when there is no demand for the pleasure of experience.

So a mind that is seeking is not a passionate mind. And without passion which is without motive, you cannot love. Because, as we said the other day, love is not desire, love is not pleasure, love is not jealousy; nor is love the denial of hate. Because when you deny hate, violence, when you put these away from you, it does not necessarily mean that there will be love. Love is something entirely different—like silence; silence is not the outcome of the cessation of noise.

So we are asking, as at the beginning, can the mind come to that extraordinary seeing, not from the periphery, from the outside, from the boundary, but come upon it without any seeking? And to come upon it without seeking is the only way to find it. Because in coming upon it unknowingly, there is no effort, no seeking, no experience; and there is the total denial of all the normal practices to come into that center, to that flowering. So the mind is highly sharpened, highly awake, and is no longer dependent upon any experience to keep itself awake.

When one asks oneself, one may ask verbally; for most people, naturally, it must be verbal. And one has to realize that the word is not the thing—like the word *tree* is not the tree, is not the actual fact. The actual fact is when one touches it, not through the word, but when one actually comes into contact with it. Then it is an actuality—which means the word has lost its power to mesmerize people. For example, the word *God* is so loaded and it has mesmerized people so much that they will accept or deny, and function like a squirrel in a cage! So the word and the symbol must be set aside.

Now, is it possible to work, live, act from the center? Do you understand what I mean by the center? Not the center created by the mind, not a center artificially produced by some philosopher, some theologian, but a state of mind—we will not even call it a center—which has not been through all the tor-

tures, and which sustains its innocency, its passion, though it goes through all the turmoils of life, so that the turmoils never touch it. One may make a mistake, one may lie, but one sets that aside and goes far; there is never a sense of guilt, never a sense of conflict. But this requires tremendous honesty.

Honesty is humility. It is only the dishonest that are pretending to be humble. The moment you have this sense of humility seriously, deeply, then there is never a climbing, there is never a reaching, there is never a state of arriving. Therefore a mind that seeks is not a humble mind. It does not know what humility is. But a mind that makes itself, reduces itself, to be humble, to have that perfume of humility, becomes a harsh mind. And you have had saints galore in this country who were harsh people because essentially they were vain people.

So, if one is serious, one asks oneself whether it is at all possible to live in this world from that state—to go to an office, if necessary, or not earn a livelihood at all. There are lots of people who are not saying, "I must earn a livelihood," and they do not approach that dimension through the usual practices which promise that dimension.

Now, how does one come upon it? You understand my question? We have meditated, sacrificed, remained a celibate or not celibate; we have accepted traditions, rituals; we have got tremendously excited over perfume, idols; we have gone round the temples several times and prostrated—we have done all those childish things. And if we have done all that, we have seen the utter futility of all that because they are born out of fear, born out of the sense of wanting some hope, because most of us are in despair. But to be free of despair is not through hope. To be free of despair, you have to understand despair itself, and not introduce the idea of hope. It is very important to understand this because then you create a duality, and there is no end to the corridor of duality. But if you say, "I am in despair," find out why, go into it, use your brain to find out. One can see why you are in despair. It is because life, as it is lived, has no meaning; it is terribly boring—breeding a family, going into an office, a few moments of delight in looking at a picture, hearing music, or seeing a lovely sunset; otherwise, life has no meaning at all. And we try to impose a meaning upon it, and that imposition is an intellectual trick. And at the end of it you become despairing, hopeless. Whereas you must go into despair, and not create the opposite; you have to find out why you are in despair. You are in despair because you want to fulfill, and in fulfillment there is always frustration. Or you are in despair because you don't understand; or because your son, your mother, your wife, your husband, or somebody dies, and you have no understanding of that; or because you are not loved. You are not loved because you don't know how to love. And so you are everlastingly in battle, and out of this battle, a frustration, an endless misery, despair, comes. And to escape from that endless despair, you create a false illusion of hope, and therefore you build an endless corridor of hope, whereas despair goes on.

So we come to the point: Can the mind come upon it without discipline, without thought, without enforcement, without any book, without any leader, without any teacher, without anything? Can the mind come upon it as you come upon that lovely sunset? When can one come upon it? Not, how can one come upon it? Not the machinery which will make you come upon it—then, it is just another trick.

It seems to me there are certain absolute things that are necessary—not something to be gained, something you practice, something you do day after day. That is, there must be passion without motive. You understand? Passion which is not the result of some com-

mitment or attachment or a motive, because without passion you cannot see beauty. Not the beauty of a sunset like that, not the beauty of a structure, beauty of a poem, beauty of a bird on the wing, but a beauty that is not an intellectual, comparative, social thing. And to come upon that beauty there must be passion. To have that passion there must be love. Just listen. You cannot do a thing about all this; you cannot practice love—then it becomes mere kindliness, generosity, gentleness, a state of nonviolence, peace; but it has nothing whatsoever to do with love. And without passion and beauty, there is no love. Just listen to it. Don't argue, don't discuss "how?"

It is like leaving a door open. If you leave the door open, the breeze of an evening comes in. You cannot invite it; you cannot prepare for it; you cannot say, "I must, I must not"; you cannot go to rituals and so on; but just leave the door open. This means a very simple act, an act which is not of the will, which is not of pleasure, which is not projected by a cunning mind. Just to leave the door open—that is all you can do; you cannot do anything else. You cannot sit down to meditate, to make the mind silent by force, by compulsion, by discipline. Such a silence is noise and endless misery. All that you can do is to leave the door of your mind open. And you cannot leave that door open if you are not free.

So you begin to disentangle yourself from all the stupid psychological inventions that the mind has created—to be free from all that, not in order to leave the door open, but just to be free. It is like keeping a room clean, tidy, and orderly; that is all. Then when you leave the door open without any intention, without any purpose, without any motive, without any longing, then through that door comes something which cannot be measured by time or by experience; it is not related to any activity of the mind. Then you will know for yourself, beyond all doubt, that there is something far beyond all the imagination of man, beyond time, beyond all inquiry.

January 25, 1967

Bombay, India, 1967

--- ✳ ---

First Talk in Bombay

It seems to me that it is always good to be serious, especially when we are sitting down here talking about serious things. We need a certain attention, a certain quality of penetration, and a deep inquiry into the various problems that each one of us has and into the problems that the world is facing. As one observes, not only in this country, but right throughout the world, there is chaos, a great deal of confusion and human misery in every form, that does not seem to diminish. Though there is great prosperity in the West, the West has many problems, not only at the economic and social levels, but at a much deeper level. There is a revolt going on there among the young; they no longer accept the tradition, the authority, the pattern of society.

And when one comes to this country, as we do every year, one sees the rapid decline, the poverty, the utter disregard for human beings, the political chicanery, the absolute cessation of any religious, deep inquiry, the tribal warfare between various groups, and fasting over some trivial affair. When the house is burning, when there is such chaos, when there is such misery, to spend one's life or even make an exhibition of oneself over some trivial affair indicates the state of mind of those who are supposed to be leaders, religious or political.

When one observes all these facts, not only outwardly, organizationally, economically, socially, but also inwardly, apart from all the repetition of traditions, apart from the accepted norms of thought and the innumerable platitudes that one utters, and when one goes deeply beyond all this inwardly, one will find that there is also great chaos, contradiction.

One does not know what to do. One is always seeking endlessly, going from one book to another, from one philosophy to another, from one teacher to another. And what we are really seeking is not clarity, is not the understanding of the actual state of mind, but rather we are searching for ways and means to escape from ourselves. Religions in different forms throughout the world have offered this escape, and we are satisfied in trying to find out a convenient, pleasurable, satisfying retreat. When one observes all this—the increasing population, the utter callousness of human beings, the utter disregard for others' feelings, for others' lives, the utter neglect of the social structure—one wonders if order out of this chaos can be brought about. Not political order—politics can never bring about order; neither an economic structure nor a different ideology can bring about order. But we do need order. For, there is a great deal of disorder, both outwardly and inwardly, of which one is vaguely, speculatively, casually aware. One feels the problems are too immense. The population is exploding so fast that one asks oneself, "What can I do as a human being living in this chaotic misery, violence, stupidity? What can I do?" Surely, you must have asked this question of yourself if you are at all serious. And if one has asked oneself this very serious question, "What can one do oneself?" the invariable answer is, "I am afraid I can do very little to alter the structure of society, to bring about order, not only within, but also outwardly."

And generally one asks the question, "What can I do?" and invariably the answer is "very little." There one stops. But the problem demands a much deeper answer. The challenge is so great that every one of us must respond to it totally, not with some conditioned reply—not as a Hindu, as a Buddhist, as a Muslim, as a Parsi, as a Christian; all these are dead, gone, finished; they have no longer any meaning except for the politician who exploits ignorance and superstition. The scriptures, what has been said by the philosophers, by the authorities in religion with their sanctions and with their demands that you obey, that you follow—these have totally lost all meaning for any man who is aware, who is conscious of the problems of the world.

You know, man has lost faith in what he has believed; he no longer follows anybody. You understand what is happening politically when the audience throws shoes and stones at the speaker? It means that they are discarding leadership. They do not want to be told what to do any more. Man is in despair. Man is in confusion. There is a great deal of sorrow. And no ideology, whether of the left or the right, has any meaning. All ideologies are idiotic anyhow. They have no meaning when they are faced with the actual fact of *what is.* So we can disregard not only the authority of leadership but also the authority of the priest, the authority of the book, the

authority of religion. We can totally disregard all these, and we have to disregard them in order to find out what is true. Nor can you go back to what has been. You know, one hears often in this country about the heritage of India, what India has been. They are everlastingly talking about the past, what India was. And the people who generally talk about the cultures of the past have very little thought; they can repeat what has been, what the books have said, and it is a convenient dope with which to lull the people. So we can disregard all those, sweep them completely away; we have to because we have problems that demand tremendous attention, deep thought, and inquiry, not a repetition of what somebody has said, however great he may be. So, when you put away all the things that have been, that have brought about this immense misery, this utter brutality and violence, then we are confronted with facts, actually with *what is,* both outwardly and inwardly, not with 'what should be'. The 'what should be' has no meaning.

You know, revolutions—like the French Revolution, the Russian Revolution, the Communist Revolution—have been made on ideologies of 'what should be'. And after killing millions and millions of people, they are discovering that people are tired of ideologies. So you are no longer ideologists, no longer leaders; you have no longer anybody to tell you what to do. You are now facing the world by yourself, alone, and you have to act. So our problem becomes immensely great, frightening. You, as a human being, alone, without any support from anybody, have to think out the problems clearly, and act without any confusion so that you become an oasis in a desert of ideas. Do you know what an oasis is? It is a place with a few trees, water, and a little pasturage in a vast desert where there is nothing but sand and confusion. That is what each one of us has to be at the present time—an oasis, where we are—so that each one of us is free, clear, not confused, and can act, not according to personal inclination or according to one's temperament or compelled by circumstances.

So the challenge is very great, and you cannot reply to it by running away from it. It is at your door. So you have got to take stock. You have got to look around. You have got to find out what to do for yourself. And that is what we are going to do together. The speaker is not going to tell you what to do because there is, for him, no authority. And this is very important for you to understand—that all spiritual authority has come to an end because it has led to confusion, to endless misery, to conflict. It is only the most foolish that follow.

So if we can put aside all authority, then we can begin to investigate, to explore. And to explore you must have energy, not only physical energy, but mental energy, where the brain functions actively, not made dull by repetition. It is only when there is friction that energy is wasted. Please follow this a little bit. Don't accept what the speaker says, because that has no meaning. We are concerned with freedom, not a particular kind of freedom, but the total freedom of man. So we need energy, not only to bring about a great psychological, spiritual revolution in ourselves, but also to investigate, to look, to act. And as long as there is friction of any kind, friction in relationship between husband and wife, between man and man, between one community and another community, between one country and another country, outwardly or inwardly, as long as there is conflict in any form, however subtle it may be, there is a wastage of energy. And there is the summit of energy when there is freedom.

Now we are going to inquire and discover for ourselves how to be free from this fric-

tion, from this conflict. You and I are going to take a journey into it, exploring, inquiring, asking—never following. Therefore, to inquire there must be freedom. And there is no freedom when there is fear. We are burdened with fear, not only outwardly, but inwardly. There is the outward fear of losing a job, of not having enough food to eat, of losing your position, of your boss behaving in an ugly manner. Inwardly also there is a great deal of fear—the fear of not being, of not becoming a success; the fear of death; the fear of loneliness; the fear of not being loved; the fear of utter boredom, and so on. So there is this fear, and it is this fear that prevents the inquiry into all the problems and being free from them. It is this fear that prevents a deep inquiry within ourselves.

So our first problem, our really essential problem, is to be free from fear. You know what fear does? It darkens the mind. It makes the mind dull. From fear there is violence. From fear there is this worship of something which you know nothing about; therefore, you invent ideas, images—images made by the hand or by the mind and various philosophies. And the more you are clever, the more you have authority in your voice and in your gesture, the more the ignorant follow you. So our first concern is: Is it possible to be totally free from fear? Please put that question to yourselves, and find out.

During these four talks, what you are trying to do is to bring about an action on the part of a human being in a world that is a desert, that is in confusion, that is of violence, so that each one of us becomes an oasis. And to discover that and to bring about that clarity, that precision, so that the mind is capable of going far beyond all thought, there must be, first, freedom from all fear.

Now, first, there is the physical fear that is the animal response. Because we have inherited a great deal of the animal; a great part of our brain structure is the heritage of the animal. That is a scientific fact. It is not a theory, it is a fact. The animals are violent, so are human beings. The animals are greedy; they love to be flattered, they love to be petted; they like to find comfort; so do human beings. The animals are acquisitive, competitive; so are human beings. The animals live in groups; so do human beings like to function in groups. The animals have a social structure; so have human beings. We can go on much more in detail. But it is sufficient to see that there is a great deal in us which is still of the animal.

And is it possible for us not only to be free of the animal but also to go far beyond that and find out—not merely inquire verbally, but actually find out—whether the mind can go beyond the conditioning of a society, of a culture in which it is brought up? To discover, or to come upon, something which is totally of a different dimension, there must be freedom from fear.

Obviously self-protective reaction is not fear. We need food, clothes, and shelter—all of us, not only the rich, not only the high. Everybody needs them, and this cannot be solved by politicians. The politicians have divided the world into countries, like India, each with its separate sovereign government, with its separate army, and all this poisonous nonsense about nationalism. There is only one political problem, and that is to bring about human unity. And that cannot be brought about if you cling to your nationality, to your trivial divisions as the South, the North, the Telugu, the Tamil, the Gujarati, and what not—it all becomes so infantile. When the house is burning, sir, you don't talk about the man who is bringing the water, you do not talk about the color of the hair of the man who set the house on fire, but you bring water. Nationalism has divided man, as religions have divided man, and this nationalist spirit and the religious beliefs

have separated man, put man against man. And one can see why it has come into being. It is because we all like to live in a little puddle of our own.

And so, one has to be free from fear, and that is one of the most difficult things to do. Most of us are not aware that we are afraid, and we are not aware of what we are afraid. And when we know of what we are afraid, we do not know what to do. So we run away from it. You understand, sir? We run away from what we are, which is fear; and what we run away to increases fear. And we have developed, unfortunately, a network of escapes. So one has to become aware not only of the fears one has but also of the network which one has developed and through which one runs away.

Now, how does fear come into being? You are afraid of something—afraid of death, afraid of your wife, husband; afraid of losing a job, afraid of so many things. Now, take one particular fear that you have and become conscious of it. We will proceed to examine how it comes into being and what we can do about it, how to resolve it completely. Then we shall establish a right relationship between you and the speaker. This is not mass psychology, or mass self-psychoanalysis, but an inquiry into certain facts which we have to face together. How does fear come about—fear of tomorrow, fear of losing a job, fear of death, fear of falling ill, fear of pain? Fear implies a process of thought about the future or about the past. I am afraid of tomorrow, of what might happen. I am afraid of death; it is at a distance still, but I am afraid of it. Now, what brings about fear? Fear always exists in relation to something. Otherwise, there is no fear. So one is afraid of tomorrow or of what has been or what will be. What has brought fear? Isn't it thought? I think that I might lose my job tomorrow; therefore, I am afraid. I might die, and I do not want to die; I have lived a wretched, monstrous, ugly, brutal, insensitive life without any feeling, and yet I do not want to die; and thought creates the future as death, and I am frightened of that.

Do you follow all this? Please, do not merely accept words. Don't merely listen to certain words. But rather listen because it is your problem. It is your everyday problem, whether you are asleep or awake—this matter of fear. You have to solve it yourself; nobody is going to solve it for you. No mantras, no meditation, no god, no priest, no government, no analyst, nobody is going to solve it for you. So you have to understand it, you have to go beyond it. Therefore, please listen. Not with your cunning mind; don't say, "I will listen and compare what he says with what I already know, or with what has been said"—then you are not listening. To listen you must give your complete attention. To give complete attention means care. There can be only attention when you have affection, when you have love, which means that you want to resolve this problem of fear. When you have resolved it, you become a human being, a free man who can create an oasis in a world that is decaying.

So thought breeds fear. I think about my losing a job or I might lose a job, and thought creates the fear. So thought always projects itself in time, because thought is time. I think about the illness I have had and I do not like pain, and I am frightened that the pain might return again. I have had an experience of pain; thinking about it and not wanting it create fear. Fear is very closely related to pleasure. Most of us are guided by pleasure. To us, like the animals, pleasure is of the highest importance, and pleasure is part of thought. By thinking about something that has given me pleasure, that pleasure is increased. Isn't it? Have you not noticed all this? You have had an experience of pleasure—of a beautiful sunset or of sex—

and you think about it. The thinking about it increases pleasure, as thinking about what you have had as pain brings fear. So thought creates pleasure and fear. Doesn't it? So thought is responsible for the demand for, and the continuation of, pleasure; and thought is also responsible for engendering fear, bringing about fear. One sees this; this is an actual experimental fact.

Then one asks oneself, "Is it possible not to think about pleasure or pain? Is it possible to think only when thought is demanded, but not otherwise?" Sir, when you function in an office, when you are working at a job, thought is necessary; otherwise, you could not do anything. When you speak, when you write, when you talk, when you go to the office, thought is necessary. There, it must function precisely, impersonally. There, thought must not be guided by inclination, a tendency. There, thought is necessary. But is thought necessary in any other field of action?

Please follow this. For us thought is very important; that is the only instrument we have. Thought is the response of memory which has been accumulated through experience, through knowledge, through tradition; and memory is the result of time, inherited from the animal. And with this background we react. This reaction is thinking. Thought is essential at certain levels. But when thought projects itself as the future and the past psychologically, then thought creates fear as well as pleasure; and in this process the mind is made dull and, therefore, inaction is inevitable. Sir, fear, as we said, is brought about by thought—thinking about losing my job, thinking my wife might run away with somebody, thinking about death, thinking about what has been, and so on. Can thought stop thinking about the past psychologically, self-protectively, or about the future?

You understand the question? You see, sir, the mind, in which is included the brain, can invent and can overcome fear. To overcome fear is to suppress it, to discipline it, to control it, to translate it in terms of something else; but all that implies friction, doesn't it? When I am afraid, I say to myself, "I must control it, I must run away from it, I must go beyond it"—all that implies conflict, doesn't it? And that conflict is a waste of energy. But if I understood how fear comes into being, then I could deal with it. I see how thought creates fear. So I ask myself, "Is it possible for thought to stop, as otherwise fear will go on?" Then I ask myself, "Why do I think about the future? Why do I think about tomorrow?" or "Why do I think about what has been as pain or pleasure yesterday?"

Please listen quietly; we know that thought creates fear. One of the functions of thought is to be occupied, to be thinking about something all the time. Like a housewife who thinks about the food, the children, the washing up—that is all her occupation; remove that occupation, and she will be lost, she will feel totally uncomfortable, lonely, miserable. Or take away the God from the man who worships God, who is occupied with God; he will be totally lost. So thought must be occupied with something or the other, either about itself or about politics, or about how to bring about a different world, a different ideology, and so on; the mind must be occupied. And most of us want to be occupied; otherwise, we shall feel lost; otherwise, we do not know what to do, we will be lonely, we will be confronted with what we actually are. You understand? So, you are occupied, thought is occupied—which prevents you from looking at yourself, at what you actually are.

We are concerned with bringing about a different world, a different social order. We are concerned not with religious beliefs and dogmas, superstitions, and rituals but with what is true religion. And to find that out

there must be no fear. We see that thought breeds fear, and that thought must be occupied with something, as otherwise it feels itself lost. One of the reasons why we are occupied with God, with social reform, with this, with that, or with something or the other is because in ourselves we are afraid to be lonely, in ourselves we are afraid to be empty. We know what the world is: a world of brutality, ugliness, violence, wars, hatreds, class and national divisions, and so on. Knowing actually what the world is—not what we think it should be—our concern is to bring about a radical transformation in that. To bring about that transformation, the human mind has to undergo tremendous mutation; and the transformation cannot take place if there is any form of fear.

Therefore, one asks oneself, "Is it possible for thought to come to an end so that one lives completely, fully?" Have you ever noticed that when you attend completely, when you give your attention completely to anything, there is no observer and therefore no thinker, there is no center from which you are observing? Do it sometime, give your attention completely—not "concentration." Concentration is the most absurd form of thought; that any schoolboy can do. What we are talking about is "attention"—that is, to give attention. If you are listening now with all your being, with your mind, with your brain, with your nerves, with your total energy—listening; not accepting, not contradicting, not comparing, but actually listening with complete attention—is there an entity who is listening, who is observing? You will find that there is no observer at all. Now, when you look at a tree, look with complete attention. There are so many trees here, look at them. When you listen to the sound of the crows going to bed at night, listen to it completely. Don't say, "I like that sound," or "I don't like that sound." Listen to it with your heart, with your mind, with your brain, with your nerves, completely. So also see the tree without the interference of thought—which means no space between the observer and the observed. When you give such total and complete attention, there is no observer at all. And it is the observer that breeds fear because the observer is the center of thought; it is the 'me', the 'I', the self, the ego; the observer is the censor. When there is no thought, there is no observer. That state is not a blank state. That demands a great deal of inquiry—never accepting anything.

You know, you have accepted all your life; you have accepted tradition, you have accepted the family, you have accepted society as it is. You are merely an entity who says yes. You never say no to any of these things; and when you do say no, it is merely a revolt. And revolt creates its own pattern which then becomes habit, tradition. But if you have understood the whole social structure, you will see that it is based on conflict, on competition, and on the ruthless assertion of oneself at any price, either in the name of God or in the name of the country, in the name of peace, and so on.

So to be free of fear, give complete attention. Next time fear arises in your mind—fear of what is going to happen, or fear that something that has happened might come back again—give your complete attention; do not run away from it, don't try to change it, don't try to control it, don't try to suppress it, be with it totally, completely, with complete attention. Then you will see that because there is no observer, there is no fear at all.

One of our peculiar fallacies is that we think there is the unconscious, a deep-rooted thing which is going to bring fear in different forms. You understand? All consciousness has its limitations. And to go beyond the limited conscious, conditioned entity, it is no good dividing it as the "conscious" and the "unconscious." There is only the conscious

field; and if you give attention at any moment completely, then you will wipe away the unconscious as well as the limited consciousness.

Attention cannot be cultivated. There is no method, no system, no practice by which you can have attention. Because when you practice a method to become attentive, it shows that you are cultivating inattention; what you are concerned with, then, is to cultivate attention through being inattentive. When you follow a system, a method, what are you doing? You are cultivating mechanically certain habits, repeating a certain activity which only dulls the mind; it does not sharpen the mind. Whereas if you give attention even for a second or a minute, completely, then you will see that momentary total attention wipes away that which you have been afraid of. In that attention there is neither the observer nor the observed. The observer then is the observed. But to understand that, to go into that, one has to inquire into the whole problem of time and space.

But, you see, our difficulty is we are so heavily conditioned that we never look, never ask, never question, never doubt. We are all followers, we are all yes-sayers. And the present crisis demands that you do not follow anybody. You, out of your confusion, cannot follow anybody, for when you are confused and you follow somebody, you are following out of confusion, not out of clarity. If you are clear, you will never follow anybody. And when you follow somebody out of your confusion, you will create more confusion. So what you have to do is to stop first, inquire, look, listen.

Unfortunately, this country is very old in its so-called culture. "Culture" is a very good word, but it has been spoiled by the politicians, by the people who have very little thought, or very little of something original to say. So they have used this word culture to cover up their own thoughtlessness. But to bring about a different culture—which means to grow, to flower, not to remain in a static state—and to understand that, one has to begin with oneself. Because, you are the result of this culture, the culture of India, with all the traditions, with all the superstitions, with all the fears, the culture in which there is religion, social divisions, linguistic divisions. You are a part of all that, you are that; you are not separate from that. So the moment you are aware of and give your total attention to what you are, then you will see that you have dropped all that instantly. Then you are free from the past completely. It is only when you are aware of your conditioning that it falls away from you naturally—not through any volition, not through any habit, not through any reaction; but it just drops away because you are giving your attention.

But most of us walk through life inattentively. We are rarely attentive. And when we are attentive, generally we react according to our conditioning as a Hindu, a Buddhist, a communist, a socialist, or what you will. And therefore we answer from the background in which we have been brought up. Therefore, such reaction only creates further bondage, further conditioning. But when you become aware of your conditioning—just be aware, just give a little attention—then you will see that your mind is no longer divided as the conscious and the unconscious; then you will see that your mind is no longer chattering endlessly. Therefore the mind becomes extraordinarily sensitive. And it is only a very sensitive mind that can be silent—not a brutalized mind, not a mind that has been tortured through discipline, control, adjustment, or conformity; such a mind can never be quiet through repetition which it calls meditation. Meditation is something entirely different—a subject which we will perhaps go into another time.

As we said, a mind that is afraid, do what it will, will have no love whatsoever; and without love you cannot construct a new world. Without love there can be no oasis. And you, as a human being, have created this social structure in which you are caught. To break away from that—and you have to break from it completely—you have to understand yourself, just to observe yourself as you actually are. Then out of that clarity comes action. And then you will find out for yourself a different way of living, a way of life which is not repetitive, which is not conforming, which is not imitating, a life which is really free and therefore a life that opens the door to something which is beyond all thought.

February 19, 1967

Second Talk in Bombay

If we may, we will continue with what we were talking about the other day when we met here. We were saying that a radical revolution is necessary, a revolution that is not merely economic or social but at much greater depth, at the very root of consciousness. We were saying that not only do the world conditions demand that this revolution take place but also throughout the world there is a steady decline, not technologically, but in a sense religiously, if I may use that word cautiously and with a great deal of hesitancy. Because the word *religion* has been so thoroughly misused; the intellectual people discard it totally, they deny it, they run away from that word; the scientists, the intellectuals, even the humanitarians, will have nothing to do with that word, with that feeling, or with those organized beliefs which are called religion. But we are talking of a revolution in the very nature of the psyche itself, in the very structure of consciousness that has been put together through millennia, through many, many experiences, through many conditions.

We are going into this question: whether it is possible for a human being living in this world—in this brutal, violent, rather ruthless world that is becoming more and more efficient and therefore more and more ruthless—to bring about a revolution, not only outwardly in his social relationship, but also much more in his inward life. It seems to me that unless there is a fundamental revolution in the whole of consciousness—that is, in the whole field of thinking—man will not only deteriorate and so perpetuate violence, sorrow, but also create a society that will become more and more mechanical, more and more pleasure giving, and therefore he will lead a very, very superficial life. If one observes, that is what is actually taking place.

Man is having more and more leisure through automation, through the development of cybernetics, through electronic brains, and so on. And that leisure is going to be used either for entertainment—religious entertainment or entertainment through various forms of amusements—or for more and more destructive purposes in relationship between man and man; or, having that leisure, he is going to turn inwardly. There are only these three possibilities. Technologically he can go to the moon, but that will not solve the human problem. Nor will the mere use of his leisure for a religious or some other amusement solve it. Going to church or temple, beliefs, dogmas, reading sacred books—all that is really a form of amusement. Or man will go deeply into himself and question every value that man has created through the centuries, and try to find out if there is something more than the mere product of the brain. There are whole groups of people, throughout the world, that are revolting against the established order by taking various forms of drugs, denying any form of activity in society, and so on.

So, what we are talking about is whether it is possible for man living in this world to bring about a revolution, a psychological revolution which will create a different kind of society, a different kind of order. We need order, for there is a great deal of disorder. The whole social structure, as it is, is based on disorder, competition, rivalry, dog eating dog, man against man, class divisions, racial divisions, national divisions, tribal divisions, and so on, so that in the society as it is constructed there is disorder. There is no question about it. Various forms of revolution—the Russian and other forms of revolution—have tried to bring about order in society and they have invariably failed, as is shown in Russia and in China. But we need order because without order we cannot live. Even animals demand order. Their order is the order of property and sexual order. And also with us, human beings, it is the same order in property and sexual order—and we are willing to give up sexual order for rights over property; and in this field we are trying to bring about order.

Now, there can be order only when there is freedom—not as it is interpreted. Where there is no freedom, there is disorder, and therefore there is tyranny, and there are ideologies imposed upon man to bring about order which ultimately bring about disorder. So, order implies discipline. But discipline, as is generally understood, is the discipline based on conformity, on obedience, on acceptance, or brought about through fear, through punishment, through a great deal of tyrannical power to keep you in order. We are talking of a discipline that comes through the very understanding of what freedom is. The understanding of what freedom is brings about its own discipline.

So, we have to comprehend what we mean by these two words *freedom* and *understanding*. Generally we say, I understand something—that is intellectually, verbally.

When anything is clearly stated either in your own language or in a foreign language which we both understand, then you say, "I understand." That is, only a part of the human totality is used when you say, "I understand." That is to say, you understand the words intellectually, you understand what the speaker means. But we do not mean, when we use the word understand, an intellectual comprehension of a concept. We are using that word understand, totally—that is, when you understand something, you act. When you understand that there is some danger, when you see a danger very clearly, there is immediate action. The action of understanding is its own discipline. So, one has to grasp the significance of this word understand very clearly. When we understand, realize, comprehend, see the thing as it is, there is action. And to understand something, you have to apply not only your mind, your reason, your capacity, but also your total attention; otherwise, there is no understanding. I think that is fairly clear.

So, we are seeing that the understanding of freedom is entirely different from revolt. A revolt is a reaction against the established order—like the revolt of the people who grow long hair and so on. They are revolting against the set pattern; but when they revolt, they accept the pattern in which they are caught. We are talking of freedom which is not a revolt. It is not a freedom from something but a freedom which is in the very understanding of disorder. Please follow this clearly. In the very understanding of what is disorder, there comes freedom which brings about order, in which there is discipline.

That is, to understand negatively is to bring about a positive act. Not through pursuing a positive pattern will order come. There is disorder. This disorder is caused by man pursuing a certain pattern—a social pattern, an ethical pattern, a religious pattern, a pattern which is based on his own personal in-clination or pleasure, and so on. That is, this society is built on an acquisitive approach of life, on competitiveness, on obedience, on authority—which has brought about disorder. Each man is out for himself. The religious man is out for himself; the politician is out for himself, though he talks about "for the good of the country"; and the businessman is out for himself. Each man is out for himself—that is obvious. And therefore he creates disorder. There are ideologists who say that man is working for himself, and therefore he must work for the country, for society as a community, and so on. Therefore, order is imposed upon us—which brings disorder. This is fairly obvious, historically. So in understanding disorder—how each human being creates disorder—not verbally, not intellectually, but actually, in seeing actually the fact of what he is doing, then out of that perception, out of that observation of actually *what is,* and in the understanding of that, there is a discipline which brings about order.

So we have to understand, comprehend the word *freedom,* the word *understand,* and also the word *see.* Do we see anything, or do we see it through the image which we have about that thing? When you look at a tree, you are looking at the actual fact of the tree through the image you have about the tree. Please observe it yourself, watch yourself. How do you look at the tree? Do it now, as we are talking. You look at it with thought; you say, "It is a palm tree; it is this tree or that tree." The thought prevents you from looking at the actual fact of that tree. Move a little more subjectively, more inwardly. You look at your wife or your husband through the image you have created about that person. Obviously, because you have lived with her or with him for many years, and you have cultivated an image about her or him. So you look at her or him through the image you have, and the relationship is between the two images that you have cultivated—not between two human beings. So you do not actually see, but one image is seeing the other image.

And this is very important to realize because we are dealing with human relationships throughout the world. As long as these images remain, there is no relationship; hence the whole conflict between man and man. It is an actual fact that each one of us is creating an image about the other, and that when we look at the other, we are looking at the image we have about him or he has about us. You have to see this fact. To see is different from verbalizing about it. When you are hungry, you know it. Nobody needs to tell you that you are hungry. Now, if somebody were to tell you that you are hungry, and you accept that statement, it has quite a different significance other than your being actually hungry. Now, in the same way, you have actually to realize that you have an image about another, and that when you look at another as a Hindu, as a Muslim, as a communist, and so on, all human relationship ceases, and you are only looking at the opinion you have created about another.

So we are asking whether it is at all possible to bring about a revolution in this image-making. Please follow this and see the extraordinary implications involved in it. Human beings are conditioned by society, by the culture in which they live, by the religion, by the economic pressures, by the climate, by the food, by the books and by the newspapers they read. They are conditioned, their whole consciousness is conditioned. And we are going to find out if there is anything beyond that conditioning. But you can find out if there is anything beyond that conditioning only when you realize that all thinking is within the pattern of consciousness. Is this clear? Now I will proceed to explain a little more.

You see, man has always sought something beyond himself, an otherness; and he called it "God," he called it "superconsciousness" and all kinds of names. He has started from a center which is the totality of his consciousness. Look, sir, we will put it differently. The consciousness of man is the result of time. It is the result of the culture in which he lives, the culture being the literature, the music, the religion—and all has conditioned him. And he has built the society to which he is now a slave. Is that clear? So, man is conditioned by the society which he has built, and that society further conditions him; and man is always seeking a way out of this, either consciously or unconsciously. Consciously, you meditate, you read, you go to religious ceremonies and all the rest of it, trying to escape from this conditioning. Unconsciously or consciously, there is a groping, there is a seeking for something beyond the limitations of consciousness.

Thought which is the result of time is always inquiring whether it can go beyond its own conditioning, and saying that it cannot or it can, or asserting that there is something beyond. So thought which is the result of time, thought which is the whole field of consciousness—whether it is conscious or unconscious—can never discover the new. Because thought is always the old. Thought is the accumulated memory of many millennia. Thought is the result of the animal inheritance. Thought is the experience of yesterday as memory. So thought can never go beyond the limitation of consciousness.

So, when you look at a tree, you are looking at the image which thought has created about that tree. When you look at your wife or your husband, or at your political leader, or a religious guru and all that, you are looking at the image that thought has created about that person. Therefore you are never seeing anything new. And thought is controlled by pleasure. We function on the principle of pleasure—into which we went a little bit the other day. What we are asking now is whether it is at all possible to go beyond this limited consciousness. And to inquire into thought is a part of meditation which demands a tremendous discipline—not the discipline of control, suppression, imitation, following a method, and all the rest of that silly stuff.

Now, I am going to go into this process of inquiry. The speaker is going into it; but if you want to take the journey with the speaker, you have not only to attend to what he is saying, but you have to pursue with him, not verbally, but actually.

We are going to discover whether there is a field of innocence, an innocence that has not been touched by thought at all. Whether I can look at that tree as though for the first time, whether I can look at the world with all its confusion, miseries, sorrow, deceptions, brutality, dishonesty, cruelty, war, at the whole conception of the world as though for the first time—this is an important matter. Because if I can look at it as though for the first time, my action will be totally new. Unless the mind discovers that field of innocence, whatever it does—whatever the social reforms, whatever the activity—will always be contaminated by thought because it is the product of thought, and thought is always old.

And we are asking whether consciousness, being limited, we are asking whether any movement in that consciousness is a movement of thought, conscious or unconscious. When you seek God, truth, it is still thought seeking and therefore projecting itself in terms of recognition of what it has known, and therefore what you are seeking is already known, and therefore you are not seeking at all. This is very important to understand. Therefore, all seeking must totally cease—which means really, you must see actually *what is*. That is, when you see that you are angry, jealous, competitive, greedy, selfish,

brutal, violent, when you see *what is* actually as it is, not in terms of an ideal, then you remove conflict altogether. A mind that is in conflict of any kind, at any level, becomes dull. Like two people quarreling all the time—they are dull, stupid, they have become insensitive. Any conflict makes the mind dull. But when you see actually *what is* without its opposite, then there is no conflict at all.

I will show you what we mean. The animal is violent. Human beings who are the result of the animal are also violent; it is part of their being to be violent, to be angry, to be jealous, to be envious, to seek power, position, prestige, and all the rest of it, to dominate, to be aggressive. Man is violent—this is shown by thousands of wars—and he has developed an ideology which he calls "nonviolence." Please follow this closely. This country, India, has talked endlessly about it; it is one of its fanciful, ideological nonsenses. And when there is actual violence, as a war between this country and the next country, everybody is involved in it. They love it. Now, when you are actually violent and you have an ideal of nonviolence, you have a conflict. You are always trying to become nonviolent—which is a part of the conflict. You discipline yourself in order not to be violent—which, again, is a conflict, friction. So when you are violent and have the ideal of nonviolence, you are essentially violent. To realize that you are violent is the first thing to do—not try to become nonviolent. To see violence as it is, not try to translate it, not to discipline it, not to overcome it, not to suppress it, but to see it as though you are seeing it for the first time—that is to look at it without any thought.

I have explained already what we mean by looking at a tree with innocence—which is to look at it without the image. In the same way, you have to look at violence without the image which is involved in the word itself. To look at it without any movement of thought is to look at it as though you are looking at it for the first time, and therefore looking at it with innocence.

I hope you are getting this, because it is very important to understand this. If man can remove conflict within himself totally, he will create a different society altogether; and that is a radical revolution. So we are asking whether man, this conditioned entity, can break through all his conditioning so that he is no longer a Hindu, a Muslim, a communist, or a socialist with opinions or ideologies, and all that has gone. It is only possible when you begin to see things actually as they are.

You have to see the tree as the tree, not as you think the tree is. You have to look at your wife or your husband actually as she or he is, not through the image that you have built about the person. Then you are always looking at the fact, at *what is,* not trying to interpret it in terms of your personal inclination, tendency, not guided by circumstances. We are controlled by circumstances, we are guided by inclination and tendency; and, therefore, we never look at *what actually is.* To look at *what actually is* is innocence; the mind then has undergone a tremendous revolution.

I do not know whether you are following this. You teach a child that he is a Hindu, you teach a child that he is a dark man or a black man, and the other a Christian. You teach him, and so you control him and condition him. Now what we are saying is that to break through this conditioning, it is necessary never to think in terms of a Hindu, a Muslim, a communist, or a Christian, but as a human being who sees things actually as they are—which means really to die.

You know, death is, for most of us, a frightful thing. The young and the old are equally frightened of death for various reasons. Being frightened, we invent various theories—reincarnation, resurrection—and all kinds of escapes from the actual fact that there is death. Death is something unknown. As you really do not know your husband or wife but only know the image you have of the husband or the wife, so also you really do not know anything about death. You understand this? Death is something unknown, something frightening. The entity that is you has been conditioned and is full of his own anxieties, guilt, miseries, suffering, his little creative capacity, his talent to do this or that; he is all that and he is frightened to lose what he knows because his censor is the very essence of thought. If there is no thinking, there is no 'me', there is no fear at all. So, thought has brought about this fear of the unknown.

There are two things involved in death. There is not only the physical ending but also the psychological ending. So man says that there is a soul that continues, that there is something permanent in me, in you, that will continue. Now this permanent state is created by thought, whether the thought was produced by some ancient teacher, a writer, a poet, or a novelist—whom you may call a religious man, full of theories; he has created this idea of soul, of the permanent entity, by thought. And we pursue that thought and are caught by that conditioning. Like the communists—they do not believe in anything permanent; they have been taught and are thinking accordingly. In the same way as you have been taught to believe that there is something permanent, they have been taught to believe that there is nothing permanent. You are both the same, whether you believe or do not believe. You are both conditioned by belief.

Then there is another issue involved in this, which is whether thought has a continuity. Thought continues when you give strength to it. That is, thinking every day about yourself, about your family, about your country, about your work, about going to a job, working, working, thinking, thinking—by doing this you have created a center which is a bundle of memories as thought. And whether that has a continuity of its own has to be inquired into. We won't go into it now because there is no time for it.

Death is something unknown. Can we come to it with innocence? You understand? Can I look at the moon shining through those leaves, and listen to those crows as though I am seeing or listening for the first time, with complete innocence of everything I have ever known? That is to die to everything I have known as yesterday. Not to carry the memory of yesterday is to die. You have to do it actually—not theorize endlessly about it. You will do it when you see the importance of it. Then, you will see there is no method, there is no system, because as soon as you see something dangerous, you act immediately. In the same way, you will see that a mind that has merely a continuity of what has been can never possibly create anything new. Even in the field of science it is only when the mind is completely quiet that it discovers something totally new. So to die to yesterday, to the memories, to the hurts, to the pleasures, is to become innocent; and innocency is far more important than immortality. Innocency can never be touched by thought, but immortality is clothed with thought.

The machinery of image-making comes into being through energy, the energy whose principle is to seek pleasure. That is what we are doing. Are we not? We all want pleasure. On that principle we act. Our morality, our social relationship, our search for the so-called God, and the rest of it—all that is based on pleasure and the gratification of that pleasure. And pleasure is the continuation, by thought, of desire.

Madame, please do not take notes. This is not an examination where you take notes, go home, think about it, and then answer it afterwards. We are doing it together. You are acting and you have no time. When you are actually living, it is now, not tomorrow. If you are following this intensely, you have no time to take notes. Please listen.

Listening means learning, and learning is not accumulation. That is, when you have learned, you act from what you have learned; such learning is merely an accumulation. Again, having accumulated, according to what you have accumulated, you act; and therefore, you are creating friction. If you listen, there is nothing more to do. All that you have to do is to listen. Listen as you would look at that tree, or at that moon, without any thought, without any interpretation. Just listen; there is great beauty in it. And that listening is total self-abandonment. Otherwise you cannot listen.

It is only when you are passionate you listen, and there is no passion when you cannot abandon yourself totally about anything. In the same way, if you are listening with total abandonment, you have done everything you can possibly do because then you are seeing the truth as it is, the truth of every day, of every action, of every thought, of every field. If you do not know how to see the truth of everyday movement, everyday activity, everyday work, everyday thought, you will never go beyond that, you will never find out what is beyond the limitations of consciousness.

So, as we said, the understanding of freedom brings its own discipline, and that discipline is not imitation, is not conformity. For example, you look at death very attentively; that very looking is discipline. Consciousness, as we said, is limited, and this limitation is within the reach of thought. Thought cannot break through this limitation; no amount of psychoanalysis, no amount of philosophy, no physical discipline will break through this conditioning. This can only be broken through when the whole machinery of thought is understood. Thought, as we said, is old and can never discover the new. When thought realizes that it cannot do anything, then thought itself comes to an end. Therefore, there is a breaking through of the limitation of consciousness.

And this breaking through is dying to the old. This is not a theory. Don't accept it or deny it. Don't say, "It is a very good idea." Do it. Then you will find out for yourself that in dying to yesterday there comes innocency. Then from that innocency there is a totally different kind of action. As long as human beings have not found that, do what they will, all the reforms, all the worship, all the escapes, the worship of wealth—they have no meaning at all.

Where there is innocency which can only come about through self-abandonment, there is love. Without love and innocency there is no life; there is only torture, there is only misery, there is only conflict. And when there is innocency and love, you will know there is a totally different dimension, about which nobody can tell you. If they tell you, they are not telling the truth. Those who say they know—they do not know. But a man who has understood this comes darkly, unknowingly, on something which is of a totally different dimension—like removing the space between the observer and the observed; that state is entirely different from the state in which the observer is different from the observed.

February 22, 1967

Third Talk in Bombay

We were talking the other day, when we met here, about the necessity of a total revolution—a revolution both inward and outward. We were saying that order is essential to have peace in the world, not only

order without, but primarily order within. This order is not mere routine. Order is a living thing which cannot possibly be brought about by mere intellection, by ideologies, by various forms of compulsive behavior. We were saying, too, that thought, which has been the old, cannot function without the pattern which it has established in the past. Thought is always the old. Thought cannot possibly bring about order because order, as we said, is a living thing. And it is thought which has brought about disorder in the world.

We went into that sufficiently, I think, the other day. We said we must consider not what order is but rather what brings about disorder. Because the moment we can understand what disorder is and actually perceive it, and see, not merely intellectually, but actually the whole structure of disorder, then in the total understanding of that disorder, order will come about.

I think this is important to understand. Because, most of us think that order can be brought about by repetition, that if you can go to an office for the next forty years, be an engineer or a scientist functioning in a routine, you are bringing about order. But routine is not order: routine has bred disorder. We have disorder both outwardly and inwardly. I think there is no question about this. There is general chaos, both outwardly and inwardly. Man is groping to find a way out of this chaos, asking, demanding, seeking new leaders; and if he can find a new leader, political or religious, he will follow him. That is, man is willing to follow a mechanically established routine, a purpose, a system.

But when one observes how this disorder has come into being, one sees that wherever there has been authority, especially inward authority, there must be disorder. One accepts the inward authority of another, of a teacher, of a guru, of a book, and so on. That is, by following another—his precepts, his sayings, his commands, and his authority—in a mechanical way, one hopes to bring about order within oneself. Order is necessary to have peace. But the order which we create in the pursuit of, or in following, an authority breeds disorder. You can observe what is happening in the world, especially in this country where authority still reigns, where inward authority, the demand, the urge to follow somebody is very strong and is a part of the tradition, a part of the culture. That is why there are so many ashrams, little or big, which are really concentration camps. Because, there you are told exactly what to do. There is the authority of the so-called spiritual leaders. And like all concentration camps, they try to destroy you, they try to mold you into a new pattern. The communists in Russia, the regimes of dictatorship, brought about concentration camps to change opinion, to change the way of thinking, to force people. And this is exactly what is happening. The more there is chaos in the world, the more there are the so-called ashrams which are essentially concentration camps to twist the people, to mold them, to force them to a certain pattern, promising them a marvelous future. And the dullards accept this. They accept this because then they have physical security. The boss, the commissar, the guru, the authority tells them exactly what to do; and they will willingly do it because they are promised heaven or whatever it is, and in the meantime there is physical security. This type of mechanical obedience—all obedience is mechanical—does breed great disorder, as one observes from history and from the everyday incidents of life.

So, for the comprehension of disorder, one has to understand the causes of disorder. The primary cause of disorder is the pursuit or the seeking of a reality which another promises. As most of us are in confusion, as most of us are in turmoil, we would rather mechanically follow somebody who will assure us of a comfortable spiritual life. It is one of the most extraordinary things that politically we are against tyranny, dictatorship. The more liberal, the more civilized, the more free the people are, the more they abhor, they detest tyranny, politically and economically; but, inwardly, they would accept the authority, the tyranny of another. That is, we twist our minds, twist our thoughts and our way of life, to conform to a certain pattern established by another as the way to reality. When we do that, we are actually destroying clarity, because clarity or light has to be found by oneself, not through another, not through a book, not through any saint. Generally the saints are distorted human beings. Because they lead the so-called simple life, the others are greatly impressed; but their minds are twisted, and they create what they think is reality.

But actually to understand disorder one has to understand the whole structure of authority, not only inwardly, but also outwardly. One cannot deny outward authority. That is necessary. It is essential for any civilized society. But what we are saying is about the authority of another, including that of the speaker. There can be order only when we understand the disorder that each one of us brings about, because we are part of society; we have created the structure of society, and in that society we are caught. We, as human beings who have inherited animal instincts, have to find, as human beings, light and order. And we cannot find that light and order, or that understanding, through another—it does not matter who it is—because the experiences of another may be false. All experiences must be questioned, whether your own or of another. Experience is the continuation of a bundle of memories, which translates the response to a challenge according to its conditioning. That is, experience is, is it not, to respond to a challenge, and that experience can only respond according to its background. If you are a Hindu, or a Muslim, or a Christian, you are conditioned by your culture, by your religion, and that background projects every form of experience. And the more clever you are in interpreting that experience, the more you are respected, of course, with all that goes with it, all the circus.

So we must question, we must doubt, not only the experience of another, but also our own experience. To seek further experience through expansion of consciousness, which is being done through various forms of psychedelic drugs, is still within the field of consciousness and, therefore, very limited. So a person who is seeking experience in any form—especially the so-called religious, spiritual experience—must not only question it, doubt it, but must totally set it aside. A mind that is very clear, a mind that is full of attention and love—why should such a mind demand any more experience?

What is true cannot be invited. You can practice any amount of prayer, breathing, and all the rest of the tricks that human beings do in order to find some reality, some experience; but truth cannot be invited. That which is measurable can come, but not the immeasurable. And a man who is pursuing that which cannot be understood by a mind that is conditioned breeds disorder, not only outwardly, but inwardly.

So, authority must be totally set aside, and that is one of the most difficult things to do. From childhood we are led by authority—the authority of the family, the mother and the father, the authority of the school, the teacher, and so on. There must be the authority of a scientist, the authority of a technologist. But the so-called spiritual authority is an evil thing, and that is one of the major causes of disorder because that is what has divided the world into various forms of religions, into various forms of ideologies.

So to free the mind from all authority there must be self-knowing, that is, self-knowledge. I do not mean the higher self or the atma, which are all the inventions of the mind, the inventions of thought, inventions born out of fear. We are talking of self-knowing: knowing oneself actually as one is, not as one should be, to see that one is stupid, that one is afraid, that one is ambitious, that one is cruel, violent, greedy; the motives behind one's thought, the motives behind one's action—that is the beginning of knowing oneself. If you do not know yourself, how the structure of your mind operates, how you feel, what you think, what your motives are, why you do certain things and avoid other things, how you are pursuing pleasure—unless you know all this basically, you are capable of deceiving yourself, of creating great harm, not only to yourself, but to others. And without this basic self-knowing there can be no meditation, which I am going to talk about presently.

You know, the young people throughout the world are rejecting, revolting against the established order—an order which has made the world ugly, monstrous, chaotic. There have been wars, and for one job, there are thousands of people. Society has been built by the past generation with its ambitions, its greed, its violence, its ideologies. People, especially the young people, are rejecting all ideologies—perhaps not in this country; for we have not advanced enough, we are not civilized enough to reject all authority, all ideologies. But in rejecting ideologies they are creating their own pattern of ideology: long hair, and all the rest of it.

So, mere revolt does not answer the problem. What answers the problem is to bring about order within oneself, order which is living, not a routine. Routine is deadly. You go to an office the moment you pass out of your college—if you can get a job. Then for the next forty to fifty years, you go to the office every day. You know what happens to such a mind? You have established a routine, and you repeat that routine; and you encourage your child to repeat that routine. Any man alive must revolt against it. But you will say, "I have responsibility; placed as I am, I cannot leave it even though I would like to." And so the world goes on, repeating the monotony, the boredom of life, its utter emptiness. Against all this, intelligence is revolting.

So, there must be a new order, a new way of living. To bring about that new order, that new way of living, we must understand disorder. It is only through negation that you understand the positive, not by the pursuit of the positive. You understand, sir? When you deny, put aside, what is negative; when you understand the whole sociological and inward disorder that human beings have created; when you understand that as long as each human being is ambitious, greedy, invidious, competitive, seeking position, power, authority, he is creating disorder; and when you understand the structure of disorder— that very understanding brings about discipline, discipline not of suppression, not of imitation. Out of negation comes the right discipline, which is order.

So, to understand oneself is the beginning of wisdom. Wisdom does not lie in books, nor in experience, nor in following another, nor in repeating a lot of platitudes. Wisdom comes to a mind that is understanding itself, understanding how thought is born. Have you ever questioned or asked: What is the beginning of thought, how does thought come into being? That is a very important thing to understand. Because, if you can understand the beginning of thought, then perhaps you can find a mind that is not burdened with thought as a repetition of what has been. As we said, thought is always old, thought is never new.

Unless you discover for yourself—not repeat what somebody says, it doesn't matter who it is—unless you find out for yourself the beginning of thought, like a seed which puts out a green leaf, you cannot possibly go beyond the limitations of yesterday.

And to find out the beginning of thought, there must be the understanding of yourself, not through analysis. Analysis takes time, like taking off the peels of an onion bit by bit. We think we can understand through analysis, through introspection, through the pursuit of a particular idea that has arisen and examining the cause of it—all that takes time. Now when you use time as a means of understanding, then time breeds disorder. Therefore, time is sorrow. You understand? If you take time to be rid, in yourself, of violence, you have established that you must be free of violence as a goal, as an ideology, and that to reach that goal, you must have time, you must cover the space between violence and that state in which there is no violence. When you have time to rid yourself of violence, you are sowing the seeds of violence all the time—which is an obvious fact. If you say to yourself, "I will not be ambitious when I reach the top of the heap," you are in the meantime sowing the seeds of ruthlessness of an ambitious man. So, the understanding of oneself is not dependent on time; it must be instantaneous. We are going into that a little bit.

We are saying the world, as it is now, is in chaos. There are wars, repetitive activity, the business of the churches—all that has bred much mischief in the world, and the continuation of all that is disorder. To bring about order, we must understand the structure of disorder. And one of the major structures of this disorder is authority. You pursue authority because of fear. You say, "I don't know; you know, please tell me." There is no one that can tell you. When you realize that, and when you realize that you have to find out everything entirely by yourself, inwardly, psychologically, then there is no leader, no guru, no philosopher, no saint that will help you because they are still functioning on the level of thought. Thought is always old, and thought is not a guide.

So we are going to find out the origin, the beginning of thought; and this is important. Please listen to this, not just merely to the words. You know what it is to listen? You listen, not in order to learn. Do not listen to learn, but listen with self-abandonment so that you see for yourself the true or the false. It means that you neither accept nor reject. It does not mean that you have an open mind like a sieve in which everything can be poured and nothing remains. On the contrary, because you are listening, you are highly sensitive and therefore highly critical. But your criticism will not be based on your opinion as opposed to another opinion; that is the process of thought. Please listen as you listen to those crows, without like or dislike; just listen to the sound of that boy hammering at something, without getting irritated, without losing your attention. When you listen so completely, you will find that you have nothing more to do. It is only the man who is standing on the banks of the river that speculates about the beauty of the current. When he has left the bank and is in the current, then there is no speculation, then there is no thought; there is only movement.

To understand what we are going to go into—which is the origin, the beginning of thought—one has to understand oneself; that is, one has to learn about oneself. Acquiring knowledge about oneself and learning about oneself are two different things. You can accumulate knowledge about yourself by watching yourself, by examining yourself. And from what you have learned, from the accumulation you begin to act; and therefore, in that action you are further acquiring. You understand? What you have learned, what

you have accumulated is already in the past. All accumulation is in the past, and from the past you begin to observe and accumulate more. Whereas learning is not accumulation. Learning is—as you watch, you are moving with the action itself; therefore, there is no residue in your learning, but always learning. Learning is an active-present of the word, not the past-present. We are going to learn, but not from what has been accumulated. In learning a language, you have to accumulate. You have to know the words, you have to learn the various verbs, and so on; and after having learned, you begin to use them. Here it is not at all like that. Seeing a danger brings about an immediate action. When you see a danger like a precipice, there is an immediate action.

So what we are going to do is to find out, to understand the beginning, the origin of thinking. And to do that, you have to listen and go with it, which means you must give attention. Attention is possible only when you are deeply inquiring—which means, you are actually free to inquire, and you are not bound by what some people have said and so on.

Now all life is energy, it is an endless movement. And that energy in its movement creates a pattern which is based on self-protection and security—that is, survival. Energy, movement, getting caught in a pattern of survival, and the repeating of that pattern—this is the beginning of thought. Thought is mind. Energy is movement, that movement caught in the pattern of survival, and the repetition of survival in the sense of pleasure, of fear—that is the beginning of thought.

Thought is the response of accumulated memory, accumulated patterns—which is what you are doing as a Hindu, a Muslim, a Parsi, a Christian, a communist, a socialist, and so on. We function in patterns, and the repetition of that pattern is the repetition of thought, repeating over and over again. That is what you are doing as a Hindu, a Muslim, or a Parsi—the pattern established by repetition as survival, in the framework of a culture which is Hindu, Muslim, or Parsi. This is actually what is going on within each one. Thought has always established a pattern, and if the old pattern is not suitable, it establishes another pattern. If capitalism is not right, then communism is right; that is a new pattern. Or if Hinduism or Christianity is not convenient, you form another pattern.

So the repetition of that pattern conditions the brain cells themselves, which are matter. Thought is matter. One can discover this for oneself. You must discover it, not because the speaker is telling you—that has no value whatsoever. It is like a man who is hungry being told how marvelous the food is, and being fed on theories. That is what is happening in this country; you are fed on theories and ideologies—the Buddhist ideology, the Hindu ideology, the Shankaracharya ideology, and all the rest of it. Therefore, your minds are empty. You are fed on words; that is why there is disorder. That is why all this must be thrown away, so that we start anew. To start anew one must understand this whole structure of thought. Now, you understand this structure of thought only when you begin to understand yourself as a living movement—not "having understood, you add more to it"; then it becomes a dead thing. You are a living thing within the framework of a culture; and that culture, that tradition, that authority holds you. And within that framework of consciousness is disorder. To understand this whole process and to go very much further—which we are going to do now—is meditation.

Meditation is not the repetitive formula of mantras, of breathing regularly, of sitting in a certain posture, practicing awareness, practicing attention—these are all utterly mechanical. We are talking of a living thing. And you have practiced these mechanical things for centuries upon centuries. Those who have practiced them are dead, and their visions are projections from their own past, from their own conditioning. But we are talking of a living meditation, not a mechanical, repetitive, disciplinary meditation. Unless you know what meditation is—like unless you know what death is—there is no new culture, nothing new is born.

You know, culture is one of the most marvelous things, not the dead culture about which you talk endlessly—the Indian culture, the Hindu culture; that is buried, gone, finished. The living culture is what is actually taking place now. To see the confusion, the mess, the terrible misery, and out of that to grow and to flower—that is culture, not going back to your dead parents.

So we are going to find out together and take a journey together into this question of what is meditation. You can only ask that question when you have gone through knowing yourself. You cannot ask, "What is meditation?" unless you know yourself, unless you have an understanding of yourself, unless you have looked at yourself as much as possible. As I said, "looking at yourself" is instantaneous; the totality of yourself is revealed in the instant, not in time. You can actually see with your eyes a tree, a flower, a human being next to you. You cannot see the totality of that tree or the totality of the human being next to you if you have an image about that tree or about that person. This is obvious. It is only when the image is not, that you can see completely. The image is the observer, is the center from which you observe. When there is a center from which you observe, there is a space between the observer and the observed. You do not have to pay such enormous attention to what is being said, you can observe this yourself. As long as there is an image about your wife, about your husband, about a tree, about anything, it is the image which is the center which is looking. So there is separation between the observer and the observed. This is important to understand. We are going into it presently.

First of all, let us remove erroneous ideas about concentration. It is one of the favorite sayings of the meditator or the teacher who practices or teaches meditation that people must learn concentration—that is, to concentrate on one thought, drive out every other thought and fix your mind on that one thought only. This is a most stupid thing to do. Because, when you do that, you are merely resisting, you are having a battle between the demand that you must concentrate on one thing, and your mind wandering to all kinds of other things. Whereas you have to be attentive not only to the one thought but also to where the mind is wandering, totally attentive to every movement of the mind. This is possible only when you don't deny any movement, when you don't say, "My mind wanders away, my mind is distracted." There is no such thing as distraction. Because, when the mind wanders off, it indicates that it is interested in something else.

So, one has to understand the whole question of control. But, unfortunately, we cannot go into this this evening, as there is no time. We human beings are such controlled, dead entities. This does not mean that we must explode in doing what we want to do—which we do anyhow secretly. But there comes a discipline with love. So I will go into it very quickly.

Meditation is not control of thought. Meditation, when thought is controlled, only breeds conflict in the mind. But when you understand the structure of thought and the origin of thought, then thought will not interfere, as I have explained to you just now. Therefore, you will see that thought has its place—which is, you must go to the office, you must go to your house, speak a lan-

guage; there thought must function. But when you have understood the whole structure of thinking, that very understanding of the structure of thinking is its own discipline, which is not imitation, which has nothing to do with suppression.

The cells of the brain have been conditioned to survive within a given pattern, as a Hindu, a Muslim, a Parsi, a Christian, a Catholic, or a communist. As the brain has been conditioned to survive for centuries upon centuries, it has the pattern of repetition; so the brain itself becomes the major factor of restless inquiry. You will see it for yourself when you go into it.

So the problem is to bring about absolute quietness in the brain cells themselves, which means no seeking of self-importance and of self-continuance. You understand? We must survive at the physical level, and we must die at the psychological level. It is only when there is death, at the psychological level, of a thousand yesterdays that the brain cells are quiet. And this does not come about through any form of manipulation of thought, repetition of mantras—all that is immature. But it comes about only when you understand the whole movement of thought, which is yourself. So the brain cells become extraordinarily quiet, without any movement, except to respond to the outward reactions.

So the brain itself being quiet, the totality of the mind is completely silent, and that silence is a living thing. It is not the product of any guru, of any book, of any ashram, of any leader, of any authority, or of any drug. You can take a drug, a chemical, to make your mind quiet, or you can mesmerize yourself to be quiet. But that is not the living stillness of a mind that has gone into itself deeply, and therefore is tremendously attentive and highly sensitive. It is only such a mind that can understand what love is. Love is not desire or pleasure. All that we have is desire and pleasure, which we call love. "I love my wife, I love my God," and so on—all that is based on fear, pleasure, and sensation.

So a man who has understood and really gone into this will bring about order, first, within himself. If there is order in oneself, there is order in the world. If each one of you will really bring about order in yourself, you will have a living order, a new society, a new life. But to do that, you have to destroy the old patterns of life. The old patterns of life cannot be broken except through understanding yourself, and out of that understanding comes love.

You know, man has talked about love endlessly: love your neighbor, love God, be kind. But, now, you are neither kind nor generous. You are so concentrated on yourself that you have no love. And without love there is only sorrow. This is not a mere aphorism for you to repeat. You have to find that, you have to come upon it. You have to work hard for it. You have to work with the understanding of yourself, ceaselessly, with a passion. Passion is not lust; a man who does not know what passion is will never know love. Love can come into being only when there is total self-abandonment. And it is only love that can bring about order, a new culture, a new way of life.

February 26, 1967

Fourth Talk in Bombay

This is the last talk. I think, during the last three meetings that we have had here and the two discussions that took place in the little hall, we have more or less indicated in what direction one has to make one's way. Because, the world, as we see now, is becoming more and more chaotic, more and more violent, almost anarchical, antisocial. There is war, there is such exploitation, ruthless efficiency, mismanagement, bad government,

and so on. We can enumerate the many problems that we—each one of us—have to face: a world that we have created out of our greed, out of our sorrow, conflict, and the desire for pleasure, the urge to dominate, to seek a position.

We could go on enumerating all the many problems in more detail. But description and explanation have very little value when we are confronted with the problem. And unfortunately, we are so easily satisfied with explanations. We think words will actually solve our problems, and so there is a Niagara of words, not only at this meeting, but also right throughout the world. Everybody talks endlessly, and there are innumerable theories, new ideologies and, unfortunately, new leaders—both political and religious—and there is every form of propaganda to convince another of what he should do, of what he should think. And it is one of the most difficult things to find out how to think. Our problem is not only social, economic, and so on, but much more a religious problem, a problem of crisis in the whole of consciousness. And, there, it almost becomes meaningless if one depends on words, explanations, or definitions. Perhaps these talks may have pointed out not what to think but how to think. We are slaves of propaganda. We have been told what to think—the Gita, the Koran, the Bible, the priest, Marx-Lenin theories, the innumerable ideologies. But we do not know, I am afraid, how to think very deeply and to see the limitation of thought.

One of our major problems, probably the only problem, is sorrow. Man has tried through every form to resolve, to end sorrow; he has tried to escape from it, he has worshiped it, he has given many explanations. But man, endlessly, from the moment he is born until he dies, lives in this sorrow, in this grief. It seems to me that unless one resolves that issue not verbally, not by ideas or by explanations, but actually by stepping out of the stream of this incessant sorrow, one's problems will multiply. You may be very rich, you may have power, position, prestige, status, and you may be very clever, you may have all the brains in the world, with great information, but, I am afraid, all those things are not going to resolve the human demands, the human urgency of resolving one of the most fundamental questions, which is sorrow. Because, with the ending of sorrow is the beginning of wisdom. Wisdom—not cunningness, not knowledge, not ideologies—comes only with the ending of sorrow; and without wisdom we cannot solve our human problem, not only outwardly, but also inwardly.

Man, as one observes historically and also from one's own life or one's own everyday activity, is caught in the principle of pleasure and sorrow. We are guided by pleasure. Most of us want pleasure only, and we are pursuing it most subtly. When we seek truth—as people say they do when they are religious—we are still seeking this principle of pleasure. Where there is pleasure in any form, there must also be sorrow: one cannot be pursued without the other. There is not only sensuous pleasure, sensuous enjoyment, but also—if one is a little more refined, a little more cultured, a little more intellectual—the pleasure of reformation, of doing good, of altering society. Writing books, entering into politics, and other endless activities of the fulfillment of desire—all that is the continuation of pleasure. If one observes one's own life, if one is at all aware, even casually, one will find that we are guided by our inclination, by our tendency. Inclination and tendency are the outcome of this constant demand for greater and greater satisfaction of pleasure. After all, all virtue is based on this principle of pleasure. Without understanding this pleasure, there is no ending of sorrow. I would like to go into it rather deeply.

Is all life a pleasure? Is all life a conflict and misery, an endless series of battles, out-side and inside? A life which is made into a battlefield—that is all we know. We may spin theories, we may endlessly talk about theological concepts, social improvements, and criticism of what shall be. But unless we understand this extraordinary demand for pleasure, it seems to me, we shall be caught in the current of endless conflict and sorrow. To understand pleasure is not to deny it, because pleasure is one of the basic demands of life, like enjoyment. When you see a beautiful tree, a lovely sunset, a nice smile on a face, light on a leaf, then you really enjoy it, there is a great delight.

Beauty is something that is not pleasure. The sense of beauty is not in a building, in a picture, in a poem, in holding the hand of another, in looking at a mountain or a river—these are still sensations, however pleasurable. Beauty is something entirely different. To understand actually what beauty is—not intellectually, not verbally—one must understand pleasure.

You know, man has been denied pleasure through religion, through worship of an idea, through the saints and the missionaries, by the sannyasis and the monks throughout the world. They have consistently denied pleasure to man. They say it is wrong, it is something evil, something to be put away. They say that a mind that is full of pleasure, or is seeking pleasure, can never find reality, God, and that therefore you should torture yourself. But such persons come to God with a twisted, tortured, petty, little mind. A mind that has been squeezed by society, by culture, is no longer a mind free, alive, vibrant, capable, unafraid. And most human minds are tortured. They may not know it, they may not be aware of it. They may be so completely occupied with their families, with earning a livelihood, with achieving a position, that they may not be aware of the total content of their being.

Man is always seeking: seeking a purpose, seeking a goal, seeking satisfaction; and the satisfaction in the highest he calls God. So we are always seeking, seeking, seeking. We are always feeling that something is missing, and so we try to fill that void in ourselves, that loneliness, that emptiness, that weary, exhausting, meaningless existence of life with lots of ideas, with significance, with purposes, ultimately seeking satisfaction in a permanency which will never be disturbed. And that state of permanency we call by a thousand names—God, *samadhi,* and so on; one can invent names. We are endlessly seeking, and we never ask why we are seeking. The obvious answer is that we are dissatisfied, unhappy, unfortunate, lonely, unloved, fearful. We need something to cling to, we need somebody to protect us—the father, the mother, and so on—and so we are seeking. When we are seeking, we are always finding. Unfortunately, we will always find when we are seeking.

So, the first thing is not to seek. You understand? You all have been told that you must seek, experiment with truth, find out truth, go after it, pursue it, chase it, and that you must discipline, control yourself. And then somebody comes along and says, "Don't do all that. Don't seek at all." Naturally, your reaction is either to ask him to go away or you turn your back, or you find out for yourself why he says such a thing—not accept, not deny, but question. And what are you seeking?

Inquire about yourself. You are seeking; you are saying that you are missing something in this life inwardly—not at the level of technique or having a petty job or more money. What is it that we are seeking? We are seeking because in us there is such deep dissatisfaction with our family, with society, with culture, with our own selves, and we want to satisfy, to go beyond this gnawing discontent that is destroying. And why are

we discontented? I know discontent can very easily be satisfied. Give a young man who has been discontented—a communist or a revolutionary—a good job, and he forgets all about it. Give him a nice house, a nice car, a nice garden, a good position, and you will see that discontent disappears. If he can achieve an ideological success, that discontent disappears too. But you never ask why you are discontented—not the people who have jobs, and who want better jobs. We must understand the root cause of discontent before we can examine the whole structure and the meaning of pleasure and, therefore, of sorrow.

You know, sirs, from school days until one dies, we are educated, we are conditioned in comparison. I compare myself with somebody else. Do watch yourself; please listen to what I am saying, and see how your mind works. You have a double task: you have not only to listen to the speaker but also, in listening to him, to observe your own state of mind actually. So you need a certain attention, a certain awareness of both the speaker and what he is saying, and observing yourself. But if you are listening—actually listening in the sense of not trying to understand, not trying to translate what the speaker is speaking, not condemning, not adjusting, not denying or accepting—you will see that there is neither the speaker nor yourself, but there is only the fact, there is only *what is.* That is the art of listening: not listening to the speaker or to your own opinions and judgments, but to *what actually is.* We are always comparing ourselves with somebody else. If I am dull, I want to be more clever. If I am shallow, I want to be deep. If I am ignorant, I want to be more clever, more knowledgeable. I am always comparing myself, measuring myself against others—a better car, better food, a better home, a better way of thinking. Comparison breeds conflict. And do you understand through comparison?

When you compare two pictures, two pieces of music, two sunsets, when you compare that tree with another tree, do you understand either? Or do you understand something only when there is no comparison at all?

So, is it possible to live without comparison of any kind, never translating yourself in terms of comparison with another or with some idea or with some hero or with some example? Because when you are comparing, when you are measuring yourself with 'what should be' or 'what has been', you are not seeing *what is*. Please listen to this. It is very simple, and therefore probably you, being clever, cunning, will miss it. We are asking whether it is possible to live in this world without any comparison at all. Don't say no. You have never done it. You won't say, "I cannot do it; it is impossible because all my conditioning is to compare." In a schoolroom a boy is compared with another, and the teacher says, "You are not as clever as the other." The teacher destroys B when he is comparing B with A. That process goes on through life.

We think that comparison is essential for progress, for understanding, for intellectual development. I don't think it is. When you are comparing one picture with the other, you are not looking at either of them. You can only look at one picture when there is no comparison. So, in the same way, is it possible to live a life never comparing, psychologically, yourself with another? Never comparing with Rama, Sita, Gita, whoever it is, with the hero, with your gods, with your ideals. A mind that is not comparing at all, at any level, becomes extraordinarily efficient, becomes extraordinarily alive, because then it is looking at *what is*.

Look, sir, I am shallow; I compare myself with another who is supposed to be very deep, capable, and profound in his thinking and in his way of living. I, being shallow, narrow, limited, compare myself with that

person, and I struggle to be like him. I imitate, quote, follow, and try to destroy myself in order to be like him; and this conflict goes on endlessly. Whereas if there is no comparison at all, how do I know I am dull? Because you tell me? Because I cannot get a job? Because I am no good at school? How do I know I am dull if there is no comparison at all? Therefore, I am what I am; I am in that state from which I can move, I can discover, I can change. But when I am comparing myself with another, the change will invariably be superficial. Please do listen to all this, it is your life. Whereas if there is no comparison, *what is* is; from there I move. This is one of the fundamental principles of life, that modern life has conditioned man to compare, to compete, to struggle endlessly, caught in a battle with another. I can only look at *what is* when there is no comparison. So, I understand, not verbally, but actually, that comparison is a most childish, immature thing.

Sir, where there is love, is there a comparison? When you love somebody with your heart, with your mind, with your body, with your entire being—not be possessive, not be dominating, not say, "It is mine"—is there any comparison? Only when there is no comparison, can you look at *what is*. If we understand that, then we can proceed to find out, to inquire into the whole structure of pleasure.

Not to compare *what is*, not only with the future, but also with what has been the past—this demands tremendous attention. You understand? I had a pleasure yesterday—sensuous pleasure, an idea which has brought an extraordinary light, a cloud which I saw full of light yesterday, but which now I don't see at all—and I want that back. So I compare the present with what has been and I am going to compare the present with what should be. It requires extraordinary intelligence and sensitivity to be free of this comparative evaluation. One must have intelligence and sensitivity completely; then only can one understand *what is*. Then you see you are passionate, and then you have the energy to pursue *what is*. But you lose that energy when you are comparing *what is* with 'what has been' or 'what should be'.

Now, I hope that is clear—not intellectually because that has no meaning at all; you may just as well get up and go away. But if you really understand this, then you can look at pleasure; you do not compare it with the pleasure that you have had yesterday, or with the pleasure that you are going to have tomorrow, but you look at the actual mind that is seeking pleasure. Man has to understand this principle of pleasure, not just say, "I want pleasure." If you want pleasure, you must also have pain and also sorrow with it; you cannot have one without the other. And if you pursue pleasure in any form, you are creating a world of conflict. When you say, "I am a Hindu"—you know all the rest of the labels one gives to oneself—then you become very important. Like when you worship one river, you deny all other rivers; when one family becomes all-important, you deny all the other families, and that is why families are a danger; when you worship one tree, one god, then you deny all trees, all gods. And that is what is happening: when you worship your own particular little nation, then you deny all other nations; then you are ready to fight, to go to battle and kill each other.

So, pleasure is embedded in the worship of gods, searching for truth, saying, "my nation," "my family," "my position"; in all this, pleasure is involved, and this pleasure is creating untold mischief. We have to understand this, not deny it, because the moment you deny, it is like cutting your arm off or blinding yourself so that you will not have the pleasure of seeing a beautiful cloud, a beautiful woman, or a lovely tree. So we

have to understand the extraordinary importance of pleasure and how it comes into being. And when you understand it, you see what significance pleasure has, as we are going to see now.

You know, you have been told by the religious people of the world that you must be without desire. It is one of the edicts of the so-called religious people that you must strive to be without desire, to be desireless. That is sheer nonsense because when you see anything, you have already desire. Desire is a reaction. When you see a brilliant color, look at it. You know, one of the most beautiful things is color; color is God. Look at it, do not say, "I like red," or "I like blue"; but just watch the color of a cloud, the color of a sari, the color of a leaf that has just come in the spring. When you do look, you will find that there is no pleasure at all, but sheer beauty. Beauty, like love, is not desire, is not pleasure.

And it is important to understand this whole question of desire, which is quite simple. I do not know why people make such a lot of ado about it. You can see how it comes into being. There is perception; then sensation, contact, and desire. Do you follow? I see a beautiful car—first, perception. Then the sensation of it, then you touch it, and there is the desire to own it—desire. First seeing, perception; then observation, sensation, contact, desire. It is as simple as that. Now the problem begins. Then thought comes in and thinks about that desire, which becomes pleasure. That is, sir, I see a beautiful mountain with deep valleys, covered with snow, bright in the morning light, full of aloofness and splendor. I see it. Then thought begins to say, "How beautiful! I wish I could always be seeing it!" Thought—which is memory responding to what it sees—says, "I wish I could live there!" Or, I see a beautiful face; I think about that face; then thinking constantly about it creates the pleasure. Sex—the pleasure that you had, and you think about it, the image—the more you think about it, the more the pleasure; so then desire. Thought brings about the continuity of pleasure. It is very simple when you look into it.

Then one asks, "Is it possible for thought not to touch desire?" You follow it? That is your problem. When you see something extraordinarily beautiful, full of life and beauty, you must never let thought come in, because the moment thought touches it, thought being old, it will pervert it into pleasure and, therefore, there arises the demand for pleasure and for more and more of pleasure; and when it is not given, there is conflict, there is fear. So, is it possible to look at a thing without thought? To look you must be tremendously alive, not paralyzed. But the religious people have said to you, "Be paralyzed, come to reality crippled." But you can never come to reality crippled. To see reality, you must have a clear mind, unperverted, innocent, unconfused, untortured, free; then only can you see reality. If you see a tree, you must look at it with clear eyes, without the image. When thought thinks about desire—and thought will always think about desire—out of that, it derives pleasure. There is the image which thought has created about the object, and constant thinking about that image, that symbol, that picture, gives rise to pleasure. You see a beautiful head, you look at it. Thought says, "It is a beautiful head, it's a nice head, it has got nice hair." It begins to think about it, and it is pleasurable.

To see something without thought does not mean that you should stop thinking—that is not the point. But you must be aware when thought interferes with desire, knowing that desire is perception, sensation, contact. You must be aware of the whole mechanism of desire, and also when thought precipitates instantly on it. And that requires not only intelligence but awareness, so that you are aware

when you see something extraordinarily beautiful or extraordinarily ugly. Then, the mind is not comparing: beauty is not ugliness and ugliness is not beauty. So with the understanding of pleasure you can investigate sorrow.

Without knowing sorrow, do what you will—climb the highest social ladder or the bureaucratic ladder or the religious ladder or the political ladder—you will always be creating mischief, either in the name of God or in the name of your country, or your party, or your society, or your ideology; you will be a mischief monger. This is obvious.

So, what is sorrow? Again, please look at *what is,* not at 'what should be'. Because, now if you have gone into it, you are not comparing any more, but you are actually looking at *what is.* Therefore, you have got energy to look, and that energy is not being dissipated in comparing. One of the problems of man is how to have energy. Again, the religious people with their petty, little minds have said, "To have energy, you must be a bachelor; to have energy you must starve, fast, eat one meal, wear a loincloth, get up at two in the morning and pray"—it is all idiotic because you are thereby destroying yourself, you are destroying energy. Energy comes when you look at actually *what is,* which means no dissipation of energy in comparison.

We are saying, "What is sorrow?" Man has tried to overcome sorrow in so many ways—through worship, through escape, through drink, through entertainment—but it is always there. Sorrow has to be understood as you would understand any other thing. Do not deny it, do not suppress it, do not try to overcome it; but understand it, look at what it is. What is sorrow? Do you know what sorrow is? Must I tell you? Sorrow is when you lose somebody whom you think you love; sorrow is when you cannot fulfill totally, completely; sorrow is when you are denied opportunity, capacity; sorrow is when you want to fulfill and there is no way to fulfill; sorrow is when you are confronted by your own utter emptiness, loneliness; and sorrow is burdened with self-pity. Do you know what "self-pity" is? Self-pity is when you complain about yourself unconsciously or consciously, when you are pitying yourself, when you say, "I can't do anything against the environment in which I am, placed as I am"; when you call yourself a pest, bemoaning your own lot. And so, there is sorrow.

To understand sorrow, first, one has to be aware of this self-pity. It is one of the factors of sorrow. When someone dies, you are left and you become aware of how lonely you are. Or, if someone dies, you are left without any money, you are insecure. You have lived on others and you begin to complain, you begin to have self-pity. So one of the causes of sorrow is self-pity. That is a fact, like the fact that you are lonely; that is *what is*. Look at self-pity, do not try to overcome it, do not deny it or say, "What am I to do with it?" The fact is: There is self-pity. The fact is: You are lonely. Can you look at it without any comparison of how extraordinarily secure you were yesterday, when you had that money or that person or that capacity—whatever it is? Just look at it; then you will see that self-pity has no place at all. That does not mean that you accept the condition as it is.

One of the factors of sorrow is the extraordinary loneliness of man. You may have companions, you may have gods, you may have a great deal of knowledge, you may be extraordinarily active socially, talking endless gossip about politics—and most politicians gossip anyhow—and still this loneliness remains. Therefore, man seeks to find significance in life and invents a significance, a meaning. But the loneliness still remains. So can you look at it without any comparison,

just see it as it is, without trying to run away from it, without trying to cover it up, or to escape from it? Then you will see that loneliness becomes something entirely different.

Man must be alone. We are not alone. We are the result of a thousand influences, a thousand conditionings, psychological inheritances, propaganda, culture. We are not alone, and therefore we are secondhand human beings. When one is alone, totally alone, neither belonging to any family, though one may have a family, nor belonging to any nation, to any culture, to any particular commitment, there is the sense of being an outsider—outsider to every form of thought, action, family, nation. And it is only the one who is completely alone who is innocent. It is this innocency that frees the mind from sorrow.

And a mind ridden with sorrow will never know what love is. Do you know what love is? There is no love when there is space between the observer and the observed.

You know what space is? The space between you and that tree, between you and what you think you should be. There is space when there is the center or the observer. You understand this? Again, this is very simple, and this becomes extraordinarily complex much later. But first begin with it simply. There is this microphone in front of the speaker. That microphone is in space. But the microphone also creates the space. There is a house with four walls. There is not only space outside but there is also space within the four walls. And there is space between you and the tree, between you and your neighbor, and between you and your wife. As long as there is this space between you and your neighbor, your wife, your husband, or anybody, this space implies that there is a center which creates the space. Are you following this? When you look at the stars, there is you who are looking at the stars and the marvelous sky of an evening with brilliant stars, clear, cool air—you, the observer, and the observed.

So you are the center who is creating the space. When you look at that tree, you have an image about yourself and about the tree; that image is the center which is looking, and therefore there is space. And as we said, love is when there is no space—that is, when there is no space which the observer creates between himself and the tree. You have an image about your wife, and your wife has an image about you. You have built up that image for ten years or for two years or for a day, through her pleasure, your pleasure, through her insults, your insults; you have built it up through nagging, dominating, and all the rest of it. And the contact between these two images is called "relationship." It is only when there is no image that there is love—which means there is no space, not sensuous space, not physical space; but, inwardly, there is no space, just as there is beauty when there is no space.

There is space when there is no self-abandonment. You know, we are talking about something you do not understand. You have never done it. You have never removed the space between yourself and your wife, between yourself and the tree, or between yourself and the stars and the sky or the clouds; you have never actually looked. You don't know what beauty is because you don't know what love is. You talk about it, you write about it, but you have never felt it because you have never known, except probably at rare intervals, this total self-abandonment. Because it is that center that creates the space round itself. And as long as there is that space, there is neither love nor beauty. That is why our lives are so empty, so callous.

You go to an office—I don't know why. You say, "I have to go because I have responsibility, I have to earn, I have to support my family." I don't know why you

must do anything. You are slaves, that is all. You have never observed when you are looking at a tree or looking at the face of a person opposite to you. When you do look at that face, you are looking from a center. The center creates the space between yourself and that person. And to overcome that space, people are taking drugs like LSD. When you take that drug, it makes your mind extraordinarily sensitive; a chemical change takes place, and then you see that space disappears completely. Not that I have taken it. (Laughter) Those are artificial means and, therefore, not real. Those are all instant happiness, instant paradise, instant bliss. You can't get it that way.

So without love and beauty, there is no truth. Your saints, your gods, your priests, your books have denied this. That is why you are in such a sorrowful plight. You would rather talk about the Gita, the Koran, the Bible, than love. This means you look at the dirty roads, the squalor, the filth along these roads, and you put up with it. You cooperate with dirt, and you do not know when not to cooperate. You cooperate with the system, and you do not know when to say, "No, I won't cooperate, and it does not matter what happens." But when you say so, it is because you love, because you have beauty, not because you revolt. Then you will know, when you have this, there is beauty, love, and there is the perception of *what is* which is love. Then the mind can go immeasurably beyond itself.

But you have to work, you have to work like fury every day, as you go to your office every day. You have to work hard, not to achieve love, because you cannot achieve love any more than you can achieve humility—it is only the vain man that talks and achieves humility, but he is always vain. Like humility, you cannot cultivate love, not cultivate beauty; without being aware you cannot see what is truth. But if you are aware—not awareness of some mysterious nature—if you are just aware of what you are doing, of what you are thinking, how you look, how you walk, how you eat, what you talk about, then out of that awareness you will begin to see the nature of pleasure, desire, and sorrow, and the utter loneliness and boredom of man. And then you will begin to come upon that thing called the 'space'. And where there is space between yourself and the object, then you know there is no love.

Without love, do what you will—reform, bring about a new social order, talk about endless ideological improvement—all that creates agony. So it is up to you. There is no leader, there is no guru. There is nobody to tell you what to do. You have to be a light unto yourself. Therefore, you are alone, alone amidst the mad, brutal world. That is why one has to be an oasis in a desert of ideas. And the oasis comes into being when there is love.

March 1, 1967

Rishi Valley, India, 1967

✳

Talk to Students

There is a great deal of discontent in the world, which expresses itself in many ways—in America, in Europe, in China, in Russia, in Japan, and in India too. There is enormous discontent in the world, discontent with the establishment. The establishment is the established order, a group of people who rule, who have a tradition. Here that discontent, if it does exist, is with the "holy cow." You know what the holy cow is? That again is the established order. So there is this discontent, this dissatisfaction with things as they are.

In America there are the hippies who wear extravagant clothes and grow beards, and amongst them there are people who are very serious, young boys and girls who want to lead a different kind of life, who want to create a different kind of society. They are in tremendous revolt, and the revolt takes the form of growing long hair, putting on odd clothes, not washing, not going to offices, not passing examinations, not knowing exactly what they are going to do in the future. Amongst them there are boys and girls who have formed a small group, in which one of them earns money and the rest of them live on what that single person has earned—a kind of community. In England it is the same thing—long hair, beards, dirty clothes, unwashed faces—and it is difficult to distinguish between a boy and a girl because the boys have very long hair down to their shoulders, and the girls have long hair too. In Italy, they are called *capellonis,* the "long-haired ones." They are against the church, against the government, against the established order. Here in India it is probably not so violently expressed, except in the universities; but even there the revolt is very superficial.

Throughout the world there is a revolt against things as they are. But they don't understand the real depths of what is involved—emotionally, psychologically, inwardly. So, knowing what is going on in different parts of the world and in this country too, I wonder to what extent each one of us who is being educated here is discontented? And how are we going to express that discontent? You know what discontent, being dissatisfied, is?—you feel that things aren't right, that they don't answer the real problem of life. One may pass an examination, have a job, get married, have children, but that's not the end. Most people are satisfied with that; they are caught up in society and just drift. But if one is rightly educated, one must have a tremendous discontent.

You know, discontent is one thing, revolt is another, and revolution is quite a different thing. Most of us are discontented with little things: we would like to have a better house, a better car; we would like to look nicer than

189

some other person; we would like to get more marks and so on. That is a superficial discontent; it results generally in nothing and is very easily satisfied. When one gets what one wants, one says, "Everything is all right, it's a lovely day. I am satisfied." That's one form of discontent which soon finds satisfaction and settles down.

Then there is revolt against society, against the established order. There is so much poverty in the world, not only physically, but inwardly; there is such misery and so many wars. There is no peace in the world, no real freedom, so that there is a constant ache and agony in the human mind and heart. Everyone revolts against all that. That revolt is a reaction, which doesn't bring about the right order. So one asks oneself: What will bring about right order in the world?

I am sorry I don't speak very good Hindi, Tamil, or any other Indian language, because I left India when I was a small boy. I hope you don't mind hearing English, though English is, I believe, taboo in this country.

So, seeing all this confusion in the world, seeing this discontent which soon finds satisfaction and settles down, and seeing this revolt which doesn't fundamentally answer all the problems of life, one asks oneself—as you must, if you are being educated—how does one bring about order? There is outward order, having peace in the world—not fighting one another, as Pakistan and India, Vietnam and the Americans—and inward order, living peacefully with one another, with affection, with kindliness. This is totally lacking in the world. The world is brutal, full of hatred, antagonism, jealousy, envy—"You have got to get a job, but I want that job too; you have got more money than I, so I want more money; you are clever, so I also want to be clever"—fight, fight, all life long. Seeing all that, how does one bring about

order so that we can live peacefully with one another, work together, cooperate?

You know the Russian communist revolution tried to bring this about. They said, "No more army, no division of classes, no private property; the means of earning a livelihood belongs solely to the government, to the state." They developed an ideology, and they worked according to that ideology. They made people conform to it, whether they liked it or not, and if they resisted, they were killed, or sent to concentration camps, to Siberia, by the millions. That was a revolution based on an ideology; and all ideologies are idiotic, whether it is the ideology of the communist or of the Hindu, the Christian, or the capitalist.

Do you know what an idea is?

Comment: No.

KRISHNAMURTI: An idea is thought organized—a reasoned-out idea. That idea becomes the ideology—that man should live this way or that way, that the government should be this way, that there should be no class distinction, and so on. So an ideology is developed, ignoring what is actual.

Revolutions, social upheavals, have not answered this question of man living with man peacefully. Religions throughout the world have also failed, for Christianity and Islam have produced a great many wars. Probably only Buddhism and, after that, Hinduism have not been responsible for wars. Economic and social revolutions have not produced order, nor has time.

So one asks: How will a human being bring about order within himself and outwardly? That's the only revolution—not the economic one. Russia, after fifty years of butchery, forcing people to conform to the pattern of an ideology, sending them to concentration camps, liquidating them, is now becoming more and more bourgeois, more and more like a capitalist society, with a profit motive and so on.

Seeing this throughout the world—and it is your job while you are being educated to see this whole pattern—how will you bring about order? An inner revolution is necessary so as to bring about right relationship between human beings; every other form of revolution brings about more misery. The question is how to bring about right relationship between man and man, not through force, not with bayonets, not through organized religions, not through ideologies— for these have all failed. So how is that revolution, that right relationship to take place? You understand my question?

Now how do you think it should take place, if there is no ideology, no idea of "we should do this" or "we should do that"? How are we, seeing all this, to change our relationship with our neighbor—without an ideology? An idea, an ideology, is not the actual, you understand? Take this country for instance, where they have talked for forty years about nonviolence. They have been preaching that unfortunate thing right up and down the land—north, south, east, west—for forty years. And when there was a war between Pakistan and India, these very people, who had been talking about nonviolence, never opened their mouths. They never said, "Oh, it's all wrong. Don't kill, don't fight, nationalism is brutal." They kept quiet. They had the ideology of nonviolence, and when the actuality of violence came along, they kept quiet. I don't believe there was one Indian who stood up against it. So ideologies have no meaning whatsoever; throw them over—ideas, ideologies, formulas, systems— they have no meaning! What has meaning is the actuality, that man is violent. He is violent in business, competitive; he is violent in anger, hatred, brutality, wanting to hurt others, creating enmity. If there is money, he must have more of it; he will fight, deceive

people, play the hypocrite. So how are you and I to change—to bring about a revolutionary spirit without an ideology and yet to change? Have you understood my question? Now if you have no ideas, no ideology at all, then you are faced with the fact. Then you can't escape through an ideology. When you are faced with actuality, words have no meaning; when you are faced with an actuality, you have to do something. You understand? When you are faced with the actuality of not having water, a drought in this valley, you do something; but if you have an ideology, it has no meaning. So can you and I be free of all ideologies and look at what we are—the fact, the actual?

If you can do that, it is the greatest revolution, for it demands instant action; whereas, if you have an ideology you can postpone action. You say, "I am trying to be nonviolent although I still hate people; I am trying to be unselfish although I am really selfish." But if you face the fact that you are really brutal, violent, selfish, then you can do something about it—why not? Then there is no pretense. "I am selfish; I am going to have a good time!" But if you have an ideology, you pretend that all the time you are not selfish; you pretend that you are not violent, but your heart, your mind is full of hatred.

So order is only possible socially and economically, and in the human mind and heart, when the fact, the actual, the *what is* is faced. Then out of that perception, order can come into being. Then you can create a new society, not based on an ideology, but on what actually is. That needs a tremendous revolution in our ways of thinking. It is like pure science. The pure scientist doesn't work on a hypothesis, on ideas; he says, "I am going to investigate," and without any emotional or sentimental feeling about it, without any ideas he investigates. He proceeds step by step. In the same way we can be free of this violence, which is in the heart of most of us, by confronting it and working at it step by step. And I think that brings about a tremendous inward, as well as outward, revolution.

You see, world planning is only possible when you have no nationality, which is something based on an ideology. The world is caught up in these ideologies, of "my country" and "your country," "my party" and "your party." When people have divided themselves like this, they are not interested in peace, in bringing about order. World planning, which is absolutely necessary so that man can live with enough food, clothes, and shelter for everybody, not just for the rich alone, can only come about when there are no ideologies, no nationalities. Nationalities are rampant throughout the world, and therefore there is going to be more misery.

So what are you going to do about it? You are being educated here in this lovely valley. I don't know if you saw the sunset yesterday evening, did you? You know there were clouds from the east moving in through that gap and they were piling up against the hills, and the sun was just setting and the clouds caught the light of the evening sun. Did you see it? How extraordinarily beautiful, vital, marvelous it was! Now in this place you are being educated. If you are going to be discontented merely because you haven't got a better house or a better car, then you will belong to the stupid crowd. Or if you revolt because you want a different ideology, then again you are caught in the mesh of nonsense. But it is different if you say, "Look, we want order in this world, and order is not possible when there are ideologies, nationalities, separate religions." So it's your job. You are the coming generation, you have to change, you have to work at it, and that is part of your education, isn't it?

Will you ask some questions? (Pause) May I ask you a question then? While you are waiting to ask, I will ask you a question. You know, at the end of this so-called learning, which isn't actually learning at all but merely stocking up the mind with a lot of knowledge, you are going to pass exams, go to university and so on. Then what are you all going to do? Do you know already, or don't you know?

Comment: Become a dancer.

KRISHNAMURTI: If you say, "I am going to be a dancer," have you found out why? Why do you want to be a dancer? Don't give emotional answers: "Because I like it, sir"— that's not an answer. Or do you say, "I am going to be a doctor because the country needs doctors"; or, "I am going to be an engineer" because you say, "I'll get more money." Do you say to yourself, "I want to be an engineer because then I'll have a better car, a better house"? Is that what you want?

You see, really achieving what you want, getting what you want, isn't the end of life. Life is something enormous and very complex, and to say, "Well, I just want to get what I like; either I will be a doctor or a scientist or this or that"—isn't this rather futile? So what do you want? What do you think you will be? You can be a sannyasi. Ah, you laugh at that, don't you? You can become a teacher in a school. No? Why not? Think it out, why not? You know what a teacher's job is—creating a new generation, not just passing on some information, but creating a new generation of people, and you are not interested in that? So what? I can't answer for you, so I will have to leave the question with you.

Now you ask me questions. (Long pause) All right then, I'll ask you another question. When you look at those hills and the trees down there, how do you look at them? Do think it out. Do you look at them with your eyes? Obviously you do, don't you? You look at them with your eyes, but is that all? Or do you look at that tree, at that extraordinary light, the beauty of the hills, and the green leaves and the flowers, do you look at them also with your mind, with your heart? How do you look at them? Do answer me. Or do you never look at them at all because you are too busy playing, talking, chatting. And when you do look, by chance, how do you look at them? If you look at them completely with your mind, with your heart, with your eyes—that is, giving your complete attention when you look—then there is no idea, is there? You look and your whole being is occupied with looking. When you are so attentive, then there is no division between you and the thing you look at. You know, there is a drug called LSD; have you heard about it? I know some friends who have taken it. They say when you take it, immediately, or a few minutes afterwards, the division between you and the thing which you are looking at disappears; the space disappears. Does this interest you? Do you know what takes place when the space between you and that plant disappears? It is not that you identify yourself with the plant or with the flower, but the quality of separation ceases. Now that is right relationship. So when you know how to look at a tree, then you also know how to look at a human being. And when there is no separation between human beings, then you can't hate anybody.

Are you going to ask questions?

They are talking in Europe and America about meditation; it is written about in the papers. One of these yogis goes there and talks about meditation. Do you know anything about it? You don't, do you? Why don't you, I wonder. You know about mathematics, you know how to read and write, how to pass examinations, you do P.T., you do this and that, but you know nothing about this, do you? Why not? What is called

meditation is generally a traditional thing. You sit or stand in a corner, or sit under a tree, and you close your eyes, control your thoughts, or repeat some mantra and get some excitement out of it. That's what is generally called meditation, but that is self-hypnosis. Now, to find out what meditation is, first of all one has to have a very quiet mind. That means that the body has to have its own intelligence. Generally what we do is to dictate to the body what we think is pleasurable or painful. We tell it what to do—that it must get up at a certain time, that it must sit this way or walk that way—the mind tells the body. So the mind is always controlling the body and therefore depriving it of its intelligence, for the body has its own intelligence. So part of meditation is to allow the intelligence of the body to function. Which means that the body will become quiet when necessary, and active when that is demanded. I won't go into it further; it is very complicated. So one has to cultivate the intelligence of the body, which means non-interference of the mind with the body, and that demands a tremendous attention. So before you try something, sit absolutely quiet, absolutely quiet without opening your eyes, without moving your eyeballs or your eyelids, your fingers, or your feet—there should be no movement of any kind—not because you think, "I must sit quietly," but because it is nice to sit quietly.

In the evening when the sun is setting, it is extraordinarily quiet, isn't it? It has withdrawn for the night. In the same way sit very quietly, close your eyes, don't see who is sitting next to you; then see what happens. Then you will find, if you sit fairly quietly for a little while, that your mind wanders. That is, you say to yourself, "I ought to have done this or I ought to have done that, or I must do this or that"—the mind wanders. Then watch the mind. Don't control it, don't say it mustn't wander. Just watch it and find out why it wanders. Then out of this sitting very quietly—without forcing the body—seeing the mind and its operations, without telling it what it should think or what it should not think, out of this extraordinary complex observation comes quite a different kind of meditation.

Comment: Sir, those who take LSD are bound to be satisfied; they take LSD to be satisfied. I'd be satisfied after taking LSD.

KRISHNAMURTI: You'll want more LSD. It is like taking a drink, alcohol; to take it relieves you. It does various things to the body, and you feel relieved. Later on you want more because that thing has gone, and so you keep on drinking.

Try sometime to look at the tree—just to look at it. And also when you have time and you feel like it, sit very quietly, not only here, but when you are by yourself; or look at a tree, sitting quietly. You'll find a lot of things that you have never seen before.

October 30, 1967

First Talk in Rishi Valley

One has to use words to communicate and exchange not only ideas but something much more worthwhile and, I feel, profound. In using words we notice that certain words have special significance and are loaded; when one hears these words, one translates them according to the associations which one has formed in relation to one's particular inclination and tradition. When one uses a Sanskrit word, that word, obviously, is heavily loaded. It has its own associations and when one hears it, one falls back into the traditional meaning of that word, and one thinks one understands that word when one translates it or interprets it in traditional terms; one thinks one has really understood

what that word means. But fortunately we are not using any Sanskrit words; we are speaking in ordinary English and without any particular jargon, so there is little possibility of interpreting or translating any word according to a particular traditional background. When one uses the word *awareness,* one understands—if one is at all inclined to go into it—what it means; but the corresponding word in Sanskrit immediately awakens, in those people who are traditionally conditioned by Sanskrit, all kinds of associated ideas. So I would suggest that when we are communicating with each other—as we shall be during these talks and discussions—one should not translate these words of special significance into Sanskrit or Tamil, or whatever one is used to, and interpret them according to one's tradition. Accept these words freely, examine them critically—that examination and understanding has extraordinary vitality. But if one merely translates these words into a particular idiomatic, linguistic, traditional meaning, then I am afraid communication becomes rather difficult. After all, you have taken the trouble to come all this way to listen to a series of talks and discussions, and we must communicate with each other—you have to understand the speaker and the speaker has to understand you. So we have a common language like English, and when we use certain English words, they are ordinary English words without all the loaded associations of tradition—they can be used freely.

Now having stated that, we can proceed to examine the primary, essential issue—the crisis that is taking place in the world. I feel that this crisis is not a momentary crisis. There is always a crisis if one is willing to look at life freely, but as most of us are unwilling to look critically, unemotionally, objectively, we pass such crises by. A special crisis, a special challenge, has to arise to make us change. We are confronted with a series of crises throughout the world: there is the extraordinary crisis of violence, brutality, hatred, war, and so on; there is the economic crisis, not only as it is in this country, but in different forms in other countries; there is a social crisis, and the crisis in the relationship between man and man. And there is also a religious crisis because through education one examines and questions belief—belief has gone, belief has become a superstition. And those people who are really serious, not just accepting a double standard of life, have rejected all ideologies, systems, and formulas.

There is a crisis all through our existence, and observing closely one finds the crisis is not only in the outside world of phenomena but also inwardly. Inwardly we are very confused; we have not any longer a belief which will hold us, a standard to guide us, no longer any principles; so inwardly—if one is at all conscious of this problem—there is a great deal of contradiction and confusion. One may not observe this, one may not be aware of it, but it is there; and one may not acknowledge to oneself that all religions and systems have failed—whether the communist or other forms of systems—they have not produced what they have promised, they no longer have any meaning. Whether one is aware of it or not, there is, inwardly, psychologically, in the totality of our consciousness, a great deal of disturbance. When one is aware of this extraordinary disturbance, one sees it both outwardly and inwardly. Now, when one uses the word *disturbance,* how does one listen to it? Does one merely hear the word with all its associations, or does one hear that word without any contradiction, without any dual process of association taking place? I hope I am making myself clear on this question. If I hear that word disturbance with all its associations and its contradictions—that is, being disturbed, I want peace, I want quietness, I want tranquil-

lity, a state of nondisturbance, and so on—then I am not listening at all. I am hearing certain associated ideas which the word awakens in me. Isn't it so? No? The associated acts of hearing prevent me from listening. There are two acts when you hear a word like disturbance: there is the act of listening, and then there is the hearing of the reaction to that word—the reaction being the idea of tranquillity, peace, quietness, and all the rest of it. That word awakens certain associated ideas, and if one is caught in the associated ideas, one is actually not listening. I don't know if you are—actually listening—now.

Look, when you use the word *God,* immediately you have a series of reactions about it—that you believe or you don't believe, that it is stupid or idiotic to believe, or that there is God whose protection we must seek—which prevent you from the act of listening. For when you truly listen, there is no interpretation, there is no reaction at all; there is just the act of listening. Such an act of listening demands a great deal of discipline in order not to be caught in verbal associations with all the duality that that implies. Such an act of listening is an act as positive as the act of hearing and being carried away emotionally by a particular word. If one can listen without being caught in any process of duality, conflict, emotional attachment, or sentimental demand, then one can look very clearly at the whole issue; this is what we are going to discuss. We are not concerned with bringing about more ideas, more formulas, or the denial of formulas or systems. What we are concerned with is the act of listening which will see the truth and which will see the false by actual perception, without any judgment.

Is this at all clear, or am I talking Greek, Chinese—is it clear, somewhat?

Understanding, in ordinary relationships, can only come about when one is actually listening, not when one is arguing, not when one is trying to influence another, not when one is contradicting or when we are annoyed with each other. We understand each other when we are actually listening to each other, and that is only possible when there is a certain quality of affection and attention; otherwise, you cannot possibly listen. If you have already an image about the speaker and the speaker has an image about you, then we are not listening to each other—each image, which is an idea, is in communication with the other image, and that is utterly idiotic. But if we could understand each other, we could not only hear the word but listen beyond the word, listen with that state of mind which sees very clearly what is true and what is false; and such perception of what is true and what is false has nothing whatsoever to do with ideas, with systems. When you see something clearly, it is so; it is like seeing something dangerous, poisonous—you see the nature of the danger, and it demands your complete attention.

So we see in the world and in ourselves a great confusion, conflict, misery, and innumerable problems that demand solution—that's an obvious fact both outwardly and psychologically. And seeing this whole content of the human situation, one asks: Is it possible to change completely? That is our question, our primary question. Can you and I—who have built a society which is brutal, which is aggressive, violent, competitive, which engenders wars and class divisions and all the rest—can we bring about in ourselves without any influence, without any persuasion, without any punishment or the fear of punishment, a total revolution so that we are no longer brutal, violent, anxious, fearful, greedy, envious, and so on? That is the real issue because if we can fundamentally and radically change, then we will create a different society, then we will no longer live on words, on beliefs, on systems which have

produced so much catastrophe and disaster in the world.

So, can I, seeing this whole situation, not verbally but actually, can I easily, spontaneously, without any persuasion, bring about a complete transformation of myself? That is the real issue—is it possible? What is, I wonder, the reaction to such a statement; is there agreement that there must be change in the psyche, a total mutation in the human mind, or do you say that it is not possible, or "How am I to do it?"? If you say it is not possible, you accept things as they are, perhaps slightly modified; then you don't want any mutation, any change, and most people don't, especially those who are fairly secure economically or socially, or secure in certain dogmatic beliefs; there is for them no question. If you say, "I don't want to change"—either you crudely put it that way or you subtly say, "Well, that's too difficult, it's not for me"—you have already blocked yourself, you have already ceased to inquire, and it is no good going any further. But if you say, "Is it possible to change?"—change in the sense of seeing the fundamental necessity of a human revolution inwardly—if you say, "Is it possible?", then the next question is, "How am I to do it? Tell me of a system, a method; help me towards it." Then of course you are not concerned with change but with what will help you to bring about change—you are not really interested in a fundamental revolution; you want to know how to do it; you are seeking a system, a method. Now, when one seeks a method or a system, what takes place—let's go into it—what actually takes place? If the speaker were foolish enough to give a system, what would happen—psychologically what would take place? If you were equally foolish enough to follow the system, then you would be merely copying, imitating, conforming. You would conform, imitate, accept, because you would have set up in yourself the authority of another, and hence there would be a conflict between yourself and the authority in you—the authority that says you must do this, and yet you find you are incapable of doing it; you have your own particular inclination, tendency, pressure of circumstance against which there is the authority of the system that says you must do this or that, so there is contradiction. You will lead a double life, the ideology of the system against the actuality of your daily life—so you develop a hypocritical attitude towards life. In imitating, you suppress yourself; you say, "By Jove, the ideology is much greater than I am, much truer; I must conform to that"—but what is actually true is what you are, not the ideology. So if you can brush aside the ideology, then what have you left? Please observe this in yourself. You no longer say, "I will follow a saint"—we'll leave that person completely out because that person is already dead; a saint is a complete washout, is finished. But the man who says, "I want to change; tell me what to do"—such a man seems to be very earnest, very serious, but he is not. He wants to be told what to do; he wants to set up an authority which he hopes will bring about order within himself.

Can authority bring about order, at all? Stalin, Hitler, Mussolini, and all the world leaders have said that by creating an ideological authority, there will be order. But one has observed throughout life that where there is any form of authority, ideological or individual, it breeds disorder, as may be perceived in Russia, in China, everywhere where there is the worship of authority. I don't know if you see it. You may intellectually see this, but do you actually apply it so that the mind is no longer projecting an authority, the authority of a book, of a guru, of a wife or a husband, of society, and so on? We have always functioned within the pattern of a formula which becomes the ideology and the authority. You can observe

this phenomena very closely, directly, in India where you see that they have talked about nonviolence for the last forty years, endlessly, up and down the land; and when there was a war, a local war between Pakistan and India, there wasn't one human entity in India—an Indian—who followed nonviolence, who stood up against it and said, "This is wrong; it is terrible to kill." Though the Indians talked a great deal about ahimsa and all that nonsense, the actual fact is that not one of them lived what he said—they lived by words, and you cannot live by words; the words create the system, the ideology. So, can one put away this demand—"I see the necessity of change, but how am I to do it?" The moment you put the "how," you have already set in process the authority, whether the authority is yourself, your own experience, or the authority of another. If you see this very clearly, you have finished with it forever. When you see the necessity of radical change and you are not asking the question "how"—I do not know if you see this central point—then what takes place? That is the real crisis—you follow, sirs?—you are no longer seeking ways and means of changing because when you seek a way to change, that becomes the authority. If you change according to the Gita, then that becomes the authority. So if you can put away all that, then what are you confronted with? I don't know if you see this point very clearly, because if you miss this point, then we shall have to go back and back, and over and over again—which will be a waste of time.

I see that I must change completely from the very roots of my being; I can no longer depend on any tradition because tradition has destroyed, tradition has brought about this colossal laziness, acceptance, obedience; also I see that I cannot possibly look to another to help me to change—no guru, no god, no belief, no systems, no outward pressure of influence, all that. When I reject all that, what has taken place? When you reject something false, that is, looking to another to help you, and also when you have no longer the authority of your particular, little experience—when you reject all that—what takes place? First of all, can you reject it?—which means you are no longer afraid. When you reject something false, which you have been carrying about with you for generations, when you throw off a burden of any kind, what takes place? You have more energy, haven't you? You have more capacity, you have more drive, you have greater intensity, vitality. Now does that actually take place?—if it doesn't, you have not thrown off the dead weight of authority. And when you have this energy, in which there is no fear at all—the fear of making a mistake, of not doing right or doing wrong—then is not that energy itself the mutation?

One needs a great deal of energy, yet we dissipate energy through fear—through the fear of not achieving, not being successful outwardly, or the psychological fears, the fears that are caused by acceptance, by obedience. Fear dissipates energy, and when we see that—not theoretically or verbally, but actually see that as a danger—then you have the energy. Then when there is that energy which has thrown off every form of fear, that energy itself produces the radical revolution. You don't have to do a thing about it.

If you change according to a pattern, it is merely a superficial change. Have you not noticed the gradual change that is taking place in Russia?—they are becoming more and more bourgeois, like the rest of the world, because they have tried to function according to a formula or an ideology; but you can't fit the human mind into an ideology; it breaks away from it, and as it breaks away, it becomes more and more like the rest of the world.

So one observes in oneself the same process that one sees in the world—chaos, brutality, aggression, and so on. There is no separate outer and inner; the outer is related to the inner, the inner is related to the outer; there is intercommunication, it is a unitary process. And observing this, one demands—if one is at all intelligent, aware, inclined to be charitable—that a fundamental mutation shall take place in the human mind. And if you are not satisfied with things as they are, you may see the need of a change; but because you have a job, a house, a family, dependence of some kind, you'll say, "Who will help me to change?" One realizes that we have depended on others throughout the millennia, on saviors, Masters, gurus, and philosophers, and that they have not brought about a fundamental change in man—so you reject them totally; you don't play with them any more. So you are left with yourself; that is the actual state for a man who is very serious about all this. You are no longer looking to anybody for help, or assistance; therefore, you are already free to look. And when there is freedom, there is energy; and when there is freedom, there is never the doing of something wrong. Please understand this very clearly because freedom is entirely different from revolt—rather there is no such thing as doing right or wrong when there is freedom. You are free, and from that center you act; hence there is no fear, and a mind that has no fear is capable of great love, and it can do what it will. But a mind that is caught in fear lives in darkness and confusion—"What to do? Tell me, what is the right course to follow?"—then from that there is aggression, violence, and all the rest.

So if one demands, as one must, a total revolution in the psyche, one has to be aware of what is actually taking place in the world, not the world of America or Russia or China, but the world in which you are living—the world of aggression, your aggression, your desire for dominance, your desire for power, position, your corruption, that little world, whether you live in Madanapalle, Madras, Delhi, or in Moscow or wherever—so, be aware of it and from there move.

Would you like to ask any questions?

Question: What is the Sanskrit word for awareness?

KRISHNAMURTI: I really don't know; I don't want to know. I have explained, just now, what takes place in your mind when you use the word *awareness* and the equivalent in Sanskrit. This gentleman says *Jagrat*—you hear that word, what takes place? You think you understand the meaning of that word in Sanskrit, but you really don't. To understand that word you should be aware, that is, be aware of the people around you—their faces, of how they sit, how they yawn, how they scratch, how bored they are—be aware of the flowers, of the trees, the skies, the hills, and from there move inwardly to your reactions to the hills, to the colors, to the trees, to the skies, to the dry sand of the river, and to why you have these reactions; and all this can be immediately understood, observed, without going step by step. But if you say, "Tell me the meaning of that word in Sanskrit," you are not actually aware—you may have understood the word, but who cares what word you use as long as you understand in action.

One of our difficulties, it seems to me, is to ask a right question, and if you do see the right question to ask, probably you will never ask it. Because in order to ask the right question, you must have already gone into it very deeply; and when you have inquired deeply into a question, the answer is there, already. But most of us are not sufficiently serious; we would rather rely on somebody who is an authority—at least on somebody who we think is an authority—to tell us the answer.

To a really fundamental question there is no answer—anybody who answers it, offers an opinion, is a fool. And if you follow an opinion, you are equally foolish. How does one ask a right question, or rather, what is a right question—not "how," but "what" is a right question? A right question, it seems to me, must be directly related to yourself; it does not come from a dialectical search for opinions and the truth of opinions. So, can one ask the right question?—which doesn't mean that we are trying to prevent you from asking questions at all.

Question: Can we face violence with fearlessness?

KRISHNAMURTI: It is rather, "What has produced violence?"—not, "Can we face it?" Why are we, as human beings, violent, and why have we been violent for millennia, not merely just now—why are we violent, not how can we face it? Violence is part of the animal which we have inherited. Animals are violent—haven't you noticed them?—the bigger dog attacking the lesser dog. There is the violence of animals protecting their territorial rights and their sexual rights, haven't you noticed it? And territorial rights are much more important to them than their sexual rights, although they are exactly the same. Attack your property—my lord, you are all as violent as animals. Your wife looks at somebody else—you become violent. So violence is inherited and is part of the structure of human beings. One has to become aware of that; one has to know one is violent, not "how to face it." If you can eliminate violence, there is no need to face it at all.

We are also violent because we live in crowded societies, crowded urban cities; man demands space both outwardly and inwardly, but we have no outward space, and obviously we have no inward space. You know they are conducting research into the question of how much space human beings demand, must have. In crowded cities like Tokyo, London, New York, and other cities like Bombay, there is very little space—yet like birds and animals, we need space; otherwise, we will lose all sense of proportion. So one of the causes of violence is that lack of space, both outwardly and inwardly. Also there is violence because we are, like the ants, so colossally greedy, acquisitive; we want power, we want position; each of us wants to be the chief man in the village or the chief of whatever it is. So these are the causes of violence, and you can enlarge on them and go into them. Unless the mind frees itself from all that, it is no good talking about how to face violence. You can't resist violence; you have tried to resist violence with non-violence, and you haven't succeeded at all; you have only developed hypocrisy. But if you actually face violence in your daily life, observe the causes of violence—when you dominate your wife or the wife dominates you, for that is a form of violence—you will then see if it is at all possible to be free from such violence; one has to be aware of every movement of feeling, thought, action.

Question: If you have self-energy. . .

KRISHNAMURTI: Sir, you can't assume that you have this self-energy, as you call it; you know nothing about it, it's just an idea. If you have not actually rejected all authority, then every other form of inquiry with regard to freedom from authority is obviously a verbal statement; it has no actuality.

Look, sir, we want order in the world. Order is necessary, but there is great disorder outwardly and inwardly, right? Now what is, perhaps, the major cause of this disorder? You seek an authority that will bring about order in the disorder, don't you?—either the authority is a system or a formula, a dictator,

a law. Will such authority bring order, or will it only increase disorder? Obviously, authority will only increase disorder. And when you see that actually, then you see that there is no authority to clear this disorder; you see also this disorder is brought about by each one of us. So, can I clear up this disorder by no longer seeking any form of authority, in any direction?—for when I no longer seek authority to help to bring about order, I alone am responsible. You understand?—I am responsible for this disorder, nobody else. So what causes disorder? One of the major factors is the acceptance of authority and following the authority; another, and complementary cause, is the desire for power, position, prestige, and the rest of it. So, can I eliminate all that inside myself? If I do, there is actual energy, not theoretical energy.

November 4, 1967

Second Talk in Rishi Valley

If I may, I would like to talk this morning about conduct and what is involved in it; and perhaps, if we have time, I would like also to go into the question of what is called love.

All human activity is behavior. Through the centuries we have developed codes of conduct; these become laid down by the society, by the culture in which we live, and by the so-called saints and religious teachers; this code or pattern, this norm of behavior becomes traditional and automatic, that is, mechanical. This you can observe throughout the world, whether the code is Christian, Buddhist, Hindu, or Islamic—behavior is according to an established pattern. And human beings throughout the world have fixed ideas about conduct, an ideology as to how human beings should behave which is the norm, the accepted traditional authority; this is to be seen among the primitive as well as the highly civilized, sophisticated, and industrialized societies. But the actuality of behavior, the everyday actual behavior, is entirely different from the ideological behavior. One can observe this not only outwardly but in oneself.

As we were saying the other day, we are not merely hearing a few ideas or reasoned-out conclusions and so on, but we are in the very act of listening—which is different from hearing—actually experiencing what is going on within ourselves, not as ideas or as something that one should or should not do, but directly experiencing that which is being said. Otherwise, it seems to me, these talks will be like the wind passing through the leaves, and one cannot live on noise, however pleasant or unpleasant the noise may be; one has to live, and living is behavior in relationship. This is what we are going to talk over together this morning.

So there are codes of conduct which we human beings, throughout the world, have accepted: the traditional, religious, and social morality, and so on. And one observes that they have become mechanical, and it is part of our tradition as Hindus or Muslims or Christians to accept ideologically what is considered to be right conduct and try to live up to that standard, according to that code. That's what each one of us is doing all the time. And conduct becomes mechanical and behavioristic within the pattern that lays down what is right and what is wrong behavior, whether it be in the communist society or in the so-called free society. So we are going to find out if there is behavior or conduct which is not based on a code, on tradition, on mere repetition.

For most of us life is a constant battle, a constant struggle from the moment we wake until we go to sleep again. And in the battlefield called living, we try to set a formula, a code of conduct on how to behave every day; and the following of this code—however pleasant, however religious—breeds automatic responses; one can observe this within oneself. But is behavior necessarily merely automatic, mechanical, or can it be something which has nothing whatsoever to do with tradition and mechanical responses? If so, is such behavior the outcome of a certain freedom? For if behavior is not born out of freedom, must it not be always mechanical? Please, it is very—if I may point out—very important for us to understand this thing; and by that word *understand* I do not mean intellectually because there is no intellectual understanding of this matter; either one understands it completely or not at all; there is not first intellectual understanding and then actual understanding.

We are trying to find out if there is a conduct which does not become mechanical, repetitive, conditioned to a certain pattern—whether that pattern be ancient, modern, or the pattern of yesterday which one has set for oneself. If I behave now as I behaved yesterday, it is repetitive behavior and therefore mechanical. Or if I behave according to the tradition established by society, then again it becomes repetitive.

Is repetitive action virtuous action? If behavior and conduct are merely repetitive processes, then all human relationships actually cease. If I behave mechanically every day, repeating a certain code of conduct which I have learned, which I found profitable, or which is pleasant—repeating that over and over again—my relationship with you ceases, completely; I have become a machine.

If my behavior is according to either the code of the Hindu, the Muslim, the Buddhist or the Christian or the communist, then I must be in opposition to other cultures. But the world is no longer so rigidly divided into the Hindu, the Muslim, the Catholic, and all the rest of it; must there not be a behavior which is completely human and yet free beyond all nationalistic, linguistic, geographical divisions?

One can see that behavior is repetitive—doing something automatically and mechanically, how I behaved in a certain way yesterday, it was pleasant, I think it is right and I repeat that today and I will repeat it tomorrow—but this repetition of behavior, is it virtue?—virtue being order. A certain mechanical repetition does bring about a kind of order. But is not such order, because it is repetitive, disorder? This is seen, politically, when the tyrant, when the dictator, when the party says, "You must think that way, you must behave that way"—as do also the religious leaders; and repeatedly enforcing that, they hope to bring about order, but actually they create disorder, as is evidenced historically—every day. So order is not brought about by repetition, by a code, by a pattern of behavior; yet if there is no order, man cannot live at peace. We must have order, but one sees that order can only come about when there is no disorder. I cannot pursue the pattern of order by repetition, but I can see that that pursuit creates disorder. And if I understand the fundamental causes of disorder, then out of that understanding there is order, not the other way round.

One sees that disorder is produced by this mechanical process of repetition and that our conduct is based on that. I have an ideology according to which I try to live; by repeatedly trying to conform, I hope that I will eventually establish order within myself and outwardly. Then how is it possible to behave without the time element?—for repetition is time. Giving continuity to what I did yesterday, through today and tomorrow, is time. Is this getting too difficult, abstract?

Look, time has established—centuries of time—a code of conduct, and if I repeat that over and over again—mechanical behavior—that repetition is a form of time, isn't it? Such repetitive behavior makes us slaves to time and is also disorder. So we must find a conduct which is not of time and which is not according to any code, for they are both repetitive.

To put it differently, is virtue or morality within the pattern of time? We see that conduct and behavior are based on the principle of pleasure. And we see that when the principle of pleasure is active, the principle of pain is also active. Is there a code of behavior which is not based on the principle of pleasure and hence also the generation of pain? Is there behavior which doesn't belong to this category? Let us leave it there for the moment and approach it differently.

What is love? Can we understand it verbally and intellectually, or is it something that cannot be put into words? And what is it that each one of us calls love? Is love sentiment? Is love emotion? Can love be divided as divine and human? Is there love when there is jealousy or hatred, or competitive drive? Is there love when each one of us is seeking his own security, both psychological as well as worldly, outwardly? Don't agree or disagree, because you are caught in this. We are not talking of some love which is abstract—an abstract idea of love has no value at all. You and I can have a lot of theories about it, but actually, the thing that we call love—what is it? There is pleasure, sexual pleasure; then in that there is jealousy, the possessive factor, the dominating factor, the desire to possess, to hold, to control, to interfere with what another thinks. Knowing all the complexity of this, we say that there must be love that is divine, that is so beautiful, untouched, uncorrupted; we meditate about it and get into a devotional, sentimental, emotional attitude and are lost. Because we can't fathom this human thing called love, we run away into abstractions which have absolutely no validity at all. Right? So what is love? Is it pleasure and desire? Is it love of the one and not of the many?

To understand the question—what is love?—one must go into the problem of pleasure, whether sexual pleasure or the pleasure of dominating another, of controlling or suppressing another, and whether love is of the one denying the love of the other. If one says, "I love you"—does it exclude the other? Is love personal or impersonal? And we think that if one loves one, one can't love the whole; and if one loves mankind, then one can't possibly love the particular. This all indicates, does it not, that we have ideas about what love should be. This is again the pattern, the code developed by the culture in which we live, or the pattern that one has cultivated for oneself. So ideas about love matter much more than the fact—ideas of what love is, what it should be, what it is not. The religious saints, unfortunately for mankind, have established that to love a woman is something totally wrong; you cannot possibly come near their idea of God if you love someone—it is sex, and taboo, it is pushed aside by the saints, but they are eaten up with it, generally. So to go into this question of what love is, one must first put away all ideas, all ideologies of what love is, or should be, or should not be, and the division as the divine and the not-divine. Can we do that? And they are doing that, mind you—the hippies, the Beatles, the Italian *capellonis,* and various others say, "All that is rubbish, wipe it out; that is the invention of the creeps"; the creeps are the older generation! Yet they have ideas and talk a great deal about love, in which is involved sex and all the rest. And also they say when you love, there is no war and so on and on and on.

Now can we—not as a reaction, but because we understand this whole process of division between the idea and the fact—can we put away the ideas and actually face the fact, the actuality? Otherwise, this division between 'what should be' and *what is* is the most deceptive way of dealing with life. The Gita, the Bible, Jesus, Krishna, all these people, these books, say you should, should, should; put away all that, completely—it is all ideas, ideology, the 'what should be'— then we can look at the actuality. Then one can see that neither emotion nor sentiment has any place at all where love is concerned. Sentimentality and emotion are merely reactions of like or dislike. I like you and I get terribly enthusiastic about you; I like this place, oh, it is lovely and all the rest—which implies that I don't like the other and so on. Thus sentiment and emotion breed cruelty. Have you ever looked at it? Identification with the rag called the national flag is an emotional and sentimental factor, and for that factor you are willing to kill another—and that is called the love of your country, love of the neighbor, love of your whatever. One can see that where sentiment and emotion come in, love is not. It is emotion and sentiment that breed the cruelty of like and dislike. And one can see also that where there is jealousy, there is no love, obviously. I am envious of you because you have a better position, better job, better house; you look nicer, more intelligent, more awake, and I am jealous of you. I don't in fact say I am jealous of you, but I compete with you, which is a form of jealousy, envy. So envy and jealousy are not love, and I wipe them out; I don't go on talking about how to wipe them out and in the meantime continue to be envious—I actually wipe them out as the rain washes the dust of many days off a leaf; I just wash them away.

Is love pleasure and desire, in which is sex—just look what is involved in it—is love pleasure? You know, that word *love* is so loaded—I love my country, I love that book, I love that valley, I love my king, I love my wife, love of God—it is so heavily loaded. Can we free that word—for we must use that word—can we free that word from all these encrustations of centuries? We can do that only when we go into this question: Is love pleasure and desire? Conduct, we said, is based on the principle of pleasure; even when we sacrifice, it is still based on pleasure. You observe it throughout life. We behave in a certain way because it pleases us, essentially. And we say, if we have not thought about it a great deal, that love is pleasure. So we are going to find out whether love is beyond pleasure and if it therefore includes pleasure.

What is pleasure? From where I am sitting, through the division in those trees, I can see the hill and the rock on top of it; it is somewhat like the Italian countryside with a castle and village on the hill. I can see the flowers with sparkling leaves in the bright sunlight—it is a great delight, it is a great pleasure, isn't it? That scene is really most beautiful. There is the perception and the tremendous delight in it; that is pleasure, isn't it? And what is wrong with it? I look at that, and the mind says, "How lovely, I wish I could always look at that, not live in filthy towns, live here quietly and stagnate." I want it to be repeated, and tomorrow I'll come and sit here—whether you are here or not—and look at that because I enjoyed it yesterday, and I want to enjoy it today. So there is pleasure in repetition. Right? There was the sexual enjoyment of yesterday; I want it repeated today and tomorrow. Right? I see that scene of the hill, the trees, the flowers, and there is at that moment complete enjoyment, the enjoyment of great beauty. What's wrong with it? There is nothing wrong with it; but when thought comes in and says, "By Jove, how marvelous that was, I want it repeated again"—that repetition is the beginning of the desire, the looking for pleasure, for tomorrow. Then the pleasure of tomorrow becomes mechanical. Thought is always mechanical, and it builds an image of that hill, of those trees; it is the memory of it all, and the pleasure which I had must be repeated; that repetition is the continuity of

desire strengthened by thought. We say love is pleasure, love is desire—but is it? Is love the product of thought? The product of thought is the continuity of desire as pleasure. Thought has produced this pleasure by thinking about what was pleasurable yesterday, which I want repeated today. So is love a continuity of thought, or has thought nothing whatsoever to do with love? And one can only say thought has nothing whatsoever to do with love, but one can say it authentically only when one has really understood this whole question of pleasure, desire, time, thought—which means there is freedom. Conduct can only be immediate in freedom. Sirs, look, as we said earlier, repetitive conduct, behavior or a pattern breeds not only mechanical, repetitive relationship but desire; in that there is a time element. And we have inquired if there is a behavior, a conduct, which is completely free, each minute, each second; it is only in that complete behavior, in each moment, that there is virtue, having no continuity as yesterday and tomorrow.

So freedom is in the moment of action, which is behavior; it is not related to yesterday or tomorrow. Sirs, look at it the other way. Has love roots in yesterday and tomorrow? What has root in yesterday is thought. Thought is the response of memory, and if love is merely memory, obviously it is not the real thing. I love you because you were nice to me yesterday, or I don't like you because you didn't give me an opportunity for this or that—then it is a form of thought which accepts and denies.

Can there be love which has no emotion, no sentiment, which is not of time?—this is not theoretical but actual, if you really face it. Then you will find that such love is both personal and impersonal, is both the one and the many, is like the flower that has perfume; you can smell it or you can pass it by; that flower is for everybody, and for the one who takes the trouble to breathe it deeply and look at it, a great delight.

Can we talk about this, ask questions and go into it more deeply, go into more detail, if you want to?

Question: When there is conflict from pressures, it is impossible to bring about that state in which love is not personal. If I may also say so, in that state the word love *disappears and many other words we are using all the time. Could we discuss that?*

KRISHNAMURTI: When there is no conflict in love, it being impersonal, would you call it by another name? Sir, again you see, we are using that word *conflict*. When does conflict arise in love? That's a dreadful statement, isn't it? Do you see that? It's a dreadful statement, that there is conflict in love. All our human relationships are a conflict, with the wife, the husband, with the neighbor, and so on. Why does conflict exist at all between two human beings, between husband and wife, and so on, in that relationship which we call love? Why? What does that word *relationship* mean—to be related, what does that mean? I am related to you; that means that I can touch you, actually physically or mentally; we meet each other. There is no barrier between us. There is an immediate contact even as I can touch this microphone. But in human relationship there is no such immediate contact because you as the husband or the wife have an image about the wife or the husband. Don't you have an image about the speaker? Obviously, otherwise many of you wouldn't be here. So you have a relationship with the image, and if that image is not according to your pattern, then you say, "He is not the right man"— you have actually no contact with the speaker at all. You have a contact with the image which you have created about the speaker, just as you have an image about

your wife and your husband; and the contact, the relationship between these two images is what you call relationship. The conflict is between these two images, and as long as these images exist, there must be conflict. But if there is no image at all—which is something extraordinary, into which one has to go very, very deeply—if there is no image at all, there is no conflict. If you have no image about me and I have no image about you, then we meet. But if you insist that I am a foreigner and you are a dogmatic Hindu soaked in tradition, well, it becomes impossible. So where there is love, there is no conflict because love has no image. Love doesn't build images because love is not touched by thought, love is not of time.

As you have pointed out, sir, we are slaves to words as we are slaves to images, to symbols. The word, the symbol, is not the actuality; and to find the actuality, see the actuality, one must be free of the word and the symbol.

Question: Can there be spontaneity in love?

KRISHNAMURTI: Now, I don't know what you mean by those words, *love* and *spontaneous*. Are we ever spontaneous? Is there such a thing as being spontaneous? Have you ever been spontaneous? Have you? Ah, wait sir, don't agree or disagree. Look at the word, what is implied in it. To be spontaneous means you have never been conditioned; you are not reacting, you are not being influenced; that means you are really a free human being, without anger, hatred, without having a purpose in view—can you be so free? Only then could you say, "I am spontaneous." To be really spontaneous involves not only the understanding of the superficial consciousness but also the deeper layers of consciousness, because all consciousness is behavior, pattern. Any action within the field of consciousness is limited and therefore not action which is free, spontaneous.

Comment: Repetition of action is necessary to life.

KRISHNAMURTI: Obviously. Taking one step after the other, when you walk, is a repetitive action. Technological knowledge is repetitive action; all accumulated knowledge is repetitive. You are going home, knowing the address, taking that road which goes to your home—it is repetitive. And such repetitive action is obviously necessary; otherwise, you will be unbalanced. But if that repetitive action is the whole of our existence, which we try to make it, then we are just machines, repeating the Gita, going to the same house, to the same office, the same sexual relations—you know, repeat, repeat, repeat. Probably most of us do prefer such a quiet, dull, dead life of repetition, and this is what industrial society is producing; and the communist world is also producing that—"Don't be disturbed, don't disturb the status quo. We are in power, we know what is right. We are the providence and for God's sake don't interfere; we'll tell you what to do, be a machine."

We said that technological knowledge, all accumulation of knowledge, is a process of repetition. Cybernetics, electronics, every branch of knowledge is accumulated, repetitive. Now do we reduce all life to repetition, mechanical process? I know we do because that is the safest way of living. That is the safest course to follow, and if one is so completely mechanized, there is no answer. You understand, sirs? Take a devout Catholic, practicing Catholic; he believes dogmas, performs rituals, completely without any thought, like many Hindus do. But in the office he behaves like a human being, destroying others, cheating others, and so on. Most of us do not want to be disturbed because we have reduced ourselves to machines. It is so obvious.

Question: What is the final state, sir?

KRISHNAMURTI: Ah! (Laughter) What is the final stage when there is not a mechanical, repetitive process? We see what a repetitive process does. But how will you find out what the other state is which is not repetitive? Can you? If I were foolish enough to tell you, then it would be a theory, which you would be foolish to accept. So can't you experiment, live, see what happens for yourself?

Question: But I want the final thing that a guru has, you understand?

KRISHNAMURTI: Oh, it's very simple sir. The final thing is—climb the mountain and look over. You sit here and say, "Please tell me the final thing you see on the top of the hill."

Comment: The man who is there can tell about it.

KRISHNAMURTI: So you sit here, and he is on top of the hill and describes to you what he sees. Right? And you are quite satisfied! You don't say, "Well, let me climb up there and see what it looks like"—you are satisfied by the image given by the interpreter who is on the top of the hill. And that is what we have done throughout centuries. Shankara and others—you know, they have described, and we say, "perfect"; we are very happy with the description, which is to live on words. And a man who lives on words has no substance; he is a dead man. Right, sirs!

November 8, 1967

Third Talk in Rishi Valley

The other day we were talking over together the question of love, and we came to a point, I think, which needed much greater penetration, a greater awareness of the issue.

Most of us have lost touch with nature; we are urban people living in crowded cities with all their problems, having little space both outwardly and inwardly, living in crowded apartments or small houses, and having very little space even to look at the sky of an evening or morning. The lack of space creates psychological problems, and as civilization tends more and more towards large cities, man, I feel, is completely losing touch with nature and thereby a great source of beauty. I do not know if you have observed how very few of us look at a sunset, or the moonlight, or look on the reflection of light on the water. And if we have lost touch with nature, naturally we tend to develop intellectual capacities; we go to museums, concerts, and various amusements, probably hoping, thereby, to experience something more, to feel a little more vital than we do in the daily routine and boredom. I do not know if you have noticed, in yourself, how little you are in actual touch with nature, and how closely we all live, and whether this circumstance has any significance, except for utilitarian purposes.

Most of us have no sense of beauty—I am distinguishing between beauty and good taste. Good taste is not necessarily the appreciation of something very beautiful; good taste can be cultivated, copied, imitated; but the feeling for beauty cannot be copied; one cannot possibly have a system to cultivate beauty, or go to school to be taught to appreciate beauty. And without this quality, this sense of beauty, I do not see how there can be love.

Most of us have developed intellectual capacities—so-called intellectual capacities,
which are not really intellectual capacities at all—we read so many books, filled with what other people have said, their many theories and ideas. We think we are very intellectual if we can quote innumerable books by innumerable authors, if we have read many different varieties of books, and have the capacity to correlate and to explain. But none of us, or very few, have original, intellectual conception. Having cultivated the intellect—so-called—every other capacity, every other feeling has been lost, and we have the problem of how to bring about a balance in our lives so as to have not only the highest intellectual capacity and be able to reason objectively, to see things exactly as they are, not to endlessly offer opinions about theories and codes, but to think for ourselves, to see for ourselves very closely the false and the true. And this, it seems to me, is one of our difficulties: the incapacity to see, not only outward things, but also such inward life that one has, if one has any at all.

I think we ought to inquire into what we mean by the word *see*. When we say we see a tree or a flower or a person—do we actually see the tree, or do we see the image that that word has created? This is to say, when you look at a tree, or a cloud of an evening that is full of light and delight, do you actually see with your eyes, and also intellectually, with feeling—totally, completely? Or do you merely see with the word and its associations so that you do not actually see the tree at all? Have you ever experimented with that, with seeing an objective thing like a tree, or a flower, or a bird, without any association? If you see it with an associated image, then that image, word, or concept, prevents you from looking at the tree, actually. As you are sitting here, there are so many trees around you, hills and the light—do look. Look, see how you perceive it, and notice what actually takes place when you look. Do you look at it without space or with space? Do you look at it with a verbal concept, or do you look at it without the word, without the association, without the mental picture or image? Is it possible to look without the "observer" and therefore without a space between the "seer" and that which is seen? It is important to understand this because we are going to go into something that requires careful investigation, and if we cannot really see—"see" in the true sense of that word, see without any preconception, without any prejudice, without condemnation or justification—then we shall not be able to proceed. It is only then that it is possible to be directly in contact with anything in life. If I have an image about you and you have an image about me, naturally we do not see each other at all. What we actually see are the images which we have about each other, that's all. My image prevents me from actually being in contact with you. Do please go into it as we are talking. Observe it in yourself and see how far you can be free of the image; to look and be free of the image so that you can see directly demands its own discipline, not a self-imposed or externally imposed discipline.

So, we are to investigate together—without any sense of authority, without any sense of "You know and I don't know," or "I know and you don't know"—the question of whether it is possible to be free of the space which we create—not only outside of ourselves, but also in ourselves—which divides people, which separates, in all relationships. Am I making myself fairly clear?

Without love and the sense of beauty, there is no virtue; without love all action must inevitably lead to mischief, but when there is that love and beauty, you can do what you will, whatever you do is right, whatever you do has order. Without love, any theory, any formula or concept about reality has no meaning whatsoever.

And this morning we are going to find out for ourselves what this quality of love is; we shall not find out or come upon it if we approach with deliberation, with intent, because conscious effort to understand something prevents understanding. There must be freedom to look, and there is no such freedom if there is a conceptual idea, or image, or a symbol, for that prevents you from looking. Can we look at ourselves, that is, not at the images that we have created about ourselves, the myths, the ideas of what we ourselves are—which are not real—but actually observe what we are, the actuality, not the theory? The Hindu, through centuries, has created formulas; he is the atma, or this, or that; he lives according to a concept that there is a permanent entity, a permanent god, or whatever you like to call it, in himself—that is just a theory, it is not an actuality. Some poor, intellectual, religious, unbalanced person stipulated that, invented that idea, whether Shankara or somebody else, and we just accept it. We don't know, and to find out, we must completely brush all that aside.

And we are going to look at ourselves actually as we are, not as we should be, because there is always conflict when there is this duality—that is, when we are unwilling to face the actual and are looking at its opposite. I am unwilling to face the fact that as a human being, there is violence in me, that I am angry, brutal, aggressive, ambitious, greedy, envious—those are facts; but I have a conceptual idea that I should not be greedy, I should not be violent, so I develop a conceptual world and live there. So there is a conflict between *what is* and the opposite, 'what should be'. Now, is it possible to be free of the concept and actually face the actual? Is it? The actual is what we have to deal with, not the conceptual, not the fictitious world of ideas.

Human beings are violent, and our problem is how to be completely free of violence.

Because wherever there is any form of violence—please follow this—any form of violence, whether from suppression or from self-imposed discipline to conform, to imitate, that violence is contrary to love; and to find out what love is, we must be free of all that violence. Is it possible to be so completely free of violence—not only consciously, but at the deeper layers of consciousness? Am I putting the question clearly? Otherwise violence is a distortion and I can't see clearly. When I have the ideal of nonviolence, it creates a conflict between the actual and that fictitious ideal; and any conflict, any effort, is a form of distortion.

Is it possible to live only with the actual and not with the conceptual?—the conceptual being the belief in God, the ideological, the theoretical, the intellectual formulas. Is it possible only to deal with that which actually is and hence remove conflict altogether? Now, let us take the question of fear. Most people are afraid—thousands of fears they have, from the most petty to the deepest fears—and they cultivate bravery, the opposite. Or they escape from fear, through drink, through sex, through amusements, through entertainment, and so on and so on. Now is it possible not to escape, not to create its opposite, but actually remain with the fact of fear and understand it and completely be free of it? So what takes place? When there is no escape from the fact of fear, there is no opposite of fear—then all condemnation and judgment ceases. Right? I am just afraid, not, "I should not be afraid," not, "I must be free of fear," or, "I don't understand what to do and I am in conflict with it"; I actually remain with the fact, and hence there is no conflict at all with the fact. Now what takes place when you have no opposite of fear, when there is no conflict in the sense of condemning it, justifying it, or accepting it, when you are not escaping from it—what actually takes place? You understand? Now

who is it that is afraid?—and is the observer who says, "I am afraid" different from the thing observed, which is fear? Most of us say, for example, when angry, "I am angry," as though anger were something different from 'me', and hence we try to do something about anger—suppress it, get rid of it, or enjoy it. But is there such separation? Is not the person who says, "I am angry," anger himself? So if there is no separation between the observer and the thing observed, you remove conflict and effort altogether. And with regard to fear, is there the observer who is different from that which he feels as fear? Please watch this in yourself. If there is a separation between you as the observer and the fear, then in that division there is conflict. There is the desire to be free from it. You make an effort to overcome it. But the actual fact is: The observer is the fear—so the observer is the observed, the fear, and hence there is no conflict at all but simply the fact. Then what takes place? What actually takes place when there is no dissipation of energy through conflict, through separation, through justification, or through condemnation? You eliminate all that totally—then what takes place? Please, I wish you would discuss this point with the speaker because then you would go into it much deeper.

What actually takes place?

Comment: It's only theory.

KRISHNAMURTI: You see, you are really not seeing this. Just listen.

Comment: Please talk more about the observer and the observed being the same.

KRISHNAMURTI: All right sir, let's go into it a little more. Is the observer static? Or is the observer constantly undergoing change, moving, in a flux? And when he says, "I am afraid," and there is no division between the fact and the observer, has not the observer undergone a tremendous change? I don't know if you are following all this.

The observer is a living entity, isn't he? Not the higher self and atma and all that nonsense; cut all that out. But in actual fact the observer is a living entity; he thinks, he feels, he has reactions, he condemns, he justifies, he accepts, he disciplines himself—he is a living thing. The observer is a living thing, vital, and when he says, "I am afraid," he has not only separated that fear from himself, but what further has he done? He has made fear something static, has he not? Right? Is what we are saying reasonable, or is it fictitious and unreal—or do you merely accept anything the speaker says?

Look, sirs, the whole problem is this: Our life is a constant struggle, a battlefield, an endless movement of achievement, fear, despair, agony, sorrow. That's our life, that's the fact; is it possible to be completely free of all that, not in heaven, not through the gods we have conceived, and all the rest of that nonsense? If the mind is not free of that, you cannot go any further. You can merely invent, you can speculate, you can live in a dream world without any reality. So, is it possible to be free from all effort?—which doesn't mean one lives in a kind of vague, negative state, on the contrary. Now to find that out, one must investigate the observer and the observed. And we ask: What is the observer? The observer is the thinker, the experiencer, and so on. The observer is the result of many experiences, many incidents, accidents, influences, strains, stresses, knowledge, accumulated memory, tradition—all that. He, as the observer, is always adding and subtracting; it is a living movement of like and dislike, of weighing, comparing, judging, evaluating—he is all the time living. He is living within the field of what he calls consciousness, within the field of his own knowledge, influences, and innumerable accumulations. That's an obvious fact. Then what is the thing observed? The observer looks at a tree—let's go step by step—the observer looks at a tree with all the botanical knowledge he has about that tree, saying that is a beautiful tree, it gives a great shadow; or if he is a merchant of ideas, he wants to translate that idea of that tree into various word pictures and so on; or he is a timber merchant, and he wants to cut that tree down and sell it for timber and so on. So the observer, when he looks at the tree—please do it with me; look at the tree there, or any tree—when you, the observer, look at that tree, you are looking with all the knowledge you have accumulated about that tree, with your like and dislike. Now, the observer is all that, and the tree is naturally static, static in the sense it remains there, right? What takes place when I look at that tree with all my accumulated knowledge, botanical and otherwise—what actually takes place? I am looking at that tree through the image I have about that tree; I am not actually looking at the tree. Now can I look at that tree, can the observer look at that tree, without any image, knowledge? Can you? And if you do, what takes place? Without any sense of evaluating, judging, condemning, of like and so on—just to look. Then what takes place? You see you have never done it; that's why you can't answer.

Comment: There would be no thought at all.

KRISHNAMURTI: Oh no, no.

Comment: No image.

KRISHNAMURTI: Sirs, what are you saying? I am talking of looking at the tree, not thought or images.

Comment: You are the tree.

KRISHNAMURTI: You are not—you begin to invent. Sirs, you are really not even intellectual; you are just verbal. Now look at that tree without the image, without the associated ideas that you have about the tree. Your mind is free to look, isn't it?—is free to look. Right? So the first thing is that there is freedom to observe.

Now move—we have looked at the tree—now move within. You have an image about your wife or your husband or your friend or about the speaker. Now can you look at yourself without the image; can you look at another, whom you know fairly well, without the image, without any formula? If you can't do this, you cannot possibly go a step further. You can merely spin a lot of theories, write endlessly about democracy, politics, what Shankara said, or this or that. Then what takes place? You see that the observer is the result of time because he has accumulated, he is the accumulation of man whether in America, Russia, or India—and the accumulation is time. The observer is time, and as long as he functions within the field of time, there must be separation between himself and the thing he observes.

The observer can only look when there is freedom. So he can look at fear—please follow this—he can look at fear only when there is freedom from the accumulated conditioning which says, "I must be free, I must go beyond it, I must suppress it, I must escape from it"—right? When there is freedom, he can look at fear; then there is no separation between himself and the fact which is fear. Therefore all conflict ceases—and when there is a cessation of conflict, is

there fear? Don't agree, sir; do it and you will find out.

In order to look, as we said, there must be freedom. Freedom to look implies care, and the attention which is involved in that. Then there is a sense of protection, love. Do it and you will see the extraordinary beauty of this. Then, in that state, when we look out of freedom, in which there is care and attention, which implies affection and love—is there fear? There is fear only when the observer is different from the thing which he observes.

So, can I look at myself actually as I am?—which is learning about myself, not according to some philosopher, not according to some analyst, not according to Shankara, or anybody, but actually learning about myself—because if I don't learn about myself, if I don't know myself, I cannot go very far. To learn about myself there must be freedom to look; to look there must be care and attention, with no sense of condemnation at all. So, self-knowing—I am using the word *self* not with the big *S* or the little *s,* just the ordinary self; don't translate it into higher self, the atma, and the rigmarole that one has developed for so many centuries—self-knowing, to learn about oneself, is very important. And oneself is moving, living, all the time undergoing a change; but if you try to learn about it with accumulated knowledge, you don't learn. What is learning? Can I learn about something if I know already what it is? I can only learn something which I don't know—let's say the Russian language—so I learn. I accumulate words, verbs, adjectives, how to place the verb, and so on; I learn. That means I accumulate verbal knowledge about the language—Russian—and at the end of a certain time, if I am fairly proficient, I begin to speak it. I can then add more words, or modify words, or invent new words—but can I use the same method with regard to something which is living? I am a living thing, changing, changing under different pressures, circumstances, strains; every impact, every influence modifies me. There is a living thing and I want to learn about it. To learn about it, to learn about a living thing, I must come to it with a freshness of mind, not with an accumulated knowledge about myself.

I learned something about myself yesterday; I learned—it's the past tense—and with what I learned I come to the fresh living of myself today and try to understand that living thing with yesterday's knowledge. What happens? I don't learn at all. I am looking at the living thing with the past knowledge, with what I learned yesterday; so I must be free of what I learned yesterday in order to look at the living thing, which is actuality, today. So to learn about myself there must be freedom from what I learned about myself yesterday; in that way there is always a new, fresh contact with today and what actually is. Well, sirs?—and is not love like that? Love is not the product of thought. Love is not pleasure or desire—which we went into the other day—love is a living thing; it is not hedged about, caught in jealousy; jealousy is the past. Is not love a living thing?—and therefore there is no thought as yesterday or tomorrow.

I know what many of you are probably thinking, which is: If that is so, what is my relationship with my wife, my husband—right?

Comment: Exactly!

KRISHNAMURTI: I thought so! (Laughter) You understand, sir? Listen exactly to what I said. I said love is a living thing; it has no yesterday nor tomorrow, it is always the active present. Not, I will love, or I have loved. And when there is that quality of love, what is your relationship to your wife or husband or to your neighbor? It's your problem, not mine—don't wait for me to answer it—be-

cause you are married, you have children, husbands. It's your problem; how are you going to deal with it? You have to find out, first, if you really love your wife or husband. Do you? Love—not the pleasure you get out of your wife or husband, sexual or otherwise. Not the desire, not the comfort, not the keeping the house, cook and servant—all that is comfort, which you call love. You call that love. Therefore to you, love is pleasure, love is comfort, love is security, a guarantee for the rest of your life—unless you get divorced—a continuous sexual or emotional satisfaction. And all that you call love. Right? And somebody like the speaker comes along and says, "Look, is that love?" and questions you, asks you to look inside it. Of course you refuse to look because it is very disturbing; you would rather discuss the atma or the political situation in India, or the economic condition. But when you are driven into a corner to look, you realize it's really not love at all; it's mutual gratification, mutual exploitation.

And when you begin to inquire into love, to find out, feel the extraordinary nature of it, you must come to it with a fresh mind, mustn't you? Not say, "I am married, what is my relationship with my wife? Must I leave her, or stay with her, if love has no past or tomorrow?" When the speaker says love has no yesterday or tomorrow, that is a reality to the speaker, not to you. You may quote it and make it into an idea, but that has no validity at all. But if you inquire, investigate, explore into what love is, try to find out, learn, with freedom from all condemnation, from all judgment, so that the mind is unconditioned already, then you can look; and when you can look with such freedom, you will see that there is neither the observer nor the observed.

Question: Is there an end to desire?

KRISHNAMURTI: Why do you put that question? Do you find that desire is very painful? Or do you find desire rather pleasurable? If it is pleasurable, do you want to put an end to something which is pleasurable?—certainly not, nobody does. To the politician when he reaches the top of the heap, it is a great pleasure, it is great ambition and desire fulfilled; he wants to continue with that pleasure, he doesn't want to end desire. But when desire becomes painful, creates trouble, brings sorrow, anxiety, then you want to put an end to desire. So one has to find out what desire is before you ask if it has an end or if it must everlastingly continue. What is desire? I know all the scriptures have said you must work without desire, you must be desireless—you know all that stuff; throw all that overboard and let's find out.

What is desire? You see a beautiful house, really well proportioned, with a lovely garden; you look at it—then what takes place? You see with your eyes this beautiful house, with a lovely garden, and there is a reaction, there is a sensation, and you say, "I wish I had that house." There is perception, sensation, and thought comes in and says, "I wish I had that house." I don't know if you are following all this—it is simple, is it not? I see that beautiful sari; I haven't got such a sari and I say, "I wish I had." So, thought strengthens and gives continuity to the pleasure which has arisen from the perception, which has become my desire.

The question then is, and it's quite important to understand this: Can there be perception of a beautiful house, a beautiful face, a beautiful car—and to react to the perception is normal; if there is no reaction at all, you are dead—without thought interfering at all? The moment thought interferes, you have begun the battle. I see that you are much more intelligent, bright, clear, than I am; I compare myself with you. You are more

learned—I don't know why but you are, and erudition is respected, and I don't know why either—and I compare myself with you, and I want to be like you, and I think becoming like you is progress, evolution; but if I don't compare myself with you in any way at all, what happens? Am I then dull? You understand what I am saying?—that I know dullness only because I compare myself with you. Am I dull because I have compared myself with you, who are cleverer; if not, then how do I know that I am dull?

Comment: I am aware of it.

KRISHNAMURTI: No, no, you have invented it. Sir, do observe yourself. Look, I compare myself with you and I say I am dull. But if I don't compare myself with you, how do I know I am dull? I don't—right? I don't know. When I say, "I don't know"—what does that mean? Am I waiting to become as clever as you are? I am hungry today—do I know I am hungry today because I was hungry yesterday? The memory of yesterday's hunger, does it tell me that I am hungry today? It doesn't, does it? So I have no comparison there at all. The actual fact is I am hungry today, and I know it without comparing it with the hunger which I had yesterday. Right? Now do I know I am dull because I compare myself with you, who are cleverer? Of course I do, but if I don't compare, am I dull? Now go into it, go into it slowly. I am what I am—I see what I am; I don't call it dull or clever; I don't use words, which are comparative; I am that, I am what I am—then what takes place? What takes place, sir, when I make no comparison whatsoever?

Comment: Satisfaction.

KRISHNAMURTI: Oh! Satisfaction? To be satisfied is to become—first of all, sir, can you remove from within yourself all sense of measurement? I am more clever than you are, I am more beautiful, less beautiful—can you remove all sense of comparison, all sense of measurement? You can't, can you? You have been conditioned from childhood to compare. In the class, A is cleverer than B, and B struggles furiously to be as clever as A; yet B, who is struggling, destroys himself in imitating A or another. That is what we call education—but that is irrelevant, for the time being. So you are conditioned to compare, and if you don't compare, what takes place? Not satisfaction.

Comment: We stop struggling.

KRISHNAMURTI: You stop struggling—if you stop struggling, will you go to sleep? You see, you can't answer this unless you have no comparison, which means having no ideal, no hero, no Gita—no book will ever tell you about the comparative relation of yourself to somebody else. When there is complete cessation of all measurement of yourself and of another, then what takes place?

Comment: We see ourselves.

KRISHNAMURTI: No. You just invent, sir, you just throw out a lot of words; you don't do it. You do it, sir, and you will answer it rightly. When there is no measurement at all within yourself which compares yourself with another—what takes place?

Comment: We see what we are and do things according to that.

KRISHNAMURTI: We see what we are and do things according to what we see! We are not talking of . . . we must be talking Greek or Chinese!

Comment: If I don't compare, then I am happy.

Question: But I do compare; I see that you are much greater and happier than myself, and therefore I compare. That's why I come here—because I realize that I am sorrowful, and I come to listen to you because you are happy. How can I stop comparing?

KRISHNAMURTI: If you are in sorrow, sir, then are you free from sorrow by comparing yourself with another who you say is not in sorrow?

Comment: No, but I want to be like you.

KRISHNAMURTI: Ah, wait. You want to be like him, which is, you want to go beyond sorrow, which means what?—that you must understand sorrow, not be "like" him. You must understand your sorrow, not the happiness of another. You must understand the thing that you call sorrow—how do you understand sorrow? By understanding yourself—what you are, what has brought about this sorrow, whether it is self-pity or a sense of loneliness, whether it is a sense of complete isolation, and so on—you have to understand yourself, and you cannot possibly understand yourself if you say, "I must be like the man who is happy."

To understand oneself there is no need for comparison or measurement at all; then you look at yourself and there is no self at all. In the same way, sir, meditation is the understanding of oneself, understanding oneself every day, what one says, what one does, how one thinks, what one thinks, one's secret thoughts—to be aware of all that choicelessly, without condemning, without judging. To be aware of all that is meditation; then in that state of meditation one can go—the mind can go—beyond all time.

November 11, 1967

New Delhi, India, 1967

✳

First Talk in New Delhi

Considering there is so much violence, disorder, and confusion in the world, not only in this country, but almost everywhere, it becomes more and more important to become very serious. Not serious according to one's own fancy or inclination, or according to any particular plan or system; because systems, organized belief, organized conduct, have completely failed, they have no meaning any more. Unfortunately what apparently has meaning in this world at the present time is lawlessness, and in this country there is inefficiency, corruption, and each man, especially in the political world, is seeking his own fulfillment through ambition.

We all know this, and we have become totally indifferent to it. We have lost our moorings, we are confused, and it seems to me that it is very important that each one of us should become extraordinarily serious. One of the things that we are serious about is when our pleasure is threatened or taken away; then we become not only violent but somewhat serious. But we are talking about seriousness that demands complete attention, attention to what we are doing, what we are thinking, to our way of life. Because as one observes, all leadership has failed; there is no authority to tell us what to do, and if there is, we don't pay attention, we go on in our own pleasant way. Organized belief as religion

has no longer any meaning whatsoever. And systems, whether the communist system or any other system or religion, or a system that one has developed for oneself according to which one functions and thinks—again these have failed. I think this is fairly obvious. It is obvious to anybody who is at all aware of what is going on in the world—not only in the world outside, but also in the world in which we live, in the family circle, the world of our own secret longings, secret desires and pleasures.

As there is so much confusion and violence, so much disorder and lawlessness, we—at least those of us who are somewhat earnest—must commit ourselves, not to any particular belief, not to any particular system, but commit ourselves to a serious inquiry which will help us to live totally differently. Because what is needed, surely, is a way of life that will be completely orderly, which we as individuals and as human beings can find by inquiring, by seeking, questioning, by doubting, by totally discarding. Orderly, not according to a formula, but according to a serious attention which begins to inquire into every activity of our life. Such commitment is essential. I do not know if we realize, not only outwardly, but also inwardly, how shoddy our lives are, how empty, meaningless, though we may well repeat some authority or a religious book over and over again, or follow some religious leader. If we examine the way we live, we shall find that it is very empty, lonely, miserable, confused, and utterly meaningless. No temple, no book, no leader, no belief of any kind, nor any authority is going to solve this problem for us. Realizing this, seeing what is actually taking place both outwardly and inwardly, one has to become extraordinarily serious, and the commitment is to be serious.

I don't think we realize sufficiently clearly or see objectively what is actually going on outwardly and inwardly, both psychologically and objectively. We are incapable of looking because we are so frightened. We think others will do something to take us out of this mire—some political leader or some guru, or by going back to the past, reviving the past, or by forming parties and hating other people. This is what is actually going on. And as one observes, there is a general decline, not only morally, ethically, but also intellectually. Intellectually, we repeat what others have said, endlessly. We compare various clever intellectual authorities, specialists, with others. We read endlessly, and we think we are very intellectual when we can compare dialectically one theory with another, one opinion with another. So intellectually we are almost dead. Please do observe, listen to what is being said, neither agree nor disagree, but see the actual fact: how intellectually, mentally, we are hedged in. There is no space, there is no mentality of critical awareness. Intellectually one is educated to perform technical jobs, pass some examination, add a few letters after one's name to get a job, and the rest of one's life is totally neglected. But to think clearly, objectively, forcefully, vitally, is denied. Obviously we have no feelings at all; we have become callous, not only in this country—but perhaps more so in this country because of the population, the poverty, the inefficiency. The self-concern prevents strong feelings,

passionate desire to understand, to change one's life, and without passion one cannot be serious, without passion one cannot do anything. And you know what is obviously happening in the world: there is starvation, there is physical fear, insecurity, a slow decline intellectually, emotionally, and physically.

Will you listen to what the speaker is saying—not to find out whether what he is saying is false or true, or if he is exaggerating, but listen to find out if that is not your own life? Use the speaker as a mirror in which you see yourself actually as you are; otherwise, if you merely listen, or hear a few words or a few ideas, then this talk will be utterly meaningless. But listen with care and attention so that as you listen you actually see what you are, how empty your own life is, how dull, how stupid, how meaningless it is—though you go to the office every day—how your thoughts function in a formula, how your whole attitude towards life is conditioned by your circumstances. If in listening you can discover that, discover it for yourself, not because you are told about it, but discover it for yourself, then it will have an extraordinary significance. But if you are told about it and then discover it or agree with it, then it is secondhand, it is not original.

It seems to me that one has to commit oneself to be very serious. I mean by that word *serious,* to give attention; and you cannot give total attention if you do not see actually what is taking place in yourself. Attention surely implies care, that is, to look with care, to look at one's own life, at one's own way of thinking, one's activities, with care; and you cannot care if there is no affection. If there is no love, you cannot possibly care. If you have affection, then you do not compare, you observe. It is only when there is no love that there is comparison, that there is the drive of ambition. And especially in this country—and when I say "in this country" I am not comparing this country with the West, nor with Russia nor China nor America; I am saying "this country" non-comparatively—there is no love at all. You might think that is a very strong statement, but it is not. And in this country—though you have talked endlessly about violence and nonviolence—you are very violent people. Though you have talked endlessly about God and spirituality, going to temples, and having your own sectarian beliefs, you are really not spiritual people at all. Please listen very carefully; I am not criticizing, I am not taking the "almighty" attitude; I am merely observing the facts as they are. But belief in God is a superstition, and you can be superstitious endlessly, and you will never know what reality is. To find out what reality is, there must be the cessation of all superstition, including your gods, your rituals, your temples, your sacred books; to find out, everything must come to an end. And so when you talk about the Gita, the Koran, the various books, and are endlessly explaining, commenting, you are obviously escaping from reality, and therefore you are not spiritual at all. If you were, this country would be entirely different; then you would know what love is, then you would not be caught in the intellectual dissection of what love is.

There is a general decline morally; it may be because of tradition, because everyone is conditioned in a particular form of tradition—and functioning in a pattern is not morality. There can be no morality if there is no love, and as love cannot possibly be cultivated anymore than you can cultivate the sense of beauty, one is lost. One has functioned all one's life in a formula, in an ideal, in an ideology, and you think that to have an ideal is the greatest of all intellectual strivings. But all ideology—whether it is of the left or of the right or of the center, whether religious or not—is idiotic because it does not face the facts. When there is danger,

physical danger, you see it actually; it is there, right in front of you; you don't theorize! There is this great danger which we refuse to see, the danger that we are in, because of the climate, superstition, tradition, the divisions of religions, caste, the over-population—there are a thousand reasons for not being aware of the implications involved in all this. We think we shall solve this problem by leaving it to somebody else, either to a political leader or to a religious teacher, or by returning to the past, which is dead and gone. Those who want to revive the past are dead people. Seeing all this—actually in our life as it is—it seems to me that it is very important to become serious, and in that seriousness commit ourselves. Not to join some particular party, not to follow a particular leader, nor a particular course of action, because leaders, systems, activities, have brought man to this terrible confusion, to this extraordinary anarchy and disorder. One has to commit oneself to become serious—so that one lives a totally different kind of life, so that one brings about a total revolution in oneself, a psychological mutation, and that is the only commitment that has deep and vital significance.

To commit oneself to freedom and to find out what love is—those are the only two things that matter: freedom and that thing called "love." Without total freedom there cannot possibly be love; and a serious man is committed to these two things only, and to nothing else. Freedom implies, does it not, that the mind frees itself totally from all conditioning. That is, to uncondition itself—from being a Hindu, a Sikh, a Muslim, a Christian, or a communist—the mind must be in complete freedom, because this division between man as the Hindu, the Buddhist, the Muslim, the Christian, or the American, the communist, the socialist, the capitalist, and so on, has brought disaster, confusion, misery, wars.

So what is necessary first of all is for the mind to free itself from conditioning. You may say it is not possible. If you say it is not possible, then there is no way out. It is like a man living in a prison and saying, "I cannot get out." All that he can do is decorate the prison, polish it, make it more comfortable, more convenient, limit himself and his activities within the four walls of his own making. There are many who say it is not possible—the whole communist world says it is not possible; therefore, let us condition the mind in a different way, brainwash it first, then condition it according to the communist system. And the religious people have done exactly the same thing; from childhood they are brainwashed and conditioned to believe they are Hindus, Sikhs, Muslims, Catholics. Religions talk about love and freedom, but they insist on conditioning the mind. So if you say man is not capable of freeing himself from his conditioning, then you have no problem. Then you accept the prison and live in the prison, with the wars, with the confusion, with the conflicts, with the misery, the agony, and the loneliness of life, with its violence, brutality, and hatred—which is what you actually do. But if you say, "It must be possible to uncondition the mind," then we can go into it; then we are together—not some authority leading you to it, not the speaker taking your hand and leading you step by step, because when there is freedom there is no authority. Freedom is at the beginning as well as at the end, and if you accept an authority at the beginning, you will always be a slave at the end. So one has to inquire together in freedom; please do understand this. The speaker is not telling you what to do, not setting himself up as an authority—you have had authorities, all you can stomach, with all their absurdities, with all their immaturities—but if you are inquiring—and there is no authority when you inquire—then we can take the journey together,

sharing together, not being led. A real scientist is not committed to any government; he has no nationality; he is not seeking an end. As a pure scientist, he is investigating objectively right to the end, without projecting his personality, his nationality, his ambitions.

So inquire into this question of freedom, not intellectually, but actually, with your blood, with your mind, and with your heart! It is only in freedom that you can live, and only when there is freedom is there peace. Then in that freedom the mind has immense peace to wander, but a mind that is not free—tethered to a belief, tethered to an ambition, tethered to a family or to some petty little god of its own invention—such a mind can never understand the extraordinary beauty or the love that comes out of this freedom. And this freedom can only come about naturally, easily, when we begin to understand conditioning, and you cannot be aware of this conditioning when you are held tightly by the four walls of your particular religion, or by ambitions; and to inquire into this conditioning one must first become aware. To be aware: this means to observe, to look—to look at your own thoughts, to look at your beliefs, to look at your feelings. But when we do look, we condemn, or justify, or say, "That is natural." We don't look with choicelessness; we are not aware of our conditioning. We are aware of our conditioning with choice, with likes and dislikes of what is pleasurable and what is not pleasurable. But we are not actually aware of our conditioning as it is, without any choice at all.

Have you ever observed a tree or a cloud, or a bird sitting on the lawn or on a branch? Have you observed what actually takes place? What actually do you feel when you see a tree or a bird or a cloud? Do you see the cloud, or do you see the image you have about that cloud? Do please find out. You see a bird and you give it a name, or you say, "I don't like that bird"; or you say, "How beautiful that bird is." So, when you say these things, you are not actually seeing the bird at all; your words, your thoughts—whether you like it or not—prevent you from looking. But there is a choiceless awareness to look at something without all the interference of what you already know. After all, to be in communion with another is only possible when you listen without any acceptance or denial, just listen. In the same way, look at yourself as if in a mirror—what you actually are, not what you should be, or what you want to be. We dare not look; if we do look we say, "How ugly I am," or "How angry I am"—this or that. To look, to see, and to listen is only possible when there is freedom from thoughts, emotions, condemnation, and judgment.

Probably you have never looked at your wife or your husband without the image that you have about him or about her. Please observe this in your own life. You have an image of him, or she has an image of you, and the relationship is between these two images; and these images have been built up through many years of pleasure and of wrangles, bitterness, anger, criticism, annoyance, irritation, frustration. And so we look at things through the images that we have built about them. You are listening to the speaker, but you have an image about him; therefore, you are listening to the image, and you are not directly in contact with him, nor with anything in life. When one is in direct contact, do you know what happens? Space disappears, the space between two people disappears, and therefore there is immense peace, and this is only possible when there is freedom—freedom from the making of images, from the myths, the ideologies, so that you are directly in contact. Then, when you are directly in contact with the actual, there is a transformation.

You know what is happening in the world. They are experimenting, taking drugs, and when you take certain drugs, the space between the observer and the observed disappears. Have you ever watched a bouquet of flowers on a table? If you have looked at it attentively, you will have seen that there is a space between you and the thing observed. The space is time, and the drug chemically removes that space and time; therefore, you become extraordinarily sensitive, and being very sensitive, you feel much more because then you are directly in contact with the flower. But such contact is temporary; you have to go on taking drug after drug. When one observes oneself, one sees how narrowly one is conditioned, believing in so many things, like a savage with too many superstitions to be directly in contact with things. But you will see if you are directly in contact that there is then no observer at all. It is the observer that makes the division.

When one is angry, anger is apparently something different from the entity that says, "I am angry"; so anger is different from the observer. But is that so? Is not the observer himself anger? And when this division comes totally to an end, then the observer is the observed, and therefore anger is no longer possible. Anger and violence only exist when there is the division between the observer and the observed. We will go into that another time because it is a very complex question that requires a great deal of inquiry, penetration, insight. It is only when there is freedom from all conflict that there is peace, and out of that peace comes love. But one cannot possibly know that quality of love unless the mind is aware of itself and has unconditioned itself and therefore is free.

Perhaps you might like to ask questions, and we can go over it together; but to ask questions is one of the most difficult things. To ask the right question implies that you have already thought about it, that you have already inquired, that your mind is already sharp, clear. Anybody can ask a question, but in asking the right question, in the very asking of that question is the right answer. Please see the importance of this. Because we must ask questions, we must doubt everything, criticize everything, find out and not accept; we have accepted for so long, we obey instinctively not only the policeman but what we are told to do. We are slaves to propaganda, and out of this confusion we ask questions for somebody to clarify. So if you are going to ask questions, first be clear what you are asking and whom you are asking. Are you waiting for an answer from the speaker, or are you asking the question to find out for yourself and therefore exposing yourself? You understand? I can ask, but behind that asking I can hide myself, behind the words I can shelter myself. But if you ask a question, ask it with deliberation, with attention, which means that you are exposing yourself, and it is good to expose oneself, not always live behind a wall of fear.

Question: Is this choiceless awareness possible in daily life . . . when you are doing all the activities of life?

KRISHNAMURTI: Whom are you asking, and who is going to tell you? The speaker has said choiceless awareness is a state of mind that sees what is actually taking place, factually, without any condemnation or justification, which means that it is very attentive; and you say, "Is this possible in life?" Isn't it possible? There are only two states: either you are attentive or you are not attentive, and most of us are inattentive. We are inattentive because we have developed various faults or habits of activity, and we function in those habits and mechanically carry on, which is inattention. To be attentive means to be attentive to inattention, not to cultivate attention. If you cultivate attention,

then you are cultivating duality. That is, sirs, one is inattentive—in the office or at home, most of the time we are inattentive—daydreaming, wishing, imagining. Wishing that things were different, complaining of the conditions we live in, feeling envious of somebody else, wishing one were in their position—all that is inattention. If one becomes aware of this inattention, then one says, "I will become attentive, I must cultivate attention." So you begin to cultivate attention, which is not attention at all; it is merely the opposite of inattention. I don't know if I am making myself clear. Wait, I'll show it to you.

Question: Sir?

KRISHNAMURTI: Just a minute, sir, I have not finished. You see, sir, we are so eager to ask our questions that we don't even listen to what is being said—and we talk about attention. (Laughter) That's just it, sir! Look, for many, many years this country with its sayings has preached nonviolence. And when there was a war between this country and Pakistan, not one of you stood up against it, right? Although you have preached nonviolence, not one of you said, "It is wrong to kill." What was factual was the violence. Human beings are violent because they have inherited animal instincts; animals are violent, and man has developed from the animal. Part of this violence is the animal, and instead of tackling violence, looking at it, going into it, understanding it, uprooting it completely in oneself, you escape into "nonviolence," into an ideology which is nonexistent; it is just an idea. So if you are cultivating attention, it is an escape from inattention, because you will still be inattentive; but if you are aware of the nature of inattention, then you are attentive; you don't have to cultivate it. Is this clear or not at all?

Comment: None of it is clear.

KRISHNAMURTI: Look, sir, is it clear? What do you mean by clear? No please, this is not a clever question. Just inquire when you say, "It is clear," what you mean. Is it clear verbally or have you actually understood it? If you have actually understood it, then you are attentive. Without cultivating attention you are attentive. And being attentive, you will know when you are not attentive, which is inattention. You see, sir, this whole problem of cultivation, of becoming something, is because one is dull and stupid and one wants to become clever, sharper. This sharpness, this brightness is the opposite of dullness, and therefore the cleverness contains its own opposite. All right, sir, you don't see it, all right.

As one can observe in one's daily life, one can be choicelessly aware, but not practice choiceless awareness; there is no such thing as practicing something which you don't know. What one can know is that one is inattentive. The moment you become aware that you are inattentive, you become attentive, you are attentive; and this is very important to understand because if you cultivate attention, or if you cultivate bravery, there is an interval between the fact and what you want to be, and in that interval there is conflict; in that interval is hypocrisy. If you say, "I am violent, I want to understand it," then there is no hypocrisy. But if you say, "I am violent, I must become nonviolent," during the interval between violence and becoming nonviolent, you are sowing the seeds of violence.

So what is important is not what others say but to find out for oneself; to actually observe, see, listen for oneself. In that you will discover reality. Then if one is a liar one will admit: "I am a liar"—not pretend and deny and say this and that. When one is angry, one is angry. But to say I must not be

angry is an avoidance of anger because you will be angry again. But if you could go into anger, into the whole question of anger, why you are angry, not why you shouldn't be angry, but why you are angry!—perhaps you have not had enough sleep, you have not had enough calcium, probably you have pet beliefs which are being shaken, questioned. There are probably many reasons why you are angry. But to escape from it and say, "I must not be angry," has no meaning. In the same way, if you begin to inquire into inattention, why you are not attentive in your office, at home, in the street, in the bus, why you are not attentive to watch, to look, then out of that inattention comes an extraordinary fact of attention—quite naturally.

November 19, 1967

Second Talk in New Delhi

Before we continue, I think it is important that we understand what we mean by communication. In communication, it seems to me there is not only a sense of communion, that is, an intimacy of exchange of feeling, of ideas, of exposing oneself totally, but we have to use words; and as the speaker uses English, it is fairly simple if you understand the meaning of the words in English. But most of us when we hear a particular word, or a particular phrase, or a particular expression, are apt to translate it into our own language. And as most of the languages in India are loaded with Sanskrit words, they have their own particular meaning. So when you hear a certain word or a certain idea, a phrase, you are apt to translate it into your own particular expression of language, into your own terminology, and thereby you think you understand, but actually you don't. What takes place when you translate what you hear into your particular language is that you go back to the pattern of your conditioned thinking.

The other day, when we discussed awareness, you will have naturally translated it into your language, into a certain Sanskrit word which you think you have understood. But what has actually taken place is you have fallen back into the groove, into the pattern which the mind is used to. Whereas if you do not do that but actually try to understand the meaning of that word in English itself, then you have to struggle to understand.

So communication becomes extremely difficult when you translate what you hear into your own particular language and thereby think that you understand it; you do not, you have merely gone back to the old pattern of your thinking, which is tradition. So could we abstain from that, stop translating, and actually listen to the English words themselves? Unfortunately the speaker doesn't know any Indian language, so he has to speak in English, though it is rather unfortunate at the present time. If you will kindly not translate what you hear into your own language, then our communication will be much easier. And in communication, as I have already said, there is also communion, when two minds meet at the same time, at the same level, with the same intensity. That is, your mind and the speaker's mind meeting with a passion which is intense. Then there is a possibility of communion. You know, when you love somebody, there is a communion without words, without a gesture there is a communication taking place, and that is much more significant than intellectual understanding.

Intellectual understanding is really not understanding at all; it is only a series of words, and we think we understand those words and the content of those words, and we seem to think we understand the idea intellectually. But what you hear is unrelated to daily action, to a total limit, and communion is only possible when there is a direct relationship; communication then becomes much more interesting, much more vital, more significant, meaningful.

As we were saying the other day, we are concerned with actual living, not with ideas or ideologies, because we live in a world that is greatly in confusion. There is misery, a great deal of wildness, despair, anxiety, a sense of hopeless loneliness; and without fundamentally bringing about a revolution in the actual quality of the mind, mere ideas, ideologies, have very little meaning. Ideas, which are organized thought, and ideologies, that is, ideational, conceptual thinking, have no validity at all because we have to deal with actual daily living. Our actual daily psychological living is so confused, so miserable—our daily life is like living in a battlefield. Not only is there a conflict deeply within but also outwardly, until we resolve this conflict totally. Any pretension or ideational thinking becomes hypocritical; it is like the politicians, not only in this country, but everywhere else, who evoke God—then you know some shady work is going on. So what we are concerned with is to bring about, if possible—and it is possible—a total revolution, a psychological revolution, a psychological mutation in the very core of our being. And that is, I feel, the crisis in our lives. It is a crisis in consciousness, not an economic, social, or political crisis; it is a crisis in ourselves, as human beings. Without understanding and resolving that crisis, merely to bring about economic amelioration, a social improvement, has very little meaning.

So our question is whether it is possible as human beings to bring about, not only intellectually, but actually, a complete mutation, a complete revolution in the way of our thinking, living, feeling. You know there is a difference between individuality and humanity, between a human being and an individual. Primarily we are human beings, not individuals at all. Human beings, whether they live in America, Russia, Europe, or here, have their problems; they are miserable, un-happy, lonely, anxious, fearful—which is common to man—violent, in deep despair, trying to escape from the utter meaningless-ness of life. They either go to churches or temples, or read books, take to drink or drugs, and all the various forms of escape. We are human beings and individuality is only a local entity. The local person, that is, a Hindu, a Buddhist, a communist, a socialist, a Muslim—conditioned locally by the climate, by the culture, by the food, by the clothes, by manners, and so on—he func-tions as an individual. But primarily he is a human being: one of the human beings that exist in America, in Russia, in China, in India, who are in travail, who are in deep sorrow. And in understanding the larger, that is, the human, we shall be able to understand the individual. But the understanding of the individual will not necessarily bring about comprehension of the human. What we are concerned with is the mutation of the human mind, because the mind is capable of extraor-dinary things. And we are only using a very small part which has become the individual, which has become the traditional, the condi-tioned, and in that limited, conditioned state we function, forgetting the vast capacity of the mind. So one has to understand the fun-damental difference between the human and the individual—the individual in society and the human as a total entity—and when we are concerned with the greater, then the lesser will be understood.

We were saying the other day that there are fundamentally only two problems for man, for the human: freedom and love. Freedom implies order. But order, social order, is now chaotic, contradictory; it is dis-order. As you observe the society in which you live, what you call order is essentially disorder because there is violence. Each human being is in competition with another; there is brutality, there is competition to

destroy the other, and so on, which essential-ly is disorder. War, hate, ambition are disor-der, and we accept this disorder as order, don't we? We accept this morality, the social morality, as orderly, but when you observe it very closely, it is disorder. I think that is fairly clear, unless one is totally blinded by tradition, by one's own convenience, and so on.

To be free from this disorder is order. Please follow this a little bit. To be free from disorder, which is the social order, is to be actually in order. So one cannot seek order. Order is a living thing; it is changing, it is moving, it is vital, creative; it isn't just functioning within a pattern established by society, by culture. That society, that culture has produced great disorder, great misery, conflict, and this conflict, this confusion, however supposedly moral, is immoral; it is disorder. If the mind can understand this dis-order, and free itself from it, then naturally there will be order. Then the mind won't seek a pattern of order. I don't know if I am making myself clear on this point. This is really very important to understand. Through negation of what is disorder, there is order. But if you pursue order, positively, then you will have disorder. If you will negate com-pletely that which is not order—which we consider positive—then out of that negation comes the positive order, which is living. When I see, when the mind understands very clearly that hate is not love, or that jealousy is not love, when you completely deny jealousy anywhere, then you may come upon what love is. You cannot cultivate love, but you can deny that which it is not. So out of denial of that which is not true comes what is true, and what is true, what is order, can-not be preestablished; if you do, then you are merely suppressing disorder, which will burst out again at another time. Look, all the tyran-nies, the dictatorships—the Russian, the Chinese, the Hitlerian, Mussolinian, and so on—they said, "This is order; this is the way you must think, act, function." And Stalin and others have liquidated millions, literally millions, to bring about order—what they considered order—which is bringing disorder, obviously, because there is the demand for freedom. There is the demand that the mind shall be free, not be suppressed, not be ordered about by a dictator.

So, in the understanding of our life, which is disorder—not an idea of disorder—out of that understanding comes order. Order is not an idea; there is no concept about order; order is virtue, and one cannot have a preconception of virtue, of what virtue is. Please do follow this a little bit because just as you cannot possibly cultivate humility, that is, follow a certain system or method—if you do, then it is not humility—so order cannot be cultivated as an ideology according to which you live; this brings about conflict, and conflict is essentially disorder. Do follow this. Conflict within or without is disorder. So the question is: Is it possible to understand this whole structure of disorder without creating its opposite, for when you create the opposite it breeds disorder. So can you understand disorder without conflict? The moment there is conflict, there is the indication of its opposite—that you must be orderly. Order is virtue, but when these two opposites exist there is conflict. Can the mind, without creating the opposite, understand disorder without conflict? This is not an intellectual question, this is not something of a puzzle, but it is essentially our problem. We live in a state of disorder—in your own houses there is disorder, confusion, the mess and the dirt, the squalor, which is projected outwardly in your office and in your way of thinking, walking, sitting, spitting, and everything that goes on.

Can one be aware of that and of whether that awareness will bring about a radical revolution, now! Freedom is not from something—please do understand, we are going through rather difficult things, and explanation is never the actual thing; unfortunately we think that by explaining we understand something, but we don't. Explanation is one thing and actuality is another. The word *tree* is not the tree, but we confuse the word with the tree. So freedom, what we call freedom, is freedom from something: freedom from anger, freedom from violence, freedom from this utter despair. And when you are free from something, are you actually free? Please do go into it in yourselves, observe it. Or is freedom something entirely different and not from something? Being free from something is a reaction, and the reaction can go on repeating itself indefinitely. But the freedom we are talking about is entirely different, the sense of being completely free—not from anything. And this quality of awareness of what is implied in being free from something, awareness of the whole structure of it, will naturally bring about a freedom which is not a reaction. Is this all getting rather too complicated? Yes?

Now we have to examine what we mean by awareness. Don't translate it into Sanskrit, don't say, "I must practice it." Just try to understand what that English word means and what is implied—the structure and the nature of that word.

As we sit here we see, are aware, conscious of, the various colors of the tent. You observe it, you see the various colors, and as you see it you respond, have your reactions of like or dislike to those colors. That is the simple beginning of awareness, of being aware of what you see. Most of us do not see at all; we pass a tree every day of our life and never stop to look at it. We see the squalor on the road, and we do nothing about it. So we are not observing outwardly the trees, the birds, the sky, the clouds, the beauty of a sunset, the curve of a hill, the smile on a face. We are not aware of these at all, outwardly. But it becomes much more difficult to be aware inwardly, of what actually is going on. There, outwardly, it doesn't much matter, but inwardly it matters very much because the moment you are aware of yourself, your thoughts, your feelings, your confusion, then you get agitated, you are anxious, you want to change them. But first what is important is just to observe, without any reaction.

Suppose I am angry—I observe it, I do not condemn it, I do not think it is right or wrong. I want to understand it, and to understand anything—it doesn't matter what it is—there must be neither condemnation nor justification; to understand something the mind must be completely quiet. If I want to understand you, I must not have any prejudice about you. I must not say I like or dislike your face, your color, your race, your language, the way you talk, the way you move. I must just observe you. And to observe very clearly, the mind must be quiet. It is not a question of how to make the mind quiet, which becomes absurd; the mind cannot be made quiet. If you do, there are dualities: there is the man who says, "I must make the mind quiet," and there is the actuality of the mind which wanders all over the place. This is a conflict. Whereas if one wants to understand oneself, the mind has to be quiet to look; and you cannot look if you condemn, if you justify, if you falsify, if you are not honest. And as most of us are trained to be dishonest, never to look at things directly, it becomes extraordinarily difficult for people who have not actually looked—observed a tree, a cloud, the beauty of light on the water.

So awareness is this quality of mind which observes without any justification or condemnation, approval or disapproval, like or dislike—it merely observes. And it becomes rather difficult when you are stirred up emotionally, when your security, when

your family, when your opinions, judgments, and beliefs are shaken—and they will be shaken. There is nothing whatsoever that is secure; everything is in change and we refuse to accept this change, and hence the battle in ourselves. So when you observe yourself very quietly and the world about you, then out of this observation comes freedom—not the freedom from something. Is this fairly clear?

Now we are going to examine this question of fear. There are two things involved in this: there is the idea of fear and actual fear. With most of us it is fear as an idea, not the actual fact. Can I look at fear without the idea of fear, without the word with its associations related to fear? Most of us are afraid of the dark, of what people say, of losing a job, of not achieving, not becoming successful—fear of your wife, or the husband, and so on. There are dozens of fears: fear of death, fear of living—we are a mass of fear!

Fear doesn't exist by itself; it exists in relation to something. We are going to examine fear without bringing in its opposite—courage, bravery, and so on—actually looking at fear and not escaping from it. Most of us do escape because we do not know how to tackle it, how to come to grips with it; so we take to drink, go to temples, churches, mosques, do all kinds of things. It is all an escape from the actual fact that one is afraid. So to understand fear, there must be no escape, not verbally, but actually no escape. And can I look at fear—fear of death, fear of losing my job, fear of not accomplishing, not becoming successful, not being clever, or whatever it is? Can you actually look at it? That is, become aware of it, without any choice—look at it. Now, it is not possible to look at it if you have an idea about fear. When you are hungry, you do not compare hunger with yesterday's hunger; yesterday's hunger is an idea, a memory, and that idea or that memory does not make you hungry now.

If you are hungry actually now, it is not the idea or the memory of the hunger of yesterday. Right? So as hunger is immediate, not provoked by a memory, can you in the same way look at fear which is not the result of a memory? Please go slowly, this is a very complex problem. Does the idea and the association with a particular incident create fear, or is fear independent of association?

What is important in this is to find out how you are listening. What is actually taking place as you listen? Are you merely hearing words and are those words creating a certain memory, arousing certain feelings, or are you actually listening to the words and therefore listening to the actual fact of your own fear? I do not know if you are following this. Is the fear caused by the image you have in your mind about death, the memory of deaths that you have seen, the associations with those incidents—are they making you afraid? Which means, the image is creating fear. Right? Or are you actually afraid of coming to an end—not the image creating fear of the end? Is the word *death* causing you fear—the word—or is it the actual ending? If the word is causing fear, then it is not fear at all. Do listen to this very carefully. Are you afraid because of a memory?—I was ill two years ago and the memory of that pain, of that illness, remains, and that memory, now functioning, says, "Be careful, don't get ill." That memory creates fear. The memory with its associations is bringing about fear, which is not fear at all because I am not afraid actually; I have very good health, but the mind with its memory through time is creating fear. Thought, which is always the old, engenders fear because thought is the response of memory, and memories are always old. There is nothing new in thought; thought creates in time the feeling that you are afraid, which is not an actual fact. The actual fact is you are well. But the thought which has experienced already, the ex-

perience which has remained in the mind as a memory, from that the thought arises, "Be careful, don't fall ill." And therefore one is afraid. So thought engenders fear. Right? That is one kind of fear. Is there fear at all, apart from that? Is fear the result of thought, and if it is, is there no other form of fear?

I do not know if you are meeting this point. "I am afraid of death," that is, something that is going to happen tomorrow, or the day after tomorrow, in time. There is a distance from actuality to what will be. Thought has experienced this state by observing death; it says, "I am going to die." Thought creates the fear of death, and if it does not, is there any fear at all? So is fear the result of thought?—thought being old, fear is always old. Please follow this carefully. Thought is old; there is no new thought. If you recognize a new thought, it is already the old. So what we are afraid of is the repetition of the old—thought projecting into the future what has been. So thought is responsible for fear, and this is so; you can see it for yourself. When you are confronted with something immediately, there is no fear. It is only when thought comes in, then there is fear. So, our question is: Is it possible for the mind to live so completely, so totally in the present that there is neither the past nor the future?—and it is only such a mind that has no fear. But to understand this you have to understand the structure of thought, memory, time. And without understanding it, not intellectually, not verbally, but actually with your heart, with your mind, there is no freedom. But when there is total freedom, then the mind can use thought without creating fear.

So freedom from fear is absolutely necessary. Freedom is absolutely necessary because if there is no freedom, there is no peace, there is no order, and therefore there is no love; and when there is love then you can do what you will. Then there is no sin, then there is no conflict. But to understand freedom and love, one has to understand non-verbally the quality of freedom that comes when disorder is understood. This disorder is understood when you understand the structure and the nature of thought, not according to the speaker, nor according to some psychologist. When you are understanding them you are not understanding yourself; you are understanding yourself according to some authority. To understand yourself there must be a complete throwing away of all authority. Don't please agree, that agreement is merely verbal, it has no meaning; but see why it is important, because all the authorities, your Gitas, your books, your gurus, your mahatmas have led you to this terrible state of complete despair, loneliness, misery, confusion. You have followed them; at least you have pretended to follow them, and now you have to take the journey by yourself; there is no authority that is going to lead you, lead you to a bliss that is not to be found in any book, in any temple. You have to take the journey entirely by yourself. You can't trust anybody; why should you trust anybody? Why should you trust any authority? You say, "I am confused, I don't know, you know, so please tell me." Which means what? You are escaping from your own confusion, and to understand your confusion you cannot look to somebody to help you out of that confusion. That confusion has come into being because of this outward authority. Look at it, it is so clear.

There must be this sense of complete abandonment of all authority, which means a great deal of fear. Because, before, you have leaned on people, on your guru, on your book, on whatever you lean on. You put your faith in them, and what has taken place in your life? There is confusion, violence, misery, and untold agony going on in your daily life. So no authority of any kind is going to help you. This abandonment of authority brings about a sense of complete aloneness, a sense of not being able to depend on any book, or any authority. You know what it does to you when you do that? Then you travel lightly. Then you do not carry other people's burdens and their authority; you are alone to find out, and you must be alone to find out what is true. What other people say truth is, is not true; that truth, that something beyond all time and space, is only possible when the mind is completely alone. I do not know if you have ever noticed that being alone means being innocent. But we are not innocent; we carry the burden of what thousands of people have said; we carry the memories of our own misfortunes. To abandon all that totally, both at the conscious and at the unconscious level, is to be alone, and the mind that is alone is innocent and therefore young. And it is only the young mind—not in time, not in age—the innocent, alive mind that can see truth and that which is not measurable in words. And this can only come about naturally, not through your wishing, wanting, longing; all that is so immature—it can only come about when we understand the nature of freedom. The mind that is burdened with authority, with quotations, with knowledge of what has been—except technologically—such a mind is burdened with fear.

So what is important is the understanding and the structure of thought, not what other people say, but what you think. And when you think, if you are a Sikh, or a Hindu, a Muslim, or a communist, or whatever it is, why do you think those things? Because you have been told, brought up in a certain culture, conditioned, and you keep on repeating like a gramophone record. That is not freedom. And because you are not free, you are creating disorder. Do please see this, see it passionately, with great intensity, and you will be out of it. You are conditioned, and that conditioning is creating disorder, and in that limited conditioning you can never find order; there is order only when you have observed the structure and the nature of disorder in yourself. You yourself are the result of a thousand yesterdays, a thousand influences, a thousand authorities, of newspapers, radio, of your wife, of your husband, the culture you live in. As long as you live in that, there must be increasing disorder and therefore increasing misery.

Can we ask questions about what we have discussed this evening?

Question: What is your opinion about what ideals human beings should have?

KRISHNAMURTI: I have no opinions. That's the most unintelligent thing to say, "What is your opinion about something?" Why do you have opinions at all? Isn't it a waste of time to have opinions about what some people do or don't do, or say or don't say? So, the question is, if you can put away dialectical opinions altogether and the search through opinions—truth cannot be found through opinions—then we are confronted with the problem of human beings—must human beings have ideals? Why should they have ideals? You have your ideals, all of you, I am sure, haven't you? That you must be good, that you must be noble, that you must love the violent, that you must be charitable, that you must be kind, loving, that you must be this and that. But are you actually? You have ideals galore, by the thousand, but what actually are you? What matters is what you are, not what your ideals are, but what your actual daily life is. Your daily life is violent, brutal, and what is the good of having an ideal of nonviolence?—that is a cheap escape. What matters is to face what you are. When you have an ideal, it is the opposite of what you are, and therefore you have conflict, you waste energy, there is escape; it is a brutal thing to have ideals. See the fact, not

what the speaker says, which is totally unimportant. What is important is to see the fact. And the fact is, in your daily life you are violent, ambitious, greedy. Face that, and you can only face it if you have energy. You waste energy through ideals, and all ideals—whether the ideal of Buddhism or communism or any other ideals—are idiotic because they do not deal with the fact of what you actually are. Man has lived on ideals, which are words; words do not feed your mind or heart, they are just ashes. What is important is to face the fact. Face the fact that you are angry, envious, brutal, with an occasional flash of affection; that you are sexual, sensual. I don't say it's right or wrong, just look at it.

Question: How do you define human beings and the individual?

KRISHNAMURTI: Do we need a definition to find out what a human being is? The dictionary will give you the definition; is that going to explain, reveal, what you actually are as a human being? So the danger is being caught in explanations and definitions. You are a human being, sir, with all the troubles, with all the misery, with the agony of life and the conflicts, just as they are in America, Russia, China, everywhere. We are human beings, without any nationality; but the nationality, the culture, the climate, that is what conditions—which becomes the human, which becomes the individual. The individual is always limited, but when we understand human nature—the human being, what you are—then in that understanding, the individual can be understood, and it has its own right place.

Question: How can the conditioned mind understand the unconditioned?

KRISHNAMURTI: It cannot. What it can understand is its own conditioning, not the unconditioned. The unconditioned is an idea, a utopia, an ideology—that you must be unconditioned. Yet the fact is you are conditioned. Can you be aware that you function, think, feel as a Sikh, as a Muslim, as a Hindu, and so on? To be aware, which is to come directly into contact with it; and if you come directly into contact with it, then you will never be a Sikh or a Hindu; you throw away all that rubbish. That is what is dividing human beings: nationalities, frontiers, religions, ideologies. You have your ideology and another has his ideology; therefore, you are in conflict with him. So throw away all that, make a clean sweep, and that means to live anew. Live a life which you have never lived before, a life of total freedom. It is only such a mind, such a life that can come upon this extraordinary thing called truth. That truth has no word, it has no image, it is not to be found in any book, in any temple, in any church. You all know this, but you all go back to your old ways. This demands an earnest life; it demands clarity on your part, not on the part of the speaker. It is your life, and in your life you have to bring about this total revolution.

Comment: Our daily life is one thing, and the ideology of what you are talking about— freedom—is another.

KRISHNAMURTI: I have no ideology, as I have told you. I am just pointing out what is actually taking place in your daily life. Your daily life is what it is. You can forget peace, a state of mind in which there is no thought, all that—forget it—it has no importance whatsoever; throw it overboard, drown it, wipe it away. But what is real is your daily life. The way you walk in your office, the way you talk to your servant—if you have a servant. The way you treat your wife, your husband, your children, your neighbor. And if you don't know what you are doing, then you are totally blind, and blind people have no right at all to have ideals; they are a tremendous escape from their blindness. Sir, you know you can multiply words, but words do not bring about love. I can talk endlessly about being generous, kind, but you will not be generous or kind because you listen to me. You will be kind and generous and full of delight when you have understood the structure and the nature of yourself, and to understand yourself, there is no need for another. You just have to look.

Question: Will you answer a question from me? Sir, I have read your works and now want to ask you this: What has been your experience with people coming together to exchange their understanding and to read your works. Do you approve of this? What has been your experience of this?

KRISHNAMURTI: "Do you approve of group formation, round what we have talked about, and do you think it is worthwhile?" Is that the question, sir?

Do whatever you want to do! If you want to form a group, form it. If you don't, don't form it. If you want to understand yourself through a group, form a group. And if you say, "Well that will not help me to understand myself, to live a different kind of life," then don't join a group. You are responsible for yourself and for nobody else. It is your life. You stand completely alone, never asking, never begging, never seeking truth, because truth does not come to the seeker. You cannot invite it. It is like the wind, or the breezes that come if you leave the windows open—you cannot invite the breeze—and if you are lucky it might come, and I hope you are lucky.

November 23, 1967

Third Talk in New Delhi

If we may, we will continue with what we were talking about the last time that we met here. We were saying how essential it is to be completely free from fear. Fear, conscious or unconscious, dissipates energy, and we need a great deal of energy, not only to live with all the innumerable problems we have, but also to go beyond these problems. Most of us have very little energy because we dissipate it in so many ways: we don't eat properly; we are confused, struggling, in constant battle with ourselves and with the world. We need an abundance of energy to penetrate through all these conflicting problems and come to a state of mind that is not at all distorted, that is not tortured, that is in balance and capable of clarity and penetration; for that, energy is wholly necessary. But unfortunately we waste our energy in effort.

We are going to go into this question of effort: what is involved in it, the nature of it, the structure of it, and whether it is possible for the mind never to be in conflict, not ultimately, but every day, in everything that we do. Is it possible for the mind, which is the result of time, of experience, of accumulated knowledge, to live without any struggle, without any conflict, and therefore without any effort? I am sure it must have happened to you in your daily life—there are rare moments when you function as though you were completely abandoned, completely in harmony with yourself, with the world, with everything about you, so that there is no struggle, no effort, no striving after something. When you see the clarity of an evening or of the morning very clearly, when you are completely one with nature, when every tree says something to you, and every flower is a delight—you must have had these moments, when the mind is not disturbed—is it possible to live like that? Is it possible to function efficiently, technologically, almost like a computer, without a battle within oneself?

Because I feel we human beings are tortured entities, driven by innumerable, contradictory desires, driven by our demand to fulfill, to achieve, to succeed, to compete—we are always comparing *what is* with 'what should be'. And this comparison is one of the factors of conflict.

As we said the other day—I hope you will not mind it being repeated—this is not a talk to which you listen and go home with a few sets of ideas, agreeing or disagreeing. We are thinking out together our problems; we are taking a journey together into ourselves, into our lives, into our conflicts, into our miseries, into our unutterable loneliness and despair. You are not merely listening to a few words but listening so that you really hear your own mind working, operating, functioning, so that you see yourself very clearly; not "what is good" or "what is bad," but actually see *what is*. If one could listen in such a manner, not only to what the speaker is saying, but also to the birds, to what your neighbor says, to your boss in the office, to yourselves when you are soliloquizing, talking to yourself—listen so that you find out, so that you learn! And I hope you will listen that way, because we are not making any propaganda, we are not telling you what to do. It is a terrible thing to rely on another about the way of life, to be told what to do, how to behave, what righteousness is or is not—this seems to me a state of immaturity, and no one can make you mature; all that one can do is to listen and learn. But learning is a very difficult art. Most of us know how to accumulate knowledge and from that knowledge act. Please observe what we are talking about in yourselves. We learn, we accumulate knowledge and experience; we have a great many memories, and from those memories, that knowledge, experience, we act, and from that acting learn more and add to what has already been accumulated. This is our daily life. But is that learning? Is not learning something from moment to moment?—not accumulating and then adding more to that accumulation. If one doesn't know a particular language, one learns the grammar, reads, and gradually accumulates words, phrases, learns how to use the words, and so on; from that accumulation one begins to speak the language, adding more words. And that is what we generally do in daily life: accumulate and then act, and from that action, learn to add more, or to take away. But one must question whether such a process is actually learning. To learn means, does it not, that you are learning about something that you don't know. You are learning about something which you don't know, and from that state of learning you are acting. So learning is always in the present, in the active present, not a thing which you have accumulated and from which you act. I think there is a great deal of difference between these two. One is mechanical, that is, having accumulated knowledge, acting from that; and the other is non-mechanical, it is an active present, which is always learning and not accumulating. And that is the only way to live: in the present. Perhaps, if there is time, we can go into it.

As we were saying, we need energy to look, to listen, to learn, but that energy is limited when we look or listen from particular knowledge, from an accumulated burden; and this energy is dissipated through effort. Now what does effort mean—actually, not according to the dictionary, but when do we make an effort? When we do something that is pleasurable there is no effort, we do it easily. When there is something which you are obliged to do, which is rather a strain and painful, which is not satisfying, then it is an effort to do it. Effort implies, does it not, a state of mind in which there is duality: wanting something and not wanting it. When there is a contradiction in ourselves, then this contradiction creates a dual activity, and to

understand this dual activity, to go beyond it, is effort. As we said just now, when we do something which is pleasurable, there is no effort involved at all; we do it easily because it is satisfactory, it gives pleasure; there is no struggle. But in pleasure there is always pain—isn't there? Pleasure doesn't exist by itself; it brings with it a certain movement which is contradictory to what is pleasurable. And this contradiction in pleasure itself brings about this battle of the opposites.

One is violent, and the opposite of it is nonviolence; there is a contradiction in it, violence and nonviolence; this contradiction is the cause of conflict, which means effort. Now if one could remain with violence and not with its opposite, then there would be no contradiction. Please listen, this is very important to understand. Why do we have duality at all? There is duality—man, woman, light, shade, and all the rest of it—but inwardly, psychologically, why do we have duality at all? Please think it out with me, don't wait for me to tell you, we are examining it together—there is no authority here at all. I am not an authority; therefore, you need to exercise your mind as much as the speaker to find out why we have this duality, psychologically. Is it our conditioning? Is it that we have been brought up to compare *what is* with 'what should be'? We have been conditioned in what is right and what is wrong, what is good and what is bad, that "this should be" and "that should not be", that "this is moral" and "that is immoral"—is that one of the many reasons? Why has this duality come into being at all? Is it because we believe that by thinking about the opposite, it will help us to get rid of *what is?* Are you following this? Do we use the opposite as a lever to get rid of *what is?* Or is it an escape from *what is?* That is, human beings are violent; that violence is shown in many different ways; the opposite of that is nonviolence. We think that by practicing nonviolence or thinking about non-violence, we will be rid of violence. But is that a fact? That is the ideal, that is what has been preached; that is one of the commodities which India exports which nobody believes in. So, is the opposite an escape from the actual, which is violence? Please examine it; it is your life, it is not my life.

So we use the opposite as a means of avoiding the actual about which we do not know what to do. If I know what to do about violence, I will not think about its opposite. If I have the capacity, the energy, the clarity, the passion to actually understand violence, then there is no need for the ideal—is there? So do we have the opposite in order to escape from *what is* because we don't know how to deal with *what is?* Is it because we have been told for thousands of years that you must have the ideal, the opposite, in order to deal with the present? Can the mind be free of the opposite when it is dealing with violence? Because one sees that one may preach nonviolence for the rest of one's life and practice it, and yet be sowing the seeds of violence all the time. So if the mind can remain actually with *what is,* then there is no opposite. Can the mind never compare? Can it stop comparing *what is* with 'what should be', comparing your own state with somebody else's, so that it is always dealing with *what is,* never with 'what should be'— so that you have no ideal at all? Because it is the ideal that is creating the opposites. If I know how to be with *what is,* then the opposite is not necessary. Then one has removed the fundamental cause of effort, of duality, and therefore one has the energy to face actually *what is*—right?

Can one do that? Can one—not theoretically, not verbally, not intellectually—say, "That's perfectly true," and then carry on with the daily opposites; can one actually cease to compare? You know, it is one of the most difficult things to do, not to compare yourself with somebody. This comparison has been taught from childhood; in every school you are told you are not as clever as the other. What actually takes place when A compares himself with B, the hero, the saint, and so on—what happens? When this comparison takes place, what actually happens to A? A is destroying himself in order to be like B—isn't he? Do observe this, sirs, in your own life. Becoming like somebody else is one of the causes of contradiction and hence waste of energy. But if you do not compare, will you vegetate, will you go to sleep? That's what we are afraid of. So, is it possible to remain actually with *what is* without bringing in the ideal, or the opposite, or comparing? When you do not compare, when there is no ideal, no opposite, then is *what is* the actual? Does it exist at all? Is my question fairly clear?

I am violent, and I see that the opposite does not help me to get rid of this violence; or I compare myself and my violence with somebody who has no violence at all. I see very clearly that in comparison there is conflict, that I introduce thereby a factor of duality, which is a waste of energy—so what have I left? Is it violence? Or is it a state of mind—please follow this—a state of mind that has become highly sensitive, highly intelligent, capable of immense passion, because then there is no effort? Effort is a dissipation of passion, which is vital energy; you can't do anything without passion. If that is so, when that actually takes place, because there are no ideals, no opposites, then the thing that I have called violence—does it exist at all? So you have to go into yourself, you have to examine it, you have to find out.

Let's put it differently. My mind is dull, I am insensitive, and so on; and I compare myself with somebody who is very clever, intelligent, bright, alive. I strive to be like him, to become brighter, sharpen my mind through comparison. Now, if I don't compare at all, if I don't struggle to be different from my dullness, will my dullness remain? Because what have I done? I have ceased to compare, which is an act of intelligence. I have ceased to create the opposite, and therefore there is no effort and therefore no contradiction. So what has happened to my mind? My mind has become extraordinarily alive, sharp, clear. It is only the dull mind that is violent; it is only the mind that is not capable of dealing with *what is* that becomes violent, ugly, stupid. So as long as there is a duality psychologically in any form, there must be conflict; and conflict is violence. Now one sees very clearly that as long as one is seeking pleasure, there must be duality—right? Because love is not pleasure, love is not desire—please don't agree with this. One has to find out what pleasure is and what desire is, because we said we are concerned with freedom and that strange thing called love. We went into it, into the question of freedom. Perhaps we can devote a little of the time that is left this evening to this inquiry into what love is.

How do we inquire? What is the state of the mind that inquires? You cannot possibly inquire if you are not free, that is, if you are not free from saying, "Love is not this or that," or "Love should be this and should not be that." To examine, explore, anything, there must be the quality of freedom from all your prejudices, conditioning, and so on, even from your own experience; only then can you begin to explore, to inquire, to find out. Otherwise you are merely examining from your own conditioning, and you can't go very far. And the word *love* is heavily loaded; we say, "Love is divine and not profane, it is sacred; it is this, it is that"—love of God, love of country, love of the flag—"I love my family; I love my wife, my husband." And we say, when there is love, we must love everybody, and not one, the particular.

To inquire into this is really an immense problem; one must approach it freely—free, not from anything, but free to look, that is, to look without an image. Can you look at your neighbor, at your wife or husband without the image? And if you have no image, are you then related? Or is there relationship only because you have images? And can one put an end to the machinery that builds images?—the image about yourself, what you are, what you should be. As long as you have an image, you cannot possibly see what you are; if you think you are paramatma, or some image which has been handed down to you through generations, obviously such an image prevents you from finding out what is real. It is only the free mind, not a mind that is loaded with images, that can find whatever is to be found. In inquiring into this question we must unfortunately use that word love; but it is such a hackneyed, brutalized word—the politician uses it, the husband says, "I love you," or speaks of the love of the family. Can one look at it, explore it, find out what that word indicates and go beyond the word? We are going to try and find out.

To find out what it is, there must be a dying. Love is something that is not mechanical. What is mechanical is pleasurable, such as sexual experience—you want it to be repeated over and over again; thought has created images, symbols, ideas; and thinking about it will increase and strengthen pleasure. This is what actually takes place. I have had an experience of the sunset yesterday, a lovely streak across the sky, full of light and beauty, and the birds were flying into it; there is that momentary pleasure, delight, a great enjoyment of beauty. Then thought accepts it and begins to think about it, judge, compare, and say, "I must have it again tomorrow." The continuity of an experience which has given a great delight for a second is sustained by thought, nourished by thought. When you look at that streak of light across the sky, at that moment there is no pleasure, no joy; there is an absolute sense of beauty, but the moment thought comes in, then you begin to enjoy it, you begin to say, "How lovely, I wish I could have more of it." So thought, which is always the old—thought is never new; it is the response of memory, experience, knowledge, and so on—thought, because it is old, makes this thing which you have looked at and felt old, and from the old you derive pleasure, never from the new. Do you understand this? There is no time in the new; in the instant there is something new, there is no time to enjoy or to take delight in it; only when thought comes in, which is old, it gives it a continuity.

Is love pleasure? Please think it out, don't say yes or no. That is, is love the product of thought? Can love be cultivated by thought? Thought can cultivate pleasure; thought can strengthen desire. But when the mind, through sensation and sensuality, seeks pleasure by thinking about it, is that love? And is love desire? I see something very beautiful, a lovely house, a nice face, then thought captures it, makes it the old, and out of that comes desire. You can see this in yourself, if you observe; if you see a car, a beautiful, highly polished car, there is visual perception, there is sensation, touch; and thought comes in and says, "How nice it would be to have it." But is love desire and pleasure? One has to find out; one has to work hard to find out, and you cannot work passionately to find out if it becomes an effort because then you are trying to find out because you are in sorrow; then your effort is an escape from sorrow. So to find out what love is, we must die to the past, to past memories. You know there is something extraordinary about living and dying—they are very close together although thought keeps them miles apart. We consider living is one thing and dying is another. We think living is

always in the present, and dying is something that awaits in a distant time. But living is not the battle of everyday life—that's not living at all, that is destruction. The way we live is all that we know: the daily battle, daily despair, the agony of life, the loneliness, anxiety, the immeasurable sorrow that one has—this is what we call living. We have never questioned whether this is living at all; we have accepted it, and when you accept anything you get used to it, as one gets used to a lovely sunset. You can see it a thousand times, and because you have seen it every day, you can get used to loveliness and also to something which is not lovely.

So what we call living is a battlefield, and death is something to be carefully avoided. But surely in our life, living and dying are always close together; you cannot live without dying. This is not an intellectual or paradoxical statement but the actual fact. To live completely, wholly, every day as though it were a new loveliness, there must be a dying of everything of yesterday; otherwise, you live mechanically, and a mechanical mind can never know what love is or what freedom is. Most of us are afraid of dying because we don't know what it means. We don't know what it means because we don't know what it means to live; therefore, we don't know how to die. Because we are afraid of death, we have all the innumerable beliefs, which are an escape from the actual. So is it possible for the mind, which is the result of time, experience, and knowledge, to die to itself—just to empty itself completely? It is only the innocent mind that knows what love is, and the innocent mind can live in a world which is not innocent.

Perhaps some of you might like to ask questions about what we have talked about.

Question: Sir, what is the function of thought in everyday life?

KRISHNAMURTI: The function of thought is to be reasonable, to think clearly, objectively, efficiently, precisely; and you cannot think precisely, clearly, efficiently if you are tethered to your own personal vanity, to your own success, to your own fulfillment.

Question: You have said we do not know what dying is; could you explain what dying is for our benefit?

KRISHNAMURTI: You see, sir, I haven't finished answering that question. We are always so eager with our own questions, we have no respect for other people's questions.

Comment: I apologize.

KRISHNAMURTI: Please, sir, you are not apologizing to me. I am nobody. All that we are saying is: When there is love there is no respect; it is only the disrespectful people who have respect. You have no respect for your servant, for your neighbor, for anybody, and therefore you are full of disrespect. But when there is love there is neither respect nor disrespect; there is only that quality of mind that loves.

Now that gentleman asked a question about thought: "What is its function in daily life?" Either we can use thought mechanically or thought can become extraordinarily active, and it cannot be active if it is merely functioning from a memory. I learn a technique, as an engineer or whatever you will, and that technique has given me certain qualities of proficiency, and I keep on functioning with that technique. I live in a mechanical world, but I must understand the whole mechanism of thought, the structure of it, how thought begins—not come upon it after it has begun—understand whether it begins from a memory or begins out of total silence. If it begins from memory, it is al-

ways old, and that's how we function in daily life. Thought is old, and the mind becomes old with it because we function mechanically, in the family, in the office, when we walk, when we talk—it is always mechanical. Can the mind be freed from the mechanical habit so that thought functions actively all the time, every day, in your office, in your home, when you look at your wife, husband, children?

And the question that gentleman asked is: "Would you please go into the question of what is death." Isn't that right, sir? Again it's a vast, complex problem; there are several factors in it. There is actual physical dying, when the heart stops beating, either through accident, through disease, or normal old age. We don't die of normal old age; most of us die through accident, or we have lived such a stupid life, with so much strain and pressure that emotionally we are worn out, the heart is worn out. So there is actual, physical dying, coming to an end; that one knows, that doesn't demand a great deal of thought. But one is more afraid of psychological dying, the dying to everything I know—my family, children, house, furniture, my knowledge, gods, character, the "what I have done," "what I have not done," and the book I have not finished; the things I wanted to do and that I have not done. That is, we are frightened, not of the unknown, but of leaving the things, dying to the things that we know—right?

Comment: Let me try again, my point is. . .

KRISHNAMURTI: Yes, sir, please, sir, we are going into that, but we can't go into it if you don't understand this: that we are frightened of leaving things which we know, not of the unknown. You cannot be frightened of the unknown because you don't know what the unknown is—so there is nothing to be frightened of. If I don't know about something, how can I be frightened of it? If I don't know the danger, how can I be frightened of danger? I am only frightened of leaving the things which I know: daily life, daily associations, daily contacts, daily sensations, daily pleasures, daily pains. And we ask: When I die will not all these daily pains, agonies, brutalities, violence, despairs, go over into the next life? Or do you say: In all this turmoil, chaos, misery, confusion, sorrow, there is a spiritual entity which will go over? I don't know what you believe; I don't know why you should believe in anything. If you believe that there is a spiritual entity in you, which is timeless, which you call by various names such as soul, atma, God; if it is in you and if you have thought about it, then it is thought that has created it and therefore it is not new; therefore, it is not spiritual, it is the product of thought; it is the product of tradition, knowledge, experience, fear. What you actually know is your daily, unhappy, tortured life—you don't want to face that. And the living that you know, you want to take into the next life. But if you die to everything you know, including your family, your memory, everything that you have felt, then death is a purification, death then is a rejuvenating process; then death brings innocence, and it is only the innocent who are passionate, not the people who believe, or want to find out what happens after death. What can probably happen is—I think it is so, but one mustn't be dogmatic about anything or assert anything—thought goes on. If I am attached to my house—just think of that, attached to your house, attached to your family, attached to your office, to your books, which is your life—then that attachment (which is the result of thought) that thought may go on like any other wave or vibration, but it has very little validity; what has validity is to die to all the things of one's petty life, petty demands, security, possessions, power, prestige. Die to it so that your

mind is cleansed and is fresh and is made new, so that it remains young and therefore timeless. What creates time is thought rooted in the past.

Question: Sir, my point is whether this body is the end of everything, or is there a spiritual entity, our soul, which goes beyond it?

KRISHNAMURTI: Sir, who is going to tell you? Me? As I said at the beginning, I am not an authority. Oh no, no, you have misunderstood.

Comment: Your belief.

KRISHNAMURTI: The gentleman wants to know my beliefs. (Laughter) I have no beliefs about anything.

Question: When you die, what will happen?

KRISHNAMURTI: I really don't care. (Laughter) Sirs, how easily you laugh. What will happen to you when you die, will you laugh? (Laughter) When you leave your family, when you leave your tortured life, if you have lived a shoddy, petty life, when you die, will you laugh and say, "I really don't care"? Because you do care; otherwise, you wouldn't live like this; if you really know, you would be revolutionary, not in the economic sense, but inwardly, tremendously, caught in a movement that is limitless. So, sirs, to find out what actually takes place when you die, you must die (laughter)—no, sirs, don't laugh—you must die psychologically, inwardly. Die to the things that you have cherished, to the things that you are bitter about, die to your pleasure—have you ever tried to die to one pleasure, not reasoned it out, but actually died to it? Then you will find out, if you have died to one pleasure, naturally, without any enforcement, what it means to die. But you see, to die means to be made completely new, which is to have a mind that is totally empty of itself, empty of daily longings, pleasures, and agonies.

November 26, 1967

Fourth Talk in New Delhi

I would like to talk about something this evening which I think is rather important. It is concerned with a problem that I am sure most of us are worried about. It is the question of how a small, mediocre mind, which seems to be so powerful in the world, how such a mind can become something totally different. It seems to me most of us live on words—words have become extraordinarily important. Words are used to cover up deceit, words are used to befuddle another, words are used to convey meanings which may have a double meaning, words are used in a political world where hypocrisy exists and is supposed to be democratic, and so on. To us, words have become extraordinarily important, like the words *Hindu, communist, Sikh,*—they are just words, but to us these words are loaded with a great deal of significance and tradition.

So the problem is, amongst other problems, how to empty the mind of all words, because we are actually slaves to words. When you mention *India* to a patriotic human being—and I am sorry there are such human beings—to them that word is an intoxication, as is the word *God*. This evening our question is whether it is at all possible for a mind which is so filled with thought, endless varieties and contradictions of thought—worries, issues, problems that cannot possibly be solved—whether such a mind can find out for itself if there is a state in which the word does not interfere.

The word *meditation* means a great deal to many people, and a petty, shallow, narrow mind, a mind that is heavily conditioned, such a mind can repeat words and think it will have some fantastic, mysterious experiences. Words must be used to communicate, but is there thinking without the word? We are going to find out this evening, if we can, what that word meditation actually means; not the word that is used by the Hindu, the Muslim, the Christian, or by the yogis, the mahatmas, but we are going to find out for ourselves what is implied in that word. People are taking various drugs, psychedelic drugs, and by using them, they hope to expand their minds and thereby live in a different world, have different experiences. We are going to go into it very carefully, but if you already have an opinion of what meditation is, or what you think meditation should be, then I am afraid you and I will have very little to say to each other. But if we are going to inquire into this extraordinarily interesting issue, then we must both be free to inquire, to find out, and not be committed to any particular form or system of meditation.

First of all, there must not only be freedom from the word but there must also be austerity. The word *austere, austerity,* comes from a Greek word which means harsh, dried up. And most of the people who practice austerity—the saints, the yogis, the mahatmas, the so-called spiritual people who have one meal a day, or have one thought, or one principle, or one idea and practice it deliberately day after day, suppressing, controlling their minds—they obviously have harsh minds, they soon become dry inwardly. So what is austerity? To examine that word and its meaning, we must put aside all formulas or concepts that we have about that word. In India, the saints, the teachers have established a certain pattern of austerities, and they think that if you practice these, you will arrive at a certain level. And there are thousands of people who practice austerity, hoping thereby to come to some extraordinary experience.

To "experience"—that word means to "go through," to go through a problem until you have finished with it. But most of us, when we have had experiences, we do not go through them; they leave a mark on the mind, and therefore there is never an ending to experience; and the experiencing of austerity needs a very close examination by each one of us. First of all, we must doubt every saint, every yogi, every mahatma—all the books about the state of mind that is austere, or about the practice of austerity which will ultimately lead man to some reality. To understand austerity needs intelligence; intelligence creates its own austerity. And we must ask, what is intelligence? What do you mean by that word? If you ask the meaning of that word or the explanation of that word, you can look it up in a dictionary. It will tell you the origin, it will tell you from what Greek or Latin word it comes, the root of it; but we can more or less investigate for ourselves what true intelligence is. Intelligence is not opinion. Intelligence is not a state of mind that is always comparing, not a mind that is measuring, but a mind that can see very clearly, dealing only with facts, with *what is* and not with ideas. That is, intelligence comes about through the negation of what it is not—by the denial of what it is not, you come upon intelligence. One observes throughout the world how human beings are conditioned: the communist in his way, the religious person in his way. If you are a Hindu or a Sikh or a Muslim or a Christian, you are conditioned according to that pattern, to that tradition, to that culture. These divisions of human beings into categories of religious, political, geographical groups, obviously imply a state of nonintelligence. So a mind which denies this religious, political,

national division is really an intelligent mind; that is, not denying verbally, but actually, inwardly, psychologically; it is not attached to any country. And a mind that calls itself nationalistic, a Hindu, and so on, is not intelligent. So through negation of what is not intelligence, one can be in a state of intelligence. That is, to find out what is not intelligence, you need a highly sensitive mind, not a dogmatic nor a dialectical mind, which is a mind that is seeking truth through opinions, which is dialectic. To be sensitive is to be intelligent; the greater the sensitivity, the greater the intelligence. And you cannot be sensitive if you are bigoted, narrow, petty, shallow. A man who is only concerned with his own problems, totally unaware of the problems of others, obviously does not have a sensitive mind. A mind that is unaware of its environment, the squalor, the dirt, the sloppiness, such a mind is not a sensitive mind—all this is very important when we are exploring what meditation is. And I feel, without understanding that quality of the mind that is meditative, life has really very little meaning. So in inquiring into what is meditation, we are going to find out what it is to be sensitive, which means to be intelligent.

So you observe in your daily life—not theoretically, but actually—the things that you talk about, the endless, useless chatter, the thoughts, the opinions, the judgments, the condemnations that you have about others or about yourself. If you are not aware of them, obviously you are not sensitive, you are asleep. And if you have any belief whatever, political or religious, obviously such a mind, being tethered to a particular formula or an ideology, is not an intelligent mind. So to find out what it is to be austere—and one must be austere, not outwardly, having few clothes or one meal a day, but to find out what inward austerity means—one must have a very sharp mind, a mind that sees very clearly. And what is it to be austere? Obviously, it is not suppressing any desire—please follow this very carefully—nor indulging in any desire, but understanding desire. One can suppress a desire, a want; one can control it—that is fairly easy; but to understand desire, to understand it not intellectually, not as a fragment, but as a total way of life (which most of us indulge in) needs not only intelligence but also the quality of austerity, to look at the thing as it is, not as you wish it to be.

You know, to look is to act. To see is to do; when you see danger you are acting. So the seeing is the doing, and to see there must be tremendous attention, which brings its own austerity—to see the whole structure of desire and the nature of desire, how it comes into being. Examine it, which means be aware of your desires and look at them without condemning, without judging, without saying, "this is right," or, "this is wrong," nor indulging in any desire, but just to look. That demands a discipline which is completely different from the discipline of suppression.

You are listening, I hope, not merely to words, but are actually examining your own minds, your own lives, not the life of somebody else, but actually your lives.

So, this austerity means order; it means precise thinking, and there can be no austerity, which is order, if there is not awareness—not only of things outwardly, but also psychologically, inwardly. Most of us live in disorder both outwardly as well as inwardly. Disorder is a state of mind in which there is conflict, and conflict exists because of contradiction both outward and inward; there is contradiction between two desires, two demands, and hence there is conflict. And without understanding the nature and the structure of desire, merely to suppress desire is the most unintelligent thing to do.

Because what you suppress festers and will explode in some neurotic way.

The understanding of desire is fairly simple: Look at desire and see how it arises. It arises through the process of thought. I see something pleasant and I think about it; the thinking about it is the cultivation of desire as pleasure—is that somewhat clear? Intelligence brings about its own austerity, its own order, not the order which anybody has established, nor the order of any society—the order of any particular society or community is disorder. Please, these are not dogmatic statements; you can watch this. Every society wants order and talks a great deal about establishing order, politically, religiously; outwardly it establishes morality, but its morality is disorder. You can be greedy, envious, seeking power, position, and prestige and yet be so-called "orderly." But are you not cultivating disorder when you are envious, greedy, jealous, obsessed by ambition? Order is virtue, and order is a living thing, as is virtue. It is not an idea, a discipline which you establish, practicing it day by day; it is something alive, active, not a mechanical thing, and order can only come about when there is intelligence. Intelligence comes when there is the understanding of disorder and the denial in oneself of the disorder; and this denial is not suppression but observation, seeing actually how you are creating disorder in yourself.

So, to understand meditation, of which we are going to talk, first there must be order in oneself, not order according to a formula, a pattern, but order which you have brought about in yourself through your own intelligence—not the intelligence of the Gita or the Koran or any other book; one has lived on these printed words that have no meaning any more. If you would understand meditation, there must be order in yourself, which is virtue; and that virtue is not according to any pattern or any society, because society says: Be as greedy, envious, ambitious as you like—which is the very essence of disorder. So virtue, austerity, order, intelligence are necessary to understand what meditation is. Without that you cannot possibly go into this question, which is of immense significance; you can repeat words: Om, om, or Jesus—Coca-Cola would do just as well—a hundred times, and put yourself in a state of hypnosis, but that is not meditation. Without going through all that, you can take a drug and put yourself to sleep. Repetition of any experience or of any word, inwardly—whether it is om or amen—such a repetition creates a mechanical process of thought, an established formula, system, and therefore your mind becomes narrow, shallow, dull. So one has to understand this repetitive process and put it away. And to understand meditation one needs a very clear, sharp mind, a mind that can reason and be logical, not sentimental, emotional, because sentimentality and emotionalism have nothing whatsoever to do with love. As we said the other evening, love is not desire or pleasure; but to understand love, one has to understand what desire and pleasure are.

Meditation is something which demands a very alert mind; that is, a mind that is aware, aware of things outside as well as inside. We are aware of things that give us pleasure, and we are aware of things that cause pain; we avoid the one and want to pursue the other. To be aware of both of them demands a mind that is without choice—please follow this. Just listen, because most of you won't do any of this; it is much too quick and sharp and clear, needing a driving energy, and most people haven't got it. Just listen, do nothing, don't say, "How am I to do it?" or "What am I to do? Tell me what to do," because then you are not listening. But if you just listen quietly, without effort, easily, without any strain, then the thing will happen to you. A petty, little mind inquiring about an enor-

mous thing cannot possibly understand it. But if that petty, little mind is quiet, actually listening, then perhaps it will be lucky enough to come upon something that cannot be put into words. So, if I may suggest, just listen, don't ask "how to" or investigate, just listen with your mind, with your heart, so that you give your attention completely.

As we were saying, be aware easily, without choice, because it is only the confused mind that has choice; a mind that sees clearly has no choice whatsoever. It is only the confused that are always asking, seeking, demanding, looking, searching; a confused mind can only choose, and its choice will invariably lead to further confusion. Be aware of the squalor on the road, the inefficiency in the office, the utter callousness of people, of the politicians with their greed and ambition, not caring one pin for the people—be aware of all that. Be aware of the beauty of the sunset, of the light on the water, the bird on the wing, just look without any choice, without any condemnation. If you can do that outwardly, then turn inwardly and be aware of yourself without condemning, without judging, without saying, "This is ugly, this is wrong, this is right, this is good, this is bad"—just look, look at yourself. Then out of that choiceless awareness comes attention.

You know, there is a great deal of difference between attention and concentration. Concentration is an exclusive process—just listen, don't accept or deny, just listen—when you concentrate, your mind is fixed on one thing, one idea, one image, or a symbol, or the meaning of a phrase; it is concentrating, which means you are excluding every other thought, every other movement—right? When you concentrate, it is a process of exclusion. But when you are aware, when there is attention, there is no exclusion whatsoever; you are aware of the world—the ugliness, the brutality, the violence, the hideous callousness, the cruelty to animals—you are aware of all that outwardly. In that there is no condemnation. Also be aware inwardly, and you will see that out of that awareness you become tremendously attentive, without any compulsion, without any effort. That is, you can only be attentive when there is complete abandonment of the observer. When the observer abandons himself totally, then you will see, if you have gone that far, that because there is abandonment, not forgetfulness, the self, the center, which is memory, experience, knowledge, the everlasting strife and sorrow, which is the essence of the observer—when that is not, then there is total, complete attention.

Now in that attention, there being no observer, there is space. You know what space is? There is space between you and me. There is space outside the tent and inside the tent, but the mind has very little space. In crowded cities human beings are put into cages with very little space to live in; they live in flats, and being an urban civilization, living in these crowded cities, that lack of space produces a great deal of violence, neurotic conditions, and so on. Man must have space, and as space is denied outwardly, one must have space inwardly. So one has to find out what that inward space is—space, which is both time and distance, between the observer and the observed.

When you look at a tree or the sky or a bird or the face of your wife or husband, there is space between you two. There is space between people, between objects, and there is space because there is an observer, the center from which one is looking. When you look at the tree or the sky or at another person, the center is looking, isn't it?—the center, which is memory, which is experience, which is knowledge, which is striving, demanding, which seeks to fulfill, which seeks success, and so on and so on; that is the center, the self, the ego, the me; and from that center, from that entity which is

the observer, you look at something, and so there is a space between the observer and the observed. Between the experiencer and the experienced, or the thinker and the thought—when you say, "I must be," or "I must not be"—there is space, a time interval. Now, when there is the observer who creates space round himself, he may expand that space through drugs, through various forms of repetition of words, and so on—he may expand the space, but there is always the center, and therefore his expansion of space is the expansion of a prison—are you understanding this? Just listen!

So our minds are crowded with words, with chatter, with experience, with memory, with the whole human sorrow of the past; that is the center from which we look at life. Now that space is very limited, very narrow, confined, it is like a prison; and is it possible to free the mind from its own center which it has built up? It is only possible when you can look at the tree, at the bird, at the face of your wife or husband, or at the face of your boss and so on, without the image. Can you look at your wife or your husband without the images that you have about her or him, just to look without the image—have you ever tried? Probably you never have. If you do, you may shatter your relationship, because what we are related to is the image— one image to the other, one memory, one experience to another. When one becomes aware of this image, relationship becomes entirely different. There may be no so-called relationships as they exist now. So the point is: Can the mind empty itself of the image, of the center? Then you will find space is limitless—and that is part of meditation. It is not having visions, because that is fairly simple to explain. If you are born, conditioned, in a Catholic world, a Christian world, and are a so-called religious person, obviously you will have Christian visions; if you are born in this country with all its superstitions, saints, heroes, gods and goddesses—innumerable entities—you are obviously conditioned and you will have experiences according to your conditioning. But they are not realities. What is real can never be experienced by the experiencer. When you love—actually love with your heart, not with your mind—when you totally abandon yourself in that love, then the other is not.

Meditation, then, is emptying the mind of the past, not as an idea, not as an ideology which you are going to practice day after day—to empty the mind of the past. Because the man or the entity who empties the mind of the past is the result of the past. But to understand this whole structure of the mind, which is the result of the past, and to empty the mind of the past demands a deep awareness of it. To be aware of your conditioning, your way of talking, your gestures, the callousness, the brutality, the violence, just to be aware of it without condemning it—then out of that awareness comes a state of mind which is completely quiet. To understand this quietness, the silence of the mind, you must understand sorrow, because most of us live in sorrow; whether we are aware of it or not, we have never put an end to sorrow; it is like our shadow, it is with us night and day. Sorrow is not only the loss of somebody whom you think you like—I won't use the word *love*—you shed tears at the loss of somebody whom you like. Are those tears for yourself or the one that is dead?—in sorrow there is a great deal of self-pity, concern with one's own loneliness, emptiness; and when one becomes aware of that emptiness, loneliness, there is self-pity, and that self-pity we call sorrow. So as long as there is sorrow, conscious or unconscious, within the mind, there is no quietness of the mind, there is no stillness of the mind. The stillness of the mind comes where there is beauty and love; you cannot separate beauty from love. Beauty is not an ornament, nor good taste. It does not

lie in the line of the hills, nor in architecture. There is beauty when you know what love is, and you cannot possibly know what love is when there is not intelligence, austerity, and order. And nobody can give this to you, no saint, no god, no mahatma—nobody! No authority in the world can give it to you. You as a human being have to understand this whole structure—the structure and the nature of your life of every day, what you do, what you think, what your motives are, how you behave, how you are caught in your own conclusions, in your own conditioning. It must begin there, in daily life, and if you cannot alter that totally, completely, bring about a total mutation in yourself, you will never know that still mind. And it is only the still mind that can find out; it is only the still mind that knows what truth is. Because that still mind has no imagination; it does not project its desires; it is a still mind—and it is only then that there is the bliss of something that cannot be put into words.

Question: Are we aware. . .

KRISHNAMURTI: Sit still, quietly, for a minute. I know you have many questions, many problems. Life is a torture; life is boredom, routine, an agony, and you have to understand that—not what the speaker says; what the speaker says has very little value. You will forget it the moment you leave the tent; what will remain outside the tent is yourself, your life, your pettiness, your shallowness, your brutality, your violence, your greed, your ambitions, your endless sorrow— that is what you have to understand, and nobody on earth, or in heaven, is going to save you from it. Therefore, to ask a question is to question yourself, not the speaker. What the speaker has said is of very little importance. You can throw it out, or you can repeat certain phrases and think you have understood it—you haven't! Or you will compare what you have heard with the Gita, with some book; but you will not face your own life. That is what matters: your daily agony, your daily despair, and the hopeless misery that one lives in. You may have occasional joy, but that joy becomes a memory, and then begins again the battle to capture that which has been. So when you ask questions, please remember you are asking the question of yourself and not of the speaker. And when you do ask, listen—listen to the question which you are putting and also listen to the speaker. Which means not respect for the speaker or yourself or another, but listen to understand. It doesn't matter who asks the question; it doesn't matter how silly the question is, you are listening to find out—not the other's silliness, but one's own silliness. Because life demands enormous observations. Life is a movement, an endless movement, and we want a corner of security out of that movement, and there is no security in life, psychologically. You must have security outwardly—food, clothes, shelter; every human being must have that, and it can only come about through world planning, a world state, not India planning for herself or another country planning for itself. Everyone can have food, clothes, and shelter if we forget our own nationalities, religions, divisions and become human beings without a label.

So, sirs, if you are going to ask questions, please bear in mind that you have to listen to your own question first and also listen to the speaker's reply, or explanation, or investigation.

Comment: To observe, one part of the mind must observe the other part of the mind, and that observation is destructive.

KRISHNAMURTI: One fragment of the mind looking at another fragment, and hence there is a contradiction, conflict, and the question is: "Is it possible to look totally?" That is the question, isn't it?

We live in fragments; if you are a politician, you are one thing in politics and something different at home. You may talk as a liberal, you may talk about democracy; yet in your heart you are autocratic, brutal, violent, ambitious. There is one part looking and working separately from the other part. You talk about loving the neighbor and then in the office about killing. So we function, we live, in fragments, and each fragment is looking at the other fragment—right? That is fairly simple. So the question is: Is it possible to live without any fragmentation, to be a total human being, to look at everything completely, totally? Isn't that right, sir? That is the question.

Now, of whom are you asking this? Are you asking the speaker, or are you asking because you are aware of your own fragmentation? You are aware of your life, one thing in the office, another thing in the street; you are respectful to the boss, and you kick the servant—which is to act fragmentarily. Are you aware of this fragmentary existence in yourself, and are you therefore asking whether it is possible not to function in fragments but wholly? Or do you want the speaker to tell you how to live wholly? Please follow this carefully. If he were foolish enough to tell you, would you live that way? Functioning in fragments, you would not. It is only fools that give advice. But if you looked at your fragments, not condemning, not identifying with one fragment that is pleasurable, that gives you delight, but if you were aware of each fragment—how one thinks politically and entirely differently religiously, how one treats one's wife or husband—if you were aware of these fragments without identifying with any fragment, then you would ask: Who is the observer? Is not the observer also a fragment which looks at other fragments? When one becomes aware of that fragment which looks at another fragment, one becomes totally aware of every fragment and also of the observer, who is the result of the fragmentation. So you will find, when you are so aware, that there is no fragmentation at all.

Question: Would you kindly tell us what to think of the processes of learning, knowing, remembering, and understanding. And I would like you to tell us how do we get people together who have the right values, in the sense you have been describing in meditation. How do we get together people who are meditating in the sense that you are meditating?

KRISHNAMURTI: How do we get people together who are meditating rightly? That is one of the questions. I don't know why you want to get people together who are meditating rightly. If you are meditating rightly, in the way we have talked about, you are with the people—right? It is only when you do not know what is right meditation, then you want to collect people and do propaganda.

Are there any other questions, sirs?

Question: What are learning, knowing, remembering, and understanding? I want you to make a reply to me.

KRISHNAMURTI: I will, sir. The question is: "What is learning, what is knowledge, and what is remembering?"

Question: And what is understanding?

KRISHNAMURTI: All right, sir, "What is understanding?"

When do you understand? Is understanding intellectual? When you read a book or a phrase and say, "I understand it," what do you mean by that word *understand?* Do you understand it intellectually, like understanding a mechanical problem? You can study a machine and you can say, "Yes, I know how it functions, how it works; I have understood it." And when we use that phrase, "I understand you," what does it mean? What do you understand—the complexity of something? Is it intellectual? Or is it emotional? Or merely sentimental? Can you understand something? Can you understand another, or can you understand yourself if you are sentimental, if you look at yourself fragmentarily? When you look at yourself with an ideology, with a formula, which is intellectual, do you understand yourself? You understand yourself when you look without the formula, see yourself actually as you are. So understanding comes only when the mind is quiet. You understand, sir? When I look at you and you look at me, when your mind is chattering, is elsewhere, comparing, judging, evaluating, and you aren't listening, then you won't understand. But if you listen with attention, then that attention is not fragmentary; it is a total process, and out of that quiet attention comes understanding.

The other question is: "What is learning?" Are you tired? You are not tired?

Comment: Go ahead.

KRISHNAMURTI: "Go ahead"? So typical! That means you sit there, and I do all the work. (Laughter) You don't work, you want to be spoon-fed. That is what has been done, that is how they have treated you for centuries; you have been spoon-fed by your teachers, by your authorities, by your books, by your saints—you don't want to work. You say, "Tell me all about it, what lies beyond the hills and the mountains and the earth," and you are satisfied with the description. That means you live on words, and your life is shallow and empty. To understand you have to work, and you haven't worked this evening; the speaker has worked. If you had worked a little, you would have taken the journey and gone on.

Learning is one of the most complex things. To learn a language, to learn a technique is one thing; to become a first-class engineer, acquire a technique, knowledge, whether that knowledge is your experience or the experience of thousands of others, it is knowledge, scientific knowledge, technological knowledge, knowledge of language, knowledge that you acquire through criticism, comparison, and so on—all that is knowledge, stored up. But knowledge is not learning. Learning is always in the active present; knowledge is always of the past, and we live on the past, are satisfied with the past. To us knowledge is extraordinarily important; that is why we worship the erudite, the clever, the cunning. But if you are learning—that means "learning all the time," which is an active present, learning every minute, learning by watching and listening, learning by seeing and doing—then you will see that learning is a constant movement without the past. Whereas knowledge is always of the past—I "have known," it is "my knowledge," "my remembrance," "my memory"—the past. But we are saying that a mind that is burdened with the past is a sorrowful mind, and to understand sorrow is the beginning of enlightenment. And when you end sorrow there is bliss.

November 30, 1967

Fifth Talk in New Delhi

I think everyone is more or less agreed that the older generation has made a terrible mess of the world, not only in this country, but elsewhere. There is still poverty, brutality, war, fear, and complete disorder. The young are especially aware of it; they say, "You can't teach us anymore because of what you have made of the world; you have no right to teach us anything; you don't know how to live, so why do you bother to teach us anything?" There is a great revolt going on, not only here, but also in other parts of the world. Man is seeking order, not only outside himself, but also within. Each generation tries to bring about such order, and each generation obviously fails and so resorts to revolution—physical, economic, and social upheaval. There have been many revolutions, including the Russian, and they have not produced order; they are still piling up armaments, there is still division of class, and so on. There is poverty all over the world. So the mind says, "What is the way out of all this?" I am sure you have asked yourself this question—not how to escape into some ideological world, or some mystical world, or a world of make-belief, but actually how does one bring about order? Because without order you cannot have peace, both outwardly and inwardly. So where is one to begin to bring about this order?

Surely order means to have no conflict in our relationship with people, with ideas, in all of our existence. Only then is there a possibility of order. And to end conflict, surely one must begin with oneself. Man—you and I—are responsible for this disorder, this chaos, this contradictory existence, this meaningless striving—either striving to find a reality, which becomes merely an intellectual concept, or striving for a better position, prestige, power, which is also quite meaningless. Surely this order can only be brought about first within oneself, and then there will be order outwardly. Inwardly, psychologically, we are in contradiction, we are in conflict; we are brutal people, each one seeking his own end; we are violent people, though we have talked endlessly of nonviolence. Each one of us is seeking his own personal or family security; each one of us segregates himself by his own particular belief or dogma, or by belonging to a particular class. So inwardly there is disorder, and outward order cannot possibly be brought about by mere legislation. We have innumerable laws, an efficient police, but such order eventually brings about disorder. Tyranny cannot possibly bring this order; one cannot brainwash people endlessly so that they remain docile, obedient, accepting what the authorities say. That again doesn't produce order; nor does the so-called religious pursuit. Those who believe in God, those who practice rituals or follow a certain method of what they call meditation do not produce order inwardly because those who practice meditation are in conflict within themselves all the time. And those who pursue power, position, prestige—politically, economically—obviously must be in conflict; they bring about chaos both in themselves and outwardly.

One realizes this; perhaps most of us realize it intellectually. One sees it and says, "Yes, that is so," but actually in daily life we are part of this social, economic, cultural structure which breeds great disorder. And I feel it is only the religious mind that can bring about order within itself. I do not mean those who profess religious beliefs, those who endlessly quote the various sacred books; they are not religious at all; they are using the books for their own profit. When a politician talks about God, you know very well that there is some dirty work going on. Religion is not belief, religion is not dogma. You cannot be religious and yet be a Hindu, a Muslim, or a Sikh; those who are religious, so-called, obviously function within an area of their own projection, of their own conditioning. A religious mind has no belief whatsoever, does not indulge in ideologies because ideologies are not factual; they are hypothetical, they offer an escape from actuality. A religious mind does not belong to any organized religion; it has no tradition, and it has no culture in the accepted sense of that

word, nor does it belong to any country. One can see why. It is not that the speaker is asserting dogmatically, but one can see why a religious mind cannot possibly belong to any nationality, to any organized religion, or have any belief, dogma, ritual. The reason is very simple; when you have dogma, belief, ritual, you are separating yourself, you are limiting the functioning of the mind, which is capable of enormous things. When you call yourself a Sikh, a Hindu, a Parsi, or a communist, you are limiting your own capacities to feel profoundly, to be intense, to have great passion, because behind these beliefs, rituals, dogmas, there is fear, and a mind that is afraid is an irreligious mind. To escape from fear through some ritual, or some belief, or some ideology, not only brings about disorder within oneself, but also outwardly. When you call yourself a Hindu, you must obviously be against the Muslim or the Christian, and when you separate, segregate yourself into nationalities, it must obviously bring about further disorder. One can see this very clearly, intellectually at least—that is, verbally. But one must realize this actually in daily life—which is not to belong to any group, not to follow any leader, not to have the authority of any book, sacred or profane, because all that has led man to utter destruction.

Living in this country, I wonder if you realize what is actually happening here. Perhaps you look at it as something you have to put up with; you get used to this disorder, to this chaos, to the utter callousness of human beings. But if you looked, not intellectually, but if you felt it in your heart, not through words, but by actual observation, you would see what a decline there has been in the last twenty years. Yet you are completely indifferent to it; you say, "I can't do anything." So when you feel that you can't do anything, you accept disorder within yourself as inevitable. And to bring about order within oneself, there must be honesty. When we follow an ideology—and most people have some kind of ideology, some kind of conceptual outlook on life—such an outlook does breed dishonesty.

Please don't accept or deny what the speaker is saying; examine it, look at it; give your heart and mind to find out, not intellectually or verbally. When the house is burning—and your house is actually burning—you don't discuss how to put the fire out, you are not concerned with who set the house on fire, but you actually do something, you act. And when you act you have energy—you have tremendous energy. But when you theorize, discuss intellectually, then action is not possible.

As we said, there must be honesty right through our being, never to say a word that we don't mean, never doubletalk, believe one thing and do another. So when you act according to principles you are dishonest—doesn't that shock you? You accept it? Apparently you do. You know, when you act according to a principle, according to an ideology, according to what you think you should be, you actually are not honest. When you think in terms of nonviolence—an ideology, a principle—you are dishonest because actually you are violent; what matters is that you face that violence, and you cannot face that violence if you are acting according to a principle. When you act according to a principle, you are cultivating dishonesty, hypocrisy. Do observe it in yourself. You can only be honest right through your being, passionately, when you see things in yourself actually as they are, not as you wish them to be; and if you have a principle, a belief, an ideology, then you cannot possibly look at yourself directly—they prevent you, and hence one becomes hypocritical, dishonest.

One must have order, because without order deeply within oneself, there is no peace. And order can only come about when you know what disorder is. When you know your thoughts, your feelings are creating disorder, then deny that disorder. Deny your nationality, deny your gods—they have no meaning; they are the invention of a frightened mind. Deny all spiritual authority, which has bred disorder. Look what has happened to religion in this country, as in other parts of the world. You have followed authority because it offers security: you don't know, and your guru, your teacher, your Masters, your books know, and you follow them. Observe it in yourself, sir. You follow them because you are confused, in disorder; the gurus, mahatmas, and all the rest of those people say they know, that they will lead you to truth, and you follow them, you accept them. Nobody, no outside agency whatsoever can lead you to truth; it doesn't matter what authority it is. And this country is burdened with the authority of tradition, of teachers, and of gurus. When a man says he knows, then you may be sure he does not know, except in technological matters. But when a guru, when a teacher says he knows and that he will lead you, then he will lead you to your own destruction, to disorder within yourself, because one cannot follow anybody; one has to find that truth for oneself, not through somebody else. So many people talk about truth, including the politicians: "experiments in truth," "following truth," somebody who has "realized truth," and if they put on professional garb, then you follow them blindly. Truth is something living, it cannot be found; you cannot seek it, it must come to you. It cannot come to you if there is no order within yourself, and nobody can give you that order; that order only comes when you have understood the whole structure of disorder. In the understanding and in the freeing of the mind itself from disorder, there is the living order, not an order according to a blueprint.

So, what causes disorder inwardly? Because there is the first resolution of disorder—not outwardly what causes disorder within each one of us? Have you ever gone into it, considered in yourself whether it is possible to come upon this extraordinary, absolute order? Pure mathematics is pure order, and to find that extraordinary state of order, there must be inwardly a living order, which is virtue, austerity—austerity is not harsh, brutal. What causes disorder? Primarily it is division between action and idea, isn't it? Because, as we said at the beginning, there is disorder as long as there is conflict, as long as there is contradiction within oneself, and this contradiction exists primarily between action and idea.

Please listen to discover what is true and what is false. You cannot discover what is true or what is false if you are merely agreeing or comparing; you have to listen, and you cannot listen if your mind is interpreting, judging, evaluating, comparing, agreeing, or disagreeing. If you want to understand anything, your mind must be empty of everything that it has projected, so that your whole brain is quiet. When you are listening to the speaker, listen with your heart and mind, not with your thoughts—thought merely separates. But if you listen with your heart—unemotionally, not sentimentally—then perhaps you will find order in yourself without going through all the processes of analyzing disorder. Most of us are inclined to the analytical process; we think we will come to order through analysis, and obviously the analytical process does not bring order; you may be clever at analyzing, but the analyzer is an entity separate from the thing which he analyzes, and so there is conflict between the analyzer and the thing analyzed.

As we were saying, one of the fundamental causes of disorder is the separation between idea and action. What is action—the doing? Is it related to an idea, to an ideol-ogy? If it is, then there is a division between what you think should be and what you are actually doing, isn't there? When you think that you should be nonviolent—"should be" in the future, as an idea, as a concept—but actually you are violent, then there is a division between the two, the idea and the actuality; hence there is a contradiction. It is this contradiction that brings conflict, and conflict is invariably disorder. When you suppress anger or envy as an idea, then this is opposed to the fact, and hence there is contradiction and therefore conflict. That is how most human beings live; they live in the conceptual world, the world of ideas, and hence they are not actually living; so their action is an approximation to the idea and brings conflict. And so the question arises: Is it possible to act without the process of ideation? Please follow this, don't jump to any conclusion, because a mind that concludes is a dead mind; it is only the free mind that inquires, lives, finds out. Why does the mind live in ideas; why does it make ideas, concepts, ideologies, principles, beliefs the most important things in life? Why? Obviously the principles, the ideas, the ideologies are a contradiction to the fact, to the fact of what actually is every day.

Now why is there this conceptual living? I do not know if you have gone into it at all; probably you have never even questioned it, and if you are questioning it now, if you are inquiring into it seriously and earnestly, then perhaps we can go into it together. That is, one must be tremendously honest with oneself, in the sense that one knows that one has ideas which are contradictory to one's life, to everyday living. So which is more important, the ideas or the living? When you call yourself a Hindu, a Buddhist, a Muslim, who cares whether you put on a turban or not, whether you are this or that—what does matter is what you are, how you live. And as long as there are ideologies, principles, concepts, there must be contradiction in action. Please, if you can understand this basically, then you live in fact and in action, never in an ideology. Ideologies, surely, come into being only when we do not know how to act, or when we want to escape from the fact of action—right? If I knew what to do with my anger, with my jealousy, with my brutality, violence, hatred, then where would be the need for an ideology? Because I don't know what to do with my violence, I escape into an ideology, hoping thereby to get rid of my violence; so there is a contradiction between the fact—*what is*—and 'what should be'. Cannot the mind push aside for-ever 'what should be'? You can only do it when you face the fact, when you accept, see directly for yourself that you are violent. When you are ambitious you are violent, when you are seeking power you are violent, when you have your god as opposed to another god you are violent; division by ideologies breeds violence. So when you realize that, there is no need for ideologies and concepts at all.

Then what is action without the idea? I hope some of you are following this. There is the doing and the non-doing person. The non-doing person is someone who is wrapped up in ideas, concepts. Can one act without the process of ideation? Because, as we said, conflict breeds disorder, and as long as we are in conflict inwardly, we not only produce disorder in ourselves but also in the world. And one of the primary reasons for disorder is this conceptual way of living. And, if there is no concept whatsoever—this requires tremendous understanding—what then is action? Now, your action is based on an idea derived from experience, from knowledge, on a reasoned-out thought, which is idea—organized thought is idea—and according to that you try to act. But you can never act according to the idea, because the idea is the result of past experience, past memories; it is of time. Action is always in the present, and

when you approximate action to past experience, there must be conflict and therefore confusion. I wonder if you are getting this? And is it possible to be completely free from all ideation, so that you are acting without conflict?

To put it differently: there is the experiencer and the experienced, which is the thinker and the thought. The thinker is separate, at least thinks he is separate from thought— please see this, observe it in yourself. There is the thinker and the thought; is there a thinker without thought at all? Obviously not. Don't say, "Which began first?"—that is a clever argument which leads nowhere. But one can observe within oneself that as long as there is no thought derived from memory, experience, knowledge—which are all of the past—as long as there is no thought, which does not mean a state of amnesia, there is no thinker at all. Can one function, act, without this division into the thinker and the thought? And besides, when you observe, the thinker is the thought, the two are not separate. It is only when there is conflict between the thinker and the thought, then there is a separation. When I say "I am angry," then the observer is different from the observed; but when the observer is anger there is no division and hence no conflict. When the observer says he himself is anger, and you eliminate the conflict, then you have energy to deal with the fact.

Sirs, most of us know what anger or jealousy or envy is. When you are jealous, for whatever reason, there is the entity that says, "I am jealous," as though jealousy were different from the thinker, the feeler, the observer—right? The two are separate, but is that so? Is the entity different from that which it feels as jealousy, or is the entity itself jealousy? Please follow this. If the entity itself, the observer himself is jealousy, then what can he do? And if he does anything, he becomes the observer and hence creates conflict. I wonder if you are follow-ing this? So one begins to inquire: is anger associated with the word *anger,* or are you dealing with the thing as it actually takes place, not a second after?

We will come upon it differently. As we were saying, action is different from the con-cept, the idea, and one has to act in life—living is action in relationship—otherwise there is no living at all. The sannyasi who retires and renounces the world is living in a relationship with his ideas. Life can only exist in relationship, and relationship means action; I can act according to an image, a symbol, or I can act in that state of affection and love which is not an idea. Is love an idea? If it is an idea, it can be cultivated, it can be nourished, cherished, pushed around, twisted as you like it. But if it is not an idea and it cannot be cultivated, then what is love? First of all, when you say you love somebody or you love your country—and God knows why you say you love your country or your God—what is that love? When you say you love God, what does that mean? To love something which you have projected, which gives you safety, which gives you hope, which gives you a certain sense of well-being, which helps you to es-cape from fear, that "love of God" is ab-solute nonsense. What has actually taken place is that you have projected an image of yourself according to your wishes, as some-thing worthwhile, great, noble; so when you worship God, you are actually worshiping yourself. That is not love.

Look at yourselves, sirs, observe your-selves; use the speaker as a mirror in which you see yourselves honestly, undistorted. You will see that there is confusion only when there is an idea which predominates action. And what is action without idea? Go into it, sirs. What is action, what does it mean "to do"? I am not talking about spontaneity. Man is not spontaneous; he has a thousand

years of tradition behind him, a thousand in-fluences which have conditioned him, fears, hopes, despairs, anxieties, guilt, ambition—how can such an entity be spontaneous? It cannot. But if you begin to inquire, not be told by another, whether you can live without a concept, without a formula, without the in-terference of thought, which is always the old, then you will inevitably come upon ac-tion which is born out of love. Love is not old, love is not the product of thought; thought is always old, thought is memory, thought is the result of past experience. But love is something always new, and love is al-ways in the present; it is not time-binding.

It is only the religious mind that has un-derstood this whole structure of conflict and disorder—it is only such a mind that can be a religious mind. And a religious mind does not seek; it cannot experiment with truth. It is only such a mind that can perceive what is true, because such a mind understands the whole structure and the nature of pleasure. Truth is not something dictated by your pleasure or pain, nor your conditioning as a Hindu, a Christian, a Buddhist, a Muslim. To understand pleasure—not to deny pleasure—one must go into this whole question of what is thought. And this understanding is self-knowing—knowing yourself, not realizing some higher entity of the self, which again is sheer nonsense. What is factual is yourself: your ideas, your way of life, your feeling, your ambition, your greed, your envy, your cruelty, and the despair, the loneliness, the boredom. Unless you bring about order within yourself, you can pray, you can wor-ship, you can read all the books and follow all the gurus, but it will have no meaning whatsoever.

So order comes through the understanding of disorder, and disorder comes only when there is conflict, when thought, which is the response of memory and always old, inter-feres with action, which is always a "doing in the present." And seeking truth has no meaning. Why do you seek? I do not know if you have gone into this question. Why do you seek at all? And how do you know when you find it? To say, "I know this is the truth," you must have had an experience of it in the past; therefore, you are capable of recognizing it. If it is the recognition of the past, it is not truth; it is still the projection of your own inclination, pleasure. So the religious mind alone can find that which is truth. It doesn't "find" it—that is the wrong word to use—the religious mind is in the state of that unnameable thing which cannot be sought because that thing is a living thing and therefore timeless; therefore, it is complete order. A mind that is petty, small, ambitious, seeking position, suffering, and in agony—such a mind never knows what love is, do what it will; and without love there is no beauty, without love there is no order.

When you ask questions, what is important? To find out what your state of mind is, or are you asking questions with regard to a problem that you have? If you have a problem and are seeking an answer, who is going to answer it—the speaker? He can put it into words and explain, but the explanation, the answer, does not solve your problem. Whatever your problem is—death, love, loneliness, despair, the agony of life, the boredom of existence—whatever it is, you have to face it, not somebody else; and when you seek an answer from somebody else, you are not facing the fact, and that is what this country has done for centuries upon centuries. That is why you are secondhand thinkers; you have been spoon-fed; you want somebody else to solve your life. That is why you have these politicians, these gurus, and they will never, under any circumstances, solve the human problem. The solution of the human problem needs care, affection. What was it you wanted, sir?

Question: Last time in answering a question about death, you said that thought continues after death, but that it has no validity. Sir, is it not thought that incarnates? Is reincarnation not a fact?

KRISHNAMURTI: First of all, why do you want to know if reincarnation is a fact? (Laughter) Please, sirs, don't laugh, this is a serious matter. Why do you want to know? Because you have lived fully? Because you know the beauty of life, because you have lived so completely, with such ecstasy and passion—is that why you say, "Look, what will happen when I die? Will I go on with this ecstasy, this delight, this thing that I have felt when I looked at the blue sky, and the bird on the wing, and that face of a man or a woman, which has delighted me—when I die will all that go on?" Or are you asking the question because you want to know if there is hope in the future, if there is reincarnation, a next life? One has led a miserable existence, a shoddy, meaningless life, and that is what we call living, isn't it? That's your life, isn't it? Going to the office—not that one shouldn't go to the office, you have to unfortunately—going to the office until you are sixty or sixty-five. Just think of it, day after day, the routine, the routine of sex, the machine-like routine, doing things over and over again, with misery, with a stricken heart, a darkened mind, dull-witted, lonely—that is your life isn't it? And you say, "Will this life, which is of sorrow and agony, with an occasional flash of joy, will this reincarnate, will this go on?"

Question: Will action without thought. . .

KRISHNAMURTI: Wait, sir! You see, sir, you haven't listened to what the speaker has said. You know it is a sad world; there is so much misery and sorrow in the world to which each one is contributing, and you want to know what will happen in the next life, when you don't know how to live. You want to know the truth about reincarnation, the proof. You have the psychical research assertions, or the assertions of clairvoyants who have had a past life and all that, but you never ask how to live—to live with delight, with enchantment, with beauty, every day! But you never ask that—and if you asked, then you would find it, then you would come upon it passionately. But to ask, one mustn't be frightened of life; that means not to be frightened of being completely insecure without becoming neurotic; for life is insecure, psychologically. You may go back to the same house, the same wife and children, but inwardly there is no security at all. And when there is no security, then there is a movement, then life is endless, then life and death are similar. The man who is frightened of life is frightened of death. And the one who lives without conflict, with beauty and love, is not frightened of death, because to love is to die.

Question: What is action without thought?

KRISHNAMURTI: Did the speaker say that, or did he say, "See the nature of thought and action; see the structure and nature of thought, how it functions; observe it in yourself"? Thought is of time. Memory is accumulated experience, and from that there is the reaction which is thought. Action is something that is active, that is being done all the time, living. And when you separate thought and action, there is conflict. Sir, to act you must be passionate. Do you know what it means to be passionate?—total self-abandonment. That word *passion* comes from a root which means sorrow, and as long as you are in sorrow, there is no passion. The ending of sorrow is the understanding of yourself as you are, not according to some yogi or some psychologist. When you under-

stand yourself there is the ending of sorrow; and when sorrow ends you will know what love is.

Question: What is the difference between awareness and introspection?

KRISHNAMURTI: What is introspection? To analyze, to examine, to dissect oneself: "This is right, I have done wrong, this is good." That is, it is inwardly inspecting—right? Now, when you are inspecting inwardly, who is the sergeant? When you are inspecting—that is, looking, analyzing, searching, questioning—who is the questioner, who is the censor? Is not the censor, the observer, the examiner, the introspector, the thing which he introspects himself? Don't agree, sir, this is meditation, not just agreement. Now, awareness is not that at all. Awareness is to be aware without introspection—it is to look. Sir, have you ever looked at a bird or a tree—have you? I am afraid you haven't because you haven't time, you are too indifferent, you have never looked; and if you look next time, do look at a tree, at the foliage, at the beauty of the line of a limb—look at it against the dark sky, at the real quality of the tree, look at it. But when you look, what takes place? You are interpreting it according to the image you have of that tree, aren't you? So what are you looking at?—at the image you have, not at the tree. And you can only look at the tree when you have no image; the image is the result of thought. So awareness is to look, to observe, to see actually *what is,* without any interpretation, without any image. Look at your husband or wife, or your children, and, if you must, at your politicians without the image. Do look at them—you understand? Look without the memories, without the pleasure, without the annoyance, the anger, the habitual things you have become accustomed to. Then, when you look that way, you have a different kind of relationship. But if you look with your image—the image that you have built up for thirty, twenty, ten years, or days, or a day—then you are not related, then the relationship is only between image and image, which is an idea, a memory, and not a living thing.

So action and awareness and living are the same; you cannot live if you are not aware, choicelessly. You are not living when you are not completely in action—of course not all the time—and you cannot act if there is no love; and love is not the result of thought.

As most of us have empty hearts and empty minds—though we may be very clever and quote the Gita upside down, or the Koran, or what you will—we do not know what it means to love our wives and our children. If you loved your children you would have no wars; there would be no division between you and the Muslim or the Christian. But you don't love. If you love, then do what you will, and there is beauty in what you do.

December 3, 1967

Banaras, India, 1967

---　*　---

First Talk at Rajghat

As one observes in the world, not only in this country, but also in Europe, in America, in Russia, and in China, one sees a growing violence, not only in individual lives, but also in the collective. People seem to get violent over such trivial things. In this country they are violent about language, regional language; and they are violent in other parts of the world over war, destruction, revolt, or, as in America, the black against the white—and so on. There is a general tendency towards anarchy, disruption, destruction, and there is more and more aggression. And, as one sees this happening, one asks oneself, why? What are the causes of this terrible, destructive, brutal violence right through the world? I wonder if you have asked yourself this question, why? Or do you accept it as inevitable, as part of life?

Each one of us in his private life is also violent. We get angry; we do not like people to criticize us; we do not brook any interference with our own particular lives; we are very defensive, and therefore aggressive, when we hold on to a particular belief or dogma, or when we worship our particular nationality, with the rag that is called the flag. So, individually, in our private secret lives, we are aggressive, we are violent; and also outwardly, in our relationship with others. When we are ambitious, greedy, ac-quisitive, we are also outwardly, collectively aggressive, violent, and destructive.

I wonder why this is happening now, during this present period in history, and why it has always happened in the past? There have been so many wars, so many disruptive, destructive forces let loose on the world; why? What is the reason for it? Not that knowing the cause and the reason for it will ever free the mind from violence. But it is right to inquire into why human beings throughout the ages have been so violent, brutal, aggressive, cruel, destructive—destroying their own species. If you ask why, what do you think is the reason for it?—bearing in mind that explanations and conclusions do not in any way remove violence. We'll go into the question of freedom from violence, but first we must inquire why these violent reactions exist.

I think one of the reasons is the instinct which we have inherited throughout the ages, which is derived from the animals. You have seen dogs fighting, or little bulls—the stronger fighting the weaker. The animals are aggressive and violent in nature. And as we human beings have evolved from them, we have also inherited this aggressive violence and hatred, which exists when we have territorial rights—rights over a piece of land—or sexual rights, as in the animal. So that is one of the causes. Then another cause is environment—the society in which we live, the culture in which we have been brought up, the education we have received. We are compelled by the society in which we live to be aggressive—each man fighting for himself, each man wanting a position, power, prestige. His concern is about himself. Though he may also be concerned with the family, with the group, with the nation, and so on, essentially he is concerned with himself. He may work through the family, through the group, through the nation, but always he puts himself first. So the society in which we live is one of the contributory causes of this violence—that is, the behavior which it imposes on us. In order to survive, it is said, you must be aggressive, you must fight. So environment has an extraordinary importance as a cause of violence, and this society in which we live is the product of all of us human beings; we ourselves have produced it.

Another of these causes is overpopulation. Throughout the world this is becoming a problem, but especially in this country. More and more people are inhabiting the world, and all of them demand, and must have, employment, food, clothes, and shelter. They are going to fight for these things, and they are going to fight much more when they live in big towns, which are already overcrowded, with no space between human beings. It is one of the most extraordinary things that the more we have become sophisticated, the more we have become so-called civilized, the less space we have. Go round any of the streets in Banaras, or in Rome, or in London, or in New York—see how crowded it all is; and in the dwellings in these cities there is hardly any space between human beings. They have experimented with putting thousands of rats in a small space. When they do that the rats lose all sense of proportion, of value. The mothers with little babies neglect them; violence and disorder increase.

So, lack of space is one of the contributory causes of this extraordinary violence.

But the major cause of violence, I think, is that each one of us is inwardly, psychologically, seeking security. In each one of us the urge for psychological security, that inward sense of being safe, projects the demand, the outward demand, for security. Inwardly each one of us wants to be secure, sure, certain. That is why we have all these marriage laws—in order that we may possess a woman, or a man, and so be secure in our relationship. If that relationship is attacked, we become violent, which is the psychological demand, the inward demand, to be certain of our relationship to everything. But there is no such thing as certainty, security, in any relationship. Inwardly, psychologically, we should like to be secure, but there is no such thing as permanent security. Your wife, your husband, may turn against you; your property may be taken away from you in a revolution.

So all these are the contributory causes of the violence which is prevalent, rampaging throughout the world. I think anybody who has observed, even if only a little, what is going on in the world, and especially in this unfortunate country, can also, without a great deal of intellectual study, observe and find out in himself those things which, projected outwardly, are the causes of this extraordinary brutality, callousness, indifference, violence.

Now these are the explanations—and we can have more of them, or go into them in greater detail—these are some of the major factors in bringing about this enormous, destructive, cruel relationship between man and man. Then what shall we do? Having more or less established the causes of violence, both of inward violence and outward, then the problem arises: How do we free the mind from violence?

We were talking the other day to a very prominent politician—and God save the world from politicians!—and he was saying that violence was a necessary part of life. When a government official accepts violence as the norm, then there is something radically wrong, because the world needs peace, not violence. Man must be peaceful, for it is only through peace that he can find out what is true, what is beauty, what is love. Through violence you can never find out what love is, you can never find out, without peace, what beauty is. So to accept violence as an essential part of daily life is a most perverse way of thinking.

The word *violence* needs a great deal of explanation, too, because we think violence is merely such things as the burning of a house by crazy people, fighting the policeman, marching off with a whole mob of people shouting "You shall not!" or, "You must!" or war. That is what we call violence. But violence is much more subtle than that. When, for example, you compare yourself with another, that is part of violence; when you are imitating or trying to surpass another, which is competitiveness, that is also part of violence. The whole social and religious structure is based on this principle of comparison. Measuring yourself against another and so competing with him is part of this violence. It is also part of violence when you suppress your desires. That does not mean that you must indulge your desires. It means that when you imitate, conform to a pattern, whether the pattern be established by society or by yourself—that is, when you are imitating, conforming, controlling, disciplining yourself, forcing yourself—that is also a part of violence. When you obey, that again is a part of violence—and most human beings are trained to obey. And again, this whole Indian structure—Hindu or Muslim or Catholic or what you will—this religious structure based on obedience, acceptance, authority; all this is part of violence.

So, violence to what?—you understand my question? I am being violent against what? If it is violence against society, it becomes revolt; that is one kind of violence. Then there is the violence of obedience, which says, "I do not know, but you do." So you become my authority and I follow you. Please do go into this in yourself, and don't just hear what the speaker is saying. Find out! Is it not a kind of violence when you set up another—it does not matter who it is—as your guru, your teacher, your saint? Whoever it is, once you accept him as your authority, inevitably you must be violent. Why? Why do you become violent when you accept authority? Because, since there are other kinds of authority—dozens of authorities—you feel impelled to assert that your authority is greater than the others. So we have to find out why, in accepting any kind of authority—whether it is social authority, or the spiritual authority of a guru or of a book—this breeds violence. It has, throughout the world; why? When you accept the authority of the Koran, or of the Bible, or of Jesus, or whoever it may be, why does that cause violence?

What is violence? It is division, isn't it? When you accept the authority of the Gita and I accept the authority of the Koran, you and I are bound to be separated by our beliefs, by our dogmas. Any form of separateness, of division, breeds violence. I hold to my book, to my authority, and you hold to yours. Superficially we may tolerate each other, living, perhaps, together in the same street, or going to the same office, but inwardly we are separate, inwardly there is division between you and me—you the Hindu and I the Muslim, the Christian, the Buddhist, the communist, or whatever it may be. So, essentially, this division, brought about through belief, through authority, through psychological exclusiveness, does breed violence, and not only breeds violence, but must exclude every form of affection and love. Please, sirs, observe it in your own hearts; do not merely listen to the speaker. Look how you regard someone who is not of the same culture, the same way of looking at things, who thinks differently from you, the occasions when you consider yourself slightly superior to someone else. When there is prejudice, there is division, and prejudice is the most stupid form of thought, and being prejudiced the most stupid way of living.

So what is one to do? Knowing that we human beings are violent, are separative—and these are facts, not ideas, not theories, but actual facts—what are we to do? Outwardly there must be one universal language—outwardly, you understand. There must be one government caring for the whole world, not separate governments concerned only with separate countries—India, China, Russia, or America—because that always breeds division, economic, social, and class division.

So, first, outwardly, one language—not Hindu or English, but one universal language. Then, again outwardly, a world-planning for the whole of mankind. Inwardly, then, it becomes much more interesting, much more vital, much more demanding.

Then how is a human being—that is, you—to be free of this violence? People have tried every way, for when the monk, the sannyasi, renounces the world, he hopes to renounce not only worldly things but also all the brutalities of life. But he doesn't. You cannot escape from violence by repeating some mantra, all the rest of that ritual; you cannot possibly escape from the fact of anything. I cannot possibly escape from what I actually am. I can invent a series of networks of escapes, but those escapes will inevitably become extraordinarily important and therefore separative, and so again produce violence. So the first thing is not to escape from the fact. Do please listen to this—not to

escape from the fact that I am violent. Nonviolence has no place whatsoever; it is a romantic, unrealistic formula. All ideation, all ideology—'what should be' as the opposite of *what is*—is romantic and not factual. Therefore one must put away all ideals—completely. Can we do that? If we are thinking in terms of nonviolence, which is what most of us are thinking, and yet, being violent, we say, "I must not be violent," that "must not" breeds a pattern of being nonviolent, that is, nonviolence becomes an ideal. But the fact is you are violent, so why bother with romantic, idiotic ideals? So, then, can you be with the fact and not with the escape?

First, then, there must be order outwardly, and there cannot be order unless there is a universal language and a planning for the whole of mankind, which means the ending of all nationalities. Then, inwardly, there must be a freeing of the mind from all escapes so that it faces the fact of *what is*. Can I look at the fact of my being violent and not say, "I must not be violent," and not condemn it or justify it—just look at the fact of my being violent?

This brings us to a very important question, I think perhaps the crucial question: What does it mean to look, to listen? For if I do not know how to look, then I am bound to condemn or justify, or to seek some form of escape. It is because I do not know how to look at anything that I begin to condemn it, to justify it, to say "It is right, it is wrong; this must not be, this should be." So I must first learn to look, not only objectively, outwardly, but also inwardly.

Look at a tree; please, sirs, this is very important. You may have heard the speaker say this often, but really to look at a tree is one of the most difficult things to do. You can look at a tree because it is objective, away from the center—over there. When you look at that tree, how do you look at it? Do you look at it with your mind, or do you look at it with your eyes?—or do you look at it with your eyes plus your mind? Are you following this? If you look at a tree, you see it not only visually, with your eyes, but your looking also evokes certain memories, certain associations. I look at that tree and say, "That is a tamarind." When I say it is a tamarind, or a mimosa, or whatever it is, I have already stopped looking. Do observe it in yourselves. My mind is already distracted by saying, "That is a tamarind," whereas to look at a tree I must give complete attention to the looking. So, to look is only possible when thought in no way interferes with the looking. Thought is memory, experience, knowledge, and when all that comes in, it is interfering with looking, with attention.

Now, it is fairly easy to look at a tree because it is something outside. But to look at oneself, to see actually what one is—to look at this violence without any condemnation, justification, explanation; just to look at it—to do that you must have plenty of energy, mustn't you?

Now, observe what is happening here. The speaker is saying something to you, and to listen you have to give your whole attention. To find out exactly what he is saying, you must give attention, but if you are taking notes, if you are looking at somebody else, if you are tired, if you are sleepy, if you are yawning or scratching, or agreeing or disagreeing, then you are not giving complete attention. So, to listen to the word, to the train that is going over that bridge, to listen to the movement of the wind in the leaves, not casually, but to listen to it, you must have tremendous energy. That can only come into being when there is no explanation—when thought doesn't say, "The tree is pleasant," or, "That noise of the train is interfering with my listening," and so on.

So, can I, and can you, look at this violence, whose cause we have explained

somewhat; can we look at this violence without any justification? Without condemning it, can we look at it as it is?

What takes place when you give complete attention to the thing that we call violence?—violence being not only what separates human beings, through belief, conditioning, and so on, but also what comes into being when we are seeking personal security, or the security of individuality through a pattern of society. Can you look at that violence with complete attention? And when you look at that violence with complete attention, what takes place? When you give complete attention to anything—your learning of history or mathematics, looking at your wife or your husband—what takes place? I do not know if you have gone into it—probably most of us have never given complete attention to anything—but when you do, what takes place? Sirs, what is attention? Surely when you are giving complete attention, there is care, and you cannot care if you have no affection, no love. And when you give attention in which there is love, is there violence? You are following? Formerly, I have condemned violence, I have escaped from it, I have justified it, I have said it is natural. All these things are inattention. But when I give attention to what I have called violence—and in that attention there is care, affection, love—where is there space for violence?

So it is important when we are going into this question of violence to understand, very deeply, what is attention.

Attention is not concentration. Concentration is a most stupid way of dealing with anything. When a schoolboy wants to—rather, is forced to—concentrate on a book when he wants to look out of the window, what takes place? He wants to look out of the window and the teacher says, "Look at your book—concentrate." What takes place? There is a conflict, isn't there? He wants to look at the beauty of a tree, or just to look at it casually, or to see who is going by, or to watch a bird preening itself; and at the same time he feels he must look at the book. So what takes place? There is a conflict, isn't there? He wants to look over there, and at the same time he wants to look at the book. In that conflict he is neither looking at the book nor looking at the tree or the bird; whereas, if he were really attentive he would be attentive to both, to everything—to the color, to the people sitting next to him, to what they are doing, to how they are scratching their heads, or taking notes, or not paying attention; he would be aware of everything.

So violence is not to be fought against, is not to be suppressed, not to be transcended, transmuted, gone above and beyond. Violence is to be looked at. When you look at something with care, with attention, you begin to understand it, and therefore there is then no place for violence at all. It is only the inattentive, the thoughtless, the prejudiced who are violent. So the stupid man is violent, not the man who is attentive, who looks, cares, has love; for this man there is no place for violence, either in gesture, or in word, or in action.

Question: Sir, when we are violent, how can we look at it?

KRISHNAMURTI: Just a minute! Take a breather! I have just finished and you are ready with a question. Just wait a minute, have patience. Because, you see, if you had listened to what I have been saying, you would have spent a little thought on it, wouldn't you? You would have asked yourself, "Is what he is saying right or wrong?" You would be looking, you would be questioning, you would not be accepting or denying; you would be just looking. But if you pop up immediately with a question, you are really more concerned with your question than with listening, aren't you? Surely. I am not criticizing you, please. So, it is better, if I may suggest it, first to listen. You have your question—put it by, keep to it. I am not saying you mustn't ask; on the contrary, you must ask, you must question, you must doubt. But first listen. Listen to the bird, listen to the train, listen to the voice of the teacher, listen to your father, to your mother, to your government. Listen, do not judge. Just find out what is true—and you can only find out what is true when you are listening, and not agreeing or disagreeing or condemning or justifying. And when you know how to listen, then there is no problem at all.

So your question is, "Can I look when I am violent?" At the moment of violence, at the precise moment of anger, you are obviously not looking. Our reactions are very quick. Somebody says to me, "You are a fool!" and I immediately react. Then I say something out of violence, out of anger, because he has hurt me. At that precise moment of anger, obviously I am not looking. So how is one to look, to be attentive, so that there is no moment of inattention? You understand?—you follow it, sirs? You say that I am a fool, and I get angry because I think I am not a fool. I have put myself on a pedestal, and I want to protect my dignity—you know, all that silly stuff. So I react very quickly and I get angry. The reaction is normal—if you tread on my toe, I must react. I am not dead or paralyzed, so a reaction is normal. But what follows from the reaction comes from inattention, doesn't it? I don't know if you are following all this. Wait a minute—I'll go into it a little more.

Most of us, most of the time, are inattentive. In that state of inattention you tread on my toe or call me a fool, and I react, which is natural. But if I also get angry, it is out of an inattentive condition, isn't it? Now—please listen carefully—how is that inattentive condition to be in a state of attention?

How is it to be, not become, attentive?—for inattention can never become attention, just as hatred can never become love. So how is inattention to be attentive? Is that clear? Now, when you are inattentive, know that you are inattentive. Say to yourself, "Yes, I am inattentive and I am sorry that I am angry." Apologize and forget it. That means what? It means that you are attentive of inattention. So, though inattention can never be made to become attention, and you cannot cultivate attention, what you can do is to be aware, to know, when you are inattentive. The moment you know you are inattentive, there is attention.

Question: Sir, is it possible to be aware when we are inattentive?

KRISHNAMURTI: Most of us aren't. Most of us are unaware that we are inattentive; why? Find out why we have become inattentive—this is a very important question—why we have become inattentive to everything—to the dirt, to the squalor, to the ugliness, to the poverty, to the brutality of society, to the absurdities of governments, to the chicanery of politicians. We are inattentive to all that; why? Find out why you are inattentive, because if you were attentive, you would do something, wouldn't you? You are frightened of doing something because you might lose your job, or quarrel with your father, or—a dozen things. So you say, "Much better to practice inattention." It is much safer to be inattentive, and that is what society wants you to be. It wants you to be completely inattentive about everything; that is, just to follow, obey, accept. Then you are a meek little citizen. You are told what to do, and like a machine you do everything you are told to do by the bosses, whether it is the political boss, or the economic boss, or the guru boss. So, since we are trained to be monkeys, we have become inattentive. But when you know

you are inattentive—it doesn't matter a single minute that you are inattentive—knowing that you are inattentive means that you are already attentive. But the man who says, "I am practicing attention," is climbing the wrong tree. You can never practice attention because attention is only possible when there is love, and you cannot possibly practice love—what a horrible idea! Is that clear?

Question: Will there be an end to these evil wars and violence?

KRISHNAMURTI: A little boy asks because he is concerned with the future, with tomorrow, with a world that is becoming more and more violent, with wars, and more wars. He says, "My future is being created by the older generation and they have produced these monstrous wars," and he asks, "Will there be an end to it?"

There will be an end only when you are nonviolent. You must begin as an individual—you cannot make the whole world nonviolent in a flash. Forget the world; be, as an individual, nonviolent. I do not know whether you have ever wondered what the older generation has done to this world. The older generation has produced this world of violence, greed, hatred; they are entirely responsible for it, not God. They have lived a life of brutality, self-concern, callousness. They have made this world, and the younger people say, "You have made a filthy world, an ugly world," and they are in revolt. And I am afraid their revolt will produce another form of violence, which is actually what is going on.

So, this problem can only be resolved—this problem of violence, of wars in the future—when you, as an individual, find out why you are angry, why you are violent, why you have prejudice, why you hate, and put them all away. You cannot put them away by revolting against them but only by understanding them. Understanding them means to look, to observe, to listen. When the older people talk about all the ugly things they have made, listen closely, give your attention, which means give your heart and your mind to this. You know, in the past five thousand years there have been about fifteen thousand wars, which means three wars every year. Though man has talked about love—love of God, love of my neighbor, love of my wife, of my husband—talked endlessly about love, they have no love in their hearts. If they had love in their hearts, there would be a different kind of education, a different kind of business, a different world.

Question: When you are attentive to inattention and you become attentive, doesn't that mean also that the attention you gave to inattention was inattention to something else?

KRISHNAMURTI: That is a good question, sir, if I may say so. What you are saying is this: that as long as there is a motive, there is no attention. Is that the question?

Comment: Right.

KRISHNAMURTI: You are quite right. As long as there is a motive for my attention, it is not attention. As long as I love you because you feed me, you flatter me, you do this or that for me, it is not love. So is there thought, or a motive—which includes the process of thinking—behind attention? Is there?—because any motive distorts. It does not matter whether it is a good motive or a wrong motive, a high motive or a low motive—any form of motive to be attentive is a distortion of attention. Can I, then, be attentive without any motive? I know that the mo-

ment I have a motive—and motive is always profitable or pleasurable—there is no possibility of attention. So, can I observe, see, listen, attend, without a motive?

Now, who is going to answer this question—you or I? You understand? The question is: Can you, can anyone—you, especially, who are the listener who put the question—can you be attentive without motive, knowing that motive is a distortion of attention? How are you going to find out? If I say, "Yes, you can be," that has no value. I say that only attention without motive is attention. Either you agree or you say, "No, it is not possible," and give it up. If you agree you say, "Now I am going to find out for myself whether I can attend to that bird, to that tree, to that noise, and to what I see is violence—without any motive." So I have got to go into the question of motives, haven't I?

Why have I motives? Motive is based on pleasure—avoiding pain and holding on to pleasure. There is no other kind of motive. What I mean is that though there are different varieties of pleasure and different varieties of pain, as long as I am seeking pleasure, in any form, I not only invite pain but also the motive becomes so deeply established in me that I demand pleasure at any price. So, can I look, observe, listen, attend, when there is a motive behind it? Obviously not. Then can I understand this motive, can I look at my motives?

Why do I have any motive at all? I do not know whether you have gone into this. Can you live without a motive? And why do you have motives? Are you listening now with a motive, to get something out of the speaker? Obviously you are; otherwise, you would not be here. You want some truth—to understand this, that, or ten different things. And when you are trying to get something, are you listening? Nobody can give you anything, except food, clothing, shelter, and perhaps transportation or technical knowledge. Psychologically, inwardly, nobody can give you anything. Do you realize that? So when you listen, knowing that nobody can give you anything—freedom, enlightenment, guidance, and all that—then what happens? Then you are listening. Then you are actually listening, since you do not want anything from anybody; then you are listening, inwardly. Therefore you have no motives. But the moment you want something, you are caught.

Question: Sir, you have told us about care, affection, and love, but how is it possible to have care between two nations?

KRISHNAMURTI: Obviously there cannot be. When you are going north and I am going south, how can there be care or attention or love? When, as one nation, you want one piece of property and another nation wants the same property for itself, how can there be care or love? There can only be war, which is what is happening. As long as there are nationalities, sovereign governments, controlled by the army and the politicians, with their idiotic ideologies, with their separateness, there must be war. As long as you worship a particular rag, called a flag, and I worship another piece of rag of another color, obviously we are going to fight each other.

It is only when there are no nationalities, when there are no divisions, such as Christians, Buddhists, Hindus, Muslims, communists, or capitalists, that there will be no war. It is only when man gives up his petty beliefs and prejudices, his worship of his own particular family, and all the rest of it, that there is a possibility of peace in the world. That peace in the world can only come about when the whole world is organized, and it cannot be organized economically or socially as long as there is a division. That means that there must be a universal language and planning—which

none of you want. Don't fool yourselves—you don't want all that. You want to remain a U.P., or whatever it is, with your Hindi and all that, for which you are fighting. But as long as you are a Hindu with your Gita, with your particular beliefs, nationalities, gods, gurus, you are bound to be at war with another. It is like a man pretending to have brotherhood when all the time he hates people.

Question: Sir, is it possible to be a functionary in the world, in society, and have a state of efficient action?

KRISHNAMURTI: "Is it possible to be a bureaucrat, a functionary, without motive, and yet be very efficient?" Is that the question?

Comment: Yes, sir.

KRISHNAMURTI: If you have motives as a functionary in society, you cannot function at the top level. It is only a man who has no motives who becomes very efficient. That is so clear.

Comment: It is very, very difficult.

KRISHNAMURTI: Ah well, sir. To be free of anything that one has carefully cultivated for so many centuries is quite obviously difficult. You understand, sir? You have been a Hindu, or a Muslim, or whichever it is, for centuries, conditioned by your mother, by your father, by your grandmother, by tradition, by society. To be free of all that, not taking time—to throw it all out immediately, without struggle, without conflict—that demands, again, a great deal of attention and observation. It demands observation of your thoughts, of what you say and how you say it, of the manner of your eating, of everything; and that requires a tremendous revolution. But who cares for all that? You want a comfortable, assured life, and that is all you are concerned about.

Question: What is your idea about a third world war?

KRISHNAMURTI: You know, there used to be a slogan which said, "This war, like the next war, is a war to end all wars." You haven't heard about that?

This boy wants to know what is my idea about the third world war. You are very silent, aren't you? The third world war—either you prepare for it or you don't. If you are going to be an Indian for the rest of your life, and say, "My India, my country, my government, my . . ."—you follow?—and another part, like Pakistan, also says, "My country," and, "I must have this, I must have that"; or if capitalists and communists both want the same thing, you are bound to have another war. But probably world war means total destruction, because now they have atom bombs which can destroy millions of people in a few minutes, and both sides can do this. America can do this and Russia can do this, and all the other nations are joining in this game, each with its own little bombs. So on that world scale of destruction I do not think there will be a third world war. They cannot afford it, since they would destroy themselves, though they might have little wars and skirmishes. But we must be concerned not with World War Three, but with whether each one of us is contributing to war in our daily life. You are contributing to war when you are a Hindu, Muslim, Christian, capitalist, communist, and all that. When there is no love in your hearts, you are bound to create wars.

Question: When man sees so much poverty and sadness, why is it that he loves his life?

KRISHNAMURTI: A little boy asks that. Why do you love your life? Because it is the only thing you have. One is afraid to die. When you grow up you are going to face this. You are going to be poor, please note this, because the population of India is increasing explosively, so that there will be a thousand people for one job. So you are going to grow up into a world of poverty and sorrow, so long as there is no world planning, so long as there is no world government. Until governments are concerned with man, with human beings—with feeding man, clothing him, educating him, giving him a way of life—there is going to be poverty and misery. And that depends on you and on nobody else.

December 10, 1967

Second Talk at Rajghat

May we continue with what we were talking about the other day when we met here? We were talking about violence, and I think we ought to approach this question from a different angle—from a total perception of the problem, understanding it comprehensively, totally—not a peripheral understanding, a fragmentary approach. We look at our problems—whether it be violence, or nationalism, or sensuality, or corruption, or our own shortcomings, our own tempers and bad manners—from a limited, fragmentary point of view. We look at each problem as though it were something separate, like meditation, for example. We think meditation is totally unrelated to daily living. We practice some mantra, hoping that by repeating this or something of the kind, we shall reach paradise, or whatever we like to call it. Again, this is all very fragmentary, not a total comprehension. And I think this question of violence and all other problems are related to one another; they are not separate. One cannot solve these problems or understand them by themselves, as though they were in watertight compartments. They all have to be tackled together from a central understanding; that is, if one is able to look at any problem totally, then I think we shall be able to solve all our problems.

Now the question is: What is total seeing? How does one see anything totally—not in broken-up little parts? How does one see something wholly? I think this is an interesting question because our minds function in fragments. How can a mind that works, thinks, acts, feels in broken-up parts, in fragments—how can such a mind see the whole issue of life, not just a particular issue? We must understand this question if we are to communicate with one another further about this.

Take, for instance, starvation. There is starvation in this country, with appalling poverty, callousness, brutality, total indifference, insensitivity. Those are obvious facts. And we want to solve the problem of starvation by a particular little plan, whereas it is an issue which involves the whole world, not merely India. You must have a feeling for man totally, a passion for man, whether the individual is an Indian, Muslim, Christian, communist, socialist, or what you will. Unlike enthusiasm, which is passion for a fragment and soon fades and is replaced by something else, this intensity, this total passion, is never fragmentary.

So the question is: How can a mind which is so broken up see the whole of life as a unit? Now, the mind functions differently in different states, at different demands, under different stresses and strains. It is one thing in the office, it is another thing when it meditates, and another thing with the family, the neighbor, and so on; that is, it is broken up. So what is the state of mind that sees the whole of life as a total unit?—because, unless one really sees life as a total unit, sees life totally, merely tackling the problem of violence has very little meaning. In the very process of understanding violence, you will create another problem.

So the question is clear: How can a mind that operates, acts, thinks in fragments—and thought is always fragmentary—how can such a mind see the whole of life and understand it as a total act? When one puts a question of this kind to oneself, how does one respond to the question? Or is this too difficult for you, for the children? A little bit, perhaps, but it doesn't matter, it can't be helped.

You understand what that word *understanding* means? To understand something— what does that word mean? Is it an intellectual understanding of a concept or of an idea? Does understanding come intellectually, verbally—or is it something emotional, sentimental? Or does understanding take place when you see the whole problem? And when does that understanding, as an act, come into being? Surely understanding comes only when the mind is very quiet, when it is not having an opinion, making a judgment or an evaluation, saying, "This is right, this is wrong"; when it is not prejudiced, angry, agitated, and so on. It is only when the mind is completely quiet—unenforced, not twisted to be made quiet—that in that quietness there is an understanding.

Look, if you want to understand what the speaker is talking about, you have to listen to him, but you cannot if your mind is looking out of the window, or there are innumerable other thoughts, other activities going on, or if your mind is chattering, wishing that you weren't here but were playing in the garden instead. If those things are happening, then you can't possibly listen to the speaker. You can only understand when your mind is really quiet in listening.

So, a total comprehension, a total understanding or seeing something, takes place as an act only when the mind is completely quiet. And this quiet is not produced, put together, by thought. You cannot say, "Well, I'll be very quiet, I'll force myself to be quiet and listen," for then you cannot listen because there is a conflict. So, to understand totally the whole of life, with all its complexities, with all its despairs, agonies, tortures, frustrations, miseries, and the beauty of the earth and the sky and the land and the river, one must look at everything from a mind that is completely at rest.

Now, to understand violence, which is so prevalent throughout the world—violence on the least provocation, as when one bursts into anger, fury, about nothing at all, every type of violence—to understand it, as we said, let us try to approach it differently.

You know, one of the most difficult things in life is to be honest. To be honest to what? You understand my question? I want to be honest—honest being the word, not the actual state of mind that is honest. The meaning of that word, the semantic meaning, is to think very clearly, precisely, and to say exactly what you mean—not to say one thing, think another thing, and do still another thing. That is what most idealists do. They think one thing, do another thing, and say something else. To me that is total dishonesty. Honesty exists only when you say exactly what you mean, without double meaning, double thinking, and not conforming to any pattern, any principle, any ideal. Then you are honest to yourself; what you think, what you do is not contradictory to what you feel, what you assert, and so on.

Most of us are quite dishonest to ourselves because we adjust ourselves very quickly to what other people want, to what other people say. We suppress our own feelings, our own ideas, our own intentions because we meet somebody who is bigger and more popular and influential; so we become hypocritical. You can observe this very clearly in the politicians throughout the world—and there is a politician in each one of us. So, is it possible to be totally honest?—not honest to an ideal or a principle, for that is not honesty. If I practice an ideal, I am leading a double life. Observe it in yourself. If I practice nonviolence because I am violent, what takes place inwardly, psychologically? The fact is one thing, the ideal is the other. Actually I am violent and I am trying not to be violent, but in doing so I am sowing the seeds of violence—for the fact is one thing, the ideal another. This may be a very drastic saying, but look at it, examine it. An idealist is dishonest. The man who follows a principle is a dishonest man. When a man is practicing something which he is not, then he is dishonest. But when he acknowledges what he is, then he is very honest. So the problem is—how to go beyond *what is*. You understand? Say, for instance, you are sensual, with all its complexity, and you try not to be sensual because you have read, or have been told, that if you are sensual you cannot possibly come to truth, that you cannot be this or cannot be that. You try to suppress sensuality, but the fact is you are sensual. And when you try not to be sensual, you are playing a dishonest game with yourself. Then the question arises: How is it possible to go beyond this sensuality? That is the question, not how to become nonsensual. If a man is angry and says, "I will not be angry," he is not playing an honest game with himself. But if he says, "I am angry; I acknowledge it; I see that I am angry. How am I to go beyond it?"—that is an honest question. Not how to become, but how to have a mind which is not capable of anger. You understand?

So the question is: Here we are, human beings who are callous, indifferent, insensitive, dishonest, caught up in so many travails and miseries—how is it possible for us to go beyond and above all these fragmentary things? You understand my question?

Suppose I want to meditate. I really do not know what it means to meditate, but I have heard some yogis and others say, "If you meditate properly, rightly, you will receive an extraordinary, transcendental experience." I do not know what it all means, but it seems to say something which appeals to me—I like something about it. So I try to meditate, force myself to control, to suppress my desires, and so on. Now, what actually takes place? There is a contradiction between *what is* and 'what should be', isn't there? No? You understand the question, sirs?

Let us take it very simply. I am angry. That is a fact. Why should I create its opposite, which is, "I must not be angry"; why? Will it help me to get over my anger to say, "I must not be angry"? Apparently it does not, for we are still angry, we are still violent, we are still brutal. So if I can face the fact that I am angry, without any excuse, without any justification, just seeing the fact that I am angry, then I can deal with it. But I cannot deal with it if I am struggling with its opposite. So, is it possible to brush aside its opposite and deal only with *what is*—which is that I am angry? The opposites not only create conflict but act as a distraction from *what is,* so that I do not have a total perception of *what is.* Can you go along?

Look, sirs; conflict in any form, whether on the battlefield, or between neighbors, or within oneself, is a process of distortion. Conflict of any kind, within or without, makes the mind unclear, distorts the mind, perverts the mind. That is an obvious fact. I can only see something very clearly when there is no distortion within the mind itself. So can I face anger, look at anger, without any distortion—which means without trying to overcome it, justify it, explain it—just ob-

serving it? When I am capable of such observation, I am looking at anger totally, at the whole structure and nature of anger, and therefore it is not a fragmentary issue but a total issue.

After all, most of us are rather callous, insensitive. Let's stick to that one thing and work to the very end of it. We are not sensitive, and the highest form of sensitivity is intelligence. We are not sensitive to nature, to the birds, to the trees, to the beauty of the earth. We do not watch, we are not sensitive to that bird, to that crow which is calling. We do not hear it. We are not sensitive enough to be in communion with nature, which means that we are callous. And we are also callous with regard to people. We are not sensitive to other people's reactions, to what other people say or feel. We are not sensitive to the poverty, to the degradations of the poor, to the squalor on the road, in the house, in ourselves. We are insensitive, which is to be callous. And also we are not sensitive to a new way of looking at life, because we are traditionally bound, or because we have our own peculiar little ideas, our own peculiar tendencies, our own conditioning, which prevent us from being sensitive. We are not sensitive to ideas, to people, or to nature, to our surroundings, so we become callous, we are callous. And a mind that is callous can worship God upside down, stand on its head, breathe, do all kinds of tricks, but it will obviously never understand the beauty of truth. It can be most learned, can quote all the shastras, the Gitas, the Bibles, or the latest prophets and all that tommyrot, but such a mind is really essentially a stupid mind.

Now, one sees that; one sees how callous, brutal, insensitive one is, because one can see the results of it in the world. If one were very sensitive, alert, intelligent, we should have a different world altogether. Now, it is a fact that human beings are self-concerned—concerned about their own particular inclinations and tendencies. They are conditioned by society, by their culture, by the climate, by the food they eat, and so on—they are all that. And how is one to become totally sensitive to the whole thing and not to the fragments? How is one to become so highly sensitive?—for it is only a very sensitive mind that is capable of love and therefore capable of beauty. How, then, is a mind that has become so brutalized, so twisted, so small, petty, shoddy—how is such a mind, on the instant, to become something entirely different, to be something totally other than what it is? You understand? A dull mind, trying to become a sensitive mind, takes time—please follow this a little bit. I am dull, my mind is dull, and I wish it were a bright, clear, sensitive, precise mind with tremendous feelings, passions; and I say it will take time to become this. So I will polish it every day; I will feel more and more sensitively each day; that is, it will take many, many days; which is a time interval—you are following? So we think time is necessary to bring about radical change within the mind itself.

We see that to learn a language or mathematics or any technological subject will take time, naturally. I don't know Russian, let's say, so I will take lessons, read, study, and it will take perhaps a year and a half to learn the language—that is, to accumulate the words, to know how to use the verbs and the adjectives, how to put sentences together, and so on. In the same way we think that through time we are going to bring about a change in ourselves; that is, through time we shall be sensitive. But time doesn't help us to be sensitive; on the contrary, time only makes us more and more insensitive—I do not know if you see that.

Change can only take place instantly, not in the field of time. Then how is this total mutation, this psychological revolution, to take place out of time? That is the only way anything happens, any fundamental change takes place—when the change is out of time. Now, how is that change to take place? The mind is insensitive and it sees the fallacy of time, it sees the fallacy of using time as a means of becoming sensitive. But does it actually see the fallacy of that, or does it merely intellectually suppose it to be a fallacy? You understand the question? Does the mind actually see the fallacy of using time as a means to bring about a mutation within itself?

You see, man has invented time as a means of improvement. We say, "Well, at least in the next life I'll be different," or, "Give me another year to work at myself, and by the end of the year I'll be different." We have used time as a means of accumulating knowledge, and through that knowledge we hope to bring about a change. But knowledge does not bring about change at all; on the contrary. We all know the terrible brutality of wars, but though man has been through thousands and thousands of wars, he has not changed. So time as a means to bring about a change, a psychological mutation, is an utter, gross fallacy. So what will make it change? And it must be immediate. I don't know if you see this. When you see this, what takes place? When you are no longer thinking in terms of time at all—time also being comparing, as when we say, "I am this and I will be that," or "I was that and I am different today" (for all measurement is a process of time)—can the mind then look at that insensitivity without measurement, without the time factor at all?

Please, sirs, these are not just ideas with which you agree or disagree. Unless you do it yourself, a mere collection of ideas is completely useless. Unless you see for yourself, directly, the fallacy of time, you cannot take the next step. Or rather, when you see the fallacy of time, that is itself the first step.

The question then is: When the mind says, "I am insensitive," how does it know it is insensitive? You understand? The mind has become callous by circumstance, by culture, by the way it lives, and so on. It has become deeply insensitive because it is so concerned with itself, but it sees the necessity of becoming completely sensitive because without sensitivity, there is no intelligence and therefore no love. When there is no love there is no beauty. So how is this realization to take place?

Now this is real meditation. This is not a trick I am playing. This is the real act of meditation—when you have seen for yourselves the structure and the nature of time, and discarded it completely, because time is thought and thought cannot possibly change a mind that has become insensitive; on the contrary, it is thought that has made the mind insensitive. Thought is the outcome of the past, the past being memories, experiences, knowledge. Thought has made the mind insensitive, and thought cannot possibly make the mind sensitive. So, does one see this fact—not the idea that the mind is sensitive or not sensitive, but the actual fact? You will see, if you do not bring a time element into it at all and have understood the structure and nature of thought, that the mind, no longer using measure, has become sensitive. The moment you have no measure, the mind is sensitive. I wonder if you are meeting this? No?

So, sirs, let's put it differently. Thought cannot possibly cultivate love—obviously— and without love you cannot be sensitive. Love is not emotionalism, love is not sentimentalism, love is not jealousy. Obviously, when you are jealous it is a fact that you are no longer loving; you are like a man who is hating, who is angry with another; you cannot possibly love. And as thought cannot possibly cultivate love, how is that state to come into being? It is only when there is real

affection that you will never be callous, never be indifferent; so how is that thing to happen to you? Only when you see for yourself that hate, jealousy, anger, brutality, violence, competition, greed, the desire for position, power, and all that must be completely discarded—only then is there the other. You do not have to search for it, you do not have to look for it; the thing just takes place. It is like leaving the window open; the air comes in when it will. But we want to keep the window closed and still talk about love.

Perhaps some of us might like to discuss or ask questions about what we have been saying?

Question: Sir, free will is the characteristic of the human organism and becomes for each an ideal. Why are you opposed to its becoming an ideal?

KRISHNAMURTI: Yes, sir, we have understood. I wonder, sir, if you listened to the talk. After all, to ask a right question is one of the most difficult things. We must ask questions. We must never, under any circumstances, accept any authority, whether the authority of the guru, the Bible, the Gita, the Upanishads—any authority. They have all led mankind to this present misery because we merely want to follow, obey; we do not want to find out the truth for ourselves. To ask a right question, about anything, at any time, is always right. When you ask a right question it means that you have already thought a great deal about that problem, or felt your way into it; and when you ask a right question you have already heard the answer—you don't have to ask anybody.

So that gentleman asks a question, which is, "Is not free will one of the fundamental elements of man? Right, sir?"

Comment: Yes, sir.

KRISHNAMURTI: Is that so? You take it for granted that man is free. Is he?

Comment: Yes, sir, in comparison with other animals, birds, and beasts, and as you say. . .

KRISHNAMURTI: Just a minute, sir! Look at it, look at it! Leave the other organisms alone. Are you free? I am not asking you personally, sir. Are you free? You are conditioned by your culture, by your climate, by your religion, by your books; are you free? You might like to be free, you might talk endlessly about free will, but have you a will that is free—and can the will ever be free? Will is the strings of desire which have become the cord, so the will, essentially, can never be free. This is not just something I am saying, sir—you do not have to accept what I am saying; that is irrelevant. But look at the fact. How can a man steeped in tradition be free?—though he might talk about it endlessly. How can a man who is frightened to be free talk about free will? Are you free from nationalism, free from brutality, anger, violence? So talking about free will is of very little importance because you are not free.

It is one of the fallacious concepts that man is free. Of course man is free to choose, but when he chooses he is already in confusion. When you see something very clearly, then you do not choose. Please look at this fact in yourselves. When you see something very clearly, where is the necessity of choice? There is no choice. It is only a confused mind that chooses, that says, "This is right, this is wrong, I must do this because it is right," and so on—not a clear precise mind that sees directly; for such a mind there is no choice. You see, we say that we choose and therefore we are free. That is one of the

absurdities we have invented, but we are not basically free at all. We are conditioned, and it requires an enormous understanding of this conditioning to be free.

When you choose to go from one guru to another, from one state to another, all that indicates a mind that is uncertain, unclear. Therefore is it possible—which is the right question—is it possible for a mind to be unconfused so that it sees truth as truth and false as false, and sees the truth in the false? When it so sees there can be no choice, there can be no mistake. So the fundamental question is: Can the mind which has been so conditioned for centuries upon centuries, through propaganda, through books, through authority, through fear—can such a mind free itself from its own conditioning? That is the real question. And if you say, "Yes, it can," how do you know? Or if you say, "It cannot," then you are already blocking yourself. All that you can do is to be aware of your own conditioning and go through it immediately, not play with it.

Question: What is the future of democracy in India, and what type of political system would be beneficial to India?

KRISHNAMURTI: Sir, to be really a democrat, not in the political sense, or in the party sense, but to be really a democrat means that you must think for yourself and not be persuaded by propaganda, nor by any leader, or guru. You must be capable of thinking directly for yourself, unpersuaded, uninfluenced by these crooked politicians or by these clever gurus. To think individually, each human being for himself, not persuaded through propaganda, radio, television, books, newspapers, is one of the most difficult things because we are all susceptible to influence. Only then can one call oneself a true democrat. And to be a true democrat a man must have right education—not merely a technical education. He must be a total human being, intellectually capable of reasoning clearly, precisely, without any personal projection into his thinking. But you are not having such education at all—even in this school you are not having it—this total development of each human being. And it is only if you are a total human being that you can be a democrat. If you are a democrat in this sense, then you will create the right administration not for India only but for the whole world.

Sir, you cannot possibly separate yourself as an Indian, as a Muslim, as a Christian, or as a communist. We are all human beings and we must plan for the whole of mankind, not just for an India. There must be universal planning, and it is only then that a true democrat can do such things. A true democrat is one who loves man, not a system.

Question: Sir, how can we make our minds completely quiet? (Laughter)

KRISHNAMURTI: Quite right, sir. I wonder why everybody laughed? Why did you all laugh? Because a little boy asked how one can have a completely quiet mind—is that why you laughed? Does that question depend on age? Would you have laughed if an older man had asked that question? I am afraid you would not have. You laugh because a small boy asked it. But, you know, a small boy can put the right question just as well as a grown-up man.

The little boy asks, "How can one have a quiet mind?" First of all, why do you want a quiet mind? Please think it out with me, go into it with me. Why do you want a quiet mind? Because it will give you greater pleasure, greater profit, or because you will see more? If you want a quiet mind out of greed, then it will not be a quiet mind. Do you want a quiet mind because you are

frightened? Then you are escaping from fear, and therefore it is not a quiet mind. Please follow all this carefully. It is through negation that you are going to come to a quiet mind, and not by a positive process of practicing a system, a method, which promises a quiet mind. Do not accept such promises from anybody because a quiet mind is not possible if you are frightened, if you are angry, if you think yourself as more important than somebody else. You cannot possibly have a quiet mind if you are an Indian or a Muslim or a Christian or a communist, for that means that you have segregated yourself, separated yourself in a shoddy, little mind—and that is the mind that wants to be quiet. A little mind thinking about God is still a little mind.

So, through denial, through negation of all those disturbing factors like anger, jealousy, brutality, violence, ambition, which prevent the fact of a quiet mind—through negation of all these you may come to it. A quiet mind must have immense space—and we have no space at all. One's mind is cluttered up with so many things—with knowledge, with fears, with hopes, with despairs, with ambitions. It is full of these things, and therefore there is no space at all within itself. A mind that is completely empty of all that it has gathered, a mind, therefore, that has immense space within itself—only such a mind is a quiet mind. Do you see? You listen to this, but you have never really tried to empty the mind of one particular desire, or rather of one particular pleasure, or to empty it of a fear. If you had you would see that space is as important as the word.

For us the word is extraordinarily important. The word is the symbol. The word *God* is a symbol but not the fact. The word *door* is not the actual door, but because it is a symbol, the word becomes extraordinarily important for us. And when the word is no longer important, it means that the symbol is no longer important; therefore, it can be put aside. Then you will find that the mind which is free of the word—which is free of the image—can look, and you can only look when there is space, not a little space but immense space, space that is not measurable. Then, in that space you can see what is true, and you do not need to have perception; there is no need for seeking.

Question: Sir, what is the more creative state—the quiet mind or the process that leads to this quiet mind?

KRISHNAMURTI: "Is the quiet mind more creative than the mind that is in process of becoming quiet?" Is that right, sir?

Now, what do we mean by that word *creative?* Look, there are three questions involved in this. First, is the quiet mind creative? Then, does not creativeness lie in the very process of becoming quiet? These are the three questions involved in this: Is the mind creative, or is the process itself creation, and what we mean by that word *creative?*

So let us settle first the meaning, or the feeling, of that word creative. Is an artist who paints a picture or writes a poem creative? He expresses what he feels on the canvas or in the words of the poem. So, is creativeness expression? You are following all this? When I feel creative must I express myself in ten different ways on canvas? And is the expression of that feeling of creativeness really creative? One must go into this very clearly, very slowly. I see a tree, the beauty of it, but only when my mind is completely quiet do I see the totality of that beauty. And why should I express it on canvas, in music, or in verse—why? Which is important—the expression of what I have seen, or the seeing? And the other question is: In the very process of becoming quiet, is that process creative? Right, sir? Now, is it a process? That is, process is gradually becoming, and can the mind gradually, slowly, through different methods, systems, persuasions, strains, stresses, conflicts, become quiet?

But there is no process at all. There is only the actual state, not a way to it. If there is a way to it, then it is static. That is, the state of mind that is peaceful is static; it is not alive, it is not dynamic, it is not moving, alive, passionate, and it is only to something that is static, dead, that there is a process. And the other question is: If there is no process at all, as obviously there is not, then how is the mind to empty itself totally and be peaceful in that extraordinary state which in itself is creative and has no need for expression? You understand? How is a mind to come upon this quietness without any effort or conflict—effort and conflict being distortion? It can only come upon it when it has understood the total negation of that which is false, when it denies time and the process—the process through which it obtains pleasure. When you totally deny all that, then it will be there, you will not have to look for it.

Question: Is denial not itself a process?

KRISHNAMURTI: Sir, how can it be a process? I see something false, dangerous, and I discard it—how can it be a process? Process involves time, gradualness.

Sir, instead of a peaceful mind put the word *love* in it; forget "peace." Do you have love through process? Can you love through the cultivation of not hating, not having desire, and so on? Gradually, as a process, will you come upon love? Or is love something which has nothing whatsoever to do with process?

Sir, most of you believe in God—I do not know why, but that is your conditioning, just as the fact that the communists do not believe in God is their conditioning. Now, you believe in God; do you think that you can come to that thing gradually, by working every day and then dying and then reincarnation and then rebirth, and so on? If there is a way to that, then both the way and that are fixed, aren't they? They are static, not living. It is only to a dead thing that there is a way, not to a living thing, not to a moving thing.

Question: How can a man be honest if he is doing the work of dishonesty?

KRISHNAMURTI: But you see, my dear child, we do not acknowledge that we are doing something dishonest. You think I am doing something dishonest, but I think I am doing something very honest. But for me to realize that I am dishonest is one of the most difficult things, because we do not want to acknowledge to ourselves that we are dishonest. I do not acknowledge to myself that I am not telling the truth, so I find various excuses, judgments—it's your fault, circumstances have forced me, and so on and so on. I never say to myself, "By Jove, I am not telling the truth!" It is only when I see that I am not telling the truth that I am honest to myself. Then I will act honestly.

December 14, 1967

Third Talk at Rajghat

Perhaps we can go on with what we were talking about the other day. We were saying that the quality of mind which recognizes a fact and pursues that fact without creating the opposite will not be in conflict. And it is important, I feel, that one should understand the structure and nature of conflict, for most of us, whether we are very worldly or have taken the robe of a monk or a sannyasi, are still in conflict—perhaps not so much with the world as with ourselves. The conflict goes on, and the mind that is in conflict, in

contradiction, is a twisted mind; it cannot see very clearly. And so the question is whether it is possible to live, not only in the outside world, but also in the world inside the skin, as it were—whether it is possible to live there completely without any conflict at all. Most of us have accepted conflict as inevitable, as part of our daily human existence, as part of our inheritance. We have accepted conflict, like war, as the way of life. But renouncing the world, or merely identifying oneself with certain mythological or ideological states, does not resolve this conflict.

So the problem is whether it is possible to live peacefully—not ideologically but actually at peace in everyday life, in thought, in feeling, in action, in movement.

When we say peacefully, we do not mean in the sense of going to sleep or accepting a dogma and living within that dogma, forgetting or being oblivious to any other question, or living in a fragment and identifying with that fragment. That, obviously, does not bring about a quality of mind that is meditatively peaceful. One must have peace, but not through drugs, not through a self-hypnotic process of repeating certain words, or by resting on tradition. Minds which do that are obviously asleep. They are dull minds which do not have the quality necessary to find out what is true. If one seeks peace with a motive, it is no longer peaceful. Peace with a motive is an escape from conflict, and so is not peace at all, but another form of violence.

So seeing all this, is it possible to be rid of conflict—completely? This is not an ideological demand, not a hypothetical searching for some state of mind which is not in conflict—for that would be another form of escape from actuality. Is it at all possible—not only consciously but deeply, in what may be called the unconscious—to be rid entirely of this everlasting struggle, strife, competition, comparison, measurement, seeking, all of which entails conflict? I do not know if you have asked that question of yourself—if you have actually put it to yourself. If you have, you either say it is impossible, and therefore block yourself from further inquiry, or you say it is possible, in which case you must have the capacity and energy for it. Capacity and energy really always go together; the two are not separate. When one has the energy one has the capacity to find out.

So, have you asked yourself whether a mind can be completely rid of conflict, and therefore live in a state which is really meditative alertness—a meditative awareness? And if you intend to go into this question, you must be quite serious, because if you are not serious you are not alive. One may think one is alive, but actually it is only the very earnest people who are alive. By earnest people I do not mean those who are committed to a certain course of action or to a certain ideological plan. An unbalanced person is quite serious, quite sincere, quite in earnest—and the hospitals are full of them. These people who are committed to a certain course of belief or action, but are neurologically and psychologically unbalanced, are dreadfully serious. The idealists, also, consider themselves serious, but I do not think they are serious at all. To be really serious is to comprehend the totality of the whole process of life, not just one fragment of it.

There are people who devote their lives to a fragment, to a part of life. They say that even if one cannot understand the totality, one can still have love in one's heart. So they say, "In the meantime I will do something. I will plan, I will help my neighbor, I will do something." They are the "meantimers"—meantime, while the house is burning, they will do something or other. They are concerned, not with the house itself which is burning, but with a side issue; and they are very serious, too.

So the question is: What is it to be serious—to be really, completely, earnest? Obviously the man who has a principle and lives according to that principle is not serious because his conception of a principle is a projection of his own desire, his own pleasure. He lives according to his pleasure, and therefore is not serious. But by the denial of what is not serious, you are serious. Through negation you find what is the positive.

Now, humility is the total denial of authority. It is not a partial denial but a total denial, because when you have no authority at all, either inwardly or outwardly, you stand alone, and then you are in a state of mind that is learning. It is only a mind which has this quality of humility that can learn. To learn, authority must obviously come to an end—the authority of a tradition, the authority of a principle, the authority of what others have said—Shankara, Buddha, Christ, it does not matter who, including the authority of the speaker. If one does not set aside authority, then one follows the path of another—and truth has no path whatsoever. The mind that accepts authority—the authority of the scripture, of its own experience, of tradition, of whatever it may be—such a mind, when it accepts authority, is basically afraid. And a mind that is afraid can never know what humility is.

So now we come to the question of whether the mind can be free of fear. You know, freedom is not from something. If there is freedom from something, it is merely a reaction, and therefore is not freedom.

I wonder if we are communicating with one another, or not? To commune with another, to understand another, there must be not only the comprehension of words but also a state of attention in which there is affection, care, love, so that you are listening with your nerves, your heart, your mind. Then we are in communication with one another and words do not matter so much. We have to be in that state of communion when we talk about a question which is quite complex—then the word is not the thing, the word does not impede.

Most of us, then, are afraid, and to understand this basic question of fear, one must give one's total attention to it so that there can then be no possibility of an escape from fear. After all, when you are afraid, it does not matter of what—of darkness, of losing your job, of what the neighbors think about you, of snakes, of death—if you escape from that fact, whether through drink, through rituals, through repetition of words, or through that cultivation of the opposite which is called courage, all such forms of escape prevent you from looking at the fact of fear. To understand something I must look. I cannot avoid it, or give it a dozen explanations, or find the cause of it. The discovery of the cause of fear does not dissolve fear. What does dissolve fear is the actual contact with it, the actual perception of what fear is.

From this question arises another—for again, so many questions are involved with one another—the question of how to look.

We look at things as the observer and the observed. You look at a tree as the observer, with the image that you have about that tree, and therefore you do not look at the tree at all. You look at the image you have about the tree; it is the image that looks. You look at your friend with the image you have about him, an image which has been built up through time, through many days. That image is made up of the insult, the hurt, the friendship, and so on, that you have experienced with him. The image is there, and with that image you look. In the same way you look at the tree with the image you have about that tree, the image being, among other things, your botanical knowledge about this particular tree. Actually it is not you who are looking at the tree but the knowledge you have about the tree that is looking. So you have no direct relationship with the tree.

Let us put it more inwardly. You have an image about your wife, or your husband—watch it in yourself, sir; don't, if I may point this out, merely listen to a lot of words. Words have no value at all. But if you are following this actually, inwardly, seeing yourself with your heart and your mind—seeing yourself as you actually are—then this has immense significance. So, then you have an image about your wife or your husband, and this image which you have built up has been put together through time—through many days of irritation, pleasure, annoyance, boredom, and so on. That image which you have about her and the image she has about you are related, aren't they? Actually you are not related; it is the images that are related. So there is no actual relationship, and—please follow this a little more—you yourself, who have built the image, are yourself part of the image.

In the same way, you have an image about fear. You, the observer, the thinker, the experiencer, have an image of what fear is—but the image is different from the fact. The image may be a symbol, a word, and that image is the actual observer. The thing he observes is looked at through the image, which is himself. So he, the observer, separates himself from the thing that he observes so that there is a division between the observer and the observed. Is this too complex? I think one has to understand this, not intellectually, but actually, if one is to go beyond and above fear; otherwise, one will be caught in it.

Is fear, then, different from the observer? Obviously not. The observer is the entity that has, through association and memory, known what is fear—otherwise he would not be able to recognize it. So the observer has become an entity, and an entity is static. Look at it this way. Memory is the accumulation of experiences, pleasant or unpleasant, and the accumulation of knowledge. It is this memory, accumulation, which responds and is the observer. Now this observer, though he may add to that memory or take away from it, is always himself static, whereas the facts which he observes are always changing.

Look—I have an image about you. You have said pleasant things to me, or unpleasant things; you have patted me on the back or you have insulted me, so I have a memory of you which is static—which is not dynamic, alive. Tomorrow, when I look at you, it will be with that memory. But tomorrow you may have changed—probably you have—but my memory of you remains what it was. So the observer, though he thinks he is alive, is always static.

So, when you observe fear, how do you observe it, how do you know it, how do you recognize it? You recognize it, know it, observe it, because you have had it before, and it is the image you have made of it from past experiences which looks at the new fear, the fear that has just taken place.

The observer, then, though he thinks he is separate, is the observed, and when the mind divides itself into the observer and the thing observed, in that division there is conflict. All division is conflict. When India says, "I am a nation," and Pakistan says it is another separate nation, there is bound to be a clash. So, nationality, with its rag which is called the flag, is really the cause of conflict.

As long as there is a division between the observer and the observed, there must be conflict, and therefore no understanding of fear. But if one examines the situation very closely, one finds that the observer is also changing, though generally he does not want to. His images are so strong, his prejudices are so vital, so energetic, his conditioning is so deep, that he does not want to change.

Yet, in spite of his conditioning, in spite of his limited, fragmentary outlook, there is also change going on in him, while what he looks at is also changing. But so long as one does not know how to observe, how to see a thing, there must always be division, and therefore there must always be conflict.

After all, love is not conflict; love does not know jealousy, hatred, anger, ambition, the desire for power and position, the demand for self-expression. And to come upon love there must be the freedom to look at that which is not love—at hatred—to look at it, to observe it, to know the whole psychological structure of it, to observe it actually. When one understands the whole business of hatred, then there is love. Hence there is no conflict between love and hatred. That is, through the denial of all that is not love, such as jealousy, envy, greed, ambition, power, hatred, and so on, by observing very closely all that is not love, in daily life—not in some mystical world but in daily existence—then out of that clear perception of what is not there takes place *what is*.

So, fear can only be understood and gone beyond—completely, totally, not fragmentarily—when the mind is no longer afraid, psychologically, about anything. If such a mind makes a mistake, it recognizes that it has made a mistake; if it has told a lie, it knows it has told a lie and is no longer afraid of it. Fear is the product of thought.

Take the question of death, which is really quite an extraordinary thing of which we are so frightened. Thought carefully avoids that thing which we call death; thought has put it at a distance, and thought says, "I do not know a thing about death. I can invent theories—you know, that there is reincarnation, resurrection, a future hope—but the actual fact is that I do not understand it, and I am afraid of it." This fear is the product of thought, for all that thought knows is what has been, not what will be. What has been is the memory, pleasant or unpleasant, of the life one has led—the turmoil, the anxiety, the guilt, the despair, the hope, the misery, the immense sorrow. That is all thought knows. But death is the unknown. You cannot be frightened of the unknown, since you do not know what that means. What you are frightened of is leaving the known—leaving your family, your house, your experiences, all that you call living. The living of every day, with all its tortures, its boredom, its loneliness, and the tricks you play upon it— the escapes through drugs, through temples, through mosques, through churches—that is what you call living; the agony of it! You are frightened of that living and you are also frightened of that death. You are frightened of life, and you are frightened of something called death. This is the actual fact.

So you do not know what living is because you are frightened of it—frightened of losing your job, of losing your wife, of losing your son, of not fulfilling, of not becoming—you know, the everlasting struggle born of fear, with occasional spots of light. So one is frightened of that and of something one calls death, of which one knows nothing. Can one then understand the fear of both these things—the fear of life and the fear of death?

You can only understand them when you comprehend, or are aware of, or see, the totality of fear, not the fragments of it. As we were saying the other day, you can see something totally only when the mind is completely quiet. You can only listen to the speaker and what he says when you give your total attention to it; that is, when your nerves are quiet, when your mind is not chattering, comparing, or saying that what the speaker says has already been said by Shankara or Buddha or by this one or that— when you are not actually translating what you hear into terms of your own technologi-

cal or linguistic comprehension, but when you are really listening.

In this same way you can look at fear— totally, completely. Then you will see a very strange thing happen—actually happen, not appearing as an idea. When there is no fear of what one calls living and no fear of what one calls death, then you will see that living is dying—that you cannot live without dying to yesterday. After all, sirs, the new is the death of the old, not the continuity of it. Life is not a continuity of yesterday—life is tremendously, passionately alive now. But if you look at life with the fear of yesterday, with its memories and knowledge, then living becomes a meaningless, frightful tangle and misery.

So, to a mind that can observe in total awareness—an awareness in which there is no choice—death is life, and living is dying to everything of yesterday. Such a mind is fresh, young, and innocent; and it is only such a mind that can see what truth is—not the Upanishads, and always comparing. All that is immature nonsense. It is only the innocent mind that can love, because it has no authority and therefore has humility.

Question: Sir, will you. . .

KRISHNAMURTI: Just a minute, sir. If I may ask, were you concerned with what was being said or with your question?

Question: I was listening to you totally.

KRISHNAMURTI: If you had been listening to the speaker totally, there would have been a space between the listening and the question.

Question: I asked. . .

KRISHNAMURTI: Just a minute, sir. What we are talking about is very serious. What we are examining is concerned not with words but with daily living. We are concerned with life, not with words and questions. When a man is tortured, or hungry, or in deep despair or sorrow, he must have space to look. He is not concerned with explanations or definitions; he is not asking anybody. That does not mean that we should not ask questions; on the contrary, we should ask, we should question, we should doubt everything everybody has said. If you do so, your mind is sharp, alive, inquiring. But if you live merely on words, then you can spin out questions endlessly. Now, sir, what was your question?

Question: My question is: What are the positive definitions of humility and freedom?

KRISHNAMURTI: I think you will find the positive definitions in the dictionary—but the definition is not freedom or humility. The word is not the thing. When you are actually in a state of humility, definition does not matter; what matters is seeing how vain you are. If you do not know or are not aware that you are vain, conceited, violent, ignorant of yourself, you may pretend to be humble, but humility, as we said, comes from the actual fact of observing honestly what you are. But it is very difficult to observe something honestly, especially yourself. To know when you are stupid, to know when you have told a lie, to know completely that when you want to help another there is in your wish ninety-nine percent of self-concern—this is honest observation of what actually is. With that observation comes humility—not a definition, positive or negative.

In the same way, the definition of freedom is in the dictionary. But to understand what it is to be a slave, what it is to be conditioned—by your food, your tradition, your culture—what it is to be held by a nationality, by a religion, by a group, actually to know that you are conditioned and to go beyond all this—not in ideas, but actually, totally denying it all—that is freedom. Totally deny that you are a Hindu, or a Muslim, or a Christian, or a communist; deny it totally. For when you call yourself a Hindu, you are separate from the Muslim, and when the Muslim calls himself a Muslim, he is separate from the Buddhist. It is these separate states of mind which cause conflict. And to be honestly aware of all this brings about that quality of freedom.

Question: Sir, if one man is honest and the others are dishonest, how can he continue in a brutal and destructive country?

KRISHNAMURTI: "How can one be honest if the other is dishonest? And how can one be honest in such a brutal and destructive country as this?" asks a little boy. Do you understand the implication of this question? This little boy is concerned about his future, the future that you of the older generation has built. You are responsible for this brutal, destructive world, and the boy says, "Am I growing up into that?" So already for him there is the despair and the fear of facing this monstrous world which the older generation has built. I think you should have tears in your eyes.

He asks, "If one is honest and the others dishonest, what is one to do?"

One cannot do anything about another. What one can do is to be honest in spite of the dishonesty around one. If you are honest because others are honest, that is dishonest, for then your honesty is a profitable thing, leading to your advancement, and so you become dishonest. Sirs, in this country, as elsewhere, there is a great deal of corruption, both outwardly and inwardly; but when one is not corrupt inwardly, no amount of outward corruption can touch that inward quality of mind that is not corrupt.

If I love you because you hate me, or if I love you because you give me food, clothes, and shelter, or give me pleasure, psychologically or sexually, is that love? So to the question that young boy asked—whether one can be honest in this dishonest world—he will find the right answer when he is completely honest with himself. Then it will not matter who is honest or who is dishonest.

But the responsibility for this brutal and destructive world is not his business; it is the responsibility of the older people. What our business is, is to see that he is educated rightly—not merely to pass some silly examination, to add a few letters after his name, which helps him to get a job in an over-populated country like this. Our business is to see that he really has right education so that intellectually and in his feelings he becomes mature. He will not become mature by reading books and gathering other people's ideas, but by being intellectually free to think, to observe, to reason, objectively, precisely, sanely. This education is something total, all around—not just the cultivation of memory. It means that he knows that he is in touch with nature—with the trees, with the birds, with the flowers, with the river—and because he is in touch with nature, he is in touch with human beings. Then, perhaps, he can create a world which is not destructive, which is not brutal.

Question: How can one see anything directly, without the help of the image?

KRISHNAMURTI: First of all, know you have an image; then discard the image. Then you will know how you can look directly.

You all have images, haven't you? You certainly have an image about the speaker; otherwise, you would not be here. Your image about the speaker is preventing you from listening to what is being said. If you had no image about the speaker, you would say, "Well, tell me. I will listen, and see if what you are saying is true or false." Or, you would see what is true in the false. So long as you have an image, you are not in relation with anything. To be free of that image, you must know how images are built up—how images, words, symbols are constructed by thought every day. You look at somebody and it gives you a delight, a pleasure. It gives you a feeling of warmth, and you think about that person and imagine what he is. So you have built an image which is giving you pleasure. If you can be free of that image, you can look at that person very clearly, very simply. But first you must know the image you have, in order to be free of that image.

Question: Science is leading mankind to destruction. How can this be changed?

KRISHNAMURTI: Is science at fault, or is it man himself who is at fault? What is wrong with atomic power? It can do enormous good, but, because we are stupid monkeys, we are using it for war—to destroy. So it is man who is wrong, not the atom bomb or science.

Man has divided himself into nationalities—the Indian, the Pakistani, the Chinese, the Russian, the American—and into separate religions based on theories, not on facts, on dogmas, not on actual living. By separating himself he creates conflict. You insist on being a Hindu because your culture, your ways of thinking and acting, and even of eating, have conditioned you to being a Hindu—just as a Catholic is conditioned by his. Yet the two of you are not very different—you are both human beings, with human agonies, miseries, loneliness, and despair. And still you insist on being a Hindu or a Muslim; who cares? What matters is what you are, not what your label is. What you are is the human being who is in agony, in despair, who is lonely, bored, frightened. The other man is also bored, frightened, and in despair. Therefore there can be a decent world without brutality only when you no longer have separative frontiers, either in the mind, or in the heart, or geographically.

Sirs, wait a minute. You have listened to this—if you have at all listened—and what are you going to do about it? Go back to your Hinduism? Go back to your tradition? Go back to your rituals? Repeat all the old tricks? Will you go back to your guru and prostrate yourself at his feet—when actually he is a stupid old man, repeating something he has learned from others? What he has learned is Hinduism, as you have. He repeats what the ancients have said—his superstitions—and you are caught in that same tradition. So you say, "Well, leave us alone," and so does the Muslim, the Catholic, or the communist; so does everybody.

So what are you going to do?—not the young people, but the older generation, who have made such an awful mess of the world. Will you go back? I am afraid you will because you do not see the danger of this. You do not actually see with your heart what you are doing, and what misery you are creating for yourself and for your sons and your daughters.

Question: All except a few do not want war, so why do they prepare for war?

KRISHNAMURTI: I am not at all sure that the majority do not want war. Do you know what war means? War means destruction—killing and maiming one another, with the noise, the brutality, the ugliness, the appalling misery of pain. You have seen it on the films; that is war. Do you know how war has come into being? It has come because in our daily lives we destroy one another. Though in the temple we talk about the love of God, in our business dealings we are cutting one another's throats. Also, we have wars because we have armies, and it is the purpose of an army to prepare for war. Do you mean to say that an army man would want to give up his position, his job, his money, in order to have peace? He would not be so stupid.

So all of us, in one way or the other, are preparing for war. You can prevent war only if, in your daily life, you realize that you are no longer a Hindu, a Christian, a Buddhist, a Muslim, or a communist. If in your daily life you are kind, generous, affectionate, loving, then you will have a different world. Then, instead of squandering money on armaments, you can make this world into a paradise. But it is up to you. You have the government you deserve because you are part of that government, because you are politicians in your daily lives, and you want position, power, and authority.

Comment: Sir, if I look at a tiger, the image and the fact are the same, but if I look at a human being, he appears different from what he really is. So I cannot establish a relationship with him.

KRISHNAMURTI: The question is this: "When I look at a tiger the image corresponds with the fact, but when I look at a man the image I have about him may contradict the fact. So how do I establish a relationship with another human being?"

The image I have about the tiger is identical with the fact—but do I want to establish a relationship with a tiger? This is very important. Have you ever come across a wild animal? If you have—as the speaker has—what takes place? You turn the corner and there it is—a bear with four cubs. The mother bear chases the cubs up a tree. They climb like little squirrels, and the mother turns round and looks at you to see what you are going to do. If you are frightened, any movement by you is a disturbance to her. She will interpret it as an attack on the cubs and on herself, and she will at once attack you. But if at that moment you have actually no fear whatever, and just look, she will leave you alone, and you can turn your back on her and go home. This has actually happened. As long as there is no fear, you have communion with nature.

Now, with regard to human beings, the question is how to establish a relationship between two people, both of whom have images about the other. These images are usually contradictory, and so there is conflict between the two people. They may be married and have sex, children, and all the rest of it, but each of them, the man and the woman, is working for himself and herself. The man wants a better position, a better job, better housing, and more and more he is driven by his ambitions, as the woman is also, by her ambitions. They may sleep together, have children together, live in the same house, but each is separately working for the self. You cannot possibly have relationship when each human being is fighting the others, which is the simple fact of what is happening in daily life. So when, in a family unit—father, mother, and children—each is separately working for himself, and also separately working for the family, that family unit becomes a danger to society. And society is built on this danger, and is therefore basically founded on disorder, in which each man is seeking to realize his own ambition through greed and envy.

The intellectuals, the communists, have seen this and said there must be a revolution, a break away from all this. This has happened in Russia, but they cannot get rid of this separative conflict. In that country there is freedom for the scientist, but the rest of the human beings there are slaves, just as they are here.

As long as you have no love in your hearts, you are going to destroy the world. Love is not a word and has no definition. It comes only when you have understood fear. When you have understood that, then you create a marvelous world.

Question: Sir, what do you believe in— peace with weapons or peace without weapons?

KRISHNAMURTI: You know that I do not believe in anything, and it is marvelous to have no belief whatsoever. But can there be peace with weapons? Why do you have weapons—armaments, cannons, guns, bayonets, airplanes loaded with bombs? To maintain peace, you say—as a defensive measure against your neighbor; and your neighbor says exactly the same about you. Pakistan says, "Well, India is arming, and therefore I must arm." But there can never be peace with armaments.

There is no such thing as a defensive war. All wars are offensive because we have created a world in which we have accepted war as a way of life. There have been within the last five thousand years about fifteen thousand wars. How the mothers have cried—how the wives, lovers, children have cried when their man has been killed! This has been going on for at least five thousand years and is going on now in this country. You will cry when your son is killed by a bomb—but you do not really care what happens to your children. What you care about is your own personal security—this security being your nationality, your religion, your gods, and your rituals. So you are perpetuating war.

Question: With regard to this definition of freedom—that one must know all aspects of fear at once and go beyond it—is this possible?

KRISHNAMURTI: "Is there any shortcut to be free of fear?" Is that it?

Question: Well, can one know all the aspects of fear?

KRISHNAMURTI: You cannot know every subtle form of fear, nor every crude form either, but what you can know is fear.

Comment: Yes, but that is not all.

KRISHNAMURTI: Sir, just listen. What you can know is one fear. If you know one fear, you know all the others. Fear may take different forms, but it is still fear. If you know the nature of desire, of one desire, and know that desire completely, in that one desire are all the other desires. Desire takes different forms with different objectives. One year I want a house, and the next year I want something more; but it is still desire.

Similarly, fear does not exist in isolation. It exists in relation to something. I am afraid of my wife, or of my husband, or of my job, or of the government, or of death. Fear is always in relation to something. Now, can I understand that one fear which I have?—because, if I understand one fear completely I have understood the whole structure and nature of fear. Let us take one fear, then. What shall we take?

Comment: The fear of death.

KRISHNAMURTI: Most extraordinary! Fear of death—not fear of living! But let us go into it very carefully, step by step.

First of all, what is fear, and how does it come into being in relation to what one calls death? It is a very complex problem. One is afraid of death. In this there are two factors—fear of something you do not know, and fear of something which you have seen, observed, and felt.

One has seen many deaths. An animal dies, brutally killed by a gun; or a leaf falls, turning yellow—beautiful, lovely to look at—veering away and absorbed into dust. One has seen other people die—the relative, the neighbor—taken away, buried, cremated. So thought asks, "What is going to happen to me? Am I also going to disappear like that?" Follow this carefully. It is thought which has put this question to itself. It says, "Am I, who have lived a miserable struggling life, or who want to write a book, or paint, or fulfill myself in some way but have never done it, or I, who have cultivated my character but have lived sloppily, sluggishly, and have been frightened of so many things—am I going suddenly to come to an end?" So it is thought, not the fact of death, which is responsible for that fear. Thought, dwelling on something which implies an ending, is frightened of that. But thought is not frightened about pleasure. I think about a lovely tree, or about the river with its reflection, and the light on the water, and it gives me great pleasure. One thinks about the sexual experiences one has had—with the images, the pictures, the stimulations—and that creates pleasure. But thought, which creates pleasure, also creates the pain of death, which is fear. So it is thought which is responsible for the fear of death.

December 17, 1967

Questions

New York, 1966

Ojai, 1966

New Delhi, 1966

Madras, 1967

Rishi Valley, 1967

New Delhi, 1967

Rajghat School, Banaras, 1967

Index

Made in the USA
San Bernardino, CA
17 March 2016